Aaron Henry of Mississippi

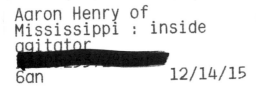
Aaron Henry
of Mississippi

INSIDE AGITATOR

Minion K. C. Morrison

The University of Arkansas Press
FAYETTEVILLE
2015

To the memory of my wife,
Johnetta Wade Morrison

Contents

Preface

I hardly knew when this project came up in a casual conversation with my good friend, the writer and poet Jerry Ward, that it would occupy me for the next fifteen years. The subject arose as we discussed the Mississippi civil rights movement and the necessity of documenting and assessing the period. Ward noted that Aaron Henry's life cried out for biographical treatment. At the time I was leaving a senior-level administrative position at the University of Missouri to return to research, and pondering the next project. I assumed I would again go off to West Africa to pursue the newly reemergent political parties, a project I did subsequently pursue (and finished before the Henry biography!).

Yet I opted to undertake a biography on Henry, never imagining the time investment and what I would have to learn about the historian's craft to pull it off. Henry intrigued me for a variety of reasons. I had been active at the tail end of the civil rights movement in Mississippi and worked in a number of Delta towns. It struck me that an exploration of Henry's long life of activism would provide an opportunity to make a professional assessment of events that had moved me to political action as I left high school in the mid-1960s. Moreover, there was a natural attraction to the subject because I have produced some scholarship on post-movement electoral politics in Mississippi, in particular black mayors in the 1970s. At the same time, because Henry spanned the movement of the 1950s and 1960s, and the succeeding electoral politics phase, an extended study of his work seemed to be an opportunity to interrogate the degree to which an activist could move into electoral politics and maintain integrity to the vision of social movement. Thus inspired, I took up the proposition that Ward offered, and this product is the result.

The pursuit of the project became a great deal easier when the first proposal I wrote attracted funding. The Research Board of the University of Missouri System provided an award allowing me to begin a preliminary investigation of the substantial body of Aaron Henry's personal papers. Only then did I begin to understand something of the scope of this undertaking. Henry preserved a treasure trove of material (notwithstanding a substantial loss of early documents in a fire bombing of his drugstore). Happily, much of this material had already been organized and catalogued by the staff at the Coleman Library of Tougaloo College, which houses a substantial additional civil rights collection, also relevant to Henry's life. This Lillian Benbow collection is now stored at the Mississippi Department of Archives and History (MDAH) and largely curated by Clarence

Hunter. The trove made it easy to become immersed in the subject as I undertook even a mere perusal of the collection. That proved just the tip of the iceberg. Henry was substantively engaged with many other networks and organizations, leading to major papers and documentation about him in research repositories all over the country. Therefore, I found myself chasing after these materials wherever I found important leads.

In the process of discovery, librarians and archivists in the Tougaloo Coleman Library, especially Clarence Hunter and Alma Fischer, ably assisted me. Ann Harper exercised due diligence in keeping up with graduate students from the University of Missouri (Kevin Anderson and Richard Middleton IV), as well as a number of Tougaloo undergraduate students who helped me explore these archives. The MDAH and its tremendous staff assisted me in developing a film on Aaron Henry's life from its filmstrips collection and in locating and processing documentation. The Mitchell Library at Mississippi State University and its special collections staff (Mattie Abraham, in particular) were especially helpful in getting me access to its civil rights collection and to acquire permission to see the Patricia Derian Papers (then not publicly available). Similarly, the Oral History Collection at Mississippi Southern University made a substantial amount of material available during a personal visit and via its online collection. Archivists and librarians at the State Historical Society of Wisconsin; the Wayne State University Walter Reuther Library–Aaron Henry Papers; the University of North Carolina–Chapel Hill Wilson Collection, where the Allard Lowenstein Papers are housed; the Oral History Collection at Columbia University; and the Library of Congress all provided important documentation.

I am grateful to many sources in Clarksdale, Mississippi, including members of the Henry family who submitted to interviews. In addition, I conducted many interviews with activists, business partners, friends, and politicians who worked with Henry in the movement, the Democratic Party, and the Mississippi legislature. I am lucky that many of his confreres in the movement remained alive and proved willing to share their recollections about Henry.

A project that extends as long as this one obviously has many graduate students, secretaries and other clerical assistants, and family members whose contributions must be noted. The Department of Political Science at the University of Missouri was supportive during my tenure there. I was afforded leaves of absence and good support from a number of graduate students. Among them were Leah Graham, Dursun Peksen, and Rollin Tusalem. Similarly, Sarah Turner of the clerical staff did an excellent job transcribing interviews. I enjoyed excellent support from the Department of Political Science and Public Administration and the African American Studies Program at Mississippi State University, which also provided assistance from several graduate and undergraduate students (among them Hannah Carlen, Kaleb Gipson, and D'Andrea Latham). The clerical staff of Quintara Miller and Kamicca Brown also provided welcome technical support. My wife and daughter, Johnetta and Iyabo, maintained high, steady interest and support throughout a project that must have seemed unending.

INTRODUCTION

The racial system in Mississippi in the 1940s made any project for social change a tall order, unlikely to be carried off by a single individual. The organized repression and the deeply ingrained rituals inevitably required a variety of forces to overturn this system. Even so, among the multiple leaders that eventually emerged, Aaron Henry played an outsized role that makes telling his personal story so compelling. His is a story when viewed from beginning to end that reveals a core vision for the racial transformation of Mississippi society and politics. At the outset he possessed a distinctive set of personal skills that allowed him to help compose and sustain a confederation of early movement activists and other supporters. Following a social movement of notable achievements, he then helped acquire and largely oversaw distribution of a vast array of resources that overwhelmed the day-to-day, formal, and customary aspects of the racial system in Mississippi (and beyond). This work is the story of his singular importance in transforming arguably the most intractable racial system in the country.

Biography, and especially political biography, is challenging to write. In the latter case the aim is not merely to make an account of an individual's life, but to isolate a particular portion of that life for documentation and scrutiny. The challenge and task are even more daunting when that individual has made an autobiographical account of his life. (See Henry's own masterful autobiographical fragment organized by Constance Curry.)[1] However, his own rendering ended in 1964, long before the full flowering of his distinctive political contribution. This account is, therefore, the first comprehensive documentation of Henry's full political life, which remained active until near his death.

Henry's story is ultimately one about political mobilization—how citizens and their leaders organize and act to acquire political power and access when their demands or grievances are not addressed.[2] The substance of Henry's life provides special insight into the 1960s civil rights mobilization, much of which rested on the social movement strategies of organizations like the National Association for the Advancement of Colored People (NAACP), the Student Nonviolent Coordinating Committee (SNCC), the Congress of Racial Equality (CORE), and the Southern Christian Leadership Conference (SCLC). The Henry story, however, shows a leader who combined both social movement action and political leadership, including holding elective office, as elements of social change. Successfully combining these two roles allowed him to have a much longer impact and influence on the character of the racial transformation in Mississippi. His maintenance of a consistent vision and his extensive role in its implementation make him arguably one of the most important figures in the alteration of that racial system.

In the history of U.S. race relations, Mississippi has occupied a special place. The ratio of enslaved people to the general population stood as one of the largest (at times a majority), and these African descendants endured the full range of harsh conditions associated with the U.S. chattel system: the strictest regimen for exacting labor, with extraordinary and broad proscriptions, and often enforced by horrific violence.[3] This background engendered the widely held sentiment that Mississippi was the most backward state (least "redeemed") in the nation in regard to race relations.[4] Hence even after enslavement ended and during a short Reconstruction, in reality little changed for a very long time for African Americans. A virtual system of peonage replaced enslavement, for example, where blacks remained locked in dependent relationships, oftentimes with former owners. The pattern lasted until well past Henry's birth and development in the Mississippi Delta.[5] It is this milieu that Henry tackled as a social movement leader and subsequently as an elected official with a degree of success unparalleled in the social and power relations between the races in Mississippi.

The state had a woefully truncated Reconstruction, though blacks enjoyed some political success, albeit short-lived. After a new constitution in 1867, for example, the majority African American population voted widely and had significant influence electing a sizable number of their own to some of the top legislative and executive positions during the first Reconstruction government in 1870.[6] However, Reconstruction was swept away shortly before the presidential election of 1876, with the return of the pre-Confederate elite. The primary goal of the old elite was to dismantle Reconstruction and especially to eliminate the African American electorate. It succeeded with stern determination. The means used are well known—violence, intimidation, sociocultural denigration, and terror among them.[7] The new racial order became even more stringent than the enslavement era. Jim Crow ushered in a pattern of hypersegregation that rendered blacks nearly powerless within almost totally segregated, residential quarters. A new constitution in 1890 then codified the new regimen, the "Mississippi Plan." The new franchise requirements (literacy and poll taxes) eliminated the overwhelming majority of African American voters.[8]

While the new racial system inspired one of the greatest internal migrations of African Americans in U.S. history (south to north), many of them stayed, especially in Mississippi. Born in 1922, Henry was one of those who remained. This precocious boy sported more bravado than the norm in a highly racialized system that demanded more circumspection. Lemann has said that "Deciding to stay and work for civil rights wasn't purely an intellectual matter for Aaron Henry, . . . [who] appeared to be completely implacable, as if the risks entailed

in fighting segregation simply had no place in his mind."⁹ After high school he
joined the army to help protect his country in World War II, but even there he
countenanced both the promise and peril of African American "citizenship." He
was a bonafide soldier, to be sure, but his race marked him for discriminatory
treatment, whether in Mississippi, Georgia, California, or the Pacific Islands, all
places where he served. It reflected a reality he knew all too well from growing up
in Mississippi.

After military service Henry had a determination to return to Mississippi. He
did so in 1946 and found things fairly much the same, though he had undergone
significant change. The schoolboy bravado had been replaced with a steely will
to live as a free citizen of the country he had defended. In the beginning this was
expressed by rejecting the rituals and proscriptions of the segregation system.
Perhaps unwittingly, that personal posture put him on a path of fundamental
challenge to this system. His early visit to the circuit clerk seeking to register
to vote intrinsically represented more than an expression of personal integrity;
it seemed a matter of marvel to the several black men who observed it. Henry
quickly realized that registering to vote for a single black man did not merely
represent a personal achievement; it had implications for the entire black community, whose wholesale disfranchisement remained group based. Perhaps in this
very instance the roadmap for Henry's public life began to be plotted. Its dictates
eventually outweighed all the many other roles he assumed—professional pharmacist, businessman, husband, and father, among them.

Henry dared to challenge this system when he returned. He tried to maintain
integrity to his status as a free man, though fully cognizant of the adroitness of
the segregationists in denying black freedom. Moreover, if he flaunted regulations
too boldly the punishment could be death and almost certain reprisals against his
business. He, therefore, gave significant forethought to how to function within
such confines and maintain personal integrity. In the end he developed strategies
that allowed him to speak confidently to African Americans and whites alike
about his ambitions and dreams and to seek public and private spaces into which
to interject himself to advance his social change goals. He did these with aplomb
and sustained them over a period of leadership that lasted more than fifty years.
The first period of that leadership was within the context of the ensemble of
actors that became the "Mississippi movement" in the 1960s, and the later period
was as a leader of the Democratic Party coalition in the state.

Henry's return after military service came at a propitious time for challenges
to the racial system in Mississippi and the South. The previously furtive challenges
no longer remained underground, especially in the Delta region of Henry's birth.
He immediately developed contacts with a formative group of black Delta leaders
and continued contacts he had already established with the NAACP. In time

the NAACP became the most visible and successful proponent of change with which Mississippi challengers affiliated. Its platform called for the restoration of the franchise and equal opportunity and for the destruction of segregation. The two-pronged strategy it adopted included legal challenges and lobbying. This simple program proved exceedingly threatening to the segregationists, who set out to destroy the organization and to prevent its presence in southern states like Mississippi. Yet, the simplicity of the NAACP project for racial change animated Henry and virtually all of the early post–World War II African American leadership. The program the organization presented provided a template that southern activists adapted for their own needs, elements of which became fundamental features of the broader social change movement that developed in Mississippi. Indeed, Henry subsequently led the state NAACP chapter and became prominent in the national body.

Precisely how did the social change leadership emerge in the state with the most formalized and ritualized racial system in the country? It began in the Mississippi Delta, the place of Henry's birth, a land that in its spectacular fertility and enduring flatness led to an immense concentration of African descendants as agricultural laborers. The racial system was drawn in stark relief in this vast cotton-producing Delta, fed by the waters of the mighty Mississippi River that sustained a virtual agricultural aristocracy. The sparse white population lived in its towns and hamlets, often resident in a single massive plantation house at the center of farm acreage, stretching from one side of the horizon to the other. Here the racial taboos and rituals continued to play out with a vengeance even succeeding emancipation. The system relentlessly suppressed resistance and was unforgiving in punishing disobedience. In short, this area of Henry's birth proved as hostile as any environment, with an African American majority, in the segregated South.

Later, this large, concentrated African American labor force became redundant when the plantation system shifted to mechanization. The region thus appeared ripe for a major social movement. As such, when Henry returned, it seemed hardly surprising that the makings for a resistance campaign were discernible in the Delta. This Black-Belt region produced the first visible cast of organized leaders who openly challenged the racial system. They loosely associated within the Regional Council of Negro Leadership (RCNL), led by Dr. T. R. M. Howard, a physician in the black Delta town of Mound Bayou.[10] Many of the members, like Howard and Henry, had a level of economic independence that put them somewhat beyond the reach of reprisals from the white ruling economic and political class. Howard's organization had a civil rights platform that resembled that of the NAACP. He corralled a number of change-oriented men, almost all from the Delta, who invested time and energy in the organization. It may well have been the first significant indigenous social change organization with which Henry affiliated. He certainly became ubiquitous in its affairs, serving as secretary and using his gregarious and affable personality to get to know all of the members.

Many of these individuals became a part of the vast network that Henry later commanded through the years as the NAACP emerged from the shadows and attained primacy in Mississippi. They had quite remarkable success in the forbidding conditions of the Delta. These leaders succeeded in getting some of the most vulnerable to acquire membership in the previously banned NAACP— schoolteachers among them—and in getting some of the most visible black community leaders to offer resources—among them ministers who opened their churches for meetings. Soon a critical contingent of social change activists existed in the Delta, and they joined Henry in formulating a resistance movement to invigorate individual leaders scattered elsewhere. In the beginning one of the most common markers of their activism became membership in the NAACP and leadership of a local chapter. With Henry at the helm of the state chapter, secrecy ceased to be practical or desirable, notwithstanding the formal and informal repressive measures that continued to be exercised against them.

Henry and the Mississippi activists were now emboldened by being a part of a national campaign and by having a network of powerful national allies on their side. Few could imagine this as the dawning of the long-hoped-for mobilization in Mississippi that in the next ten to fifteen years would turn the "unredeemed" state to a kind of redemption for African American political participation and racial reconciliation. Eventually other organizations came onto the scene—SNCC, CORE, and the SCLC—and formed a confederation for unified action (the Council of Federated Organizations [COFO]). Henry managed to attain a place of leadership that allowed him to have a role in or relationship with all of these entities through the years. His ubiquity and persistent vision was critical to all of them. In the end, he outlasted them and oversaw the evolution of a social and political movement of profound consequence in the state. In the process he became the single most important continuous leader in implementing a civil rights vision that transformed racialized society and politics in Mississippi.

This work is the story of Henry's rise, the scope of his monumental contribution, and how he accomplished it. The first chapter chronicles his ordinary childhood according to the rules of a rigidly segregated society. His personal circumstances reflected those of so many other young black children; an uncle and his wife, who became young Aaron's parents in virtually every respect, raised him and his siblings. Henry's early milieu did not prove exceptional in this segregated world. He lived as part of a typical family structure largely defined by tenant farming in the Mississippi Delta. However, the ordinariness of this cast did not last long because the family abandoned the plantation for a life in town. A part of their objective was to be freed of dependence on the proverbial sharecropping system and to be self-reliant in the style of Booker T. Washington, whose ideas had some currency in the area. Both of his parents subsequently became entrepreneurs, an experience that had a profound impact on Henry. He grew through elementary school into adolescence, revealing a curiosity and determination that may have signaled his destiny. Contrary to the designs of the white power structure, his inferior segregated schools nurtured his curiosity and inspired his determination for racial change. Though he learned how to survive in the system, he also learned how to challenge it. Most important, he never learned to accept it, abetted by his immediate family and courageous schoolteachers.

Chapter 2 captures Henry as he moved into adulthood, completing high school and enlisting in the army. Sullied by the segregation that followed him in the military, for the first time he openly joined the NAACP, an affiliation that continued throughout the rest of his life. He returned to Clarksdale afterward determined both to go to college and to become an entrepreneur, with sufficient independence to bring social change to his town. That change trajectory began to be implemented in the early 1950s when he received his pharmacy degree, set up a successful business (a drugstore), married a schoolteacher, and set about questioning the boundaries of racism. Henry made furtive contacts with kindred spirits in the Delta, but these soon burst into the open with the RCNL when signs of his leadership skills became apparent. His organization of the Clarksdale NAACP followed, and by the end of the decade he was poised to lead the state chapter. This perch made him perhaps the most visible African American activist in the state.

The first big press that Henry made for social change came in his hometown. Just as the entire country began to experience a major civil rights social movement by the early 1960s, Henry also led a massive campaign in Clarksdale utilizing many of the then-common tactics—public street demonstrations and assaults on segregated spaces. Chapter 3 details these activities and their evolution within the context of a national movement. At the same time a white countermobilization developed, with which Henry and his activist cohorts had to contend. However, these redoubled efforts to maintain the status quo inspired and invigorated Henry. He engaged and unleashed a wave of local and external allies from his vast arsenal of contacts that helped to propel a two-year mobilization in Clarksdale. Despite the legal-formal, local and state actions directed against them, Henry and the challengers virtually immobilized their local opposition.

In chapter 4 I show Henry working within an ensemble of other civil rights groups, including the formal organization of the COFO. This reflected an early decision among Mississippi challengers to combine social movement activity with political mobilization. It matched a vision already apparent in Henry's activity when he spearheaded a 1960 effort to field candidates to run against the white incumbents in Mississippi's congressional delegation. Meanwhile, since most would-be black voters remained disfranchised, COFO oversaw perhaps the most important symbolic event foreshadowing the evolution to political mobilization in 1963: Henry led a ticket as candidate for governor in a "mock election." This project aimed to demonstrate the potential power of the African American electorate and to dramatize its disfranchisement. By this time few could doubt the centrality of Henry's leadership to the Mississippi movement or that the challenge in the state had fundamental links to the broader civil rights campaign.

Chapter 5 focuses on the development of a "third political party," the Mississippi Freedom Democratic Party (MFDP), in many ways the successor to the mock campaign. Though the mock election event did not set out to install blacks in office, it significantly emboldened the activists to challenge the Democratic Party—the segregated, single party that controlled state government. Supported by an army of allies (many of them college students from the North), Henry became the primary leader of the ensemble that demanded ouster of the white Mississippi delegation from the national convention. The effort failed, but it effectively set Henry on a course to demolish the segregated party and subsequently to assume its leadership—a sea change in racial politics in Mississippi.

In chapter 6 I detail Henry's activity on the cusp of his taking command of the reins of the state party, despite the refusal of the traditional white elite to cooperate as the transition commenced. This part of the story includes detailed accounts of Henry's dexterity in managing and deploying the array of allies to whom he had connections in the national Democratic alliance. In this period he essentially functioned as a public entrepreneur. Henry commanded the attention of Presidents Kennedy and Johnson and their most senior aides; caused statements to be read into the *Congressional Record* and generated congressional votes on issues important to his Mississippi cadre; and helped build an array of legal experts who exploited every angle of the civil rights and civil liberties rulings emanating from a liberal Supreme Court. He was at the full height of his power, in effect, challenging and largely succeeding in dismantling the most fundamental features of segregation with the help of his allies in the ruling Democratic coalition in Washington. He tapped into the War on Poverty, delivering or influencing a bevy of programs and grants to Clarksdale and the state. The Head Start preschool program is of one of these, and it generated a monumental counter-campaign from Mississippi senator John Stennis. Though the senator's intervention virtually killed the program, the circumstances ironically lay the groundwork for an integrated party to which Senator Stennis later had to pay homage as he sought reelection.

Chapter 7 takes a step back and details a variety of other projects that paralleled Henry's social and political mobilization work. Having attained the control of the state party, he set aim at some of the other core sectors still representing and reflecting the old ways—media, education, health care, housing, and employment. With these activities he is seen contesting the state's major television station and the public schools in Clarksdale (with his daughter as a plaintiff); seeking the expansion of health care and housing for the black elderly; and seeking to break the cycle of unemployment that plagued African Americans. In short, he sought the redistribution of resources, daring to contemplate ways and means for compensation that enhanced systemic regularity for African Americans whose life chances had been truncated by racism. He enjoyed remarkable success, though not always easily or quickly.

Meanwhile, the sparring continued regarding control of the state Democratic Party. The "Regulars" (the segregationists) yielded little to Henry and the Loyalists (the challengers). This precipitated the ouster of the Regulars from the national party four years later (1968). In chapter 8 I trace these events through the eight years (and two governors) before Henry and his interracial cohorts could consummate the victory. The chapter documents the struggles to build a strong infrastructure and balance the pressures attendant to power sharing between erstwhile masters and servants, inferiors and superiors, and the powerful and powerless. Henry achieved another milestone in the scope of power at his command: for a time he was the most powerful party leader in Mississippi, with influence that stretched far beyond the state's borders. The payoffs were palpable as blacks won elective offices at virtually all levels throughout the state.

In chapter 9 I take up the culmination of Henry's career, with his election to the state legislature, representing a Delta district inclusive of Clarksdale. He held this office until shortly before his death, even as his health failed and his power waned in the party. A detailed accounting is made of his legislative work, including committee assignments, bills, and his interactions with colleagues. He had finally come full circle from social movement leader to full-time politician. His success was limited by the enduring minority status of his chief supporters—other black legislators. Nevertheless, he remained aggressive and vocal, proposing a bevy of legislation that maintained a level of integrity to the principles and vision that he sketched for racial change in Mississippi.

There is little doubt about the conclusion that Henry's extraordinary and improbable journey as an African American leader in Mississippi proved a remarkable success. He led the most fundamental change in race relations and political change in the history of the state. He brought this least "redeemed" state into the ambit of a national movement and made accomplishments that in many ways overmatched those in most other places. At his demise he left a larger number of black elected officials in Mississippi than anywhere else, and the scope of engagement across racial lines remained in large measure indistinct from patterns of engagement elsewhere in the country; for example, facilities were desegregated, and norms of public behavior vis-à-vis the races were not as fraught as prior to his leadership. The distribution of power between the races is another matter, however, with the emergence of the Republican Party. The Democratic majority that Henry helped to forge began to winnow even prior to his death. As many whites shifted their partisan identification to the Republican Party, the majority of blacks maintained a strong identification with the Democratic Party. It is a set of conditions that raises new questions about the terms on which the interracial coalition that Henry believed essential may evolve in the state.

CHAPTER ONE

Son of Sharecroppers and Entrepreneurs

Rites of Passage in a Segregated Society

The fate of an African American boy born into the Mississippi Delta of the 1920s was fairly predictable: a life of subservience in a racial caste system. Aaron Henry was born into this milieu in 1922. Webb and Clarksdale, his boyhood homes, thrived from cotton sowed, tended, and harvested by African Americans. Though enslavement was gone by 1920, that fact hardly changed the master-servant relationships between plantation owners and African American laborers. The myth of aristocracy in this flatland of alluvial soils, along the Mississippi River, seemed assured: the taming of a wilderness wrestled away from its native population in a series of treaties; the rationalization of a set of values that sustained a small white patrician class of plantation owners; an ever-increasing demand for cotton; and the post–Civil War reorganization and apparent permanence of an inexhaustible supply of cheap labor. The niche for Aaron Edd Henry seemed predetermined, so trapped in the web of deceits of the "sharecropping" system as to thwart independent thinking or action.[1]

In spite of the seemingly impermeable wall, Henry did break through to become an independent thinker and one of Mississippi's most inclusive leaders. He persisted in a belief in an integrated society and negotiated a perilous course of resistance to a system maintained by force, violence, and custom. He operated with what often appeared to be callous fearlessness, in his determination for "regularity" vis-à-vis his "white brothers." These were combined with his singular intellect, favorable demeanor, and organizing skills, which made him first among equals in the leadership of the Mississippi civil rights and political mobilization movements.

Henry's beginning in the Mississippi Delta was like any black child born to sharecroppers. He was born on the Flowers Plantation in rural Coahoma

County in the northern Mississippi Delta. His family was bound to the plantation for labor and life, where they sharecropped on forty acres. While there were
variations in the sharecropping system, Henry's family and most other African
Americans labored under the least favorable arrangement.[2] According to Henry's
own account, they were involved in the half share system where the landowner
provided the land, house, equipment, and half of all of the seed and fertilizer. The
owner also provided cash advances and commissary privileges against the crop
and either supervised the plantation or appointed an agent-manager. All of the
accounting and distribution of shares was done by the owner.[3] It was rare for the
tenants to receive cash at the final accounting. Indeed, they usually ended up in
the red, caught in a spiral of ever-escalating indebtedness.[4]

Despite the daily work regimen there was organized, independent cultural
life. Community life consisted of family groups reflecting intricate webs of
kinship. It revolved around the churches, which almost everyone attended on
Sunday. Henry's own web included an extended family of thirty-plus relatives
among which communal welfare obligations ran deep.[5] Individual households
were maintained, but everyone lived far below the margins. Young Aaron's household disintegrated rapidly when both parents died—his mother when he was
three and his father when he was five. Later in life Henry only noted their passing,
intimating nothing of the devastation it must have caused him and his sister, who
were taken in by a maternal uncle Ed Henry and his wife, Mattie. All indications
are that the arrangement resembled full parenthood. Young Aaron called them
"mother" and "father," and in his brief references to them they were described
as loving parents who spared nothing to advance themselves and their children.

Ed Henry was determined to get his household out of sharecropping. He first
moved the family nearby to Webb, a town of about one thousand. There he and
his wife became entrepreneurs—he a cobbler and she a beautician. Both thrived,
catering to the majority African American population. In the next year or two the
family moved to the bustling nearby town of Clarksdale, one of the largest in the
state. Ed Henry and Mattie bought their own property there and built a house.
Young Aaron was now suddenly launched on a different trajectory from most
other African Americans around him. His family broke away from the plantation
and became fairly independent of it. The young and precocious Aaron could then
imagine another world not linked to the plantation he so detested.

The path the Henrys took was not accidental. Despite the racial caste regimen, Ed and Mattie Henry did not live in a vacuum. In a remarkable degree
of personal industry, strategic external connections, and fortuitous location,
this family acquired a self-help ideology and entrepreneurial spirit. Both were
influenced by the work and ideals of Booker T. Washington and his school at
Tuskegee (Alabama), and a related experiment in the all-black town of Mound

Bayou (twenty miles south of Clarksdale). There is evidence that both Ed and Mattie were involved with the programs at Tuskegee and Mound Bayou. Henry noted Washington's influence on his father's interest in developing a trade,[6] and he spoke of his mother's year of study at Tuskegee.[7] Indeed, the ideas of Washington were so strong in this area that it was easy for the Henrys to come under their sway. In the first place, Washington was intensively involved in the development of the town of Mound Bayou and had deep connections to its conservative founder, Isaiah Montgomery. Mound Bayou was settled in 1887, just six years after Tuskegee. The two men met in 1885 when Washington gave his famous Atlanta Exposition speech, and their friendship and collaboration continued for much of the rest of Washington's life.[8] Louis Harlan says that "Mound Bayou . . . captured [Washington's] heart, a small town in the Yazoo-Mississippi Delta that seemed to embody the values, methods of self-help, and priorities of his own social philosophy."[9]

Meanwhile, Clarksdale also had a black entrepreneurial class, and Washington played a role in cementing that into a Delta network. For example, he knew Charles Banks (1873–1923), a black Clarksdale banker, with whom he organized the National Negro Business League in 1900. Washington referred to Banks as "the most important Negro business man in the United States" and as "the leading Negro banker in Mississippi." In short order, according to Janet Sharp Hermann, Banks and Montgomery became a team, and the former moved to Mound Bayou and established the town's first bank and a variety of other business enterprises.[10] Charles Banks was a special and enduring symbol to blacks in Clarksdale. He made a considerable fortune there before moving to Mound Bayou, a town that offered the opportunity for entrepreneurship anchored to his "race consciousness" ideals. No doubt his relocation from Clarksdale owed to his bedazzlement at this "all Negro capital" where entrepreneurs like him could execute all their trade within the racial business community with "perfect security under the rule of a Negro Mayor and a Negro Marshal." He had a prominent national identity as a Washington "lieutenant" and was deeply engaged in Republican Party politics, being a convention delegate multiple times with entrée to U.S. presidents and with influence over patronage for Mississippi's black Republicans, according to his biographer Donald Jackson.[11] This Banks-Montgomery axis made the Delta region the most influential center of black entrepreneurship in the state.

Henry's parents almost surely knew Banks and his cohorts and their business achievements, and this must have informed their vision of a world of racial independence. The close physical location of Mound Bayou to Clarksdale made for an ease of exchange of ideas. Moreover, Neil McMillen shows that Isaiah Montgomery conceived of the town as reflecting "black financial, industrial and agricultural interests that embraced not only central Bolivar County but a 'vast territory' encompassing much of the upper Delta, including Tunica, Coahoma, Quitman, Tallahatchie, and Washington Counties."[12] This reinforced whatever direct training the Henrys had in Washington's methods, coupled with the exchange of personnel between Mound Bayou and Clarksdale. Banks remained tied to his hometown, for example. A number of business families that are prominent in Clarksdale to this day are directly tied to Mound Bayou (for example, the Stringers).[13] This enduring Mound Bayou connection was not lost on Aaron Henry; both his pharmacy business and political development were partially built on such ties.[14]

Aaron Henry's new home of Clarksdale was a rich and vibrant bastion of commerce, fashion, and entertainment after the Civil War. It was favored by its central location near waterways with its soils perennially bathed by the Mississippi and Yazoo Rivers.[15] The town's founder, John Clark, acquired land there in 1848.[16] The area was described by Nicholas Lemann as a "trackless wilderness infested with snakes and alligators." The town blossomed as Mississippi Reconstruction waned in 1875 and cotton acreage increased.[17] Between incorporation in 1882 and the turn of the century, this boomtown was one of the largest and most influential in the region. As the price of cotton soared to a dollar per pound, Clarksdale was one of the towns where wealth and culture flourished with "clubs, schools, libraries, businesses, and solid homes in the towns, . . . [and] the big plantations were worth millions."[18]

Meanwhile, the African American population rose steadily in light of the failed effort to recruit whites from Europe.[19] The resident blacks were joined by a wave of freed black migrants from elsewhere, especially the Carolinas, Georgia, Alabama, and other parts of Mississippi.[20] They became the linchpin of the sharecropping system and the day laborer in the towns.

When the Henry family moved from the plantation to Webb and Clarksdale, it discovered that certain aspects of the racial system in town were organized differently. Since encounters with whites occurred more regularly and without the benefit of an established relationship, a new set of rules defined racial decorum. The difference was immediately apparent to young Aaron. On the plantation it sometimes seemed as if race did not define interactions. He said that both blacks and whites were sharecroppers who "stood in line together to get our goods in the commissary. The men stood around and chewed tobacco together and drank whiskey they sometimes made together. . . . A Negro midwife delivered white and Negro babies."[21] Henry also described Randolph Smithers, a white boy, as one of his first "friends." In Webb, however, that relationship was shattered when Henry learned a deeper meaning of racial division: he and Smithers could not go to the same school: "I was considered inferior to Randolph simply because his skin was white and mine was black."[22] Meanwhile, it was hard not to observe the difference between Randolph's brick schoolhouse and Henry's school in a church sanctuary. The racial division in Clarksdale brought home to Henry that he was a part of a majority black community controlled by whites. He lamented that "The schools were separate and unequal; movies for colored were upstairs and dingy. Negro boys could not be in the Boy Scouts, even in a separate troop. If we paid social calls on whites, it was through the back door, because it was through the front door that courtship could possibly occur."[23]

The decision of Ed and Mattie Henry to move to town and become entrepreneurs was fortuitous. Much of the population growth in Clarksdale resulted because of the significant black day laboring force that emerged in the town. Though still tied to the plantation system, their residential segregation provided a niche for African American businesses to cater to the needs of these segregated enclaves. The Henry household took advantage of this circumstance and dedicated considerable energy to developing their businesses, while abandoning their days as perennially debt-ridden sharecroppers. Soon they gained control of their finances and earned the capital to purchase a home. Their evolving independence was the environment into which Aaron was socialized, and it had an enduring impact on the path he took.

The independent energy of the Henrys found an easy resonance with the Booker T. Washington model, which they adopted. Aaron described his father as a proud man, generous and caring, with a steely dedication to advance. He recounted that his father "heard about a shoe cobbler course over at Tuskegee and all you had to do was to get there. There was no charge for it as this was the way Booker T. Washington ran his show. Well he went over and took the course and set up a shoe shop in a little town called Webb."[24] That was the start of Ed Henry's cobbler business, for which he acquired machinery and other support from a Memphis leather company.[25]

Henry's mother, Mattie, had a more formal education and actually matriculated at Tuskegee. She spent a year there after completing sixth grade in the small Quitman County town of Vance. Henry explained little else about her Tuskegee connection, except that finances prevented her continuation.[26] However, given what we know of the regimen at Tuskegee, Mattie likely took part in a variety of learning activities. First and foremost, Tuskegee education was developed to advance farm production, but there was far more for its students. The curriculum also included many academic courses in math, science, composition, and literature. Mattie was likely to have followed such a broad academic program during her time at Tuskegee.[27] She, like most students there at the time, did not complete the program. This one-year experience, meanwhile, provided a model for her that matched her husband's vision of entrepreneurship, and she later established her own business, a beauty parlor.

Both members of this "team," as Henry described them, worked tirelessly to be successful at their trades. His father kept longer hours than he had on the plantation, coming home far past sundown. His mother was equally absorbed by her job as a beautician. In addition, she soon took on another job, perhaps unique at the time, that of "real estate agent." Henry depicted her responsibility as encouraging homeownership among blacks, a job that took her away frequently. Though the full scope of her duties is not known, Henry said her real estate earnings were significant, generating a good portion of her income.[28]

Even though his parents were exceedingly busy and often absent, their rewards from entrepreneurship were palpable. At the same time they were imparting a model for their son. Cobbling and "fixing hair" were niches that required them to develop a relationship with clientele within the confines of their racial enclave. They deployed their ingenuity and drive as black entrepreneurs within the limits and rapidly attained economic "independence." With that relative independence, they could avoid some of the demands that whites placed on other blacks. Within the limits of their freedom, they carved out a space to advance themselves while serving a large segment of the black community. Their son, Aaron, took this to another level when he used the leverage of his own entrepreneurship to assert a political voice and to form a significant part of the state's African American leadership cadre.[29]

Their path, though not widely accessible to other blacks, was well known because the segregated marketplace made black entrepreneurs a practical necessity. Washington's ideals were only the most prominent during the times when the Henry family was striking out. The ideals were not new; some of his predecessors had an even broader ideal of uplift through self-help, and were dedicated to leadership and solidarity of their segregated communities.[30] Among the examples are the clergy that Richard Allen organized to serve the separate American Methodist Episcopal (AME) church following the segregation of black congregants within the mainstream Methodist congregation; or, a quasi-political party organization such as the Negro Convention Movement that sketched its own manifesto for black participation and the franchise before the Civil War.[31] Many of these were what W. E. B. Du Bois referred to as the "Talented Tenth," who had special responsibilities in uplifting the community.[32] In the main they were clergy, shop owners, morticians, and insurers, and the like, reflecting the pool of options then available.[33] Henry's path in this regard was better laid than most leaders. Mississippi may have had a greater number of such models that "embraced the hopeful ideals of racial solidarity and self-help."[34] Clarksdale, for example, was ranked as a town with one of the most prominent entrepreneurial hubs along Issaquena and Fourth Streets, where Aaron Henry established his own business cum political office.[35]

While the racial system, of which Aaron Henry was a product, rendered his parents inferior vis-à-vis whites, that system did allow them a spot in the small class of blacks to service (and inevitably to lead) their compatriots in the subaltern, segregated enclaves. Ed Henry was likely the only black cobbler for miles around, serving many white clients, too. No doubt there were many beauticians like Mrs. Henry in the African American community, for whom pressing and straightening hair was the preference at the time. The popularity of this process of hair care among blacks made beauticians some of the best-paid workers in their communities.[36] But her role as real estate agent was certainly unique because most blacks were discouraged from property ownership in favor of renting or sharecropping. In this position she traveled and acquired a kind of cosmopolitanism within the community that further elevated her status. Blacks like the Henrys who occupied these limited roles could also service whites, especially in performing tasks that no other whites would assume. The effect on young Aaron Henry was that he led a relatively privileged life within segregated Clarksdale. Both parents were not only present and working, but were engaged in fairly lucrative occupations.

Photo of three generations of the Aaron Henry Family, date unknown, left to right, mother, Mattie; wife, Noelle; Henry; and daughter, Rebecca. (Courtesy Aaron Henry Papers, Tougaloo College.)

At Henry's birth an element of the sizable independent black economic class or its influences were still present in and around Clarksdale. Charles Banks (who lived until 1923) and the Montgomery family in Mound Bayou were among those who remained. This elite continued to express strong ideas and had influence upon social and cultural life. Clearly they influenced Henry's parents, whose status and example became all important in forming the mindset and ambition of their son, though Ed and Mattie Henry did not exercise a political voice. Aaron Henry reflected their independence at an early age in goals that assumed autonomy and the aspiration of equality; he did not perceive himself as inferior to anyone. The disjuncture between the desired and the existing world made him acutely aware of the challenge in dismantling the system of virtual racial caste.

Henry's boyhood was also distinct because his parents were homeowners. Within about a year of arriving in town they bought land and a house with a loan from the Home Owner's Loan Corporation (HOLC). Henry believed that "it was fairly easy to borrow the money" because HOLC was a federal agency.[37] His parents then built their "neat little house" for about $5,000. His belief was that the only requirement for getting and maintaining the loan was having an income of "about ten dollars a week."[38] The ease that Henry perceived, however, was not the reality for most Mississippians. Though 99 percent of the state was deemed eligible for home loans, and the rate of applications was among the highest, the denial rate was over 50 percent. It is unknown how much the Henry family borrowed, but the average size of loans in the state was $1,879.[39] Data were not found showing the rate of loan approvals for African Americans. However, national data do show that their eligibility and approvals were rare. According to the Homeowners Loan Corporation: "From 1933 to 1936, the period HOLC was authorized to issue loans, 44 percent of its help went to areas designated 'native white,' 42 percent to 'native white and foreign,' and 1 percent to Negro."[40] Being from rural places may have helped black families like the Henrys since urban, inner cities (like those in Detroit and Chicago with concentrations of blacks) received fewer loans. In any case, a loan to the Henry family was fairly exceptional, and its acquisition afforded young Aaron a degree of pride and comfort that left him brimming over. "We were so thankful for that loan, and I went happily every week for five or six years to the post office for the postal money order forms we needed for payment."[41]

Now that young Aaron had a home, the next major question was his education. During his formative years, the disparity in educational opportunities for African Americans (and whites) was stark all over Mississippi. The problem for blacks was the paltry investment in facilities, especially buildings, equipment, and supplies. Professionally trained black staff was also severely limited, as was the curriculum and the time allocation for study. The disparity evident during

Reconstruction (51 grammar and 4 high schools for blacks compared to 400 and 78, respectively, for whites) continued as black enrollment and the number of teachers declined.[42] In 1899, the state superintendent acknowledged that "our public school system is designated primarily for the welfare of the white children of the state, and incidentally for the negro [sic] children."[43] According to Henry Bullock, "as late as 1910, there was not a single eighth-grade rural Negro public school. No public school, rural or urban, was approved for two years of high school work."[44] In 1928 things had not improved a great deal. There still were no accredited high schools for blacks, while there were 335 for whites. Ten years later there were 15 high schools for blacks compared to 391 for whites.[45] This was a major stumbling block for the Henrys, who desired to educate their children.

The location of Aaron's first school among church pews, therefore, was hardly a surprise. Local government financing for school construction was rare, leaving the onus on the impoverished African American community for the provision of school buildings. Even the donations from philanthropists had to be supplemented by blacks—both capital and land/facilities.[46] Often, funds allocated for black schools were actually spent on white schools. According to Charles Bolton, this was especially true in "Delta districts [that] used most of the money they received for the region's black majority to invest in educating the Delta's relatively small white population."[47] Aaron Henry was fortunate that a school existed in a church building in a nearby plantation; children too distant to travel by foot simply did not get to school.

The lack of state provisions for schools for blacks was somewhat relieved by investments from philanthropists. Such philanthropic support was critical for the development of both schools and colleges, and the list of contributors was impressive. George Peabody gave significant discretionary funds to the Conference for Education in the South for public education, and by 1909 the Rockefeller family had given over $50 million, designating a portion for blacks. Anna Jeanes created school supervisors dedicated to rural schools, providing extension-type support, and Andrew Carnegie built a string of libraries across the South in general support of education. The Julius Rosenwald Fund spent more than $28 million on buildings (over 16 percent of the total investment) and generated about 25 percent more from private black donors. The local southern states, therefore, had more than forty cents of every dollar of public money subsidized with proceeds from private sources. This freed up an incredible amount of tax money for investment in the segregated white schools.[48] In 1928, about the time that Aaron Henry started school, 376 schools were constructed at a total cost of just over $28 million.[49] Bullock shows that "the Rosenwald Fund agreed to aid in the building of thirty-six schools, seven teacher's homes, and seven vocational buildings. Most of the program was completed within a year." This single construction project was designed to provide schools in rural Mississippi to accommodate eight grades for eight months of the year.[50] The first state high school for blacks was constructed as a part of this project, which providentially for Henry was located in Coahoma County just outside Clarksdale.[51]

As Reconstruction waned and some state resources began to be invested for black education, racial segregation and the disparity of the black schools remained. One way of calculating its impact on young Aaron is by analyzing per pupil expenditures leading up to his entry at elementary school.

In 1900 Neil McMillen estimated that blacks received well under 19 percent of state funding, and that trend continued until the eve of *Brown v. Board of Education* (1954). In 1913 a mere dollar and a half was spent per pupil for blacks compared to over eight dollars for whites. When white expenditures rose to over thirty dollars in 1930, expenditures for blacks rose to about six dollars. In the next ten years the proportion declined considerably, with blacks getting a mere 13 percent share.[52] Perhaps the most egregious practice was that blacks were subsidizing white schools. As the taxpaying majority they received far less in state education expenditures. McMillen also shows that the gap between tax receipts and expenditures in Mississippi "gradually widened after 1870, pushing annual net transfers of black tax dollars to white schools to well over $1 million by 1910."[53]

School staffing was equally grim, with a paucity of trained personnel. Since there were few colleges for blacks, the first African American teachers had little more than an eighth-grade education. "In 1945, less than 10 percent of black teachers possessed a bachelor's degree; over 23 percent did not even have a high school diploma," according to Bullock.[54] Similarly, teacher pay was very low, and there were few opportunities for professional development and advanced training. For example, average annual salaries in 1945 were $399 compared to an average of $1,108 for whites; and those with a baccalaureate degree had no accessible local institutions for advanced training.[55]

There was also the matter of the curriculum. The bargain struck with the philanthropists favored the vocational model based on the assumptions that blacks had a limited capacity to learn and that industrial education was appropriate to the skills necessary for building institutions and inculcating values of discipline and a work ethic.[56] Such a model was particularly influential in Clarksdale and the surrounding Delta communities. Bullock quotes one exponent who put it as follows: "[A]void social questions; leave politics alone; continue to be patient; live moral lives; live simply; learn to work and work intelligently; . . . learn that it is a mistake to be educated out of your environment."[57] Horace Mann Bond showed that the rich benefactors often accepted such arguments. Philanthropist Rosenwald, for example, said that rural blacks needed "the ability to read and to write clearly; some skill in the use of figures; a knowledge of farming, including some general understanding of biological processes and an appreciation of nature; manual dexterity, especially in the handling of wood, fabric, and other utensils as related to simple mechanics; and a grasp of the fundamentals of sanitation and health." This evolved into a framework for the education of blacks. One of the most far-reaching and enduring projects was the Jeanes supervisors—teachers who moved from one school to another offering demonstrations to rural school-teachers, largely about industrial subjects. These roving purveyors of garden-ing, cookery, and sanitation survived well into the 1960s in Mississippi. They were so pervasive and influential that "they exercised the duties of an Assistant Superintendent in charge of Negro schools."[58]

Henry immediately encountered this disparity when he went to school. One of his first memories is how school interrupted the parallel path he and Randolph Smithers, his white playmate, seemed to share when they both lived on the plan-tation. Aaron looked forward to going to school where he and Smithers could expand their play days together. That was not to be. Their simultaneous move to town abruptly ended the camaraderie these two sharecroppers formerly enjoyed. Now segregation intervened, a fact of life little noticed before in the commonality of their plantation circumstances.

Henry was crushed to learn they could not attend school together. But that was just the beginning. The distinctions between the separate facilities the two boys inhabited, in appearance and in location, could not be missed. Smithers enrolled at an imposing brick edifice in town, near where the two boys resided within earshot of each other. Henry did not have the convenience of going to school in town. He traveled to a plantation some distance away from Webb, in a less than idyllic setting. The school was in a church, an edifice that hardly looked the part, nor was it functional. Though it was technically a "state" school, blacks owned the property—a single-room concave of pews accommodating multiples classes, not in any manner separated from one another. This archetypical struc-ture had two teachers, quite an improvement over 75 percent of similar schools in 1911 that had only one teacher.[59] Henry said that instructors "would go from one group to another while we sat on our benches and waited." Meanwhile, "[e]ach grade had a time during the day to recite and have its lessons heard by the teacher."[60] This was a cruel realization for the young boy, who in his precocity recognized the oddity of the situation.[61]

A year later the family moved to Clarksdale where Henry enrolled in school at Myrtle Hall, just across the street from his home. It was a great improvement with eight grades, each with an individual teacher. The education provided in Clarksdale was also superior, and Henry indicated that many parents on the plan-tations actually paid a small tuition to send their children there. Even so, the training level of these teachers was often little better than their rural counterparts.

Only the principal at Myrtle Hall School had some college training, according to Henry. "The best system that could be arranged was to make sure that each teacher finished at least a grade higher than he or she was teaching." He said little about schoolwork, choosing to focus on the importance of play. In the mischief and grounds play that he relates, this period in his life seemed perfectly ordinary and routine for a boy his age.[62] Nevertheless, it seems that Henry made the best of Myrtle Hall, gaining a background to do well in high school.

The chance locus of birth made high school accessible for Henry. The construction of the first public high school in the state for African Americans in close proximity to Clarksdale (Coahoma Agricultural High School) made him extremely lucky. Even though the school was not within walking distance, it was less than ten miles away, making it a reasonable day-school option until he could afford to board.[63] Therefore, when Henry finished Myrtle Hall in 1938, he proceeded to the nearby high school. He commuted there daily, and estimated that it cost about fifteen cents per day—quite a sum of money for a family that already had another child at boarding school. In the beginning he attended only part time. He worked to help defray the cost by finding a variety of odd jobs, usually in white businesses in Clarksdale. He worked very hard that first year and was able to board and become a full-time student the following year.[64]

Some of the greatest insight into the budding young man can be gleaned from his descriptions of the various jobs he worked around Clarksdale. He observed first hand what it meant to be black and unequal. He saw the routine interactions between white businessmen and their patrons, and could discern no qualitative difference between them and himself, except that they were white and had privilege and power. He also worked with young white men, whose talents were observably not superior to his own. Yet he was paid less, received the worst work assignments, and lacked any control over the terms of his service. He observed some of the worst examples of racial epithets and violent encounters from bosses and patrons. These slights and demeaning acts were sometimes directed at him personally, but as often (if not more so) at other African Americans employed in these settings.

Henry had to endure being called "nigger," though he was deeply unnerved about it. For example, while working for a white drugstore owner, Mr. Henderson, Henry saw him kick a black worker and call him "nigger." The young Henry, with as much fear as loathing, ran home to tell his father. The elder Henry subsequently met with Mr. Henderson and exacted a promise that this would not happen to his son. This approach revealed to the boy how certain assertive tactics could provide a means of negotiation within this peculiar system. Henry, however, was bothered that his father ignored or diminished the importance of the epithet, which the employer continued to use. "Perhaps father was so accustomed to this that it seemed ordinary speech. Or, maybe he was burning inside and showing no outward discomfort to protect my job. The system dictated that my father beg Mr. Henderson to let me stay on rather than storm in and say, man to man, 'I'll not have you mistreating my son.'"[65]

Henry did learn early to make challenges to the system, and sometimes he did so directly. He described an example of resistance while working at the same drugstore. His responsibility was to make deliveries. A young white man, Joe Wilson, stocked shelves, and he resented Henry's employment. Wilson seemed particularly perturbed that Henry, who was about his age, would often come into the stockroom and help with the shelving when there was nothing else to do. Henry made an even bolder challenge when "Joe decided that I should address him as 'Mr. Joe' or 'Mr. Wilson.' Since we were about the same age, I just hooted at the suggestion and told him that I wasn't going to call him 'Mr.' anything. So I continued to call him Joe, and he continued to pout, and his resentment continued as long as I knew him."[66]

However, Henry could not always avoid the punishments of the system that was sustained by constancy of suspicion, visceral hate, and often violence. He related an instance of being accosted on a Halloween night while making Henderson Drugstore deliveries by bike. A white passerby set upon him as he stopped in the street to talk to friends. The perpetrator leaned out of his car "and hollered, 'Nigger, what did you say to me?' I answered, 'I wasn't talking to you.' The white man got out of the car, busted me in the mouth, cussed me some more, and then drove away." Henry was left bleeding with a busted lip, but chalked it up as one of those routines from which there was no immediate recourse. Indeed, he illustrated how these assaults could result from seemingly simple acts deemed violations of the racial codes. "All we had to do was walk down the street and not get off the narrow sidewalks to let a White pass." In the absence of some formal means of recourse, Henry said, "I always hurried on in case he might try to do some of the things that he was threatening."[67]

Sometimes avoidance of the risks really meant resistance by other means, such as dissembling. Clearly this was involved in how Henry's father handled Mr. Henderson's use of derogatory terms for some of his black employees. Ed Henry did not contest the use of the word "nigger," but rather focused on expectations regarding the treatment of his son. This created a space for the elder Henry to establish some bounds for how disputes involving Aaron would be handled. Clearly the context for this conversation was Mr. Henderson's treatment of the other black employee, but the approach Ed Henry used allowed him to violate ordinary rules of conduct by negotiating favorable terms.[68] Others were adept at use of such tactics as well. For example, black administrators and teachers could dissemble before white administrative hierarchy with a vitality and imagination that verged on caricature. Henry gave a long description of what often happened when Mr. Crumpton, the white superintendent, visited for a countywide meeting of all black teachers. Deference was on display, even when a teacher or principal was making veiled criticisms. First, these impending visits were presaged by efforts of the staff to have the facilities clean and tidy. Then the superintendent's arrival was replete with the rituals of the racial conduct code: "'Morning, Bessie, hello Delia,' always addressing the teachers by their first names." Invariably, instead of starting with a substantive agenda Crumpton began by soliciting a spiritual from Ernestine Powell, the teacher Henry believed to be among the most competent. She duly complied, perhaps singing a hymn like "Swing Low, Sweet Chariot," which others joined. "There they were, our teachers bellowing their lungs out with spiritual and field songs, and Mr. Crumpton standing there, tipped slightly forward from the waist up, chin poked out, beaming and smiling and rubbing his hands."[69]

This was followed by reports and discussion of activities, during which teachers found means, however veiled, to make critical expressions and demands. The well-understood protocol required them to issue glowing reports about their progress and general appreciation for state resources, despite the paltry resources Crumpton actually delivered. Henry often eavesdropped on these events and observed teachers trying to maintain integrity by pressing the limits of the code. They would make oblique references to resource needs or make reports about poorly working equipment. In a narration of what could have been one such example—faulty blackboards—Henry described how the superintendent was likely to dismiss such a complaint and actually lay the blame on the schools for not properly supervising students. Even when teachers might persist in bringing up the same issue from one meeting to the next, nothing could force the superintendent to be accountable; his negation of the complaint simply became a refrain. As such the school remained grossly underfunded and underequipped.[70]

Yet this kind of fawning and sycophancy masked a broad range of alterations of the approved agricultural and home economics-oriented curriculum that caused Henry to see high school as a productive experience. The curricular alterations could not compensate for the lack of resources, but the ingenuity and energy of the teachers enhanced the educational experience. Henry argued that his conversance with literary texts and his oppositional stance toward the system were foundations established in the Coahoma Agricultural High School. This alternative project was maintained with nods and winks as school officials walked a virtual tightrope maintaining the appearance of respecting the bounds of the racial system.

Henry particularly admired a principal appointed during his matriculation, J. B. Wright. He deemed Wright responsible for integrating liberal arts studies "with the Booker T. Washington program of teaching Negroes to work with their hands." It took a short time before "Negro history and literature were being boot-legged into the high school, and we were learning in biology that the Negro race was not inferior at all." Of course, eventually the school board found the "liberal ideas" of Wright too much and fired him. This did not occur, however, before the agricultural curriculum had been fundamentally subverted, largely because the principal recruited teachers who shared Wright's views. Henry regarded the Washington-style curriculum as secondary by the time he reached his senior year. Wright "was insisting on the arts, music, and the classics. He himself taught a course in ancient and medieval history and translated enough Caesar and Chaucer for us so that we at least knew who they were."[71]

The in-depth description that Henry gave of his high school education revealed a complex, almost stealth operation, as teachers and administrators contravened the approved boundaries. After the principal was fired, the classroom teacher Henry most admired was Thelma Shelby. This graduate of Dillard University in New Orleans taught English and economics. Since she also spoke French, she taught the language to interested students as an extracurricular activity. Moreover, unbeknown to the school district hierarchy, Shelby was a member of the NAACP. She revealed this to her students, both inside and outside the classroom. Moreover, she openly criticized racial segregation, even rejecting the dissembling tactics of some of her older colleagues.[72]

Meanwhile, in her classroom assignments Shelby helped students to make a critical assessment of the racial system. Henry reflected on the meaning of her assignment of Richard Wright's raw, hard-hitting *Native Son*, partially set in Mississippi. The book had inspired widespread controversy, and its use in a black classroom in Mississippi was unimaginable. Henry said his assessment of the novel was a defining moment. He found Wright's main character, Bigger, both revolting and sympathetic—a man driven to violence by the grinding omni-presence of oppression in everyday life and yet he maintained sufficient dignity in the end to choose death over acquiescence. Henry recalled "one sentence in the book . . . the most powerful I had ever read." He said that it brought together the scope of the problem and the necessity of taking personal responsibility to change the system. "As we learned about Bigger Thomas and the oppression of Negroes everywhere, we knew we were getting a bad deal right there in the school and in Clarksdale. It was up to us to change things, and those quiet rumblings from within the high school gave hope to many of us." He and his mates took their first step under the guiding hand of Miss Shelby: "the entire class joined the youth division of the NAACP. It cost fifty cents."[73]

An assessment of the curriculum Henry pursued confirmed his autobio-graphical depiction of his experience. He pursued a curriculum not even remotely related to the specifications of the Washington model. In his high school transcript there is scant evidence that agricultural courses occupied him. He took only two courses having this subject matter—Agriculture I and II.[74] In his autobiography he discusses what appear to be these two courses with revulsion. In his first year, he, like all the other boys, had an individual project. "Mine was a corn-testing experiment, where I took several grains of corn and determined which was most fruitful." The second project was raising chickens. Otherwise, he described a five-acre plot of cotton that his freshman class had to tend after school in a work-study arrangement—"I was returned to those damn fields again and hated them as much as ever."[75]

The rest of his curriculum through high school, however, did not look especially different from a liberal arts program that students pursue in public high school today, minus the plethora of electives. He completed four years of English, which his descriptions suggest also included a heavy dose of literature.[76] There were four units of history, including individual subjects introduced by Principal Wright before he was sacked—Negro history, U.S. history, and ancient and modern history. His mathematics regimen was also quite consistent with what one might see currently—algebra I and II and geometry. The sciences completed were biology and general science. It is not clear what was included in the general science course, but Henry's detailed description suggested some chemistry in the curriculum. There was apparently only one science teacher, and the equipment was so spare that a single Bunsen burner (the teacher's) was available. His high school curriculum was filled out with music, typing, and economics.[77]

The academic record shows that Henry was an outstanding student. He turned in his best all-around performances in history—making all As, explaining the ease over the years with which he peppered his speeches with historical references. He made two grades of C in his entire high school program. He was limited only by what was not available to him as he voraciously pursued learning.[78] He gave credit to his teachers and community preachers: "Our teachers and preachers were reasonably successful in developing among us a sense of responsibility to family and race. They encouraged education, running our own homes and trying to take care of ourselves, and above all to try and be 'somebody.'"[79] The educational achievements that Henry obtained later in life are the proof that he came away in relatively good repair, notwithstanding the absence of many critical resources from a school system that was in perennially desperate straits.

Henry completed high school in 1941, and the ever-widening disparity between the schools in the dual racial system caused him to believe that something had to change. He says that about this time he began to be more aggressive in stating his objections to the status quo, studiously avoiding stepping "too far over the line."[80] He was also increasingly restless about what he would do without the resources to go to college. The answer soon came as he was drafted for military service.

Meanwhile, the winds of change were coming to segregated schools in Mississippi and elsewhere in the South as the NAACP became more aggressive in contesting the dual school system. When Henry was drafted the NAACP had already achieved several court rulings that chipped away at pieces of the system.[81] This "writing on the wall" propelled a conversation among the white power elite in Mississippi about means for better implementing separate but equal. With a consensus building against school segregation in the Supreme Court, and with pressures from black teachers, the state allocated funds in 1946 and 1948 that were designated for school construction and salary improvements. While the project was never designed to attain parity with white schools, the terminology adopted for these efforts was "equalization." The only problem was that even after funds were made available, local districts maintained authority to allocate the money. True to form, they rarely allocated funds to black schools or to black teachers. By 1947, only 35 percent of the building funds had been allocated to black schools; while by 1950, the gap between salaries for the racial groups remained basically stable.[82] Despite all the pressures to change, including an unsuccessful NAACP lawsuit instigated by Gladys Bates, a black Jackson teacher, the racial status quo Henry knew prevailed as he went to war.[83]

CHAPTER TWO

Military Service, Family, and Profession

Challenging Contested Citizenship at War and at Home

Aaron Henry received a draft notice from the army in early 1943 and reported being inducted shortly before his July 2 birthday. He initially trained at Camp Shelby outside of Hattiesburg, 240 miles south of Clarksdale.[1] He entered a military service that had not sorted out how to handle African American soldiers. However, by the time of his induction there had been high-level discussions within the federal executive about how to fashion a practical policy for the recruitment, training, and treatment of black soldiers.[2] In part this resulted from intense pressure from black leaders.[3] At the same time, this approach reflected a desire to deflect criticism from international allies, especially in the emerging power conflict with the Soviet Union.[4]

Camp Shelby proved an interesting place for Henry to begin his military service. The diverse, but segregated base built during World War I, transformed the surrounding area. The population of Hattiesburg tripled in ten years, from 4,100 in 1910 to 13,000 in 1920. The camp experienced spectacular growth during World War II.[5] Arvarh Strickland says: "In September 1940, the federal government allocated $11,000,000 for the construction of the camp, and the War Department allocated $3,200,000 for the training of two army divisions. . . . By the last months of 1940 the Camp Shelby payrolls contained some 17,000 workers and the first 10,000 soldiers had arrived."[6] Located in the heart of segregated Mississippi, the thousands of black troops that passed through for training found the camp a turbulent place.

There were daily manifestations of the rigorous application of principles of racial caste on and off the base. These could be absurd and banal. For example, in order to maintain separation of the races a black officer "reported that he and another black lieutenant were assigned their own latrine consisting of four uri-nals, seven sinks, ten showers, and sixteen commodes, enough to bathe and flush an entire company."[7] The Hattiesburg police chief warned "black servicemen that when they visited Hattiesburg, 'they were expected to conduct themselves in the same manner as [N]egro civilians residing in the city.' This included not walking in white neighborhoods at night, 'except when going to and fro from work.' Black soldiers, like black civilians, were expected to stay in the black sections of town."[8]

Conflict, often violent, occurred between the two racial groups. It increas-ingly became exaggerated because a large number of nonsouthern black recruits trained there. They were unfamiliar with or unwilling to accept the rigors of segregation. The nonsoutherners "seemed to show little awe of the white police-men," taking them on in bar brawls and such. Sometimes, too, black soldiers violated the separation codes on public buses. This often led to violent encounters between the soldiers and the local or military police. Added to this mix was the special dynamic of Japanese soldiers, who arrived in 1943. The local elite sought to manage this by declaring them honorary whites, an arrangement that might have worked except that Japanese soldiers too sometimes violated the racial codes. In other instances, local whites simply objected to the honorary status and refused to honor it.[9]

Henry sized up the general situation immediately and complained bitterly about the contradictions. He lamented the irrationality in a system that asked black soldiers to commit to the ultimate price with their lives and yet remain segregated. "The moment we got to Camp Shelby, the whites were sent to one part of the camp, the Negroes to another. The only thing not segregated were the men in charge—they were always white, and 'in charge' was the operative word."[10] Moreover, the separation only aggravated an already volatile situation. For example, "the white soldiers were learning how to fire rifles and machine guns and other necessary skills of combat; the black soldiers were performing the peaceful 'house-keeping' duties needed on the post." Their "separate but equal" facilities were reflected by the brick recreational structure built for whites versus the frame building built for blacks. The expenditure for the white structure was more than three times that expended on the black one.[11] Though Henry did not remain long in Hattiesburg, these conditions at least clarified some of the limits presented by the "opportunity" for military service.

Since soldier diaries are often sparse, it is not atypical that little is known or documented by Henry about his life as a serviceman, and if he did preserve papers on his service, it is quite likely that they were lost in a major fire at his drugstore in 1993. A part of what is gleaned came from Charles Hill, a local veteran who served with Henry. The two were inducted at the same time and served their entire military commitment together. As "homeboys" they had the rare coincidence to sustain a preexisting friendship, and their relationship occupied a major place in Henry's autobiography.

According to Hill, Henry began to assume an activist attitude and leadership role from the beginning of his military service. He said that Henry began his critique before the bus completed its 240-mile trip from Clarksdale to Camp Shelby. A particularly sore point was the segregation the conscripts endured at a restaurant enroute. Hill recalled this scene: "And so, Aaron said . . . , he was [just] talking and he said: 'We are going to call ourselves going to fight for our country, and then look at that [segregation at restaurant] . . . ' He started right then . . . "[12]

Little relief or satisfaction came when they arrived at Camp Shelby. They discovered that familiar southern-style racial segregation was the policy.[13] Hill found the separation copiously maintained, with blacks receiving the least desirable of often-makeshift accommodations and services. "We got to Hattiesburg, and we [were] segregated in a small, little place. The white inductees had a big PX, and we had a little PX that looked like a hamburger stand. And [the base] had a big movie theater, [where] the whites went in the front [door], and the colored had the side door."[14]

Within several days at Camp Shelby, Henry began using his loquacious, gregarious character and superior intellect to urge defiance of segregation. "Right there in Hattiesburg, in Camp Shelby, Aaron started talking to the colored [soldiers] and told them not to attend the show [since they] had to go through the side door . . . But they [the Army] never changed it [even] then." It is unclear if this act of defiance led to direct confrontations, though Hill indicated that Henry's stance was well received by the soldiers, some of whom would forego movies altogether in order to avoid the indignity. Moreover, according to Hill, Henry refused an invitation for Officer Candidate School because of the sense of obligation and purpose he felt to the masses of black soldiers segregated at the bottom of the military structure.[15]

The next stop for basic training put Henry at Fort McClellan in Anniston, Alabama, with racial conditions on a par with Camp Shelby. Henry remained there for six weeks. The racial conflicts appeared to be heightened in Anniston because the base was larger and conscripts served longer. A more diverse population also existed there: a larger number of blacks from the northeast joined Japanese and European prisoners of war.[16] Yet, Henry and Hill managed to get through this part of the service without major incidents.

Most of Henry's military service, however, occurred far away from the South, thus influencing what he both obtained and gave to his units. Succeeding Fort McClellan he spent the balance of his time in California and Hawaii, never seeing a combat zone. In these settings he said that he experienced perhaps the closest thing to true "separate but equal" status. Though practically everything remained segregated, at least blacks appeared to get near their share in quantity and quality. Seeing a range of things never experienced before helped to broaden his horizons, allowing him to envision new possibilities. Sometimes these were mundane things; for example, riding a train for the first time; seeing mountains and the sea; and encountering diverse recruits from all over the country.[17]

The first assignment outside the South for Henry and Charles Hill was at Camp Roberts near San Luis Obispo, California. The town, like most in California, was not segregated. However, this military base, like the others that Henry had passed through, was segregated. The large camp included both a hospital and internment section for prisoners of war. It could house 30,000, and soldiers usually trained there for seventeen weeks.[18] Henry received training for the truck-driving job he performed during his service at this camp. Like many other black soldiers, he served in one of the 1,600 "Negro" quartermaster companies and became a light truck driver.[19] He achieved the rank of staff sergeant.[20] From this vantage point little opportunity existed for advancement into higher ranks and responsibilities. Soon after training in California, the two Clarksdale soldiers again left together for an assignment in Hawaii. When they arrived at still another base to find segregation a fact of life, Henry noted with some irony that "perhaps there was little or no segregation there before the U.S. Army moved in, but the place was pretty well segregated by 1944."[21] Yet there was an ever-growing African American presence among recruits. Scholars have corroborated Hill's view that these soldiers were aware that activists back home were partly responsible for waging an increasingly vigorous campaign for racial equality in society as well as equal access in the military.[22] This seemed to have an effect on Henry, whose opposition to racial discrimination within the army became more aggressive, and he began to take on something of a leadership role.[23] Henry's location in nonsouthern military bases also helped.

Several incidents showed him assuming leadership in resisting segregation in the army. In one example, he opposed the system symbolically and directly and received the desired outcome. This occurred in California, though there is some discrepancy about the exact place. Henry reported an incident in some detail where he led a protest against a chaplain who used a racial slur to refer to blacks. Previously he had helped to organize a large group of black soldiers to attend Sunday chapel services, where he and several others sang in the choir. On the date in question the soldiers "were all sitting in the rear of the church listening to the white chaplain's sermon, when he made a reference to a day back home when it 'rained pitchfork and nigger babies.'" Henry said he and most of the others protested by walking out, flagrantly slamming the door.[24] Charles Hill said that Henry not only walked out, but also made an official complaint that led to the removal of the chaplain.[25]

In a second illustration, Henry adopted symbolic and stealth measures. Aboard ship en route to their next posting in California, Henry and Hill were again confronted with a segregated movie facility. Since there was only one theater aboard and insufficient space for blacks to occupy their usual place at the back of the hall, two viewing nights were set aside. One of these was reserved for African Americans. Henry reacted to the indignity right away, sensing that other blacks also objected. He then organized a protest; if the theater were not available on an integrated basis, then blacks would not attend movies. Hill reported that Henry issued a threat through the informal network: "'Anybody I see going to that show on Wednesday, we're going to throw them to the sharks.' And nobody went to that show."[26]

Henry sustained his aggressive attitude in part because of significant support from the NAACP, which had chapters near bases. Indeed soldiers more often lodged complaints about racial incidents to NAACP officers as opposed to military representatives. Henry said: "I always affiliated with these chapters, and many times it was helpful in working out racial disputes on the base. . . . The NAACP officials were always available and made it their business to mediate. Negro soldiers . . . became enthusiastic members and started chapters when they returned home."[27]

Henry described certain positive aspects of his military experience for the resolution of at least some racial issues. He referred to placement in an integrated trucking unit when he arrived on Sand Island, in the Midway Island chain in the northwestern part of Hawaii.[28] As a light truck driver, he became a part of an apparent early experiment in organizing a work unit without regard to race. Though this "integration" had its limits, Henry described a reasonably commodious environment. "The trucking company where I was assigned . . . was one of the army's first experiments with integration. There were four trucking companies stationed on Sand Island. One was composed of Negroes and the other three of whites, and we were all in the same battalion. We used the same PX, the same mess halls and the same recreational facilities. Some individual conflicts came up between the races, but they were usually broken up by officers."[29]

Despite the limitations for advancement while in the army, Henry also used his natural entrepreneurial spirit to seize opportunities within his reach. He sought to advance his education; for example, taking remedial and general education courses at schools near two bases: San Francisco and the University of Hawaii. He took courses in algebra I and II, philosophy, chemistry, biology, and some mathematics, supplements to courses in which he excelled at high school.[30] He said he chose no degree course because he was undecided. Later he transferred some of these credits to Xavier University.

While Henry had a short military service, the interval in his development into manhood became especially important. In the army he first began to exercise public leadership and to develop the social change vision that defined his role when he returned to Mississippi. His status in society was drawn into stark relief when he realized that even fighting as a soldier for his country did not transfer equality. Though all soldiers bore the same risks and responsibilities for the country's security, he observed, the racial hierarchy remained in place. This contradiction was particularly glaring in war being waged, at least in part, to fight Nazis and their ideology of racism. Once in the army, as the descriptions from Hill suggest, Henry rapidly grew into a position where he spoke up in defense of himself and his rights. He quickly began to do so for others and even to engage in modest organized protests against his status. More than anything else, he left the army with the resolve to fight for change when he returned to Mississippi.

Moreover, the military provided another, perhaps inadvertent advantage to Henry's development. He became a part of a cohort of similarly minded fellow veterans. Some of these men later became his collaborators in the Delta. Many of them, like Henry, affiliated with the NAACP upon their return, but most important they collaborated in working toward goals of social change. Amzie Moore, from nearby Cleveland, was one of these veterans.[31] An even more central ally was Medgar Evers, who returned from the service, moved to the Delta, and subsequently became Aaron Henry's chief partner in building a new and highly visible NAACP. Francoise Hamlin has described the important role returnees from World War II had in laying the foundation for what eventually became the widespread assault on the racial system in Mississippi. She suggests that these soldiers, all of whom went to the war at a relatively young age, returned as mature men with a heightened sense of social responsibility that matched Henry's nagging discomfort at the continuation of racial discrimination at home. They had gone to war to fight for their country, ostensibly in defense of universal freedom and human rights. They returned with an expectation, that later became a demand, for an improvement in their status. Their experience provided them an unusual vantage point for staking claims as leaders for social change.[32]

The Mississippi to which Henry returned after military service remained unremittingly segregated, and black access to power remained almost totally blocked. These conditions continued despite the organization of the Mississippi Progressive Voters' League after the war. The league was a nonpartisan group of blacks whose middle-class orientation led them to focus on moderate changes such as political education and voter registration, but not mobilization. Even registration remained mostly unchanged. Despite an active chapter in Clarksdale in 1943 the city had very few black qualified voters, mirroring a state where less than one-half of 1 percent was registered.[33] By 1947, after several successful legal challenges to disfranchisement, only 1 percent succeeded in enrolling to vote. It took another ten years to rise to 5 percent, and no significant increases occurred until 1965.[34]

Meanwhile, the means that sustained these conditions had not changed, despite the "separate but equal" policy. Aside from violence, intimidation, and terror, legal procedures played a major part. Mississippi had perhaps the most stringent voter registration requirements, including both a cumulative poll tax and a literacy test, rigorously administered by race.[35] While poor and illiterate whites were likely to be registered, even the most highly qualified blacks were unlikely to be approved since the circuit clerk made these decisions on site.[36]

Henry challenged the old order by seeking to register as soon as he returned to Clarksdale in 1946. He discovered a wall of resistance from local officials, as well as great fear among would-be black registrants. He was determined to conquer both the white resistance and the black fear. Personally, he perceived an advantage because of the special provisions that were extended to veterans. He knew, for example, that the state exempted veterans from the cumulative poll tax, though literacy was required. Initially he simply presented himself as a veteran to the circuit clerk, who denied that such an exemption existed. However, by the second visit the gregarious Henry had not only ascertained that white veterans were being given the exemption but showed up with proof. He acquired a copy of the registration certificate from one of the white veterans and produced it when the clerk again denied any such knowledge. Thereupon the clerk "told me politely that I would still have to pass various tests to show that I was qualified to vote. I read several sections of the state constitution and went through more rigmarole satisfactorily. Then he registered me to vote." Apparently after his challenge, the circuit clerk allowed other blacks to "pass" the test. According to Henry, a man who had long denied them the right to register seemed to have a change of heart, and thereafter proceeded to register many blacks. He also urged Henry to return to Clarksdale after college to help his people.[37] This was an extraordinary event insofar as Henry's persistence represented the kind of behavior that could easily have led to reprisals or even death.

It is hard to tell whether this resulted because of Henry's directness or because of the clerk's assumption that registration did not guarantee actual voting or political mobilization. Indeed, few expected mobilization to be eminent. The leadership of the local Progressive Voter's League at the time even appeared willing to focus on mere registration as an end. Perhaps being aware of the known efforts of whites to intimidate voters, the league's leader said that "[h]e urged members to register, to pay their poll taxes, and to 'work individually to get other Blacks to do the same.' Yet [he] opposed any systematic block-by-block, door to door canvassing 'for any purpose.'"[38]

Henry differed and immediately made the connection between registration and casting ballots. He used the first opportunity to exercise his personal vote, leaving some bemused and others in disbelief at how he flaunted the well-understood rules. He described that day and the audience of blacks who gathered around as observers, some of them "older men who had paid their poll tax and registered. I asked why they were standing around, why weren't they voting, and they said that they were waiting to let the veterans have the honor of voting first. Actually, I think they were waiting to see what would happen to the first Negro who tried." Henry continued, "I walked on into the voting place, signed my name, took my ballot, and voted. There was no reaction from the whites, and the other Negroes began to file in and vote. I was the first Negro in Coahoma County to vote in a Democratic primary."[39]

The emphasis Henry had on voting in a Democratic primary is also significant. Previously the few blacks who did vote only did so in national elections as members of the Republican (Black and Tan) Party.[40] Because the white primary denied them membership in the de facto ruling Democratic Party, blacks were unable to influence local elections at all.[41] These conditions remained even though the white primary had been outlawed some ten years earlier.[42] Therefore, while Henry and some other blacks voted in this 1946 municipal election for the first time, their small number had little chance of influencing the outcome. The ruling white Democratic Party elected J. W. Hopkins as mayor, a man whose influence in the all-white state Democratic Party was such that he became a delegate to the 1940 national convention, along with the rabid racist demagogue, then U.S. senator Theodore Bilbo.[43]

Henry desired to attend college prior to entering the army, and had even settled on Alcorn College, the black land-grant college that bore the name of the Reconstruction governor from Clarksdale. Unfortunately, Henry did not have the funds for tuition.[44] He did not give up, however, and decided to seek training as a pharmacist following military service. Accomplishing this in Mississippi though was even more difficult than getting a high school education in the state. In 1946 the four black colleges offered little beyond teacher training.[45] There was no option for training as a pharmacist, a subject available only at the University of Mississippi (Ole Miss), an institution open only to whites. Consequently, he, like all of the other African American lawyers, physicians, and doctorate-level trained professionals at the time, had to secure such degrees elsewhere. The state even provided funds for blacks to go out of state in order to maintain the sanctity of segregation.[46] Henry chose Xavier University, a small black Catholic college in New Orleans.[47] The educational supplement from the GI Bill eased the financial strain, paying his tuition and incidentals.

He credited the military with providing him the desire to pursue pharmacy as a career. He developed a concern about health issues after observing the performance of army medics. He felt that these trained individuals often performed their duties without any compassion. At the same time, he believed they often neglected to use the medical knowledge at their disposal to assist in the alleviation of common public health problems among soldiers, such as venereal diseases. Henry felt he could do better and was thereby motivated to pursue pharmacy.[48]

Pharmacy was an interesting choice given that all indications in the environment suggested that it was a profession rarely occupied by blacks. The professional occupations open to them were almost all in teaching, the clergy, or mortuary science. For example, in 1940 there were only fifty-five African American physicians, twenty-nine dentists, and eleven pharmacists in the state.[49] Most of these were in urban locations, including Clarksdale. The town had one physician and one dentist in 1950, but no lawyers nor scientific specialists. Though these data seem to indicate the near inaccessibility of pharmacy for a black, Henry remained determined to pursue it.

Xavier proved a good choice for Henry. As an institution organized for African Americans, it provided a nurturing environment attuned to the needs of its black students and the segregated communities they were destined to serve. It also filled an almost unique role as a professional school. The pharmacy program founded in 1927 became only the second such program in the country; Howard University had the other.[50] This characteristic of Xavier allowed Henry a degree of freedom that supported his evolving social change orientation. His interests were further fueled by the fact that Xavier was significantly involved in social change activities. At the same time, the relatively close proximity of New Orleans to his home made the school more attractive to him.

Henry had a very active student life. Though a Methodist, he easily accommodated himself to this Catholic college environment. He heavily engaged in both academic and student activities, including religious life, though it was in student life where his natural leadership tendencies emerged. During his sophomore and junior years he served as student body president, for example.[51] There is also evidence that he served twice as class president. The student newspaper, the *Xavier Herald*, carried notice of Henry's selection as class president in the junior year. A later edition featured a photograph of his senior class in May 1950, where he is again listed as president.[52] Despite his protestations that he devoted most of his time to study, it is clear that his activism spanned all phases of campus life—in academic pursuits, in extracurricular life, and in the community.

Even though he perceived defects in his previous preparation, Henry followed the rigorous academic program and excelled. The prearranged curriculum at Xavier allowed few electives, and the pharmacy track seemed especially daunting. The college bulletin produced the entire four-year "order of studies." Henry started his first semester with the history of pharmacy (101), mathematics for the profession (103), plus basic mathematics (101, likely college algebra). The basic sciences were chemistry and biology, both laboratory courses. The program was rounded out with English and religion. The second semester he had only one pharmacy course (102, Latin), while chemistry, math, biology, and English were continued. A one-credit hour first-aid course rounded out his second-year program.

This regimen of difficult course work continued for the next three years. The math and science courses predominated in his curriculum. In the sophomore year he was required to take two chemistry courses each semester, in addition to his study of drugs in pharmacognosy and physics. He continued religion, fulfilling this one- to two-credit annual requirement in each semester through graduation. The junior and senior years were the most stringent, with the addition of advanced pharmacology courses. However, in this phase philosophy and economics replaced some of the science and math.[53]

A great deal of documentation about his academic performance and extracurricular activities appeared in the university newspaper, which carried a wealth of information about the activities of students. For example, it published the honor roll and individual grade-point averages. Henry excelled from the beginning, making the honor roll his freshman year. He was not yet at the top of the class, but his 86.75 grade point ranked him seventeen in a class of twenty-eight, where the highest freshman score was 92.4. By the end of the year, however, he made considerable gain. He earned a grade point of 91.5 and a class rank of seven. A complete profile could not be compiled because the *Herald* did not systematically report the honor roll. However, subsequent editions did continue to list Henry among honor students. It is, therefore, safe to assume that his high performance was maintained throughout his pharmacy studies.[54]

The rich social change activity in the environment of Xavier became apparent within the first months of Henry's arrival. The very busy New Orleans NAACP chapter sponsored a youth conference on the Xavier campus. It featured two national officers whose civil rights work later earned national acclaim: Thurgood Marshall (then special counsel for the NAACP) and Ruby Hurley (youth secretary). Both subsequently became well known to Henry during his leadership of the Mississippi branch. It is quite likely that he first met them at this meeting because of the broad participation of the campus chapter in the event. For example, Charles Bell, an Xavier student and president of the New Orleans NAACP Youth Council, spoke at the meeting. The Xavier University Choir also performed, all of which suggests that there was institutional support for the event.[55]

Xavier proved to be an especially rich university environment for the nurture of a new black leadership class in the South. A month following Henry's arrival, several other African American community leaders and a group of liberal white civil and human rights activists arrived at Xavier to organize a conference. They represented the Southern Conference on Human Welfare (SCHW), an early southern, interracial coalition for social change. The group had a broad platform, compelling the interest of an amalgam of intellectuals and activists. Its concern for racial liberation included the full gamut of related social factors: equal education, economic justice, and civil rights. Like the NAACP, the SCHW utilized lobbying and appeals to universal humanity to make its case.[56]

The SCHW attracted several high-profile African Americans to the New Orleans meeting in 1947. Among them were Mary McLeod Bethune, the educator and President Franklin Roosevelt's director of Negro Affairs in the National Youth Administration, and Walter White, the top NAACP official.[57] It also attracted some powerful elected officials, among them Senator Claude Pepper of New York. The attendees heard Walter White denounce the state of Alabama for legally barring NAACP membership and heard Georgia governor Ellis Arnall demand the ouster of Mississippi senator Bilbo from the U.S. Senate.[58] This was a heady affair for Henry, but it put him in the mainstream of ideas and among some of the prominent citizens working for social change. This appealing and enriching environment illustrated the special experience that the black college afforded Henry while he honed skills that he later employed in pursuing social change in his own community.

Henry also worked with the progressive and interracial National Students Association (NSA) while at Xavier. Among other things, the NSA (formed in 1946) took strong stands against all forms of discrimination, especially of a racial and religious nature.[59] Ironically many of its first student organizers met at an international gathering in Prague, Czechoslovakia, that was ostensibly designed to focus on international issues. It quickly gravitated to discussions of civil rights and academic freedom, however.[60] The organization soon became an important connection and outlet for Henry, and he joined the Xavier-NSA affiliate group, attending local, regional, and national meetings. He appeared to be deeply involved in early NSA organizational activity as well. Xavier sent a delegation of six students to the first formal organizational meeting in December 1946 in Chicago.[61] It is believed that Henry was among them. In his autobiography he refers to being a part of the Xavier delegation for a founding meeting in the Midwest in 1947 (though this was more likely the 1946 meeting).[62]

The NSA provided a venue where Henry met other southern students. Some among these came from Tulane and Loyola Universities, two private New Orleans schools active in the affairs of the emerging NSA. They were especially active in the regional meetings, some of which were held in Louisiana.[63] Henry also met students from other southern schools, surprisingly including some from segregated public institutions. Among historically public black colleges were Alabama State, Johnson C. Smith (South Carolina), Florida A and M, North Carolina State, North Carolina Central, and Virginia State. Those among the private schools were Howard, Bennett, Hampton, Tuskegee, Virginia Union, and Shaw (North Carolina); and virtually all of the major private higher education white institutions were active—Vanderbilt, Emory, Duke, Mary Washington (Virginia), and Wake Forest. There were, however, major white public institutions, too, the most active of which seemed to be the University of North Carolina at Chapel Hill (its undergraduate, Al Lowenstein, subsequently led the NSA). Other schools that sent delegations to various conferences and meetings were Georgia Tech, University of Virginia, University of Tennessee, and University of South Carolina.[64]

For Henry this was a boon; talking across racial lines about common problems must have given him tremendous hope that his emerging vision was entirely practical, that there were other southerners who were willing to run the risk to seek racial progress. The richness of this environment is indicated in the way the NSA functioned. It met in annual congresses, according to William Chafe, that "were lengthy deliberative sessions: although leavened with a certain amount of frolicking and the exhilaration of meeting new friends."[65] The race question was an abiding concern for these idealistic students, making them instant allies for Aaron Henry and his cohorts from the black colleges. Indeed, it sometimes proved hard to tell whether student governance or the race question was more important. In its first meeting to organize a local chapter at UNC, the predominant issues addressed were racism and discrimination on the campuses. The students met at the parish house of an Episcopal Church where speaker after speaker hammered this home. Reverend Allyn Robinson, chairman of the North Carolina Council of Christians and Jews, stressed the fraternity of humanity, criticizing current antidiscrimination policies "as dealing with symptoms, rather than with roots and causes."[66] In this company Henry, the budding activist leader, surely felt he was among kindred spirits.

The timing could not have been more propitious for Henry to network with these emerging white leaders, among whom he could bring a distinct perspective about race, and broaden his own worldview. He discussed major national and international public policy issues and gained a perspective far beyond the racial isolation in Clarksdale. One of its benefits was that the NSA modeled racial integration by selecting an African American as its first president.[67] By 1950 Henry had become the chairman of Xavier's Student Affairs Committee and primary campus liaison to the NSA.[68] From this perch he had continuous exchanges with the diverse leadership of the NSA. This established a pattern of exchanges from which he never wavered when he became a leader of the Mississippi civil rights movement.

Despite the scope of Henry's extracurricular activities, he remained a successful and diligent pharmacy student. However, he said little about progress toward his degree, until his junior year apprenticeship. This was clearly a time he enjoyed, especially doing some practical pharmacy work. He was assigned to an African American couple, Mr. and Mrs. J. W. Lopez, who owned a drugstore. The placement provided him room and board and a kind of filial relationship with the proprietors. They gave him substantive responsibilities right away. "I worked in the store afternoons after school and on weekends and learned how to fill prescriptions and how to run a drugstore. I also placed stock orders and sold general merchandise. . . . My big moment came one summer when Mr. Lopez told me he and his wife were going on a trip for several days and that they were leaving me in charge of the store. I learned a lot and everything went smoothly."[69]

The apprenticeship and its location were profoundly important. They fit Henry's view of himself as a professional pharmacist whose mission was to enhance the lives of underserved people without regard to race. "The Lopez Pharmacy was located in the middle of a housing project for low-income whites, and I became further convinced that poor whites are not unwilling to get along with blacks, and that poverty is more common than race." He drew two lessons from the irony of the clientele. The first was that he could dedicate a professional life to the alleviation of problems for poor people. The other was that if we focused on real human need instead of the false premises of race, it was entirely possible to alter the system of racial exclusion in the South. There was no difference in the service the Lopezes provided to their impoverished clients, rather the terms on which they offered it was with sensitivity to the problems the clients faced: the extension of credit or a space for their children to play. And in the acceptance of these arrangements, these white clients displayed no obvious difference because their benefactors were African Americans. "It seemed perfectly natural that the white youngsters from impoverished homes would come daily for assistance from Negroes who were better off educationally and economically."[70]

Henry completed the pharmacy program with flying colors and on time in the spring of 1950. In the world of the black college, he was a "big man on campus." His superior academic performance had been successfully combined with leadership of student governance and social activism. He was a fixture on the honor roll and was class president multiple times. Meanwhile, he also relished Xavier's role in giving voice to civil rights issues by opening its facilities for meetings of civil rights figures and liberal activists often unwelcome elsewhere in New Orleans. He completely absorbed himself in this world, both learning and leading on issues that later completely consumed him.

All that was left was the consummation of his achievements with graduation. That proved to be a trying circumstance since Henry tried to opt out of the ceremony. He had a respectable problem—the pharmacy board examinations were scheduled in Mississippi on the same day as graduation. "The nuns at Xavier told me that nobody had ever graduated from there without attending the ceremony.

They explained that each student had to march up, receive his degree, then kiss the bishop's ring." Henry ultimately found a way to comply and to also take his board exams.[71]

Managing the board exams, however, proved the most challenging, with the sole testing site for the multiday test located at the segregated University of Mississippi at Oxford. Henry's appearance (and that of Xavier pharmacy student Joe Leonard) presented a problem and exposed the irrationalities and inefficiencies of the racial system. The eventual resolution turned the system on its head since the arrangement "integrated" the segregated examining hall. Henry said, "We sat anywhere we pleased, and at no time was there evidence of discrimination."[72] To accomplish this Henry turned to the networking skills that later became a signature. He called upon John Duddy, a white salesman he previously met in one of his part-time jobs in Clarksdale, to help. Henry flew to Memphis, and Duddy met him and then drove on to Oxford. They then called the dean, who arranged housing at a black local residence for Henry and Leonard. Still another white, John Leslie, himself a student taking the exam, helped them secure food since the commons was not open to blacks. Leslie said he sat next to Henry, though separated by three rows, and took him along to the cafeteria at lunchtime. Upon arrival, "They told us 'we can't serve him here.' I said you're going to serve Aaron! 'It's against state law,' they said. They finally ended up feeding Aaron on the back porch!"[73] None of this seemed to detract from Henry's performance. He said: "The oral test was given first, and that's where I made my mark. I like talking and whenever the man asked me a question, I had studied so much that I started talking and elaborating until he had to tell me to stop. . . . A month later I was pleased to learn that I scored the third-highest grade on the examination."[74]

After graduation Henry returned to Clarksdale to get married and begin his pharmacy business. There is not much documentation of his courtship with Noelle Michael, whom he married in 1950, though it lasted perhaps five years or more. Henry's daughter, Rebecca, recounted the story both parents related to her. Henry apparently first became aware of Noelle Michael during his military service. During a summer vacation in Clarksdale she attended Bible school at Haven Methodist Church. She happened to board with Henry's mother, a member of the church. At some point Mrs. Henry asked Noelle for a photograph, which she then promptly sent to her son. According to the story, it was not long thereafter that he started writing to the young woman and expressing an interest in a relationship. Noelle appeared not to be impressed and did not reply. Later Noelle's elder sister termed this discourteous, entreating her to reply to the young serviceman.[75] Apparently she did so since a relationship did develop, albeit from a distance.

Despite her hesitance, Henry's pursuit of Noelle Michael was intense. He even went so far as to propose before their first face-to-face meeting. According to Rebecca it seems that he simply began to announce in his correspondence that he was going to marry her. Subsequently, their first encounter, which occurred during one of his routine military leaves, went well enough that their correspondence flourished and continued until Henry ended his service. Then he almost immediately departed for pharmacy school, a period that Rebecca described as the real courtship between them.[76] On June 11, 1950, the two were married. They established a household in Clarksdale where they remained as a family until the death of Mrs. Henry in 1993.[77]

Aaron Henry and wife, Noelle Henry, Graduation day, May 1950. (Courtesy Aaron Henry Papers, Tougaloo College.)

Noelle Michael's birth on Christmas Day in 1921, just outside the capital city of Jackson, in the small community of Van Winkle, preceded the birth of the man she eventually married by seven months. She attended public schools in Jackson, received a BA degree in 1945 from Jackson State College, and subsequently did graduate work at Atlanta University.[78] The occasion for her original visit to Clarksdale reveals a part of her story. She came from a Christian family very active in the Methodist church. The Christian values by which she lived seemed fundamental to the kind and gentle personality that almost everyone attributed to her. Though she hailed from a very large family, seven girls and two boys, many of her siblings, like her, were college educated. She and all of her sisters became schoolteachers—a rare accomplishment for the time. Noelle already had her degree in 1945 and was teaching in the Jackson City schools, a career she continued in Clarksdale.

Noelle Michael also had a web of connections within the city of Clarksdale that almost surely facilitated the relationship with Henry. One of her sisters became a teacher there and was coincidentally the wife of the minister at Haven Church, Reverend Merrill Lindsey. Another sister acquired a teaching job there and lived first with the Lindsey family and later with Noelle and Aaron. Rebecca Henry described these sisters as being very close, relationships that deepened since the three now lived and worked in Clarksdale. This family relationship deepened as Henry developed a personal and political relationship with his pastor, now also his brother-in-law. They both became political activists who developed a partnership to pursue social change in Clarksdale and the state. For example, Lindsey became one of the first blacks since Reconstruction to run for Congress, with Henry as his campaign manager.[79]

This God-fearing woman adored and supported her husband, whom she called "Precious." It was no doubt a role she enjoyed fulfilling. Many sources described her as a person of extreme generosity, kindness, and gentility. Louise Bradford and Brenda Luckett used the words "sweetness" and "angelic" to characterize her personality, a portrait similar to that provided by Rebecca.[80] According to them, she never wavered through the years as her husband's life evolved and became consumed by political work. She endured his long absences, threats upon her life and the members of her family, bombings at her homestead, and eventually the loss of her job as a schoolteacher. Her support was described as steady and sturdy, though Henry's political activities disrupted their personal family life. She appeared to look after Henry's personal care with joy and had a storehouse of surrogates to see after his welfare when he traveled. She delighted in entertaining, cooking, and boarding the numerous civil rights activists and politicians who visited their home in Clarksdale. Louise Bradford, by self-description a surrogate daughter to the family, supported the view of Mrs. Henry as "a God-fearing woman. She loved her church; she loved her house; and she loved her Precious."[81]

Moreover, there was little doubt of her full support for Henry's political work. Their daughter and several others offered a similar rendering of what he told her about his commitments in the early days of their marriage: that his life's destiny was to work in the interest of enhancing the life of his people. He related this as a religious calling, being an injunction from God to use his talents in this way. Here is how Rebecca Henry remembered her mother's iteration of the pact she and Aaron made: "He told my mama that when he was in the service and saw black people being treated so bad he had promised the Lord that if He let him live to come home, he would spend his days working for his people." It was a mission that she seemed to accept as his movement activity continuously increased.[82]

The shocks that Noelle Henry endured because of her husband's chosen path could well have destroyed their marriage: the virtual abandonment of his pharmacy career, absences, efforts at intimidation, and personal threats. Perhaps one of the strongest challenges were questions about his sexuality and other aspects of his faithfulness to her. Soon after the Clarksdale movement began, a morals charge was brought in March 1962 against Henry alleging that he had offered to have sex with Sterling Eilert, a young white man.[83] While these charges (detailed in chapter 3) seem almost certainly to have been false (the Supreme Court later agreed) and designed to intimidate Henry for his civil rights work, the questions about his sexuality remained.[84] He was arrested on several other occasions at various places around the country and charged with offering to have sex with men.[85] Some of those who worked closely with him expressed no doubt that Henry was bisexual and/or had conflicts about his sexuality. Broader allegations about his sexuality were also featured prominently in John Howard's historical study of homosexuality among men in Mississippi.[86] Mrs. Henry herself raised concerns about relationships with other women that she found threatening. As will be seen below, sometimes these concerns were a product of her observations at events, or sometimes they came from awareness of cards with warm words and small gifts that Henry was known to send to other women. Often these women were clearly associates in his political work (such as Muriel Humphrey), but other relationships may have been more difficult to interpret.

There is no known evidence that Mrs. Henry communicated directly to others about the complications these possibly intimate involvements with other men and women had on their relationship. There is at least one piece of evidence that she communicated her loneliness to him and lamented the virtual loss of intimacy in their marriage. In a long, undated letter to her husband she indicated that she was deeply affected by the inattentiveness and what she referred to as the many public embarrassments he had caused her. She related that these were matters that she had brought up to him many times over thirteen years including her suspicions about relationships with other women. If she had concerns about his relationships with men, she did not mention them.

Her letter was written on a Sunday afternoon. She addressed Henry, as was her custom, as "dear precious." She asked him to "relax, read this and then think on it, after which tear it up." The letter was apparently occasioned by a complaint from Henry that she was not in a good mood when he came home. She explained that this was true, but that it was not a condition that afflicted only her. She reminded him that he too was sometimes moody. She explained that her moods might result because in their interactions he had so often been wrong about things, but refused to admit it. She reflected on her inability to get him to communicate what was going on when he was in a bad mood. Of herself, she said, "I can't pretend. When something is wrong, I feel depressed. I'm not lively during those times and most times I don't have anyone to talk to." She went on to express doubt that he loved her. She recounted, "In the last 13 years we have had sex seven times. In the last 11 years we have had sex once."[87] She wondered about other relationships and was quite specific about circumstances regarding other women that caused her to have these doubts.

> I've always trusted you and never thought about what you might be doing until this [nb: woman's name deleted] deal was rumored. Then I thought about statements she had made on various occasions. I thought about [nb: second woman's name deleted] becoming upset because you danced a good deal with someone [else] and not her. Her husband was there but she didn't want to dance with him. I thought about the lady who had been in prison, [who] called and said she was coming by. You said she was coming to see about a husband in prison. . . . [Only] When she got up to leave, she mentioned her husband. She also mentioned while here something about the nightclub you carried her to.

Clearly Mrs. Henry was anxious to give her husband the benefit of the doubt. After chastising him about not sharing his whereabouts when he was gone, she suggested that having this knowledge was beneficial to both of them. While she obviously wanted to know where he was traveling and what he was doing, she also wanted to be able to credibly provide information to his many colleagues and friends who telephoned seeking his whereabouts. As his wife, she said, she did not wish to be put in the untenable position of having people distrust her when she could not explain where he was. Yet, she made it clear that she understood his responsibilities and that "perhaps you are so wrapped up in what you are doing, that you really haven't stopped to think about what's being done to me." She continued: "As a wife I've been neglected. You could tell me sometimes 'I love you.'" She did give him credit for responding in kind when she expressed her love for him. Then, she took the occasion to also express her displeasure that hc sometimes dispatched others to purchase gifts for her. She asked that he not continue to do this, since it was his personal thoughtfulness that mattered. "It doesn't have to be much, but these are things we always cherish." Despite these concerns and hurts, she closed expressing her lifetime love while wishing him a happy new year. Her final injunction was "let us both strive to love, care and be more concerned about each other."[88]

None of these factors brought down the Henry marriage. They remained a family until Mrs. Henry preceded him in death. At the same time, these personal circumstances also did not diminish the towering leadership role he played in local, state, and national politics. In short, these aspects of his personal life did not define or become the story of his social movement life nor of his political leadership.

With a pharmacy degree and a new bride, Henry began his professional work audaciously by bending, if not breaking, the rules of the system. He entered an interracial partnership in Clarksdale with K. W. Walker, who ran a pharmacy in the Palace Drugstore. Walker had many African American clients, acquired by cultivating a relationship with the sole black physician in town, Dr. O. G. Smith. This physician directed his customers to Henry and Walker's new Fourth Street Drugstore and the cross-racial partnership flourished. Despite the obvious anomaly, Henry spoke about the arrangement in a matter-of-fact way—a business arrangement among equals. The partners did recognize certain limits, one being avoidance of an outward personal relationship. No doubt location in the black community afforded some protection. Yet what seemed most important was how Henry functioned within the arrangement. The business gave him entrée to the broadest spectrum of the local black community, where he espoused his emerging impatience with the system and sketched a vision for change, perhaps foretelling the direction he would take later in life.

From the outset, racial rules specified that the pharmacy would be an institution that catered to the African American community. This was an artifact of the post-Reconstruction Jim Crow system that gave license to the development of a class of businesses and specialists to cater to African American residential enclaves, the "Negro quarter." This domain was not exclusive to black entrepreneurs, but it sustained a class including teachers, a physician, morticians, and personal care associates, among others. As such, the Fourth Street Drugstore became the center for servicing the pharmaceutical needs of black patients.

The drugstore dispensed much more, however. It became a safe haven for people to congregate—a special space in the rural setting that paralleled urban cafes, saloons, and social clubs. In the small towns and hamlets in the South commercial spaces were as likely as anything else to serve such a function. After all, public spaces often were severely limited. In Clarksdale the Fourth Street

*Aaron Henry in Fourth Street Drugstore, October 1, 1963, Clarksdale, Mississippi.
(Courtesy The Image Works/Take Stock Image.)*

Drugstore soon became a destination for African Americans: a place of socializing, information exchange, and a conduit for the circulation of political messages.[89]

Aaron Henry gained entrée to a broader network of African American entrepreneurs through the drugstore. Many of these individuals also had personal characteristics like Henry's. Some were recently returned veterans, while others formed a small class of scientific professionals cum entrepreneurs, many compatriots of the Mississippi Delta. Like him, they were increasingly restive about the system. Perhaps the most critical part of this network can be traced to Henry's early contacts. The first parts of his regional network developed in Mound Bayou. Henry said, "one of my first efforts was to establish good relations with every medical doctor in the area. This endeavor took me to Mound Bayou, an all-Negro community located about thirty miles south of Clarksdale. I met people at the Taborian Hospital and Friendship Clinic, including Dr. T. R. M. Howard, one of the best-known Negro physicians in the state."[90] The Mound Bayou crowd put Henry into contact with other military veterans like Amzie Moore, Medgar Evers, and Emmett Stringer. Coincidentally, four of these veterans also returned in 1946 and used the GI Bill to complete college or professional education.

These returning World War II veterans who fought for freedom now showed far less tolerance of the old Mississippi ways. They were not alone. The work of an emerging African American-centered civil rights coalition greatly supplemented this local network. The first among equals in this coalition was the NAACP, whose northern secretariat belied its focus largely on issues of the South: segregation, disfranchisement, and economic disparity.[91] Its relentless pressure on the military enhanced the experience that these Mississippi veterans had in World War II.[92] Moreover, most southern blacks who had civil rights affiliations, even if furtive, had them with the NAACP. They were also aware of A. Philip Randolph's threat to march on the White House in 1941 to protest job discrimination. Similarly, black migrants to northern cities had elected the first blacks to Congress who directly associated themselves with the move to eliminate disfranchisement in the South; Charles Diggs and Adam Clayton Powell, who represented Detroit and Harlem, respectively, were particularly outspoken.[93]

Moreover, the winds of change blew across an even broader spectrum. For the first time since Reconstruction, a consensus emerged outside the South that saw Jim Crow as inconsistent with national democratic values. The open appeal to blacks by the Democratic Party in the 1940s was a part of this process.[94] At last an alternative could be discerned to the Black and Tan Party, a residual outpost of previous alignment with the Republican Party.[95] The media proved a major, if sometimes unwitting, ally of the emerging movement with their moving pictures of egregious acts of discrimination and racial violence.[96] Clergy and students became engaged.[97] Though these disparate forces had not yet congealed into a movement in the late 1940s, Henry had deep engagement with these players. He had a personality that situated him well to become a leader in the environment. His loquacious and gregariousness—a folksy, backslapping manner that can be likened to the notion of "southern hospitality"—allowed him to easily collect allies among local and external actors. He had already exhibited these traits in Clarksdale: enlisting a local white veteran to aid his voter registration quest and entering a taboo interracial partnership for his pharmacy. Courting and cumulating external allies therefore came easy to him. Soon this young pharmacist had only to deploy them generously as he negotiated the wiles of the racial divide in Mississippi.

With the independence Henry established with his pharmacy he began to publicly challenge the old ways with fearlessness, despite the often swift and devastating consequences that could result. His close associates noted this characteristic, attributing it to his commitment to principles of fairness and a belief that the right combination of biracial forces could bring change. One of his closest associates in Clarksdale, Bennie Gooden, said: "He was anxious in some ways. [However,] I never saw him very fearful. *We were fearful for him* [emphasis added] to the extent that we had voluntary guards at his house for many years. We had men who would spend the night at Aaron's house armed with shotguns and pistols and what have you."[98] In his casual, almost banal acts, Henry accomplished something quite revolutionary; he projected his rights by merely laying claim to them, assuming roles theoretically off limits. In short, in the words of Nicholas Lemann, "he appeared to be completely implacable, as if the risks entailed in fighting segregation had no place in his mind."[99] He reflected Charles Payne's new class: "[A] generation of leadership . . . [that was] largely male, relatively well-educated, frequently veterans, and ordinarily associated with the NAACP. . . . They came of age before or during the Second World War, took advantage of changing postwar economic and political conditions to increase at least temporarily, the pace and intensity of Black activism." Because they could tap into a broader, external movement "they were able to push white supremacy further than it had ever been pushed before."[100]

The black community in Clarksdale already showed signs of agitation. Just one year after Henry's return from pharmacy school, an event occurred that generated widespread outrage: the rape of Leola Tates and Erline Mills, two black women. They told a story of being assaulted by two white teenagers.[101] Previously such an event might have gone without any visible public reaction from the black community. Such rapes, according to Patricia Hills-Collins, were "one fundamental tool of sexual violence directed against African American women."[102] Stanley Gaines Jr. called the practice "sexual chattel," a phenomenon that was critical to the "institutionalization of slavery."[103] When these rapes occurred in Clarksdale the perpetrators likely assumed the old rules would apply. Instead, without fanfare, but with a heretofore-unknown certainty, the African American community expressed outrage and forced a public accounting.[104] It was an event that helped propel a movement in Clarksdale that allowed Aaron Henry to emerge as community leader.

The changing role of the local black community seemed evident from the moment this incident occurred. When the women were reported missing, their parents raised an alarm that resulted in a community search. Later when they turned up and told their stories of the rape, instead of silence a police report was made. Sensing the widespread negative reactions from blacks around the case, the authorities arrested the men. The women testified that they had been raped at gunpoint, though the men claimed that the sexual contact, which they admitted, had been consensual.[105] Despite the overwhelming evidence against them, the justice of peace court judge freed the accused perpetrators. Then something astonishing happened: the families refused to accept the verdict and appealed.

Henry is one of those who became instrumental in helping to press the case. He recalled his argument to a father of one of the girls who was worried about possible reprisals for pressing the case. "I got to the floor and said as politely as I could, 'You say you don't want any trouble—well, you are already in trouble. If you were my father and this had happened to me and you stood there and talked about trouble, I would disown you." He reminded them: "It could have been any two Negro girls or women in Clarksdale, and it's time we tried to put a stop to it. If we didn't protest, this type of thing will continue forever, and the time has come for us to be heard."[106]

He urged the families and the Progressive Voters League to press the case. About this time he assumed the leadership of the league, then the most visible organization around which a protest might be mounted. However, Henry had to first transform this organization, which Dittmer referred to as the "base for the postwar voter registration drive" in the state. However, its leadership "stressed the nonthreatening, cooperative character" of its nonpartisan activities.[107] The Clarksdale branch was particularly noted for the conservative approach of its former leader, Dr. T. W. Hill, a dentist, who resisted even going door to door to seek registrants or to establishing a chapter of the NAACP.[108] It was therefore a significant shift when Henry secured league consent to become involved in the rape case.

The community then focused on acquiring legal representation to take the case to the next level. Without a black attorney in town they could hire, the focus turned to finding someone in town who might be somewhat sympathetic to their claims and on how to pay attorney fees. They settled on George Maynard, whom Henry called "one of the most liberal white men in town." Maynard agreed to take the case, but asked for a fee of $2,000. In the absence of any treasury,

Henry had to then lead a solicitation campaign, which generated about $1,200. It was to little avail, Maynard failed to convince the judge, and the plaintiffs again lost.[109] Despite defeat, this set a new tone for how egregious racial acts would be treated in town. At the same time, this moved Henry to the center of the stage in Clarksdale for this early protest event.

The outcome of the rape case made the limits of the Progressive Voters League glaringly clear in the face of emerging demands from the black community. The community had few financial resources to help press claims and few reliable local sources of support for legal challenges. Indeed, according to Payne, many of those following the rape case in court "were not sure their expensive lawyer argued the case very well."[110] Thoughts then turned to the NAACP. The national NAACP had attained a high degree of visibility for several reasons, but mostly for challenging school segregation. It also offered expanded contacts and resources such as experienced legal counsel. Moreover, there were already some local people in Clarksdale such as teachers who were quite open about their membership in the organization as early as 1951.[111] Henry also had long familiarity with the NAACP, especially during his service years and while at pharmacy school.

The first Clarksdale NAACP chapter organized in 1953 as a response to these conditions. Aaron Henry played a central role in its development, forcefully urging action against the white-controlled legal system that absolved the accused rapists. He also became the president (though he claims he did not see himself as the natural choice) and the conduit to the national NAACP.[112] Henry says W. A. Higgins, the black high school principal, whose job did not allow him to assume such a visible role, thrust the role upon him.[113] Unlike public schoolteachers, Henry's role as an independent pharmacist made him less vulnerable. He was also well suited because of the local reputation he had earned as a spokesman and as a courageous individual with external contacts.

The highly bureaucratic nature of the NAACP required a significant amount of formal actions to establish a local chapter.[114] In consultations with Principal Higgins, who contacted the national secretariat, Henry and others arranged an organizational meeting at his church, Haven United Methodist. Ruby Hurley, the indefatigable southeastern regional director from Atlanta (Henry first met her at Xavier), arrived to assist the state president, Reverend Amos Holmes, in acquiring a charter for the Clarksdale chapter. Henry said that two hundred people showed up at this charter meeting.[115]

The chartering went smoothly. In August, Henry became president and the charter application filed in New York listed twenty-eight members. Henry and Noelle (then a public schoolteacher) became charter members. Others included Reverend H. H. Williams (pastor of Haven) and several other black ministers. Other notable Delta leaders also joined, among them "Megar [sic]" Evers, subsequently state NAACP field secretary, and T. R. M. Howard, the legendary physician/organizer in the Delta. Both had addresses in nearby Mound Bayou.[116]

In many ways this event set in process the trajectory that later evolved into the social movement in Clarksdale with Henry at its center. He began organizing a network of resource people almost as soon as he began his professional life in his hometown. Some of this was in his personal nature; he was an exceptionally gregarious man. With a trajectory set for a professional and a public role, networking became an especially valuable asset. He fused his business and public affairs work. He enhanced his business by building contacts among physicians and pharmaceutical clients, while in the public role he used these contacts as a means for gaining and exchanging ideas about social change.

From the outset Henry saw the engagement of external partners as an important means of expanding his local conflict for maximizing the potential for success.[117] One of these regional networks formed about the time of the rape cases in Mound Bayou, the nearby emblematic all-black community. Indeed the influence of the network there was longstanding in Henry's family. Many of the ideals of Booker T. Washington were incorporated into the ideals of the town's small class of ambitious professionals and entrepreneurs in Mound Bayou. For example, some of them served the needs of blacks from all over the surrounding area, creating a natural base for intercommunity linkages. Perhaps the most ambitious in this group was the physician and entrepreneur Dr. T. R. M. Howard, with whom Henry established an ongoing relationship in 1950. Howard was avowed in his aspirations for leadership of blacks, at least regionally, and perhaps beyond. His interest in carving out an arena of public participation for blacks matched the ambitions Henry had started to sketch for himself. As an independent black town, Mound Bayou provided a relatively autonomous arena for these early associates to nurture a very significant homegrown, statewide organization, modestly dedicated to social change: the Regional Council of Negro Leadership in 1951.[118] From this platform, led by Howard, the group developed the most comprehensive cadre of black leaders assembled since the early days of Reconstruction. Henry became central to the short-lived RCNL, one of the vehicles that propelled him to leadership of its successor, the statewide NAACP.

The RNLC constituted a virtual "talented tenth" insofar as it represented a group of lettered black men and entrepreneurs of means.[119] Among them were physicians (such as Howard), dentists, pharmacists (Henry), morticians, educators, ministers, and other independent businessmen.[120] They composed the upper class of the black community, a group that Howard believed he was empowered to lead because of their station. This reflected the founding ideals associated with Mound Bayou and their fidelity to the Booker T. Washington self-help scheme in Tuskegee.[121] Among other things, the RCNL focused on attaining equal education and the franchise, equal treatment in the criminal justice system, and access to jobs. Despite its practical approach in the Mississippi environment, it increased pressure on the state's power elite to a degree not seen before. Beito and Beito described the preliminary goals of Howard: "He promised that Blacks had no interest in 'social equality' but added that 'we are terribly concerned about equality at the ballot box, equality in education, equality in the courts of the states, equality in the protection of our homes and equality in chances to make our daily bread.'"[122] The role of Mound Bayou as a symbol and a safe space for the congregation of these leaders cannot be overestimated. It became a place where they had the freedom to congregate. The town ran its own government, displayed a reasonably successful social community, and had a small elite well disposed toward serving as handmaiden to this venture. Remarkably some of the public meetings there attracted thousands. When its hospital opened in 1942, for example, it is estimated that between 7,000 and 10,000 spectators showed up.[123] In 1955 with Congressman Charles Diggs of Detroit as principal speaker, about 13,000 blacks came, "some traveling by mule."[124]

Moreover the location of Mound Bayou in the Delta proved significant. The bulk of the state's African American population resided in the region. They were conspicuous in their links to the unique health services available in Mound Bayou. Dr. Howard arrived there in 1941 as the chief medical officer of the new hospital, the first completely dedicated to care for Mississippi blacks. They flocked there to purchase the insurance Howard offered that guaranteed them services and a hospital. In the way that Howard merged his professional work with entrepreneurship and racial leadership, he may also have served as a model for Henry. Aside from being chief hospital surgeon, Howard had a separate and lucrative private medical practice. He was also a farmer (owning over 1,600 acres and hiring black sharecroppers), and a part owner of a black-owned insurance company and bank in nearby Memphis.[125]

Howard found Henry's interests and skills exceedingly important for the emerging cadre he was leading. Henry possessed skills of organization and a willingness to be aggressive, and he had a strong work ethic. As a founding member and secretary, Henry quickly emerged as a prime mover in the RCNL. He also chaired the conspicuously political "Separate but Equal Committee," with the function to force the state to make good on its promise of segregated equality within the separate but equal system, even as the ground was shifting. For example, the NAACP had opened an assault on the state's belated equalization program for schools.[126]

Significant controversy accompanied the leadership of the RCNL under Dr. Howard. Making concessions to the racial status quo were as likely as the provocations and challenges he made to these norms.[127] He earned the enmity of some by appearing to seek accommodations to avowed racists like the powerful Mississippi leader Theodore Bilbo. Others perceived an inherent conflict of interest in the way he commingled private and public business.[128] However, the RCNL made profound leaps in challenging the system, and it introduced strategies that were deployed in the Mississippi movement just a few years later. Perhaps two of the most important techniques adopted were the mass meeting and the strategic boycott, both of which might have seemed improbable given the painstaking efforts of segregationists to prevent organized or individual acts of resistance to the racial in the early 1950s.

The mass meetings became perhaps the subtlest of the RCNL modules tested, bearing some elements of stealth. The RCNL turned out huge crowds for annual meetings amid panoply of fanfare and costumes, reminiscent of Marcus Garvey's 1920s nationalist parades in Harlem.[129] "Each, in the words of Myrlie Evers, was 'a huge all-day camp meeting: a combination of pep rally, old-time revival, and Sunday church picnic.'"[130] The events drew blacks from all over the state, especially from among the large plantation communities in the Delta. Agendas always included substantive discussion of racial improvement, laying a foundation for mobilization. For example, at its 1952 inaugural meeting black congressman William Dawson of Chicago served as the featured speaker. His official arrival occurred in a parade down the main street. "Black schools and colleges contributed three marching bands. An estimated seven thousand blacks crowded into a giant circus tent to hear the speakers." Later, "[s]tandard features were a big-name national speaker from the North, musical performers, and liberal helpings of food and refreshment. [They became] a life transforming experience for many younger and future civil black leaders such as Fannie Lou Hamer."[131]

The second strategy seemed to be an outward provocation, foreshadowing later activities in the 1960s—an economic boycott of segregated facilities. In 1953 the RCNL instituted a boycott against service stations for denying blacks use of restrooms. The demand was not for integrated toilets, but rather for equal facilities consistent with separate but equal policy. As chair of the Separate but Equal Committee Henry became central to the orchestration of the campaign. As Henry described it, the campaign had some success in forcing stations to provide toilet facilities for blacks, though rarely of the quality maintained for whites. The slogan for the campaign became "don't buy gas where you can't use the washroom." Dr. Howard produced fifty thousand bumper stickers displaying the slogan. Later, discovering that the wording might violate Mississippi law, Henry said the slogan was revised to read: "we don't buy where we can't use the washroom." Dr. Howard then had another fifty thousand printed. Henry gleefully recorded that "All over the state, Negroes were driving up to service stations and asking . . . for gas and to use the washroom. They would drive off when they were told that there were no washrooms available for Negroes. Most service stations were finally forced to add rest rooms to accommodate us."[132]

Aaron Henry's central role in the RCNL, subsequently led to a major leadership role in the emerging state civil rights efforts. This is evident in how thoroughly he became integrated into and interlocked with a range of organizations, interests, and individuals that challenged the status quo in Mississippi. We can observe Henry's networking skills as they formed and expanded from the initial links to the medical and entrepreneurial sector in Mound Bayou and the RCNL. For example, out of necessity in the racial system the sole black physician in Clarksdale used the Mound Bayou Taborian Hospital for his black patients. He drew Henry and his pharmaceutical business into this network, introducing Henry to this milieu.[133] Later Henry developed his own relationship with Dr. Howard. That relationship brought the young pharmacist into contact with black insurance and banking interests in Memphis. Later these contacts expanded to fraternal orders and fledgling NAACP chapters across the state. Henry was conspicuous by holding leadership positions in virtually all of these complementary

Freedom Fighters When The Going Was Really Tough

Sam Bailey, Dr. E. J. Stringer, Levi Chappelle, Dr. Aaron E. Henry, Dr. Douglas Conner, Joseph Broadwater, Robert L. T Smith, Jr., C. R. Darden, Attorney Carsie Hall, Roy Wilkins, Houston Wells, Medgar Evers, C. Q. Johnson, Dr. A. H. McCoy, A. J. Noel, Miss Mary A. Cox, A. W. Wells

Mississippi NAACP Leadership, March 16–18, 1972, Southeastern Regional NAACP Conference, Jackson, Mississippi. (Courtesy Aaron Henry Papers, Tougaloo College.)

organizations and groups. In addition to being secretary of the RCNL, he soon became founding president of the Clarksdale NAACP and a member of the Knights and Daughters of Tabor (the fraternal order that owned the Taborian Hospital). He also acquired a financial interest in the Magnolia Mutual Insurance Company, a business organized by Dr. Howard. This connection subsequently brought him together with insurance agent Medgar Evers, later his primary partner in transforming the state NAACP.[134]

The foundation for the broad leadership role that Aaron Henry eventually assumed resulted after harassment caused Dr. T. R. M. Howard to flee the state. This produced a vacuum that opened a leadership path that Henry evolved into.[135] Henry's economic independence and his equally well-honed links among this small elite made him well suited. He also had an additional attribute that later served him well—a habit of tapping into the wellsprings of his grassroots local community, seeking out its counsel, and finding ways of reflecting the nuance in local concerns and dreams. He found a way to bring people together, projecting himself as a part of the ordinary people. He also moved far beyond the early Booker T. Washington influences that he (and practically all of his cohorts) bore. His entrepreneurial success was not an end, but became an important means that provided a safe space for the pursuit of other goals.

CHAPTER THREE

Henry, the NAACP, and Indigenous Leadership

The Clarksdale Social Movement

The social movement, perhaps more easily than most other conceptualizations of massive social change, captures the spirit of contentious affairs in Mississippi of the mid-1950s. The gathering forces challenged the status quo in this deeply segregated state with its notions of ordained white supremacy and domination over blacks. Sidney Tarrow accurately captured the times: "Movements are produced when political opportunities broaden, when they demonstrate the existence of allies and when they reveal the vulnerability of opponents. By mounting collective actions, organizers become focal points that transform external opportunities, conventions and resources into movements."[1]

Aaron Henry eventually stood at the center of this movement, being propelled by events, personal sentiments, affiliation with the NAACP, and links to grassroots leaders and their communities across the state. The model example became Clarksdale, the first town with a comprehensive project in the 1960s, where a confluence of events led to a social movement. Henry served as its primary leader, and the tactics utilized there were subsequently employed all over the state. In addition, Henry became involved in virtually all of the other elements that coalesced for a statewide movement: the NAACP as the social change organization; returned black veterans of World War II; a national realignment in the Democratic Party; and the increasing presence of private and public agency allies. A vastly overplayed countermobilization of elite opponents and their constituents challenged this coalition. This chapter is the story of that local movement and Henry's emergence as its most visible leader.

In 1950, in the minds of most peoples, Mississippi remained the least likely of the former Confederate states to change its racial system. However, despite the migration of many blacks to the North, sentiments grew for social change in the state.[2] Among those who did not migrate, for example, were persons who exercised ordinary and subversive acts of resistance with a renewed vigor. They were poised to challenge a system groaning under the weight of contradictions and inefficiencies that excluded about 40 percent of its active population. In the initial phases, the acts of defiance were a matter of willful spontaneity. From one place to another local citizens took advantage of individual and situational circumstances to challenge the system. These expressions, while not organized in the sense of being directed from a central agent, were not isolated from activity elsewhere. The similarity of racial circumstances and social change events across the segregated south allowed spontaneous challenges in any one place to easily resonate across the region. In this environment, the scope of the racial divide in Mississippi provided the greatest opportunity for exploitation as the civil rights revolution gained momentum.

It is easy to place Clarksdale and the revitalized NAACP near the front of the internal state movement. The African American community in this city became a collective of challengers that generated a leader who subsequently became the glue for a statewide grassroots movement. The Clarksdale movement, anchored around the NAACP, became one of the first strong centers where opportunities were seized with consistency and sustained with high visibility. Henry emerged there riding the wave of local resistance and serving as its spokesman, learning the art of successful negotiation of the people's collective choices and arranging them into a highly organized social movement campaign.

Meanwhile, the state NAACP was enjoying a revival under the leadership of Medgar Evers, who had been appointed the state's first field secretary in 1954. (His actual service began in 1955.)[3] Evers, like Henry, known for his ubiquity in social change efforts at the time, also operated from Mound Bayou in the 1950s. He too had been associated with Dr. T. R. M. Howard's Regional Council of Negro Leadership and was employed by his insurance company. His relationship with Henry deepened because Clarksdale was within Evers's insurance territory.[4] Evers and Henry became close collaborators in establishing the leadership role for the NAACP across the state and Clarksdale, respectively. It is hardly surprising that Evers and Henry grew to share in the leadership of the NAACP-led social change movement that became discernable in the late 1950s.

Clarksdale represented an almost classic example of conditions for a social movement, defined by Tarrow as "collective challenges by people with common purposes and solidarity in sustained interactions with elites, opponents and authorities."[5] The success of the challenge is dependent on vulnerabilities when an elite comes under pressure, leaving uncertainty that creates new spaces for action. Challengers occupy these spaces and orchestrate a campaign encompassing ideas that are framed with symbols that inspire and impel others to enlist.[6] These frames provide a way of collectively explaining events that legitimate and motivate collective action or broad mobilization of participants.[7] The structures that emerge to support the group are often highly specified organizations with equally well-identified local leadership. Movements then press their claims using a repertoire of strategies. In the civil rights movement these were protest demonstrations, selective boycotts, pickets, rallies, and other demonstrative public stances.[8] In addition, routine interest group strategies were also deployed: electoral politics, lobbying, and legal challenges to the system of racial exclusion and discrimination.[9]

The state of Mississippi at the time remained dominated by ribald and provocative racists in top leadership positions whose actions exacerbated the contention.[10] Their orations were designed to sustain the old way of life and to stir the passions and fears of their constituents.[11] These stances, however, no longer occurred in a vacuum. The cotton kingdom was gone, diminishing the region's market share and labor.[12] Nor did the state remain a virtual "closed society" that could banish influences from an outside world.[13] In short, there was an environment of immense opportunities that Aaron Henry captured on the wave of African Americans' dissonance.

A combination of events in Clarksdale spawned a movement that later reverberated throughout the state. By some accounts this Delta city allowed some space for negotiating the racial divide,[14] perhaps because this wealthy planter town reflected a relatively unusual degree of diversity[15] and because it more jealously guarded its cheap labor supply against the racially demagogic leadership associated with competing yeomen farmers.[16] However, like other Mississippi towns it preserved the racial order, employing necessary measures to keep blacks in their "place."[17] Despite the contradictions there were both local opportunities and catalysts that propelled a movement. It generated a leader who worked prodigiously to frame the contentions and give leadership to a local NAACP affiliate. It helped that Henry enjoyed economic independence, which no doubt aided him in being plainspoken about racial change.[18] The latter gave him great credibility among his black compatriots. They found this affable, self-effacing leader perennially attentive and resourceful.[19]

As the Mississippi Delta reeled from the exodus of African Americans to the North, the disparity in the Delta was drawn in bold relief. While acts of racial brutality continued, they did so now in an environment where blacks did not suffer them in silence. For example, there was significant escalation in racially charged events in Clarksdale that generated citizen actions. Twice before the brutal Emmett Till murder in 1955 (an event to which Henry responded),[20] egregious acts occurred in Henry's hometown. First, there were the Leola Tates and Erline Mills rapes (recounted in chapter 2). They were followed in 1951 by wanton violence against a young black epileptic, Denzill Turner, who was having a seizure at the bus station. Some whites nearby reported that he was drunk and disturbing the peace. He allegedly "talked back" to the station master and was subsequently arrested. Entreaties for relief from his father, who explained his son's condition, went unheeded. Matters rapidly deteriorated as Turner died trying to defend himself against the police. In the succeeding legal action the police were cleared, with "the court ruling it was justifiable homicide."[21] In this event, however, the matter was not allowed to just go away. Blacks publicly protested and registered their complaint against the officers to the mayor. The desired relief did not come, and police brutality continued with impunity, though under protest.

The active objections by blacks reflected a new approach to racial relations. Increasingly exclusion based on race generated public rebuke from African Americans. While they were often unsuccessful, the standard rebuffs from white authorities now led to an escalation of challenges. Indeed, these rebuffs helped the community to develop a collective conscience and a framework to articulate its demands. Circulation of common interpretations of events throughout the community served as the recruitment tool for a grassroots campaign, as theorized by Morris and Morrison.[22] Henry aided the community in developing and deploying a toolkit in the line of attack, publicly questioning authorities about egregious behaviors and demanding accountability from public officials.

The year 1954 proved momentous insofar as strong sentiments for social change were expressed by the federal judiciary. The Supreme Court outlawing of school segregation was sweeping in its *Brown* decision, and that ruling began to be rapidly applied to the entire Jim Crow system; segregation was inherently unequal.[23] For blacks this signaled unparalleled external support for a core change in the racial system. Henry often referred to the profoundly invigorating watershed effect the decision had on the masses, notwithstanding the equally swift reactionary response from the white elites.[24]

The fledgling Clarksdale NAACP and the state organization took immediate steps to implement the decision. In consultation with the national office Henry initiated a petition asking school officials to voluntarily desegregate. The petition in fact followed soon after Medgar Evers was appointed state field secretary for the NAACP in December 1954. His appointment provided some confidence that the national office was poised to back such local efforts.[25] Myrlie Evers said a petition signed by 140 parents was also filed in her hometown of Vicksburg "less than three weeks" after the ruling. Other towns followed swiftly; Jackson and Yazoo City were joined by Clarksdale.[26] The petition became arguably the first collective action led by Henry and the new Clarksdale NAACP chapter. Meanwhile, the collaboration with Medgar Evers also signaled the partnership these two men had established as the anchors of a revitalized and more aggressive NAACP.

In Clarksdale, Henry led an informational meeting where representatives from the national office were on hand with petitions, which were subsequently distributed to local black churches and other race-exclusive venues (barbershops and beauty parlors). The petitions remained available for a month. Blacks were urged to sign up largely from pulpits on Sundays, by pastors who often organized their congregants to execute signings. All indications are that the campaign to get blacks to sign on as petitioners achieved immediate and widespread success. According to Henry, 450 names were collected.[27]

The success, however, proved to be short-lived as the segregationists resorted to well-wrought tactics to suppress participation. In a rapidly organized white backlash, a campaign of intimidation and threats ensued against petition signees. Some petitioners lost jobs; sharecroppers were rendered homeless; and some were publicly assaulted with impunity, while others were accosted in acts of terror. Many among the everyday laborers (maids and field hands) were forced to withdraw their names from the petitions. The wives of Dr. Emmett Stringer and Aaron Henry subsequently lost their teaching jobs in public schools.[28] In short, local whites left little doubt about their intentions to completely thwart the *Brown* decision and any other elements perceived to alter segregation of the races.

Local Clarksdale white elites joined others across the state to develop a new organization, the Citizens' Council, designed specifically to thwart the *Brown* decision. Congressman John Bell Williams shared its sentiments, dubbing the date of the decision's issuance as "Black Monday."[29] Chapters of the council seemed to grow overnight. Its organization, membership, and activities were all publicly acknowledged, as it sought to distinguish itself from the secretive Ku Klux Klan. Among other things, it set out a strong ideological defense of white supremacy and engaged in an intensive propaganda campaign for its white audience about the perils of integration. The NAACP and any of its associates were identified as the enemy and were constant sources of denigration and harassment.[30] A native of Clarksdale, Robert "Tut" Patterson, led the public meeting at Indianola on July 11, 1954, where the first chapter formed.[31] Henry's reading of the organization was that its "goals were to make it impossible for any Negro in favor of desegregation to find or keep a job, to cut off his credit or mortgage renewal, and to discourage Negro voting."[32]

The strong white backlash took its toll on the African American leadership for which the Delta had become the epicenter. For the most part these leaders clustered along two major highway arteries that bisected the Delta—numbers 61 and 49, and were concentrated in six towns, in seven majority black counties: Clarksdale (Coahoma) was the northernmost, being roughly 150 miles from

Vicksburg (Warren County), the southernmost town. Easily first among equals at this time was Mound Bayou (Bolivar County), the home of Dr. T. R. M. Howard, arguably the most prominent statewide black leader. It was also home base to Medgar Evers and the birth home of Dr. Emmett Stringer, then state president of the NAACP. Other very active towns whose leaders fit this profile were Indianola in Sunflower County and Yazoo City in Yazoo County. Among them were physicians, dentists, clergymen, and grocers.

Every single one of these leaders was singled out for reprisals of one kind or another. More than half of them were murdered or effectively forced into exile. Both leaders in Belzoni endured violence and efforts at intimidation. Gus Courts, a grocer, was wounded by gunfire, lost credit, and finally was forced to flee to Chicago. Reverend George Lee, a clergyman and entrepreneur, was murdered.[33] Drs. T. R. M. Howard and Clinton Battle (Mound Bayou and Indianola, respectively) were also forced to flee to Chicago after massive intimidation and threats.[34] Dr. Emmett Stringer, whose roots lay in Mound Bayou, was forced to abandon the state presidency of the NAACP because of reprisals against him and his wife, a schoolteacher. Medgar Evers did manage to survive this turbulence, but was later assassinated in 1963.[35] Amzie Moore referred to six deaths in 1955 that were believed to be a direct response to the heightened activity surrounding school desegregation. Bayard Rustin uncovered other examples of NAACP associates or just ordinary citizens who went missing or were found dead. Others were simply forced to flee, abandoning their land and other personal property.[36] Aaron Henry in Clarksdale and Amzie Moore of Cleveland both survived the period, but not without major intimidation, economic reprisals, and/or acts of violence against their persons or properties.[37] The campaign of intimidation also targeted average citizens. In every town where a petition was produced, a major campaign of harassment and intimidation targeted the signees. Yet, the Emmett Till lynching represented perhaps the most horrific act of violence within the epicenter of this activist Delta leadership in towns with revitalized chapters of the NAACP.[38]

State officials did not lag in thwarting the *Brown* decision. The legislature belatedly commenced an equalization plan to comply with the separate but equal principle. Simultaneously all legal means were deployed to prevent school desegregation. Plans were made for closure of public schools, and law enforcement tools were developed to handle protests from "outside agitators" and misguided local activists.[39] Then as the number of "provocateurs" expanded, with the federal government often acting as an ally, Governor Ross Barnett declared a state of "interposition."[40] Akin to a secessionist act, this gave the state the right to interpose itself between the citizens and the federal government, ostensibly because constitutional state power was being usurped. This culminated in 1962 when the governor assumed the role of chief admissions officer of the University of Mississippi to block the admission of James Meredith to the school.[41]

The post-1954 state backlash backfired, however. The previously fledgling NAACP grew in many large and small towns. Henry in particular prospered within the organization as his leadership spread beyond the Clarksdale chapter. He rapidly moved from state NAACP secretary to vice president. The easy rapport he had already established with now state field secretary Medgar Evers led Henry to challenge state president C. L. Darden for the presidency in 1957.[42] The outcome was close (Darden 316 and Henry 305), an illustration of the distance Henry had come in a mere five years.[43] Two years later he won easily.

Henry's election presaged a generational shift in leadership and approach. He and his youthful ally, Medgar Evers, exploited every opportunity to challenge the system, channeling the aggression and passion bubbling up from the grassroots. Dubbed "militants" by their white detractors, this younger group became the most influential interpreters of issues within the black community.

The external roles that Henry increasingly assumed, beyond the NAACP, provided a network that strengthened his position in the state and Clarksdale. He generated vital allies and resources for local projects and began to acquire independent national influence. Perhaps the most prominent link was to Martin Luther King through the RCNL. The latter supported King's Montgomery bus boycott, first following Adam Clayton Powell's call for "an hour of prayer for that Montgomery, Alabama situation" in March 1956. A month later representatives from Montgomery appeared at an RCNL meeting to discuss the boycott. This was followed in July by an RCNL financial contribution to the Montgomery campaign. The RCNL secretary Henry was the conduit for all of these transactions and privy to all of the discussions about the boycott.[44] As an indication that King regarded Henry and Evers as critical leaders in the southern coalition, both were invited to join the board of the Southern Christian Leadership Conference when it organized in 1957. Henry subsequently did so and remained an active member.[45]

Henry took full advantage of this relationship. In May 1958 he hosted King (and the SCLC board) in Clarksdale. The specter of nearly one hundred delegates holding a civil rights conclave in a small Mississippi town served as a profound provocation. On the occasion the SCLC board approved a stinging rebuke to President Eisenhower for failure to support the *Brown* decision. For Henry and the Clarksdale activists, however, this put them on the map as serious players in the civil rights leadership coalition.[46]

In a relatively short time the gregarious and ubiquitous Henry acquired a wealth of experience, a broad knowledge base about social change movements, and an unparalleled political acumen. Hardly anyone seemed more suitable to assume a major leadership role in the first sustained 1961 civil rights campaign in a Mississippi town: the "Clarksdale movement." The scope of this campaign foretold the full-blown challenge to racial exclusion in the state. It followed and built on three high-profile short-term challenges that put activists in the street: Dr. Gilbert Mason's May 1959 "wade-in" to desegregate Mississippi's Gulf Coast beaches,[47] the 1961 Freedom Riders, and the international sensation caused by these events when Henry and the demonstrators were arrested and sent to the notorious Parchman penitentiary.[48]

The opening salvos in Clarksdale paralleled the August 1961 grassroots effort that Robert Moses and the Student Nonviolent Coordinating Committee opened in McComb. It began on the strength of the NAACP chapter and its youth wing led by local beautician Vera Pigee, who, like Henry, was an entrepreneur. As the organizer of foot soldiers Mrs. Pigee became the inspiration for the first public events staged in this campaign. Also like Henry, she held a state leadership position within the NAACP, that of state youth leader.[49] The first documented Clarksdale events occurred on August 7, 1961, when three students held a sit-in at the railroad station.[50] This opened a Delta campaign that lasted three years, and it was the most comprehensive in the state at that date. This remarkable project occurred in what was deemed the most intractable stronghold of southern segregation. The community called upon the national NAACP for help, and the organization dispatched an adviser and local lawyers to handle the expected arrests. The well-planned project, much of it documented by Pigee and Hamlin, owed most to the important organizing skills of indigenous people who orchestrated the events. All of this corresponds to the way in which Aldon Morris theorized the role of indigenous people in social movements, specifically the southern civil rights movement.[51] The local people in Clarksdale plotted the route, ascertained walking time to the station, and provided support persons to monitor events. They chose the railroad station because it seemed the best venue at which the personal safety of the students might be secured. The site remained secret until the date of the event.[52]

This project represented a bold and momentous leap for blacks in Clarksdale, and it unleashed massive resistance from the local authorities. The students sitting-in at the train station were quickly jailed, in a show of force far beyond necessity. The ticket agent, rebuffed when he directed them to services in the "colored" waiting room, called the police. "Shortly after . . . three police cars arrived. The Chief of Police, Ben C. Collins, subsequently arrived on the scene. Then he turned around and told the youths to leave the station." Three times they refused and were then arrested.[53]

The arrests and possibly violence were expected, so NAACP lawyer R. Jess Brown from Jackson was on the scene. Jack Young and Carsie Hall, also from

Jackson, reflecting practically the entire complement of African American law-yers in Mississippi, later joined him. Despite the legal resources at their disposal, the students (teenagers of eighteen, sixteen, and fifteen years) were convicted of "breach of the peace." The court sentenced the oldest and presumed "ringleader" to a fine of $300 and ninety days in jail. The two others received fines of $200 and thirty days in jail.[54]

Notwithstanding the arrests, the activists believed they had the upper hand. The national and state NAACP were strong partners, providing resources, direct advice, and encouragement. Moreover, there was symbolic support with similar actions mushrooming across the region.[55] The formerly measured pace of lib-eral decisions from the Supreme Court appeared now to be keeping pace with demands in the streets. Perhaps the best example was the Boynton case in 1960 that outlawed segregation in interstate transportation (trains and buses) and pointedly included such accommodations as waiting rooms.[56] Therefore, the challengers escalated in Clarksdale. Soon after the railroad event, a sit-in followed at the Greyhound bus terminal. One demonstrator recorded what occurred after each refusal of service. "We left and filed our complaints with the NAACP, the Justice Department, the local FBI, police and Interstate Commerce Commission. We kept repeating the cycle until we won." The protesters stayed until the segre-gation signage disappeared after Christmas in 1961.[57]

The victory at neither the railroad nor the continuing bus station protest fazed Clarksdale authorities. Suddenly on Thanksgiving Day in 1961 the mayor denied black marching bands their usual participation in the annual Christmas parade. Ironically, the parade was not even a city event, though in this instance the mayor assumed the authority and informed the sponsor, the chamber of com-merce, of his decision to exclude black school bands.[58] This act became the cata-lyst that propelled a three-year-long protest campaign.

The announcement stunned African Americans. Henry reflected their gen-eral sentiment when he argued that this event hardly related to the campaign for racial change since black parade participation conformed to the existing racial order. Henry said "our community had become accustomed to seeing our band at the end of the parade, followed by our floats." In effect, the structure of the event completely segregated blacks from the main body of participants—"in the back of the bus" so to speak. The late issuance of the exclusion order at the end of November was seen as especially callous. The students were well along in their preparations. Henry continued: "Negro children spent weeks preparing the floats and learning the music, and adults took pride too because our band always out-stepped and outplayed everyone else."[59] So the rejection was not a casual matter; it was a major shift in racial understandings, even for blacks skeptical of challeng-ing the status quo.

Coming at the height of the Christmas holiday, Henry seized the opportunity to escalate demands for change by striking the thriving downtown commercial sector, which also catered to the rest of Coahoma County and towns in adjacent counties, a majority of whose patrons were African Americans. The local NAACP opened its call to the barricade with the tagline "If we can't parade downtown, we won't trade downtown."[60] This commenced a boycott of all white commercial businesses in the city.[61]

The political hierarchy and the business leadership began a counteroffensive. The chamber of commerce endorsed the mayor's ban, joining him in the belief that a boycott by blacks, even in the busiest shopping period of the year, could not be successful. Consulting with the county attorney, the police chief reasoned that charging the leaders of the boycott with restraint of trade would be sufficient intimidation to kill the movement. They deemed Henry the primary target and issued a warning about the restraint of trade option in a meeting on December 7, 1961. When he demurred, "Babe [Thomas Pearson] looked offended and bellowed for Clarksdale police chief Collins, who immediately appeared from a side room. Without looking at me, Babe said to Ben: 'Take this Nigger to jail.'" Henry described this "legal reasoning" as a mere ruse, asserting that Collins "gave no explanation for the legal process involved in such an arrest and was clearly relying on his ability to put a Negro in jail anytime he wished."[62]

The authorities identified others besides Henry as targets. Henry said they pursued legal action the same day against "the best of our leadership in Clarksdale."[63] The entire NAACP leadership was arrested, handcuffed, and charged with conspiring to direct a boycott that restrained trade. The group included Reverend Theodore Trammell, Henry's activist pastor, who later ran for Congress; several RCNL members, including R. L. Drew (a minister and SCLC board member) and John Melchor (Henry's successor as Clarksdale NAACP president); and Vera Pigee (the industrious, inveterate activist and lone woman among them). The remainder included J. W. Wright, by self-description "the oldest member of the NAACP living in Coahoma County" and Laboyd Keys.[64]

It is worth note that not all white elites agreed with the police chief. The county sheriff, L. A. Ross, apparently opposed the arrests, denouncing them in earshot of Henry as without sufficient justification or legal grounds. Taking cognizance of the reputations of those arrested, Ross was skeptical about using them as targets. "Babe [Pearson,] don't you know you have locked up some of the best citizens of Clarksdale? The Negro community makes up about half of this town, and these people are the leaders."[65]

In any case the attack of the authorities was a complete failure. Henry and the others demanded to know the law under which they were being charged, since boycotting was not illegal. They also insisted that the charge of conspiracy was patently false and asserted that they had the proof. Henry also perceived that the public disagreement between the county attorney and the police chief shifted the ground in favor of the NAACP because the arrestees were released on their own recognizance. They resolved to intensify the boycott, despite a strong admonition from the somewhat sympathetic county attorney. He accused them of being engaged in a conspiracy against the merchants, whose investments were vital to Clarksdale's development. "You all are destroying the goodwill between the white and colored . . . I am asking only one thing of each of you. Stop this foolishness. Call off this boycott! Conspiracy carries a severe punishment."[66]

This quickly exposed the fallacy in the old approach. The arrests had a catalyzing effect on the community due to the anger and frustration of parents and children alike. With such a clear grievance, leaders found it easy to get compliance with the boycott, but they also organized well. In general, according to Lemann, "nearly all the blacks in town bought their groceries and clothing elsewhere for several weeks."[67] Henry exhorted them: "Let us plan now to wear our old clothes for Easter. Those items we cannot do without, let us purchase them on the side of the railroad track or go into other communities to purchase them. The NAACP is still supplying transportation to Memphis, Helena, Arkansas, and other cities."[68]

Simultaneously as the bus station sit-ins and the boycott led to a general mobilization, a movement began to be conceptualized. Henry and the other principal leaders remained steadfast. Mrs. Pigee, who had been the main organizer of the bus station protest, moved on to organize campaigns to integrate other public transportation facilities.[69] Similarly Reverends Trammell and Davis were her chief logistical supporters. They provided vehicles to transport demonstrators to the sites and organized rides for shoppers.[70] In a very short time in Clarksdale widespread challenges against segregation occurred.

Despite the noted disagreement in the local power elite about how to respond to the movement, there was ambivalence in the outcome of the legal case against Henry and the other men deemed the leaders of the protests. Henry, Trammell, Drew, Melchor, and Wright were found guilty of restraint of trade. The group appealed their convictions to the county court, which affirmed the rulings for four of the five (Mrs. Pigee was not sentenced). They were sentenced to six months in jail with a $500 fine and received bails of $1,500.[71]

The efforts to stop the movement proved a spectacular failure. Indeed, it seemed to give inspiration for broader support. The boycott officially lasted until 1964. Its greatest moments were in the first six months to a year, when transportation was best organized.[72] By the end of 1962 there was little doubt that a full-scale social movement was underway. The grassroots NAACP membership and its youth wing provided ample foot soldiers for insurgency against the city government and the business community, the arbiters of the racial system.

Overall the boycott gave momentum to a broad desegregation campaign in town. The NAACP under Henry's leadership and its Youth League under Mrs. Pigee's leadership challenged everything from barbershops to churches. Voter registration and electoral politics became agenda items as the movement sought links with state efforts elsewhere. This revealed a striking maturity to the efforts in this Delta town, where some of the most extreme measures were used to preserve racial caste.

Meanwhile, the excessive means employed by the countermovement forces energized allies in support of Henry and his local forces. Each tactical escalation by the city authorities to derail the challengers seemed to embolden allies to publicly offer support for Henry and the NAACP. The new Kennedy administration evinced an interest in supporting civil rights to preserve stability and calm; clergy, students, and social activists sought direct engagement; and national media sought a newsworthy story. This combination of forces created a space allowing activists to formulate an ideology and to galvanize cultural frames for the interpretation of events and further mobilization. For the next two years Clarksdale faced a street campaign that stretched segregation to the breaking point.

At this juncture Henry became more than just another street challenger. He also acquired broad legitimacy as a thoroughly engaged activist. His views were consistent with those of the average citizen; he was willing to take risks; and he demonstrated a special skill at organizing, formulating ideas, and soliciting allies. When he also ascended to the presidency of the state NAACP in 1960, it was a major extension of his power. He rapidly became the element that cemented the local forces—inspiring their action, arranging meeting venues, organizing and deploying external resources, and continuing his own personal defiance.

Henry worked arduously to link the Clarksdale events to a larger movement. As Mrs. Pigee oversaw the street campaign, he was using his broad network to produce an external base of support at the highest reaches of the hierarchy and beyond. For example, following the sit-in arrests and the restraint of trade charge, Henry brought hard-hitting NAACP field secretary Medgar Evers to speak at a church mass rally. In early January 1963 he appeared at the First Baptist Church to discuss police brutality, a relevant concern given the widespread and forceful arrests following every protest.[73]

Shortly afterward, Henry made a tactical escalation to force the federal government to publicly go on record as an ally. He made an entreaty to the Justice Department for a federal investigation of local police brutality. He had a further aim of pushing the government to use its superior power to trump state authority. He surmised that conditions were ripe to elicit outright federal support or at least some symbolic action since the Kennedy administration had already sent enough signals of endorsement of civil rights or ambivalence to make Henry's opponents anxious.[74] Eventually Henry prevailed when the Civil Rights Division of the Justice Department authorized an investigation into the treatment of a young woman who alleged that she had been "stripped and beaten during questioning about a theft."[75]

Neither Medgar Evers nor the federal government, however, constituted Henry's trump card. That was left to none other than Martin Luther King Jr. It is important to recall that Henry had entrée to King as a member of the SCLC board and that King had already visited Clarksdale in 1958.[76] In energizing the local base in Clarksdale, few could surpass the charismatic King, whose every move generated national and international attention. King returned in April 1962 in direct support of Clarksdale's movement campaign.[77] With this appearance little doubt remained about Clarksdale's status in the vortex of the broader national civil rights movement. Henry demonstrated that he had the connections to command support from two of the most important civil rights organizations at the time: the NAACP and the SCLC.

For Henry these mass rallies across the state and the prominence of the speakers represented a masterstroke for mobilization. Both Evers and King drew huge audiences. The impact of the teaching-learning atmosphere they created was electric. The list of personally engaged locals expanded as people scrambled to be in King's presence. His message of defiance of Jim Crow, of moral hope, and of courage proved irresistible. Knowledge of his Montgomery accomplishments in a campaign focused on segregated public transportation seemed also to boost the increased number of people willing to go into the streets. Meanwhile, Henry's stock rose as the leader with the greatest capacity to draw on a broader array of resources with which to move the Clarksdale campaign to a comprehensive challenge to local segregation.

Henry's centrality was hardly ignored by the local authorities. Law enforcement officials admonished him to cease his activities or suffer the consequences. There were rumors of a "contract" on his head. In the nature of historical circumstances of violence, such rumors could not be discounted. The local authorities clearly saw him as the ringleader of the "restraint of trade." His treatment in the court proceedings revealed his special status. Hamlin argues that the authorities led a concentrated effort to silence him by undermining the source of his economic independence. She draws special attention to the attempt to destroy his pharmacy business.[78]

The authorities had a variety of options in its toolkit to try and immobilize Henry. Ironically, physical violence did not become the first major orchestrated plan to destroy his leadership. Instead, a fabricated morals charge, albeit a spectacular failure, became the object. On March 3, 1962, a Saturday, local authorities in Clarksdale alleged that Henry propositioned Sterling Eilert a young, white male hitchhiker, for sex. This seemed designed to disqualify him both among those he led and those he challenged. Homosexuality, equally abhorred by both races in Bible-Belt Mississippi, could easily disqualify a high-profile public figure like Henry.

The allegations seemed suspicious from the start. Henry suggested that the first charges laid against him by the officers had him seeking sex with a white woman and that only coincidentally did they reference propositioning Sterling Eilert.[79] Similarly, a gap between Henry's arrest and arrival at jail casts doubt on the supposed timing of the Eilert allegation. Henry reported that he was awakened in the early evening by Clarksdale police chief Ben Collins, who told him only that a warrant existed for his arrest for misconduct in Mound Bayou. Henry asked to see the document and was shown a paper with the name of the accuser but no other details. He was then arrested. During the evening he was interrogated by Clarksdale policemen, the mayor, and other unknown white men (later determined to be policemen from Bolivar County, the alleged scene of the misconduct). Initially in a tape-recorded session Henry was asked to account for his whereabouts that Saturday. Then, he said, the relations between him and the officers shifted. "I waited in the conference room a few minutes alone, and then the Bolivar policemen returned with an elaborate set of chains. They made me stand up, wrapped a piece of chain around my waist, and chained my hands behind my back. It was a tight arrangement, and I could do nothing more than walk."[80]

It will be recalled that Henry's initial arrest and jailing took place in Clarksdale, though the interrogation included officers from the two jurisdictions—Coahoma and Bolivar Counties. Only later did they remove him from Clarksdale (in chains) and hand him off to Bolivar County authorities. During the time he could not get permission to notify anyone of his whereabouts. Meanwhile, the Clarksdale authorities also denied knowledge of where he was. Similarly, formal charges against him were not revealed, beyond an officer's suggestion that they had something to do with Henry's alleged desire for white women.

The authorities aired the charges in court on March 14. Eilert's allegation referred to hitchhiking from Clarksdale to an unspecified place when Henry picked him up. According to the testimony, the conversation drifted to sex and Henry asked him to find a white woman for sex. This seemingly improbable conversation continued between these two strangers, of different races, in rural Mississippi. Eilert said Henry then demanded sex with him and fondled his penis. At that point, Eilert said he jumped out of the car and ran, but not before getting a portion of the tag number from the vehicle. He alleged that he subsequently walked to nearby Shelby (thirty miles south of Clarksdale) and reported his story to the authorities.[81]

The Bolivar County courts quickly convicted Henry despite the controversy about the evidence. A justice of the peace court convicted and sentenced him to sixty days in jail with a $250 fine. Three attorneys—Jack Young and R. Jess Brown of Mississippi and Robert Carter of New York—represented Henry on a failed appeal to the circuit court. Their appeal cited several irregularities that violated due process and rendered his trial impartial and unfair: the disappearance of the hitchhiker's affidavit and the court record; the use of an amended charge document; and the search of Henry's car without a warrant.[82] In any case, the charges seem almost certainly unrelated to any encounter between Henry and the hitchhiker, though many of Henry's collaborators and supporters assumed he was bisexual. Whether the charges were in some way related to local knowledge about Henry's sexual orientation, thus making such an allegation a chosen point of attack, is not known.[83]

Henry issued his own detailed rebuttal of the charges, which were corroborated by others. For example, Eilert claimed that the incident happened around 5 P.M. in Bolivar County. Henry said he was at Delta Burial Insurance office at the time. He also gave a full account of his activities on March 3. He said that his wife drove him to the drugstore early that morning, and returned the car to him there later, after which it was left at a car wash for the rest of the day. He then spent the day at the drugstore, he said, before retrieving the car and driving home. Customers at the drugstore, the car washers, and his family corroborated his version of his whereabouts. Among the witnesses were the president of Coahoma Junior College, two former NAACP branch presidents, and schoolteachers. Henry called them "unimpeachable community leaders."[84] Certainly the time frames in these accounts made it virtually impossible for Henry to have been where the alleged crime occurred. Most African Americans in town seemed not to give the accusations any credibility either. Their support for Henry was in no way diminished.[85]

Neither Henry's alibi nor the escalating activism in the community dampened the official pursuit of the case. Indeed things got worse. The Mississippi Supreme Court upheld the conviction. Henry, meanwhile, found himself in more legal trouble with the authorities when he threatened to file a complaint to trigger a Justice Department investigation of "a diabolical plot cooked up by the Coahoma County prosecutor Thomas Pearson and Collins." The two officers he named promptly sued him for defamation and just as quickly won a conviction. The court ordered Henry to pay the complainants $25,000. Henry received the legal relief he sought only after the United States Supreme Court overturned both of these decisions.[86]

The charges hardly achieved the desired effect. Henry's response was not angry, despite its defiant tone. "You can't keep evil men with evil ideas from saying evil things about you. All you can do is to be sure these things are not true." He then put them on notice: "Whatever the reason for the charges you can be assured that my activity in the field of freedom for my people and myself will continue, just as in the past."[87] Indeed, following this and a string of arrests of locals and visiting allies, it became easier to generate participation for a broad-scale assault on segregated facilities in the city.

Henry began to rise to greater prominence as Clarksdale's leader because of the bevy of resources he commanded to generate heat on the streets in Clarksdale. His position at the state NAACP put him at the very heart of movement policy formulation and decision making, and he quickly sought links to other movement elements emerging in the state such as SNCC and the Congress of Racial Equality. That broader conceptualization of the challenge always informed how he framed his work in Clarksdale. The symbolic acts deployed in sit-in protests at facilities, for example, were always part of a larger project. He sought to focus on the entire system of racial exclusion by attacking many elements simultaneously. Broad interests that Henry had ever since his return from the service came together. The assault on the Clarksdale commercial sector and sit-ins now coincided with a major initiative to mobilize blacks to register, vote, and seek office. Henry spearheaded an organized campaign to this end that immediately looked toward the outcomes of voting. In March 1962 he announced that a local minister, the Reverend Theodore Trammell, would run for the U.S. House of Representatives. Henry made the calculation that if African Americans were ever to acquire political influence, it was necessary to have familiar community candidates who would reflect local sentiments on issues. He signed on as Trammell's campaign secretary and treasurer, and was the primary organizer of activity.[88]

The focus on electoral politics significantly broadened the civil rights question to include representation. It exposed the glaring disfranchisement of African Americans. Though they constituted a majority of the population in the congressional district, their almost total disenfranchisement gave them no influence over the outcome of congressional (or any) elections. Reverend Trammell fit the bill as a prospective representative of black interests in many respects. This distinguished activist clergyman, a veteran of World War II (navy), was born in adjacent Panola County. Like several other Delta leaders, he could trace his activism to the RCNL, before settling in Clarksdale.[89] His name appeared in RCNL minutes as early as 1956. In 1957 he served as president of the board of directors, succeeding the founder T. R. M Howard, and he on several occasions represented the organization in national settings.[90] Trammell therefore had deep connections to the small group of activists around Aaron Henry and the surrounding Delta area. This known NAACP activist became among the first wave of those arrested in the Clarksdale boycott of merchants. Despite his frail health (he died before the campaign ended), accepting the challenge and risk of running for office simply revealed that he was in synchrony with Henry's aggressive pursuit of broad change in the racial system.

The death of Reverend Trammell did not diminish the effort to contest the congressional seat; Reverend Merrill Lindsey of Mound Bayou replaced him.[91] This trained theologian and activist, like Trammell, was a part of the small group of Delta leaders. After receiving a bachelor's degree from Rust College, a black Methodist institution in Holly Springs, Lindsey obtained a masters and a divinity degree from the University of Denver. He was also an educator, "having taught in the public schools of Mississippi, [including] Mississippi Vocational College" (later Mississippi Valley State University).[92] His early engagement could also be dated to the RCNL, where he held leadership positions. Lindsey and Henry were also especially close; they were brothers-in-law, having married two of the Michael sisters.[93]

Henry moved on to become the prime mover in this effort as Lindsey's organizer and campaign manager, the first independent black-led event of its kind since black disenfranchisement in the 1890 Constitution.[94] Henry and Trammell constructed a comprehensive platform, which began by endorsing the program of the national party. That resulted because they had no standing in the segregated Mississippi Democratic Party. Lindsey thus began: "I pledge support to the Kennedy administration. I feel that this administration has guided us in the direction of prosperity, peace and democracy." There were four other points: support for a foreign policy that expanded friendly relations with other nations; Delta job creation and control of flooding from the Mississippi River; agriculture stabilization; and elimination of the racial system. The latter point invoked the equal protection language from the Fourteenth Amendment: "The right to vote; justice in the courts; elimination of police brutality, intimidation, and harassment; education without discrimination or segregation; . . . the use of all public facilities to all people; and measuring all activities by the Christian ethic."[95]

Henry's provocative decision to seriously contest the congressional seat made the white elite anxious about the potential for disruption of the racial system. If the pressure against disfranchisement succeeded, there was a real prospect that the existing Delta district could be controlled by the super majority black population. Therefore the state legislators quickly moved to squelch this opportunity when the 1960 population decline caused the loss of one congressional seat. At the time Frank Smith, deemed too moderate by whites, then represented District Three in the Delta. The legislators devised a reapportionment plan that obliterated the district by consolidating it with the Second District. Smith found himself competing against another incumbent, Jamie Whitten. The new district had been gerrymandered in such a way that Whitten was guaranteed a victory.[96] The gerrymander also diluted the majority African American population and thereby eliminated its potential as a voting majority.[97] The strategy worked. In the primary Lindsey received 1,318 votes, and Whitten (35,381) beat Smith (21,327).[98] Even in defeat this nevertheless revealed the comprehensive approach that Henry brought to his leadership role at this early date.

Soon enough Henry moved to formally link the Clarksdale campaign to civil rights efforts across the state and elsewhere. It was in this context that he called for a collaborative state voter registration campaign. A structure to harness the collaboration was what came to be known as the Council of Federated Organizations. A strategy meeting was called in Clarksdale in August 1962 to initiate the campaign.[99] The event did not go unnoticed by the authorities. The Clarksdale police cordoned off the area and "stopped each person, questioned why they had gone to the meeting, and took names and addresses."[100] The importance of this emerging coalition immediately became apparent. A comprehensive voter registration drive began in Clarksdale during the summer of 1962, paralleling the commercial boycott. This also coincided with increased SNCC presence in the state, many of whose field secretaries were Mississippians. McComb was the organization's first stand. It too was a voter registration campaign, but included efforts to desegregate facilities as well.[101] Meanwhile, the national NAACP authorized a region-wide registration drive in late summer, after which the Clarksdale branch hired a staffer with the sole function of getting unregistered blacks to the circuit clerk's office. At the same time SNCC workers arrived in the city to assist with the increasingly complex street movement.[102]

This intensified effort generated increased surveillance from the authorities, and arrests increased exponentially. In September local police arrested Willie Griffin, a voter registration staffer, while she solicited registration volunteers. Charges of destruction of government property, possession of profane literature, and "restraint of trade" resulted. Henry recalled that Ms. Griffin was "placed in a cell without a bed or chair. She pulled some padding off the wall and made a seat on the floor. . . . [The] profane literature was a printed card which included a picture of a well-dressed white man and a shabbily dressed Negro. The caption was: 'The NAACP has sent me to segregate you trashy bastards.'" Subsequently, the SNCC field secretary in Ruleville, Charles McLaurin, and James Jones were also arrested while transporting people to the courthouse. Their charges were resisting arrest and blocking traffic.[103]

Meanwhile, three Delta towns (Clarksdale, Greenwood, and Ruleville) became the sites for a coordinated movement in Mississippi (sites of intense protest and voter registration). The focus in Clarksdale varied, while that in the other towns focused on voter registration. The authorities in Greenwood and especially Ruleville hastily began economic reprisals against activist churches and individuals, matching the response of law enforcement in Clarksdale.[104] Together these towns created a virtual Delta zone of challenges to Jim Crow. Henry's collaborative nature helped to maintain unity among the separate organizations, diminishing the potentially divisive tendencies that might have emerged.[105] While SNCC did most of the work on the ground, Henry helped everyone to solidify their local organizations, to share information, and to deploy their leadership in ways that strengthened one another.[106] The environment proved especially important to Clarksdale allowing it to augment its planning staff and to obtain additional foot soldiers for the broadened street campaign. On balance, it was Henry's prominence as a seasoned indigenous leader that put more of a spotlight on Clarksdale and brought more coherence to the activity. His external connections to national civil rights organizations and allies made him best able to tap into those resources to sustain the local effort.

Ironically the retaliatory actions of authorities often aided in linking discrete events in these towns. The cancellation of the federal supplementary food that subsidized poor families with surplus commodities is an example. This program that provided meal and flour, dairy products, rice, and canned vegetables was a major source of subsistence for displaced black farm laborers and welfare dependent female-headed households.[107] However, Mississippi officials opposed the program, dubbing it an unwarranted "federal handout." In Greenwood in October 1962 in a direct challenge to federal authority, the county abruptly canceled its food distribution.[108] Suddenly in the face of an increasing civil rights effort, a program that had been in place since 1957 was too expensive to run. Since this was so patently false, stopping the program was a major boost to the movement contenders, and it galvanized allies.[109] It took little time to generate foodstuffs from supporters around the country who were disdainful of this act against innocent people merely seeking the right to vote.[110]

Clarksdale figured prominently in attaining national visibility for the food project. For example, two Michigan State University students trucked an early shipment all the way from Michigan. Ivanhoe Donaldson, subsequently SNCC field secretary in Holly Springs, drove the truck, accompanied by Benjamin Brown.[111] Arriving past midnight they elected to stop in Clarksdale, a little safer than Greenwood they surmised since they knew of Henry. It proved a miscalculation because after finding Henry's Fourth Street Drugstore and parking there, their arrest soon followed. Donaldson said: "We were harassed and juggled around and thrown in jail. The charges were that we were taking narcotics across state lines, but what we had were aspirins and bandages as parts of first aid kits."[112]

The whereabouts of Donaldson and Taylor remained unknown for days, and subsequently became the basis for an intensified local and national mobilization. Donaldson eventually succeeded in smuggling a note to Henry. A fellow inmate on a work detail near his drugstore served as the conduit. Henry immediately secured legal help from the NAACP and gained their release.[113] Meanwhile, the news spread all over the Delta, and the SNCC central office in Atlanta mounted a national campaign exposing the case. The Clarksdale and Greenwood authorities inadvertently handed the civil rights forces a spectacular means for dramatizing the plight of disfranchised and now potentially starving blacks during winter months. It generated an outpouring of donations and critical examination of the Mississippi racial order by a far broader audience.[114] Two prominent entertainers became primary sources for broadcasting the events. Dick Gregory, a comedian at the height of his power, made the food issue his special cause and had tons of food airlifted in; while Harry Belafonte lent his singing talent and considerable influence in the entertainment industry to stage a Carnegie Hall benefit and traveled to Greenwood as well.[115] Locally blacks flocked to the SNCC office and to the voter registration campaign. Dittmer suggests "SNCC activists now made relief to the hungry their priority."[116]

The selection of Greenwood by SNCC as a staging area in the Delta acted to elevate and expand the conflict in Clarksdale. Henry and his Clarksdale cohorts came to conceive of the area surrounding Clarksdale as a theater of movement activity. Though events in Greenwood focused on voter registration, the mere activation provided another venue for the engagement of Clarksdale leadership and citizens with their neighbor. Indeed, in addition to the initial sit-ins at bus and train stations, Clarksdale activists also organized a set of public rallies and demonstrations in support of the voter registration project in Greenwood. As an example of the synergy emerging in this theater of Delta activism, Henry also hosted the organizational meeting to prepare the strategy for the Greenwood campaign. Subsequently a significant amount of funds were raised from external foundations to support the voter registration campaign in the area, which became a part of a broader effort known as the Voter Education Project (VEP).[117]

The engagement between the two cities intensified in late February when three civil rights workers were fired upon in Greenwood as they departed a community meeting. A bullet struck Jimmy Travis, but Robert Moses and Randolph Blackwell escaped injury. Clarksdale held a sympathy rally at Centennial Baptist Church and Dick Gregory was speaker. Despite heavy police presence all around the building, Henry referred to a packed meeting, featuring the usual singing, testimonials, and strategy sessions. "Suddenly a smoking canister came sailing through an open window and hurtled across the opposite side of the room. It struck one woman seated in a pew. Charles Newson, who was sitting nearby, lunged toward the bomb and threw it out of the window."[118]

The shooting of Travis reverberated throughout the state. Rallies were held virtually nightly in Greenwood, where information was circulated and strategies for the next day's activity were developed. Henry found himself spending almost as much time in Greenwood as in Clarksdale. He again became a central leader to the mix of planners and street participants, speaking almost every night and acting as an agent for access to legal and other resources.[119] Charles Payne documents how the mass meeting rally came into its own as an organizing and mobilizing tool. "The meetings were something new, the regular speakers, including Mrs. [Fannie Lou] Hamer, Medgar Evers, Dick Gregory, and Aaron Henry, could hold an audience." In the highly charged, often long meetings, speaker after speaker related personal experiences, usually noting increased violence or intimidation perpetrated against them by the authorities. These events served as nightly teach-ins where the gruesome and irrational nature of the Jim Crow system simply became intolerable to the least activist-oriented person. The singing was essential to the process "operat[ing] as a kind of litany against fear."[120]

Meanwhile, Henry remained attentive to Clarksdale. The many fronts of challenge to Jim Crow continued, and so did the efforts by the authorities to intim-idate him. In April Henry hosted U.S. congressman Charles Diggs (D-Detroit). Since Mississippi blacks had no standing within the local Democratic Party, con-gressmen like Diggs and Adam Clayton Powell of New York from the North became the "representatives" of black interests everywhere, especially among those disfranchised in the South.[121] In fact, the Diggs information-gathering visit arose because of a request from President Kennedy for a report on southern race rela-tions. Diggs also served as a featured speaker at what had now become the obliga-tory mass rally. He appeared on April 11 at the Jerusalem Baptist Church, and in the absence of suitable hotel accommodations, boarded at Henry's home. Late the following night after the family retired, three bombs were hurled at the house. A fire erupted and despite all the ensuing mayhem, Henry, his wife, daughter, and the congressman were evacuated uninjured.[122] This shattered the sense of security the residence ordinarily afforded his wife and daughter.

Contrary to expectations, two young white men were arrested almost imme-diately by the local authorities: Ted Carr, a college student, and Luther Cauther, someone with whom Henry said he had been acquainted "for a few years."[123] Neither their arrests nor their confessions of guilt, however, foretold the outcome. Improbably, they were not found guilty. The local paper, the *Clarksdale Register*, reported that the two men were exonerated on account of coerced confessions. The jury did not take long—fifteen minutes.[124] Apparently Cauther later apolo-gized to Henry and claimed that he and Carr were joy riding and had no plans of throwing a bomb.[125]

This bombing signaled an escalation in the campaign against Henry's person and properties. The aim appeared to be to destroy the source of this indepen-dence: his pharmacy business. This was a tried and true tactic that had silenced others or caused them to flee.[126] Several weeks after the house bombing, a serious explosion occurred at the drugstore, also believed to be a bombing. The investi-gation by the local police determined that the fire was due to a bolt of lightning, despite the gaping hole in the internal ceiling.[127] Still later in the month shots were fired at the drugstore, again shattering its front windows. In fact so frequent were these attacks that Henry incorporated it into a symbolic display at the drugstore illustrating the disjuncture between the democratic promise and its reality in Mississippi. After "March, 1963, he left for all to see the bricks, the broken glass,

Aaron Henry in bombed Clarksdale home, April 1963. (University of Memphis Libraries/ Special Collections/Memphis Press-Scimitar.)

and the displays—one of the Declaration of Independence and the other of the Emancipation Proclamation," according to James Silver.[128]

Henry survived what seemed like a determined effort to bring him down, while other targets did not. Medgar Evers, who had emerged as his major partner in the growing statewide civil rights campaign, had many of the same efforts directed at him. Indeed, Michael Williams argues that Medgar Evers's position as statewide field secretary for the NAACP made him the "face of the civil rights movement in Mississippi" at the time. His visibility and exposure were elevated because of the decision to adopt Martin Luther King-type direct-action tactics statewide. This was in opposition to the national NAACP, but it reflected a tactic that Henry and Pigee had already employed in Clarksdale.[129] Like Henry, Evers's home had been bombed and shots fired upon it.[130] The two did more than any others to transform the state NAACP into a premier role with an aggressive stance against the racial system. They displaced the old guard and assumed the two principal NAACP leadership roles and forged a promising partnership. Henry lost his major partner when Evers was murdered on the evening of June 12 after driving Henry to the Jackson airport.[131]

Henry pressed on with renewed determination as Clarksdale endured a major eruption of protests for the next two years. The circumstances reflected the crystallization of the broad Henry vision. In late February 1963 Henry sketched out the broad arenas of concern, using voting as the rubric to focus on major issues. This framework allowed activists in Clarksdale from the outset to set their horizons on dismantling segregation as a comprehensive project. This "manifesto" focused on five broad areas: (1) police brutality and racial violence; (2) voter registration; (3) elections; (4) employment; and (5) education. He took on the local law enforcement in justifying the emphasis on police brutality and violence. He challenged the Clarksdale police department, for example, to explain "the death of a Negro prisoner in the City Hall." He asserted that its attitudes and lack of action made a "thorough investigation necessary by both local and federal authorities." He held out the exercise of the franchise as the means for voting in "men and women who will administer the law fairly without regard to race or creed." Yet he remained keenly aware that many did not have the franchise. On that score he exhorted blacks to "go, time and time again, to the Circuit Clerk's office" until their registration was secured. Similarly, active black voters could also improve their chances for employment "by voting into office those who will secure industry" that will use equal standards for hiring. The same was true for education: "we can vote for a better school system—one that will obey the laws of the nation.[132]

Meanwhile, concurrent with the intensive street demonstrations, Henry and the NAACP sought to engage the city authorities. On June 4, 1963, Henry asked the mayor and board of commissioners for a meeting "to discuss and resolve grievances pertinent to interracial goodwill and understanding." His four-page memo noted that the NAACP had earlier "asked and not received permission" to appear before these authorities. The memo continued: "The solutions to the problems we wish to discuss we feel can very well be handled by the endorsement and appointment of a Bi-Racial Committee, composed of the interested leadership of both racial groups."[133]

The memorandum enumerated suggested agenda items: (1) *Law Enforcement and Courts*: persecution of blacks by the justice system (double jeopardy, false arrests, denial of routine police assistance); (2) *Employment*: the absence of black government employees; (3) *Education*: continued school segregation, deficient facilities, and unaccredited academic programs; (4) *Voting Rights*: outright denial of the franchise, for example, denying at least fifty would-be registrants per week; and (5) *Human Dignity*: segregation of public facilities that sustains "the stigma of racial inferiority."[134]

The memo featured elements of both conciliation and threat. To facilitate the biracial committee the NAACP selected fifteen African American representatives to "negotiate with responsible leaders of the white community." Anticipating a rebuff, however, Henry suggested that if a biracial committee was not appointed, then "we call upon the ministers of the white community and other responsible leaders to take the initiative in this regard." It was added ominously: *"In addition to you we plan to inform the entire community of our grievances. We intend to saturate the area of public opinion wherever an opportunity can be found or made"* [emphasis in original].[135]

As the short Delta spring turned to the sultry days of summer, Clarksdale's campaign moved into the streets. The NAACP and its Youth League attacked virtually every visible symbol of segregation: churches, the library, the city government, the federal building, businesses, and the circuit clerk. Activities reflected a comprehensive movement to alter social relations, employment, voting, and access to public facilities. By mid-June there were daily challenges in the streets.

Protesters made an early stand against local clergy and church people. They tackled Sunday worship, perhaps the most segregated hour in the country.[136] Vera Pigee, who helped facilitate the sit-ins almost a year earlier, had the central role in this campaign as well. On Father's Day, June 16, 1963, she led a picket of white churches.[137] Pigee recounted that sixteen picketers moved from the NAACP offices and formed four lines of marchers who stationed themselves at churches with placards challenging parishioners. "Our pickets read: *(1) our father; (2) our heavenly father; and (3) grant unto us our freedom.*" The group picketed seven congregations, assembling at all of the mainline protestant churches—Baptist, Methodist, Presbyterian, and Episcopalian.[138]

Their actions did not amuse the authorities, who immediately arrested them. The local newspaper reported arrests of people from sixteen to sixty-six years old.

The newspaper also printed their full names and street addresses,[139] a tactic to intimidate and harass demonstrators, Henry and his cohorts insisted. It did not work. Instead it broadcast the model, used a year later in Jackson churches when Tougaloo College Chaplain Edwin King (later to be Henry's running mate in a mock gubernatorial election) led an initiative with his students. (They too were denied entry and arrested.)[140]

The following day Clarksdale demonstrators moved on to the *Clarksdale Press Register*. Demonstrators targeted this local newspaper because it openly espoused its segregationist views in print and relentlessly attacked the protesters. Frequently the only source of news for local white citizens, the editorial page of the paper became both the information source and the interpreter of events for its readers. Its opposition to the movement and Aaron Henry were stark, often exhorting white leadership to forcefully end disruptions to what was deemed racial peace. In its view, the disruptions reflected the work of a militant minority and its external allies—"outside agitators."[141]

African Americans perceived themselves to be largely left out of the local news, except when they were being disparaged. The refusal of the paper to use the courtesy titles of "Mr." or "Mrs." and biased and unfair reporting about them incited particular grievance in the black community.[142] The demonstrators reasoned that making the newspaper accountable would create a more favorable climate for African Americans in the community. Their placards were instructive as recalled by Mrs. Pigee: *"The aid of the press will help freedom . . . May we have the press on the side of freedom . . . Freedom of the press can aid in freeing the oppressed . . . Favorable public sentiments can be moved by the press . . . Freedom of the press— freedom to petition to be free."*[143]

Over the next couple of days the picketers targeted local government regarding voter registration. NAACP members marched in groups to designated government buildings bearing placards exhorting local officials to cooperate and urging blacks to mobilize. Their placards were also designed to capture the attention of the national media, which was now often on the scene. Among the messages on the placards used over these days were some of the following: *"I only want to get a book to read"; "You say I am ignorant. How can I help it when you will not let me get a book to read."*[144]

The protesters then moved on to challenge segregation in the economic sector. They appeared at the telephone company, post office, and various merchants (already being boycotted). This issue was critical because the agricultural jobs traditionally reserved for blacks had dwindled, and most other jobs were reserved for whites. The few positions not reserved for whites were those in segregated schools; for example, teaching, food service, and custodial work.

Targeting the telephone company and post office was a part of a broader strategy; that is, to attack local operations that were subsidiaries of larger companies.

The aim was to expand the conflict to potential new allies by forcing national corporations to reject segregation or risk alienating their clients and potentially themselves being boycotted by the NAACP or other civil rights groups. Therefore picketers appeared simultaneously on June 21 at Clarksdale offices of the Southern Bell Telephone company and the U.S. Postal Service.

> *"How about a lift from Southern Bell? You are great enough to do it."* . . . *"Southern Bell has the capacity to be fair. Let's display it."* . . . *"Southern Bell and its local personnel should include us."* . . . *"My postman has walked for years. How about a job inside for him?"* . . . *"All white inside, getting whiter outside"* . . . *"This is discrimination by the Unites States Government."*[145]

The demonstrations continued almost daily through June and early July. The tactics employed became routine—picketers with placards, sit-ins, and personal confrontations with business owners. The purposes were twofold: to keep the pressure on the business leaders and public officials and to dramatize events to increase African Americans mobilization. They enjoyed considerable success since their every action generated an equally negative reaction from the local authorities. Law enforcement officials reacted with fierce determination to abort practically every demonstration. They almost always immediately arrested participants and lodged the most extreme charges in order to justify the most severe punishments. Yet, shutting down one protest venue only precipitated action elsewhere by the protesters. The choices were easy for the activists since literally everything in the town was segregated. When the arrests did not stem the tide, according to Lemann, "[t]he city responded in most cases, by taking integration out of the realm of possibility: the pool was drained, and then sold to the American Legion; the lunch counters were closed; the library removed all the chairs."[146]

Meanwhile, by July the mayor still had not responded to the NAACP request for a meeting and the creation of a biracial committee. Therefore Henry escalated the protest in dramatic fashion. He led an NAACP delegation to city hall and held a sit-in at the mayor's office. When Mayor W. S. Kincade came outside, Henry read the contents of the written petition and then handed it over. While there was no immediate response from Kincade, Henry and the demonstrators had pointedly used the opportunity to publicly air their grievances before the mayor. Still a week later when there had not been a response, the protesters made a return visit. According to Henry, the mayor said: "There was nothing in the petition that he was able to grant and added that conditions were not as bad as we claimed. He refused to set up a biracial committee or even to discuss any of the problems."[147]

An immediate reaction came from the now highly mobilized black community. Within a few days one of the largest local demonstrations ever organized took place. Henry recorded that demonstrators converged on the city hall from all directions. They made it difficult for the police to completely control the situation. "They ran to one side to stop a group and then rushed over to stop another group, but we all kept coming." Henry himself was arrested almost immediately and could hear the reaction of the agitated police radio dispatcher: "'Look at the niggers coming. There are niggers coming from everywhere.'"[148] The police nevertheless made mass arrests. According to Henry eighty-six demonstrators were jailed the first day.[149] The marchers, however, were undeterred and kept coming—men, women, and children. Henry recalled that more than two hundred arrests were ultimately made.[150] As had become the custom, convictions were rapid with jail sentences and fines imposed. In this instance the charges were parading without a permit, and the punishment was thirty-day sentences and $100 fines. The authorities had hardly considered that the demonstrators would exploit these punishments. Virtually all of those arrested did not challenge their convictions and also refused bail. Fairly soon the city jail was overfilled, and so was the county jail. This "jail-in" lasted for eleven days. Henry was assigned to the work crew to collect city garbage, undoubtedly a punishment seen as the most severe and symbolically demeaning. His description of his assignments was on "work crews to clear rubbish, dump garbage, and dig ditches for a new sewer line."[151]

In this chain-gang-style operation the city had provided a mobilization strategy that Henry himself could hardly have orchestrated. Henry made the most of his week's detail on a Clarksdale garbage truck, cheerfully chatting with observers as he swung the city's trash.[152] For his mother, Henry says, it was a devastating sight. "One morning she looked out the door of the house where she had raised me, and there I was picking up garbage. She had always encouraged my civil rights activities, but that was almost too much for her." Many African Americans also saw him and were incensed, appearing more determined than ever to break the system. "Doc Henry, the pharmacist," hauling garbage incited a visceral reaction from many who witnessed the sight. Photographs of the work detail flashed across the country engendering considerable sympathy from movement allies and ordinary citizens alike. Henry left jail after eight days, riding a crest of national sentiment that he says quickly generated $40,000 in a fundraising trip to New York.[153]

The authorities, led by the irrepressible police chief Ben Collins, used tactics reminiscent of the Stalinist Soviet Union, of which there was considerable documentary evidence.[154] Virtually all of the demonstrators were charged with parading without a permit, some being arrested while marching and others at city hall. Henry, as a notary, collected many affidavits documenting what the marchers endured. He also oversaw and often prepared the local NAACP documentary reports. For example, John Wesley Saddler reported that after marching on July 31 he was beaten during fingerprinting inside the city hall. His placard (an American flag) was snatched away, and he was charged with parading without a permit. Later when he refused to address an officer as "Mr.," he was struck every time he responded to a question, eventually being pummeled to the floor. Similarly, Percy Atkins, a Coca-Cola employee, was charged with parading without a permit, vagrancy, and resisting arrest. His arrest resulted merely for walking toward city

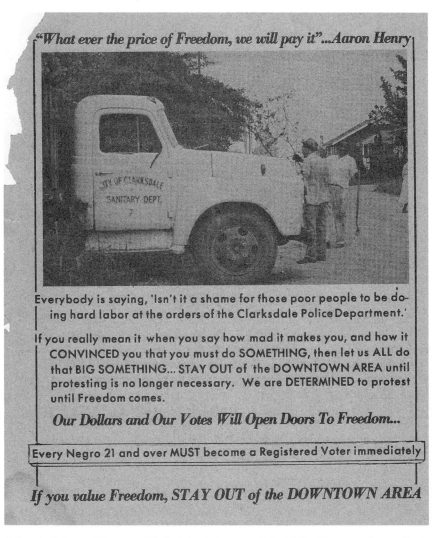

"Convict" Aaron Henry on Clarksdale chain gang, July 1963. (Courtesy Aaron Henry Papers, Tougaloo College.)

hall in apparel associated with the movement: "a tee shirt with 'Freedom Now' spelled out across the back [and] 'CORE' across the front." Later his employment and his brother's came into play when "the Chief of Police and other members of the Clarksdale Police Department . . . went to the Coca-Cola plant and succeeded in getting [them] fired."[155]

Mrs. Odessa Brooks and a group of nine other African Americans were arrested walking toward city hall on July 30, 1963. According to her affidavit they were walking in an orderly manner and "wearing anti-segregation signs." Initially an unidentified officer put them under arrest without lodging a charge. Later, however, they were "rearrested" by police chief Ben Collins because they had no permit. Mrs. Brooks described what incarceration was like. More than twenty women were placed in a single cell and received no food the first day. The next day they were "served for breakfast one spoonful of cold grits with no salt and one slice of cold bread." Then after removing the younger demonstrators that night the "heat was turned on," causing "sweat to roll down my face like rain." All that was coupled with police officers intermittently coming past and using such epithets as "nigger, bitch and cow," and threatening sexual assault. Police chief Ben Collins subsequently forced them onto a work detail, under threat of turning on the heat in the cell again. Mrs. Brooks continued: "We were made to work in the heat of the day cutting grass with swing blades and hoes."[156]

Nonlocal civil rights workers also complained of abuses from the police. Percy Lee Atkins complained of a July arrest for violating a "midnight curfew" after his car ran out of gas. He was jailed and beaten by persons allegedly brought in by the police chief, who authorized and then observed the event. In August, Lafayette Surney, a SNCC field secretary, was arrested for violating the "anti littering ordinance." He was carrying leaflets announcing a mass meeting for August 9. Surney reported that six police officers, including the chief, surrounded and beat him until he passed out. After about four hours he said he was fined and released.[157]

A challenge to school segregation also came to a head in September 1963. As elsewhere, the white Clarksdale school district officials had made no move to desegregate schools. The Coahoma NAACP announced that on September 16 twenty-one parents had filed a petition for desegregation in the interest of twenty-nine African American children. This came, they said, after being unable to get a discussion established "with our White brothers and sisters" in order "to study and resolve our problems and the problems of the community." A discussion had first been sought via an earlier petition in 1955.[158] This time Henry warned that failure to voluntarily comply with the *Brown* decision would result in a lawsuit. The warning went unheeded, and Henry instituted a legal challenge. School desegregation then became a part of the assault on racial exclusion in Clarksdale.[159]

The following summer the street campaign resumed with equal intensity. It was now part of a national civil rights mobilization. Virtually all of the original sites were struck again, as little progress had been made through the winter with the authorities and business leaders. While the recalcitrance of local officials was steady, the visibility and influence of Henry among state activists and external allies expanded the opportunities for action in the city. Observing the tremendous support and resources elsewhere for their cause, local citizens were undeterred by arrests and efforts at intimidation. The NAACP put its legal staff and financial resources at their disposal, securing their release from jail;[160] Clarksdale became a destination among civil rights sympathizers—financial supporters, community organizers, clergy, and media.[161] Clearly, the segregationists had contributed to a realignment of sentiment among many whites outside the South about the values and practices of Jim Crow. The Clarksdale stage now developed into a national stage and Aaron Henry's broad network made him more than a bit player.

Moreover, activists in Clarksdale were far from alone in their struggles in Mississippi. All over the state blacks challenged the Jim Crow system in a manner similar to what played out in Clarksdale. Other towns now had individual initiatives to desegregate facilities or more likely voter registration campaigns.[162] Their leaders were skilled operatives and vital sources of information, all having links to one another to a degree unparalleled in other state campaigns. They achieved this via the COFO, which was led by Aaron Henry. While he was not the day-to-day operator of the confederation,[163] he served as the glue that kept it together, and he used his influential status and personal flexibility and negotiating strengths to see that the focus remained on social change. None of the individual groups felt privileged or deficient in the arrangement.[164] As such a wealth of sharing, cross-fertilization, and broad agenda setting occurred that allowed local communities like Clarksdale to feel empowered by their links to a network of statewide civil rights challengers.[165]

Even as Mississippi seemed perched on the precipice of complete disruption in 1964, events in Clarksdale made that town seem at the core. Another wave of street demonstrations and protests ensued in 1964. The campaign started anew just after the July 4 celebration. First, an integrated group of COFO workers sought entry to the swimming pool reserved for African Americans. They were immediately denied entry because the facility had a blacks only policy. The entire group refused to accept these conditions and left. The city authorities then anticipated that the white pool would be the next challenge and decided to close both city facilities, avoiding integration and removing them as objects of protest.[166]

The movement forces then escalated the assault on segregated facilities, with assistance from external media, as an example below from CBS News reveals. The targets were hotels, motels, and movie theaters, with multiple simultaneous engagements. The first hotel demonstrations were at the Holiday Inn (a national chain) and the Southern Inn (owned by southern segregationists). Aaron Henry led the demonstrations, accompanied by Roy McKissick, national president of CORE. The event drew even more attention because some of the demonstrators had previously managed to get reservations, apparently booking as a CBS news team. Despite their reservations, however, the blacks were denied rooms. Meanwhile, across town a separate group was at the Alcazar seeking rooms and service at its restaurant; and further downtown others sought entry to the Paramount movie theater.[167]

The Clarksdale businesses responded as they had the previous year—deny, object, stall, even to the point of destruction of their livelihood. For example, after the initial assault, the Alcazar closed the next day.[168] Later after blacks were issued patron cards at the Carnegie Library, all the seats were removed from the facility. Meanwhile, the Paramount cinema, the local pool hall, the domino parlor, and a "whites only" service window at the Picnic-er restaurant all denied entry to black patrons.[169]

Elsewhere local and visiting demonstrators were targeted for arrest on a wide range of frivolous and bogus charges. An example is the ludicrous charge against longtime activist Vera Pigee for driving on the wrong side of the road while overtaking another vehicle.[170] The protests only escalated, however, and outsiders became special targets of the police. A CBS news employee received a charge for failing to signal a turn and driving with an expired license. A COFO worker from Colorado received a citation for taking a photograph in city hall, while a New York lawyer's traffic violation resulted "because [the] County Attorney said he almost caused him to wreck."[171]

The attacks on the demonstrators continued for the rest of July. The nearly day-by-day accounting in the *Clarksdale Press Register*, though often relegated to the back pages, indicated the scope of the protests. On July 14, for example, eight African Americans and one white tried to integrate Geneva's Coffee Shop, reported on page eight. Failing there, the group proceeded to the bus station and entered the "whites only" waiting room.[172] A day later the paper announced that while Henry had suspended demonstrations against segregated facilities, a "splinter group," identified as the Clarksdale Youth Action Movement, had continued. Then a host of return protest visits were reported at the Walker Drug Store soda fountain, the Paramount Theatre, and Geneva's Coffee Shop. Several days later, July 20, the Clarksdale Youth movement moved once again against white churches. An integrated group appeared at eight churches: First Presbyterian, Oakhurst Baptist, Clarksdale Baptist, Riverside Baptist, Oakhurst Church of Christ, First Christian, First Methodist, and the Church of the Nazarene. All of these churches refused them entry.[173] On July 21 a report came that several other blacks had been arrested the previous day after refusing to leave the Hamburger Café.[174] In short, no segregated establishments were spared. Combined with the ongoing boycott of the commercial sector, protests enveloped the entire city.

Meanwhile, Henry improved local prospects by expanding the conflict. He called on a network of friends, colleagues, supporters, and well-wishers (far broader than the NAACP) to assist with human and financial resources. Now instead of relying exclusively on the four or five local black civil rights lawyers, he called on a battery of out-of-state lawyers. Many were affiliated with two groups: "The Lawyers' Committee for Civil Rights under Law, which was formed in the aftermath of the Birmingham demonstrations . . . , and the Lawyers' Constitutional Defense Committee (LCDC) [supported by] the American Civil Liberties Union with the backing of Protestant, Catholic and Jewish leaders." The National Lawyers' Guild was already active in the state.[175] Similarly, Henry used his health professionals network to secure medical personnel for an expected increase in workers during the summer. The arrival of a team was announced on July 14, 1964, by the local paper—one physician, a nurse, and a driver. Later the paper recognized this group as a part of the Medical Committee for Human Rights, after interviewing a physician and a dentist. This group became a major supportive arm for the support of activists who otherwise had little access to health care in their activist roles.[176]

Henry seemed attuned to all the dimensions of the civil rights campaign, including its cultural elements. One of these was music, which Martin Luther King Jr. saw as vital to the civil rights struggle. He made special reference to the freedom songs (often traditional spirituals that had been adapted) performed at civil rights rallies. He said, "they gave the people new courage and a sense of unity."[177] It was a role that was equally well described by Bernice Reagon, one of the legendary singers in this genre: "civil rights workers used songs as a basic introduction to the communities . . . The song identified what the struggle was about. The presence of organizers with this body of material made for a high level of exchange between them and the communities they sought to organize."[178] Therefore, in mid-July the *Clarksdale Press Register* reported on the visit of a national group, Folksingers, who would provide music for upcoming meetings in Clarksdale. They were scheduled to appear at Henry's church, Haven Methodist, to provide music for a voter registration meeting. Among its members were Julius Lester (the writer), Len Chandler, and Cordell Reagon (both a part of the famous SNCC Freedom Singers).[179]

Oratory was just as important to the movement as music. Henry brought national movement orators to the doorsteps of Clarksdale with a veritable "who's who" among great orators. July closed with a visit from James Forman, executive director of SNCC, and keynote speaker for the Coahoma Freedom Convention in preparation for the presidential election. The local paper gave a mocking account of this thirty-five-year-old, born in nearby Marshall County: The "Hour long display of colloquial oratory which at times seemed to mesmerize a crowd of about 300 Negroes at First Baptist Church. . . . Last night he was dressed in work clothes and carried a crude weather beaten stick with which he thumped the rostrum to emphasize many of his highly emotional points."[180] Congressman Charles Diggs had long been involved with the movement in the city, but the arrival of his wife, Anna Diggs, was also noted in this period.[181] John Lewis, another SNCC chairman and Freedom Rider, appeared with James Forman in June at another of the activist black churches, First Christian.[182]

The NAACP sent its top brass, too, including board members and national staff executives. Their July visit came during the daily protests, a fact noted by the local paper, which listed them by name and state to sustain the view that "outside agitators" were dominating the movement: Dr. H. Claude Hudson (California), chair of the group; Chester Lewis (Kansas); Kivie Kaplan (Massachusetts); Dr. Eugene Reed (New York); John Davis (New Jersey); Alfred Baker (Connecticut); L. Joseph Overton (New York); and Robert Carter and Gloster Current (New York). The group was scheduled to meet at Centennial Baptist Church to take testimony of grievances.[183]

Meanwhile, the challenge to the school system that Henry promised a year earlier was fulfilled. A lawsuit was filed in federal district court in April 1964 with Henry's daughter serving as the lead plaintiff. The court issued its injunction against the school district in June requiring that a desegregation plan be put into place.

The school district submitted four optional plans for desegregation, none of which would accomplish desegregation right away. Two plans extended desegregation through 1970 and 1971, while two others offered desegregation by 1968. All of the plans included substantial delays in desegregating secondary grades and proposed moving students within zones. Plan A proposed to desegregate grades one and two by January 1965; grade three by September 1965; then one grade per year through 1968; the next three grades in 1969; and the last three grades in 1970. Plan B proposed desegregation of grade one by September 1964; then one grade per year through 1968; the next three grades in 1970; and the last three grades in 1971. Plan C proposed a 1965 start with continuation of three grades per year through grade six; then three grades per year to completion in 1968. Plan D proposed desegregation of grades one and two by September 1964; two grades per year through grade six; grades seven through nine in 1968; and grades ten through twelve in 1968.[184]

Henry and the other plaintiffs quickly rejected the plans as foot dragging. In appealing they suggested that because blacks "lived south of the Illinois Central tracks, while the great majority of the white residents have lived north of the tracks . . . no school child will cross those tracks. The result was obvious from the beginning: the zoning could produce only token desegregation." They argued that this was by design: "certain pockets of Negro residences north of the tracks were purposefully removed through deannexation, purchase, or urban renewal by public authorities so that no Negroes would reside in the attendance zones of the northern half of Clarksdale."[185] Moreover, Henry argued that the effort had been stalled too long, and therefore asked the court to impose an interim plan, effective for the school year less than two months away.[186] Though the desegregation of schools was years off, the importance of the event was that it became part of the comprehensive, simultaneous assault on segregation.

The Clarksdale movement and the emergence of Aaron Henry represented the dawning of a new era for resistance to the racial system so deeply embedded in every fabric of life in Mississippi. The grassroots activism and the leadership that developed in this Delta town became a virtual template for the broader challenge that emerged in pockets across the state over the next several years. In Aaron Henry a leader emerged who had the knowledge and skill to capture the sentiments and strategically link these to other grassroots projects and to help marshal allies and supporters that squeezed their segregationist opponents. The framework for action and the tools used in Clarksdale found maximal use later as Mississippi became blanketed with the profoundest movement for social change since Reconstruction. The organizational basis centered on a revitalized NAACP, with an identity most characterized by grassroots indigenous interests.

Aaron Henry and Medgar Evers, and then Henry alone after the murder of the latter, stood at the forefront of revitalization of the NAACP. Henry first led from the grassroots chapter in Clarksdale, and he and Medgar later took the reins of the state organization and transformed it to the forefront of the frontal challenge of segregation in Mississippi. As the organization moved from the shadows, the influence of these two men and their indigenous supporters created a local organization that tested the highly bureaucratic, slow-moving policy of the national NAACP. The organization that Henry now led threatened the parent body because he sketched a far broader, aggressive assault on segregation than the legal approach of the national organization. The tension never disappeared and recurs throughout Henry's story.

As the most prominent leader to survive the RCNL (before the ascendancy of the NAACP), Henry cemented relationships with other emerging elements within the state, while he provided a template in Clarksdale that foretold the comprehensive vision he had for transforming the racial system. It included not just altering the day-to-day indignities of segregated life (courtesy titles and seats in a train station), but also substantive changes in the representation system:

voter registration, voting, and offering black candidates for office; desegregation of schools; and equal allocation of resources to improve life chances for black families. Remarkably, the Clarksdale movement featured all of these elements that in time characterized actions all over the state.

Improbably in a rural town like Clarksdale, Mississippi, one could not be blamed for thinking that a full-blown social movement built around civil rights was not possible in the early 1960s. Mississippi after all was known for using all of its power to maintain a system of racial exclusion and discrimination. A clear and virulent backlash did indeed develop in Clarksdale. The segregationist elites and their followers deployed all of the usual elements in their toolkit to derail the movement and to disqualify its leaders, especially Henry. Yet the circumstances were especially ripe in this Delta town where African Americans proved willing to take unusually forceful, public steps to challenge its racial system. The presence of Henry within a cluster of African American leaders in the Mississippi Delta helped to propel a broad movement. It made Clarksdale seem like a virtual laboratory for a social change movement. He stood at the center of a massive wave of assaults on segregation from every angle in this small Mississippi city. The highly organized and persistent movement proved effective in exposing the system and achieving some genuine shifts in racial exclusion. While this did not mean that the comprehensive program Henry envisioned came to pass in the two years of the massive street campaign, the foundation it laid was critical to the victory that came later. The experiences Henry gained in Clarksdale proved invaluable as he moved through the various stages of his singular place of leadership in the Mississippi civil rights movement and subsequent political mobilization.

CHAPTER FOUR

Demanding Restoration of the Black Franchise

Henry Heads the Freedom Vote Ticket, a 1963 Mock Election

The scope of Aaron Henry's activity had gone beyond Clarksdale long before the heady days of statewide mobilization in 1963 and 1964. By this time, however, with the death of Medgar Evers, Henry was the indigenous leader on a trajectory to the forefront of the campaign. This made the election he won as state NAACP president in 1959 all the more important. He was head of the most active, visible state civil rights organization, which gave him a base for connections to forces for change all over the country. He used these opportunities wisely, networking to attach himself to those who could advance his cause in Mississippi, sometimes to the chagrin of the national NAACP.[1] For example, he smoothly aligned with Martin Luther King, SNCC, and CORE, facilitating their activities within the state.[2] He had a selfless approach, integrity, and a genuinely collaborative nature. Henry's ubiquity, steadiness, and resourcefulness meant that the movement in Clarksdale could no longer define him; he belonged to the entire state, becoming the major player that facilitated expansion of the conflict and the conduit for resource deployment.

At the time of Henry's emergence as the most important indigenous state leader, a variety of other civil rights organizations attained prominence on the Mississippi scene as well. An increased national spotlight also shone on the state because as activism increased, a heightened countermobilization ensued from segregationists. The dexterity that Henry already demonstrated in moving among the various civil rights groups became a great advantage in facilitating relationships that advanced the wider movement.

Early on, the activists sought an organizational form as the means for sustaining linkage, communication, and division of labor. They appropriated a name for the organization that had already been used earlier: the Council of Federated Organizations. Henry said that he and Medgar Evers first used it in combining the various movement organizations active in Coahoma County in 1960. They called it the Coahoma County Council of Federated Organizations (CCCOFO).[3] Later when a group of largely NAACP leaders sought a meeting with Governor Barnett they called themselves the Council of Federated Organizations to deflect attention from their NAACP affiliation, the organization then seen as the primary nemesis for state officials and other segregationists groups. They succeeded in getting the meeting, according to Henry, which also facilitated a gathering of "nearly all of the state's Negro leaders."[4]

The COFO framework proved handy later on as the activities of NAACP, SNCC, and CORE escalated to a point of enveloping the entire state in a civil rights movement.[5] It was both practical and logical that these leaders develop a means of linkage due to the similarity of their goals and in the similarity in the counteroffensive waged against them by segregationists. The agreement for the confederal arrangement was arrived at, according to Payne, in meetings involving "Bob Moses of SNCC, Tom Gaither and Dave Dennis from CORE, and Medgar Evers, Amzie Moore, and Aaron Henry." Their aim was to organize where large concentrations of black people lived, and to adopt a strategy of placing workers (whom they envisioned would be made up largely of students) in "small places 'to stay only a week or two at a time.'"[6]

COFO became the organizational arm for the escalating grassroots movement in Mississippi. By this time SNCC and CORE had become the most prominent organizers of the foot soldiers across the state. The group chose Henry as the president of COFO because of his prominence as an effective and steady indigenous leader. Bob Moses of SNCC became the leader of the operational day-to-day activities.[7] The NAACP continued a variety of well-organized activities of its own, no doubt in efforts to extend its influence among younger people increasingly motivated by the activism of SNCC and CORE. Henry as organizer, speaker, and resource consultant was the connecting point for all of these groups.

Joyce Ladner and Robert Moses, keen observer-participant leaders, corroborated this view of Henry. Ladner first saw Henry when she accompanied Vernon Dahmer (an NAACP stalwart later assassinated) to an NAACP state convention in Jackson.[8] She came to know him much better when she enrolled at Tougaloo College and joined SNCC. "Dr. Henry was someone that we looked up to as . . . being a warrior who had been involved in civil rights in Mississippi . . . long before the so-called invasion of the outsiders occurred." She saw him as "a mentor, as a backstop, in a way, in the community who would stand up, speak out on our behalf . . . I don't remember . . . any experiences with Dr. Henry in which he drew the lines between, say, SNCC and the NAACP."[9] Moses agrees, seeing Henry as perhaps the only person with the combination of attributes and commitment to "bridge all the camps" operating on the civil rights front. "Henry was, in many ways, the linchpin of a certain part of the operational aspect of the movement [in] which he [had] these really different organizations, with different histories, and different personalities, different structures interfacing in Mississippi."[10]

The early COFO projects concentrated on voter registration and community organizing, supported by Delta communities. It did not take long, however, for political mobilization to be added to the list. The Voter Education Project became one of the early big projects of significance associated with the work of COFO. This Field and Taconic foundations-supported effort began in 1961 following the Freedom Rides and was run by the Southern Regional Council (SRC). It had a primary aim of obtaining the franchise for blacks in the South, an idea urged by the Kennedy administration as a way of shifting activists away from more controversial and often violent street encounters with segregationists.[11] Though the administration did not fully realize its hopes, VEP became a resource for COFO efforts to boost black voter registration. It had the most immediate effect of assisting in the establishment of projects[12] in six Delta and surrounding counties—Washington, Coahoma, Sunflower, Bolivar, Marshall, and Leflore.[13] It helped to strengthen and extend indigenous Delta leadership (e.g., Fannie Lou Hamer) and existing NAACP leaders (all Henry cohorts). However, the major projects that revealed the scope of the period and Henry's major leadership role are the mock election of 1963, Freedom Summer of 1964, and the Mississippi Freedom Democratic Party. Together they culminated in the challenge to the Mississippi delegates at the National Democratic Party convention in 1964.

Gradually the Mississippi campaign expanded beyond segregated public facilities to include voting and electioneering. For the leaders of the NAACP like Henry and Medgar Evers this was all logical since politics was always quite central to their vision for African American participation. This evidence for such a direction for Henry already appeared in the failed Trammell/Lindsey campaign of 1962. SNCC then arrived and its focus on local community organization immediately led to thoughts about political organization. Voter registration simply became a conduit. Henry used two high-profile events to dramatize the devastating consequences of the lack of African American representation in the Mississippi racial system. Within a month of Lindsey's announcement of his candidacy, Henry secured state hearings of the U.S. Civil Rights Commission (CRC) by its Mississippi advisory group, and also gave riveting testimony about racial exclusion in the state before the U.S. Senate.[14]

The Mississippi Advisory Committee of the CRC scheduled its first public hearings in Clarksdale after intense pressure from Henry. He was keen to get a public airing of charges for which he had written evidence, but had not succeeded in getting the Justice Department to allow the national commission to hold hearings in the state.[15] Henry and Vera Pigee testified before the state body reciting a litany of complaints about personal arrests and harassments in Clarksdale, material that northern legislators would surely exploit. Moreover, they hoped this record would compel President Kennedy to more actively oppose the southerners.[16] They also inserted concerns about the plight of candidate Lindsey, noting with dripping irony that he was even denied the right to purchase ads on local radio stations. In short, they railed against a power structure unwilling to accommodate blacks in the electoral process.[17]

The Mississippi movement had attained a high level of visibility nationwide by 1963. Violence from segregationists' state repression often drew attention, but so did the focused efforts of VEP and the continuing arrival of external allies. The national visibility generated by state repression of the 1961 Freedom Riders (incarcerating them at the notorious Parchman penitentiary) proved just the tip of the iceberg.[18] Henry's presence there indicated that despite NAACP demurrals, he worked to harness every major civil rights event for a broad attack on the entire Mississippi system of social and political discrimination.[19] Following Medgar Evers's death, media captured Jackson protesters (in an ongoing boycott of downtown businesses) being beaten and incarcerated like cattle at the state fairgrounds.[20] Earlier, the horrific violence, including murder, was captured when the externally based SNCC began its voter registration campaign in southwest Mississippi.[21]

Soon enough Mississippi captivated activists from all over the country to contribute to a movement as it shifted from the mere exercise of social and human rights to the question of political representation. Renewed voter registration, perhaps inadvertently, signaled this transition. The Lindsey congressional campaign that Henry managed (and the campaign of another Black, Reverend R. L. T. Smith of Jackson) served as a prelude to this transition. Meanwhile, new allies emerged, the majority from outside Mississippi, who deployed a wide range of resources that advanced the local campaign: finances, legal assistance, foot soldiers, and new modules for social action.[22] This complex web of linked resources seemed the perfect match for the rapidly escalating political mobilization.[23] Henry, as chairman of COFO, did as much as anyone to channel and steady this ship. His unwavering vision for equality in Mississippi and his collaborative style gave him links across all of the activists, allies, and organizations. He virtually became the intermediary and conduit for much of the debate and action. His leadership status, executed in a selfless manner, was vital in combining the social and political activists who composed the unified COFO organization.

The 1993 mock election gave concrete form to the phase initiated with the 1962 campaign for congressional seats, and it renewed emphasis on voter registration. Dubbed "Freedom Vote," it represented an opportunity for unregistered African Americans to participate in a separate, parallel poll during the upcoming gubernatorial election. Registered and unregistered black citizens alike, however, could use the open poll. The working proposition assumed that since African Americans were unable to participate in the real election, then the simulated contest would dramatize their plight.[24] The possibility even existed that the votes might be counted. "A Harvard law student working for COFO found that under Mississippi law voters claiming to have been illegally excluded from registering could cast ballots which would be set aside until they could appeal their exclusion."[25] This started a mock election campaign that opened a major salvo in a movement that increasingly focused on political mobilization.

With the failure of Reverends Lindsey and Smith in 1962, a compelling argument could be made for dramatizing the absence of a meaningful vote. Moreover, plenty evidence existed showing the difficulties blacks encountered trying to register, let alone vote. Unita Blackwell, who subsequently became mayor of Mayersville, recounted her arduous path to register. She had to return three times before she passed the arbitrary literacy test. According to her testimony before the U.S. Civil Rights Commission, she received some of the most difficult constitutional passages to interpret.[26] This is consistent with Neil McMillen's finding: "Whites were frequently asked to interpret Article 3, Section 30 (there shall be no imprisonment for debt), and Article 12, Section 240 (All elections by the people shall be by ballot) of the state constitution. Negroes were more likely to be assigned Article 3, Sections 21 (habeas corpus) and 22 (double jeopardy)."[27]

Provenance for the mock election project has been assigned variously.[28] Henry recalled that Robert Moses (SNCC), Annelle Ponder (SCLC), David Dennis (CORE), and Allard Lowenstein (no organizational affiliation) all participated in the formulation of the idea.[29] Lowenstein, who arrived in Mississippi about this time in 1963, subsequently arranged for about one hundred white students from Stanford and Yale to join the summer effort.[30] In any case, Henry is certainly one of the central figures who helped get this off the ground. The intensified focus on electoral politics, albeit in a simulation, became a logical extension of Henry's vision for blacks to habituate themselves to expressing a preference on off-limits public business.

The leaders of Freedom Vote emerged out of the loose solidarity structure reflected in COFO, in which Henry maintained the position of chairman. He had team members that he knew well. They included the top leaders of the principal affiliated groups in COFO. Moses was named the campaign manager, in charge of the daily operations and field strategy. He became the principal decision maker in deploying forces for action around the state. Allard Lowenstein became campaign chairman, a good vantage point for engagement in major aspects of the operation. The state Executive Committee was composed of R. L. T. Smith, the

1962 congressional candidate and a longtime Jackson NAACP leader, who served as the finance chair. Charles Evers, brother of Medgar Evers and now NAACP field secretary for the state, chaired the Speakers Bureau. Dave Dennis, Delta head of CORE operations, led the Policy Committee. Henry Briggs, Tougaloo College public relations officer, had that same role for the campaign. Regional managers worked within the existing framework of Mississippi's congressional districts, and they too reflected the COFO membership, but revealed the dominance of SNCC and CORE. Three were from SNCC (Frank Smith, District One; Sam Block, District Two; and Lawrence Guyot, District Five). Two others were from CORE (David Dennis, District Three, and Matteo Suarez, District Four). The sole woman was from SCLC, Annelle Ponder in District Two, also a stronghold for the NAACP.[31]

The selection of candidates to stand for governor and lieutenant governor in the mock election became one of the first orders of business. Henry as head of the ticket seemed a foregone conclusion due to his visibility and as head of the COFO. Known all over the state owing principally to his longtime activism among the black leadership elite, he also had high popular visibility as state leader of the NAACP, then the most widespread social change organization.[32] He also had the makings of an organizational support system and foot soldiers. This came from the Delta network of activists, his Clarksdale base, and affiliate chapters of the NAACP all over the state.[33]

The selection of Edwin (Ed) King, a white minister, as lieutenant governor candidate gave credence to the aspiration for local interracial cooperation. As an indigenous white activist, he had broken all the rules of his racial caste experience in favor of civil rights.[34] And as a local, King represented the promise and the ideal of a new racially integrated Mississippi.[35] He described the request asking him to take the second spot on the ticket. "About a week after the campaign had officially begun I received a phone call from Bob Moses. . . . I assumed he wanted me to do something like a northern speaking and fund raising trip . . . But Moses wanted much more than that. In his quiet way he made his request—he wanted me to join the ticket as the candidate for Lt. Governor." He justified it by focusing on our common interest in "interracial reconciliation and understanding." Moses reasoned "if I would join Aaron Henry then we could have a ticket with two native Mississippians, one Black and one white, working together, speaking at campaign rallies, talking about problems of all people of the state."[36]

The COFO leaders developed a detailed, sophisticated, and progressive platform for the campaign focused on the four major concerns elaborated below: justice, voting, economics, and education. The justice plans sought to "abolish segregation [laws] and replace [them] with integration laws for housing and public." In place of public funds for organizations like the Citizens' Council and the State

Aaron Henry at Freedom Vote (mock election), Jackson, Mississippi. Rally, October 1, 1963. (Courtesy The Image Works/Take Stock.)

Aaron Henry and Ed King, candidates for Mississippi governor and lieutenant governor, Mock election, November 14, 1963. (Courtesy The Image Works/Take Stock.)

Sovereignty Commission the plan called for a "State Commission on Equality" to mediate racial conflicts and to investigate police brutality. Similarly, the platform sought to influence the law enforcement sector by securing appointment of a reasonable number of blacks to state and local police forces, and the elimination of "corporal punishment in jail." The document assailed other peculiarities in state policy, such as the tax on illegal liquor sales, instead proposing a referendum on liquor sales.[37] Voting had prominence in the platform. The language COFO adopted seemed almost prescient in its closeness to that handed down later by the Supreme Court, and proposed by Congress in the Civil Rights Acts of 1964 and 1965: "Establish a one-man, one vote system for all adults; criminalize [voter] intimidation and give power of investigation for same to [a] State Fairness Commission; make dismissal a punishment for [local voting] registrars that discriminate."[38]

Detailed economic and education planks included standard concerns. The economic concerns related depressed conditions for sharecroppers and day laborers, job discrimination, unemployment, and lack of access to federal farm subsidies available to large plantation owners. This included a proposal for a small loan program for small farmers (under 300 acres), together with a progressive land tax (500+ acres); cooperative farming to take advantage of the economies of scale among small black landowners; a minimum wage of $1.25/hour for a forty-hour week; and the freedom to unionize were sought. The education plank focused on the most prevalent problem of segregation: seeking to "Integrate schools as soon as possible; equalize expenditures for all aspects of education, especially strategic vocational education; guarantee academic freedom so that teachers are not dismissed for their ideas."[39]

The Freedom Vote campaign actually commenced with the August 1963 Democratic gubernatorial primary when a small number of unregistered blacks cast "mock" ballots in "makeshift polling places in their communities." However, since a primary runoff occurred (August 27), a second round of mock voting also occurred. Estimates are that between 27,000 and 38,000 ineligible blacks again cast ballots. This impressive turnout in a short time frame reflected participation largely in just three cities—Clarksdale (Henry's bailiwick); Greenwood (SNCC activism); and Jackson (the capital city with strong NAACP leadership).[40]

The actual Freedom Vote coincided with the November general gubernatorial election. Preparations got underway using the standard state procedures for organizing campaigns. COFO held a nominating convention October 6 and "officially" nominated Henry and King as its candidates. Then it organized a registration process, simplified on account that the regular state process was not just illegal, but also inefficient.[41] Robert Moses argued: "Literacy tests should not be required because the state had not provided Negroes with adequate literacy education." Henry added, "There is no right and wrong in the interpretation tests. The only standard, he said, is what satisfies the white registrar."[42] Therefore, according to Waskow, "COFO ignored all the legal requirements for paying a poll tax, proving literacy, and demonstrating the ability to understand the state constitution." In short, this orchestrated event became the equivalent of another sit-in or freedom ride: "doing outside the existing local law what could have been done legally if racial equality had been achieved."[43]

The organizers set about arranging the details for voting and constructing a ballot. Since the voting aimed to replicate as nearly as possible the options available in the general election, the names of the officially sanctioned Republican (Rubel Phillips) and Democratic (Paul Johnson) candidates also appeared on the ballot. They provided clear specifications for the selection and management of the polling stations—how to cast and count ballots, and how to resolve disputes. The ambition for coverage remained high: to "have polling stations throughout every city. . . . In as many churches and business establishments as possible."[44]

Efforts turned to maximizing turnout, including planning for anticipated transportation problems. A "votemobile" collected ballots—"an automobile with a ballot box would travel throughout the Negro residential areas to gather the votes of the persons who did not vote in the churches."[45] Voters also did not have to wait until Election Day to cast the ballot. A system permitted advance voting so as not to compromise work schedules. Similarly, ballots could be cast on the nonbusiness days of Saturday and Sunday. Many church congregants particularly preferred Sunday since they worshiped at churches that were designated voting places.[46]

The procedures offered a measure of security from harassment or reprisals at places of employment or residence. To cast a ballot one had to do two simple things: provide a name and address (held confidential) to guarantee against fraud and execute the ballot paper. Since most of the participants had never seen a ballot nor had previous voting experience, leaders found it necessary to provide descriptions of how to mark and fold the ballot papers.[47] COFO also produced and disseminated a variety of materials to socialize their new voters. As an example several documents known as "Freedom Primers" provided detailed knowledge on both procedures and the history of the black franchise in Mississippi.[48]

The campaign organizers had a deep awareness of another audience—white officials. They hoped to demonstrate that blacks had the full capability of exercising the franchise, and doing so with integrity. Like the civic education arm of political parties (e.g., the League of Women Voters), Henry campaign headquarters provided full documentation about the process—those present at the polling stations, their functions, and appropriate behavior, and so on. Publicly released documents painstakingly described the activities.[49]

Freedom Vote had another high ambition as it sought to reach 200,000 voters via newspaper, radio, and television advertisement. This too required a special effort since the segregationist-controlled media often ignored news about the movement or were biased in coverage.[50] However, a sizable number of black-owned newspapers existed and they could be tapped. Though mostly weekly editions, they proved valuable resources.[51] (Also, the *Mississippi Free Press*, "a movement-oriented weekly" with statewide distribution, while not black owned, served as another major source.[52]) Similarly, black-oriented radio stations played an inestimable role. Aside from musical entertainment, listeners acquired a bevy of information—a virtual "bulletin board" of events, including movement activity, editorials, local public service programs, syndicated programs from movement spokespeople and clergy, and encoded messages in the idiom of gab from community-based disc jockeys.[53] Perhaps the most widespread dissemination of vital information emanated from churches and political rallies, places where large groups congregated. These relatively safe havens, under the control of members of the African American community, delivered unfiltered political messages and opinion.[54]

Meanwhile, the television media proved to be a daunting challenge. The NBC network in Jackson offered one of the particularly egregious examples.[55] Consistent with the Federal Communications Commission's (FCC) "fairness doctrine," Moses asked for free time for Henry to present the "views of the Negro and liberal communities on important social issues." He added that "these views are not expressed on Jackson television—but contrary opinions have been vigorously put forth by the other gubernatorial candidates . . . during their frequent appearances on WJTV." He added that because the campaign was being run without funds, it could not afford paid advertisement.[56] The Moses request received a quick denial, and blacks remained unable to get out their alternative messages in the major television market of the state. Meanwhile, the station persisted in portraying the Henry campaign as a nuisance perpetrated by a minority of local troublemakers and outside agitators.[57]

In spite of many obstacles, a well-organized three-and-a-half-week campaign ensued (from its October 6 convention to the November 5 election). Payne says: "There was nothing mock about the way COFO approached the election. They set up an elaborate statewide campaign organization, took out newspaper and television ads, and held rallies across the state. By October Aaron Henry was making a speech a night."[58] This matched the shrewd operation of the headquarters. While it had no party organization to guarantee the kind of local- and county-level structure its congressional district scheme required, the campaign seemed hardly bereft of foot soldiers. COFO and its affiliate organizations had tentacles all over the state. The NAACP and SNCC organized much of this, making information acceptable to a large number of African Americans. Each congressional district, under the leadership of a manager and further subdivided into regions, often corresponded to populous counties. Delta District Two had the largest number of county leaders (eight). It also had perhaps the most prominent and experienced indigenous leaders, among them Amzie Moore (a longtime NAACP leader) and Fannie Lou Hamer and Charles McLaurin (more recent grassroots leaders affiliated with SNCC). District Three had four leaders, and Districts One and Four had one leader each.[59]

District leaders (the majority from SNCC and a few from CORE) gave their first reports in September 1963. The documents reveal deep organization, broad issues, and paltry resources. Frank Smith (Congressional District One leader) had a staff of three deployed in urban areas—Holly Springs (headquarters), Columbus, Batesville, and Tupelo. His plan for voter registration and the Freedom Vote was ambitious: Mass meetings advertised "by word of mouth, leaflets, announcements"; block-to-block canvassing, including "clubs, fraternities, bars, etc."; and a six-person rapid response team. Coverage of this two-hundred-mile radius district had to be accomplished with only one car, and the modest $240.00 per week budget Smith requested. He lamented: "If we had cars we could do twice as much work. We could get twice as many people registered to vote."[60]

Samuel Block headed heavily black District Two, which included some of the most activist Delta towns and important indigenous leaders like Aaron Henry, Amzie Moore, and Fannie Lou Hamer. Again, the urban places turned out to be the targets for organization: Indianola, Belzoni, Charleston, Clarksdale, Ruleville, and Cleveland. A worker had a station in rural Tunica County with its many potential voters. The project had similarities to that in the First District—"block captains, organization of clubs, churches, juke joints, beauty salons, etc." to generate maximal Freedom Vote turnout. An interesting initiative involved use of students to "hold mass meetings, evening and weekend canvassing, public speaking before church congregations, engaging their parents and friends, and preparation of weekly reports." Block's budget request was equally modest, given the many workers present in the district—$960 per month.[61]

McArthur Cotton headed District Three, encompassing the most urbanized zone of the state (Jackson, Vicksburg, and Natchez) and McComb (mobilized as the site of SNCC's first project). A considerable African American population (47 percent) also existed in the district. In addition to a cadre of NAACP activists, now joined by SNCC and CORE, especially in Jackson and Vicksburg, McArthur Cotton sought to capitalize on another base in the district—students from three senior black colleges (Tougaloo, Jackson State, and Alcorn), and three two-year colleges (Utica, Prentiss, and Campbell). He projected a weekly budget of $50 in this district, which had a single car.[62]

District Four, headed by George Greene, issued a modest report built around the same themes for a territory that spanned both the "Black-Belt" cotton region and the eastern hills: urban Meridian on the Alabama border, and several sizable towns (Philadelphia, Forest, Canton, and Newton). Greene proposed a budget of $840 per month. The least detailed report came from District Five in the Southwest led by Lawrence Guyot. Its weekly budget proposal for $240 per week covered four unspecified projects. Though it had a comparatively small African American population, the Gulfport and Biloxi area had some history of NAACP activism.[63]

Aaron Henry had presence everywhere in this campaign. While it is not possible to reconstruct a day-to-day schedule of his activity, Payne suggests that Henry indeed made a speech a night.[64] In fact, he often made multiple appearances in a day all over the state, affirming the comprehensive reach of COFO. Henry gave indications of the scale of his activity: "I spoke in Holly Springs, Oxford, Greenville, Clarksdale, Jackson, Gulfport, and Hattiesburg." Later he added Vicksburg and Lexington and as "many communities and rural areas as possible and dipped into places as yet untouched by any civil rights activity." Yet, he lamented, "there were some counties that we did not go at all because of plain fear and good sense—like Issaquena, Amite, and Neshoba, where we were afraid we would be shot."[65] Some of Henry's most memorable appearances occurred in his hometown of Clarksdale, where he always reminded his audiences of his candidacy for governor, even as he battled police brutality and fielded boycotts.[66]

A sample of two weeks of his frenetic pace and the regular venues for appearances is revealing. The period began in Clarksdale at week's end in mid-October, followed by a Monday evening speech, October 14, at Jackson's Masonic Temple.[67] Wednesday evening he was back in Clarksdale speaking to the NAACP at Haven Methodist Church with his running mate, Ed King.[68] The following Friday found him in Yazoo City at Bethel AME church. Four days later he had crisscrossed the state again, appearing in Hattiesburg.[69] Other venues of regular appearance for him included the Delta towns with active branches of the NAACP and SNCC and CORE workers—Greenwood, Greenville, Holly Springs, and Cleveland. He also had excellent contacts in Meridian and Philadelphia, and many towns in the Southwest were on the list: Natchez, Liberty, Port Gibson, Columbia, McComb, and Fayette, among them.[70]

The October 29, 1963, appearance in Hattiesburg is what a typical day could be like. Five Yale University students and two SNCC workers preceded Henry there and found themselves set upon as they attempted to interview the black proprietor of the restaurant where this integrated group had dined. According to the "Committee to Elect Aaron Henry Governor of Mississippi," police arrested the group and "ransacked the restaurant." Henry arrived and attempted to make an afternoon walk through the city accompanied by a white reporter and an integrated pair of SNCC workers. The provocation proved too much for law enforcement, who arrested the whites present. When Henry seemed ready to intervene, "the police officer said to the gubernatorial candidate, 'Nigger, I didn't tell you to stop; move on.'"[71]

The drama had just begun. The police tailed Henry though his first appearance was an evening speech. Meanwhile, already intimidation and harassment had begun of any African Americans who appeared to be collaborating with Henry and the "outside agitators." For example, two churches on Mobile Street, scheduled venues for Henry speeches, withdrew their invitations. They responded to pressure from police, who intensively patrolled the area. Undaunted, community leaders acquired the local Masonic Temple, a friendly black-controlled facility. When Henry arrived for his speech, ominously the fire department with three trucks and a police cruiser joined officers already tailing him. With sirens blaring, this convoy roared up to the Masonic Temple.[72]

The police/fire surveillance team intended to disrupt the campaign event on several levels. It sought to muddle Henry's message and to silence the audience. Consistent with these goals, the police convoy redeployed to the local SNCC office arresting a local white worker as she left the premises. Then the convoy circled back to the Masonic Temple. "During the rally, several firemen stood in the back of the meeting hall while every two or three minutes the police and fire vehicles parked outside would sound their sirens and use their loudspeakers to disrupt the meeting, and disrupt the whole neighborhood." In the face of this scene Henry admonished his hecklers: "I would like those people blowing the sirens and the firemen in the back of the room to know that there is a fire going on, but water won't put this fire out." This contest of wills continued through the speech.[73]

Ed King offered a fairly extensive account of experiences on the hustings. He recalled that because of the continuing threat of violence, early campaign rallies and meetings occurred at churches, though even these could sometimes be thwarted. Nevertheless, over time he and Henry appeared in gatherings at some public facilities or in open air. The traditional outdoor fish fry or cookout became a favorite event adapted for such events, a variation on what the regular Mississippi Democratic Party used in its campaigns. King described an early "Fish Fry for Henry" where "over 200 residents of Holmes County cheered their candidate and donated money for the campaign." Later such events, dubbed "Freedom Fish Fries," became a staple of political campaigns as the movement became more focused on electioneering.[74]

Greenville and Greenwood hosted large campaign events. The former, a large Delta town, permitted a rally at its county courthouse. Ed King provided an elaborate description of the event: "On a cool evening, over 500 black people gathered on the lawn to see their candidate standing on the Courthouse steps, flags, bunting, and posters surrounding them." As was often the case in these southern towns, irony and contradiction abounded. During the rally King observed the shadowed gaze from a statue of a Confederate soldier nearby, a presence hardly noticed or perhaps ignored by the crowd.[75] Also somewhat unpredictably, the police provided protection, perhaps in order to preserve Greenville's "good name" since a small crowd of local whites had gathered in the distance.[76] Meanwhile, in nearby Greenwood at the Elks Rest (Masonic Hall), "nearly 1000 blacks jammed" the building.[77]

The public rallies accomplished multiple and sometimes contradictory goals. Ed King's description of the Greenville Courthouse scene indicated a display of national symbols like flags and bunting. The display on turf normally "owned" by the segregationists was an act of defiance since the latter had largely disavowed the "Stars and Stripes" and adopted the Confederate flag as a symbol of their aspirations. Yet, the Henry campaign continued to remind the national government of its obligation to support blacks who remained loyal to the Republic and who sought only to affirm their membership in the face of racial exclusion. Finally, appropriating these national symbols reiterated the faith that the leadership had in the ideology and values of the U.S. democracy. As such, waving the flag was no idle act; it represented an expression of faith.

On the stump, Henry, in hard-hitting and indefatigable performances, asserted a well-honed ideology of equality. His positions always echoed the "integrationist" line of the NAACP, and struck all of the themes of the campaign platform—education, voting rights, public accommodations, jobs, freedom of expression, and cultural rights. He always invoked his Christian faith, but focused more on the issues of inequality and their consequences for African Americans. He rendered his white opponents as the "other," indistinct in their aims to maintain segregation. While he could also be mocking about the obvious contradictions and inefficiencies of the system, he always remained decorous. Nor did he ever appear to lose faith in the constitutional arrangements the founders established for democratic government. Ed King described Henry on the stump as giving the appearance of a businessman, in a suit and tie. "His eyes and voice were usually gentle, but not weak. However, on the speaker's stand, the quiet determination was often succeeded by a strong, more impassioned advocacy of the cause of the peoples whose votes he sought." King goes on to say that while Henry often referred to scripture "he never used the extreme emotionalism of most of the ministers (and other leaders) that the Mississippi Black people were used to."[78]

When Henry spoke, King continued, he exuded a confidence of "voice and presence that was easily communicated to his audience. Most . . . knew he had been jailed for his civil rights activities. His happy, easy-going style showed that prison had not broken his spirit—and this was reassuring to all those who met him."[79] Several examples from him on the stump illustrate his method and style. In the passage below he was speaking in late October in Holmes County.

> The only issues now being raised is how hard the Democrats are going to be on Negroes—and on the Republican side we hear how much harder Mr. [Rubel] Phillips and [Barry] Goldwater are going to be on us when they get into office.
> The Mississippi Negro today wants equal rights and brotherhood.
> We want freedom, law, democracy and justice.
> All of us are from loyal Christian homes, and Christianity would not have survived to this modern day if there had not been those stalwart souls who were willing to sacrifice their lives for their faith, those who took their stand regardless of consequences.
> Every right and privilege due any other American, Negroes want and are determined to have.
> . . . [T]hey will help pull the state up from the bottom of so many lists where we have been for so many years.
> We've got to stop these white men from coming into our homes and calling our wives by their first names.
> And while we are at it, we should try to make the white man understand that we don't want to be his brother-in-law, only his brother.
> If it takes bloc voting to end segregation and secure Negro rights, then we had better get ready for the bloc voting.
> [Nevertheless] We want to pick the best man for the job regardless of the color of his skin or his religion.[80]

The campaign developed an array of other strategies to utilize its standard-bearer. It featured Henry in radio advertisements and/or discussions, mostly on black-oriented stations; and election headquarters also produced a constant stream of blurbs, flyers, and so on. Hardly any of these matched the slickly produced material of the state's Democratic or Republican Parties. In this unorthodox "shoestring campaign" most material consisted of hand-drawn, mimeographed broadsides. Some blurbs featured direct quotes from Henry, while others referenced his accomplishments and civil rights involvement. Others featured photographs of him and his running mate, projecting the visual image of integration that irked the segregationists. The irony is that perhaps the most provocative of these campaign images also served as a tool of mobilization for the civil rights forces. This flyer carried a photograph of the two candidates side by side, but Ed

King had almost one-half of his face covered with a surgical bandage, the result of what he believed was a terrorist head-on vehicular collision following the street demonstrations after Medgar Evers's assassination. A car driven by a white teenager, the son of an active member of the Citizens' Council, forced another car into a collision. Ed King's critical injuries left him near death. He did survive and campaigned as he healed.[81]

However, a sizable amount of printed material had the appearance of routine campaign objects: for example, civic education pamphlets for disfranchised citizenry. In addition, excellent use was made of "free" advertisement, such as the well-timed news release or news conference. As the campaign progressed with Henry active on so many other fronts, press notices became more numerous. Even negative treatment from local media was a bonus because its credibility was always doubted.

Several examples give a flavor of the visibility Henry garnered from news conferences and other media events. He waged a major battle with the Clarksdale police just as the campaign began and dramatized this conflict for national visibility.[82] He made use of a number of affidavits collected just two months before the Freedom Vote campaign opened that charged police brutality. Many these related to the ongoing boycott of merchants in Clarksdale. In early September Henry sent a batch of the affidavits to Roy Wilkins, executive secretary of the NAACP, requesting help in securing federal intervention. Henry's letter said the "affidavits . . . set forth the facts of police brutality and the denial of civil rights by the police department and other officials of this city. In all cases the victims are Negroes, and in no instance has the interest of the Federal Government gone beyond the investigatory stage."[83] He implored Wilkins to force a status report from Washington authorities.

On October 6, Henry escalated by sending a letter to Burke Marshall, assistant attorney general for civil rights of the Justice Department. His biting charge read: "We are forced to call your attention to a reign of terror being forced upon the Negroes of the Clarksdale Community. . . . The latest in a series of horror stories as the Lynching, yes lynching of one Earnest Jells . . . on Friday night September 20, 1963. Jells was chased into a dead end alley by a local white merchant and about 12 members of the Clarksdale Police Department and gunned down to his death with no opportunity of escape."[84] Again, he attached affidavits from witnesses substantiating that charge and a variety of similar ones. Henry reminded Marshall that the nature of the local movement was nonviolent. Then, using a common tactic to tap a variety of audiences, he copied the letter to a variety of supporters (likely to publicly release it), and to others implicated in the issues raised. The copy list included the local NAACP attorney (Jack Young), Roy Wilkins, and Clarence Mitchell (NAACP lobbyist at Congress).[85]

Similarly, he used press releases to comment on events occurring elsewhere. On October 27, 1963, his election committee issued a terse statement on a "pray-in," dripping with symbolism and irony. It appealed to the African American base, but also reminded others in this Bible-Belt region of a fundamental religious contradiction—the refusal to receive other members of the faithful (clergy from outside Mississippi, and integrated groups seeking to worship freely at white churches). Henry called attention to the recent arrest of two ministers from Chicago at one of the largest white Jackson congregations, Capitol Street Methodist, whose bulletin salutation read: "To our visitors we extend a cordial welcome." He called their arrest "one [of the] more incredibly repressive violation[s] of fundamental rights," noting that the police were acting "in a manner more befitting a totalitarian state than the United States of America." He asked: "Who can decide . . . what is more equal before God? For these hypocrites to deny the house of God to their fellow men because of the color of their skin is not only a crime against humanity but a sin before God." Henry lambasted the church for its hypocrisy. "To Americans with any sense of the inherent dignity of man this statement in the program of a Church which refuses to allow Negroes and whites to worship together in it is duplicity of a sort which I shall never be able to understand or tolerate." The release included personal testimonies that the ministers recounted to their own congregations about their cruel experience in Mississippi. Distribution of the release went to the standard list of national allies.[86]

Perhaps the most significant dimension of the Henry campaign resulted when it partially generated a statewide voter registration and mobilization. Mississippi's indigenous leaders and activists became a critical element in the campaign. Henry and field secretary Medgar Evers enjoyed the highest visibility; other homegrown leaders complemented them. In the Delta alone, a bevy of indigenous leaders appeared in Greenwood, Cleveland, Mound Bayou, Ruleville, Mayersville, and the Holmes County area. Jackson and Vicksburg had long produced strong local leaders, initially associated with the NAACP, and later Jackson's importance rose because of the location of the main COFO office there.[87] When SNCC made its foray into southwest Mississippi it also found experienced leaders and foot soldiers primed to organize—C. C. Bryant, Herbert Lee, Hollis Watkins, and Curtis Hayes.[88] Significant groups of external allies became a part of the resource base for the campaign. The first of what was to be waves of allies from the North arrived, first students, then clergy, attorneys, and medical personnel. Prominent members of the national political and social elite also put their considerable prestige and links to the power structure at the disposal of the movement.

The SNCC and CORE field organizers, in concert with the homegrown leaders, consistently assumed the leadership role in grassroots organization. The students entered communities and sought to meld into the local culture, persistently questioning the status quo urging voter registration. Their early field reports hardly revealed the difficulty of their daily work—canvassing and re-canvassing to find registered voters and, alternatively, to find those registered for Freedom Vote. Jesse Sherrod expressed what became the broad mission, "organizers should use local churches and black newspapers to communicate with residents and should develop personal relations by working with youth groups including gangs, and living with local families." He added that he and his cohorts also preferred to remain as self-sufficient as possible: "We are willing to pick cotton, scrub floors, wash cars and windows, babysit, etc. for food and lodging."[89] Notwithstanding the banality of the task or its frustrating outcome, the organizers became well-known conduits for campaign information. They organized local rallies and produced the crowds to hear Henry speak.

The ambitious campaign required still more human resources to get out the projected 200,000 for the Freedom Vote. Bob Moses concluded that increased outside intervention would so dramatize the plight of black Mississippians that it might lead to a breakthrough in thwarting the segregationist backlash.[90] Allard Lowenstein was permitted to recruit help from Ivy League schools in the North.[91] It was a foregone conclusion that these students would be largely white, and this caused some debate. There was concern about how the resulting dynamic would affect a mostly southern black-led local movement and about how to manage the considerable risk to northern college students unaccustomed to often violent, racist reactionaries.[92] However, with the pressure so great to deliver a strong showing in the Freedom Vote, about one hundred students arrived in the late summer to assist.[93] Henry remained excited about their engagement because of its consistency with the logic of his integrationist vision and program. He also calculated that the presence of these allies generated a broader base of support among national elites. That could only further the long-term goal of desegregation, from his point of view.[94]

Lowenstein used contacts largely at Stanford and Yale (his workplace and alma mater, respectfully) as a base of recruitment.[95] Though always a fairly good salesman, he had help in recruitment from Robert Moses and Marian Wright (Edelman), the latter then a Yale law student. These two gave speeches about conditions in Mississippi and showed how student volunteers could contribute.[96]

The young enthusiastic workers extended the role of community organization in familiar and unexpected ways. Their mere presence did bring a great deal of attention just because most were white. The national media focused on them as the "core story," bringing a level of visibility that blacks alone rarely achieved. The students also generated their own stories, which were chronicled by their student newspapers back on campus. Their members in Mississippi included some student newspaper editors and photographers.[97]

Equally important was the reaction of local media and political elites. Virtually all dubbed the volunteers "outside agitators," precipitating an escalation of racial violence and other attacks upon the movement leaders and upon the white outsiders (as predicted). Chafe reported: "Each day new episodes of violence and intimidation were reported, some of them coming perilously close to murder." Lowenstein personally experienced this cruelty. Clarksdale police arrested him for running a nonexistent stoplight and for loitering when he sought a room at a local hotel.[98] These incidents brought considerable national publicity, generating sympathy due to the cumulative effect of media stories about temporary volunteers caught up in a web of Kafkaesque deceptions and subterfuges. The importance of these stories was elevated as Martin Luther King Jr. followed the huge August 1963 March on Washington with increasingly large mass demonstrations throughout the South. The sheer constancy of news coverage, let alone editorials, saturated the airwaves.[99] The attention had the opposite effect from that desired by the local whites—expanding the conflict to the significant advantage of the Freedom Vote campaign.[100]

Meanwhile, the volunteers brought a variety of skills that expanded the scope of the local organization. Many functioned essentially as staff in the small makeshift offices, producing written materials for civic education and campaign ads. Some of them, of course, were also involved in the day-to-day canvassing. The inherent power in such administrative work often led to internal conflicts with local volunteers, a tension that escalated as the number of volunteers increased the following year.[101] In this early venture at interracial cooperation, the Freedom Vote was greatly enhanced by the combined forces.

Henry reveled in the collaborative spirit often on display at his appearances. In his affable manner he made volunteers a part of his personal retinue, flaunting them before the police and highway patrolmen who invariably tailed him. Two of the volunteers wrote reports detailing what it felt like on a whistle-stop Henry campaign trip. Cal Arnold reported from the Gulf coast on October 7, 1963. He related his tasks on organizing for both a COFO meeting and a speech by Henry. He encountered a well-organized and "militant" community of indigenous NAACP leaders who had been mobilized since the 1959 "wade in" on the beaches.[102] After visiting all of the towns along the coast, he traveled on to help with the Henry rally in Jackson. He was arrested on both legs of his round trip for trying to integrate a lunch counter and later a bus terminal.[103]

Willie Blue provided a similar report from the road in Batesville in the northern end of the Mississippi Delta. He traveled down to Jackson for a strategy meeting with Henry, Bob Moses and representatives of the National Council of Churches, among others. Following Henry's selection as gubernatorial candidate the next day Blue returned to Batesville to organize voters, give speeches of his own, and at the same time to continue a vigorous campaign to formally enroll blacks for the state electorate. Arriving Sunday, he spoke to the Voters League; on Tuesday he spoke to the Black Beauticians Association; on Wednesday he picked cotton; and Wednesday night he returned to Clarksdale where Henry and Bob Moses spoke.[104]

The campaign adopted another major tool of using external elites as allies. Just as the students served to increase the salience of the Freedom Vote, so did the speaking appearances and intermittent protest actions of prominent visitors. They represented a wide range of social activists, movement leaders, clergy, and legal advisers, among others. Their stock in trade became the well-timed public appearance that put a national/international spotlight on the racial system. For example, two Chicago clergymen, part of an integrated group during the campaign, spontaneously dropped to their knees for a "pray-in" when denied admission to a Jackson church in late October.[105] The press captured the scene and distributed it widely, exacerbating the sense of irrationality of the segregationist forces.

The tent of allies that Henry accepted and cultivated had a wide span indeed and sometimes provoked reactions from detractors about unpatriotic elements infiltrating the movement. Undeterred, he invited Norman Thomas, a six-time Socialist Party candidate for president, to campaign for the Freedom Vote. Thomas was certainly controversial, especially for southerners, but he brought much more as an ally—the experience and travails of seeking an office that most regarded as outside the realm of possibility and a background as a clergyman dedicated to social justice. Thomas gave a rousing speech at a Delta campaign rally, which the segregationists sought to thwart. One effort included a "vigilante gang [that] followed a car they thought carried Thomas and deliberately rammed it from behind. When the car arrived at campaign headquarters, two cars blocked it, trapping the campaign workers for hours."[106] By then Thomas "started speaking at the pulpit. . . . His talk was almost a sermon; . . . the rapport between speaker and the people was absolute. He talked of faith and courage; of his admiration for what the Black people of Mississippi were doing; of his pride in what the youth in America were doing; of the past and of the present of his hopes and fears for America."[107]

Lawyers constituted a part of the prominent group of powerful external allies. They help to sustain the ever-escalating legal challenges, previously the sole preserve of the NAACP and three or four local lawyers. Almost immediately the new arrivals expanded the options for lawsuits against recalcitrant local officials. Prominent lawyers came, many originally associated with the Legal Defense Fund of the NAACP, or with other movement allies, or the federal government. Some of them came as much out of inspiration following the assassination of Medgar

Evers months earlier, as they did for the Freedom Vote. An example among them, left-wing New York lawyer William Kunstler had first come to Mississippi during the Freedom Rides in 1961 at the behest of the ACLU. He stayed on to assist in the investigation of the Evers assassination and continued work with most of the civil rights and legal organizations thereafter.[108]

There were also individual lawyers within the Justice Department who served as the legal face of an increasingly activist executive branch. Perhaps the best example of these, John Doar, held the position of deputy director of the Civil Rights Division, an office on the front lines of federal challenges to segregation. His first test came when he had to face down the governor and a virtual armed militia to desegregate the University of Mississippi.[109] Doar subsequently became the Justice Department liaison with the civil rights forces in the state. As challenges to segregation escalated across the state and put pressure on the federal government to intervene, he had a hand in many efforts in support of change, even prior to the mock election. In Greenwood he supported the SNCC-led efforts for voter registration in 1962. It was frustrating work of which Doar said: "We brought suits against the county officials and the state officials, and they were in court on these cases of intimidation. At the same time, we were trying to get more registrars to open up the rolls. We were battling. We weren't making any significant progress, but we had a lot of presence in Mississippi."[110] He appeared at the Ohio orientation conference that prepared the northern college students who descended on the state in the 1964 "Freedom Summer." He briefed them on the federal law even as he expressed his personal sentiments and commitments to their cause.[111]

However, the great wave of legal experts came through the sponsorship of legal organizations. Clearly the NAACP lawyers and the few local black lawyers were overwhelmed with the dramatic increase in arrests, assaults, and violence. A multitude of other legal needs also existed. The segregation laws became moving targets as the state legislature instituted new statutes to thwart the civil rights forces or to head off the consequences of an anticipated restoration of the franchise to blacks.[112] Moreover, lawyers had to be available to simply protect federal laws that were routinely contravened by Mississippi elected officials and local courts. Among the organizations that responded to this need were the Lawyers' Committee for Civil Rights under Law, the Lawyers' Constitutional Defense Committee, and the Lawyers' Guild.

The Lawyers' Committee for Civil Rights under Law actually began at the suggestion of President Kennedy, who sought to reduce the political consequences of street confrontations by redirecting the focus to the courtroom. Clarence Dunnaville says that Kennedy "requested that the American Bar Association recruit private lawyers to volunteer and travel to Mississippi to represent black citizens and civil rights workers. Bernard G. Segal, a former president of the ABA[,] assembled 244 prominent lawyers[,] among the most prominent lawyers in the nation."[113] The organization did its work by recruiting lawyers to volunteer to provide free legal representation on civil rights matters. In the nature of the circumstances it dedicated little time to the redirection of the focus of activism; the lawyers just became another part of an increasingly organized assault on segregation. They "filed lawsuits against individuals who deprived black citizens of their civil rights. Its lawyers represented civil rights workers who were jailed, advised on voting rights issues and provided a support system for black citizens and civil rights workers. They were the subjects of hostility, and some were physically attacked and injured during the performance of their services."[114]

All of the legal organizations generated strong reactions from the segregationists who claimed that they were simply a part of a misguided lot of outsiders who did not understand the Mississippi way. The oldest of these, the Lawyers' Guild, inspired an additional amount of invective, not just from segregationists, but also from some of the liberal civil rights organizations and lawyers. The guild had been tarred with a label perhaps more reviled than integration: communism. Founded in 1937, according to Dittmer, it "had achieved a reputation as a 'communist' organization, largely because it did not exclude communists and because its lawyers defended American communists during the witch hunts of the post–World War II era." Indeed it was among the first groups to provide legal assistance that supplemented local lawyers who took civil rights cases. For example, they "pioneered the innovative legal maneuver of using a Reconstruction statute to remove civil rights cases from local to federal jurisdiction, thereby improving the chances for favorable verdicts."[115] This refers to the 1875 Removal Act in which "Republicans authorized parties to remove cases to federal courts when they could not secure federally guaranteed rights in the state courts."[116] This became a tactic that Henry and all of the civil rights organizations subsequently used to get around the avowedly racist judges in the local courts.

Henry generously used the services of these groups through the years as the needs for attorneys increased with the virtual daily barrage of assaults on segregation continued in Clarksdale and many other sites across the state. Much of this related to the coordinated efforts of COFO, but as often included activities initiated by the members of the confederation—especially SNCC and CORE. Not being particularly wed to the exclusive use of lawyers from the NAACP, as that organization desired, Henry regularly called upon whatever sources were available as needs arose.

A host of other celebrities and representatives of the national political elite arrived in Mississippi on the eve of Freedom Vote. They put the weight of their celebrity and/or pedigree at the disposal of Henry and other activists in Mississippi.

Many of them gravitated toward Clarksdale because they were a part of the vast NAACP network or were friends Henry had collected in his multitude of organizational affiliations. Dick Gregory, perhaps the most celebrated black comedian to cast his lot with the movement, appeared regularly, making public speeches often with Henry at his side.[117] Franklin Roosevelt III came in September, evoking the spirit of his father's larger-than-life presidency. Leroy Johnson, the first black elected Georgia legislator since Reconstruction, spoke at the First Baptist Church in Clarksdale on October 30, 1963. He represented a powerful symbol of the promise of the reacquisition of the franchise.[118]

The national NAACP remained an important ally, which could always attract luminaries from its board of directors, as well as the executive director, Roy Wilkins. The latter often showed up to protect his own turf because Henry, his independent-minded state president, did not always seem to be in sync with the national office. Other NAACP board members, with whom Henry served, also lent significant personal and political weight and financial resources to the Mississippi cause. They could accomplish with the dispatch of a letter what ordinary citizens could not do.[119]

The Freedom Vote inspired a hugely negative reaction from white citizens and authorities. Some were routine efforts to thwart the campaign—such as churches that denied integrated groups admission to Sunday services and the harassment that accompanied Henry when he spoke in Hattiesburg. At other times authorities simply denied Henry the right to make appearances. Two such instances occurred in important Delta towns with sizable African American populations and some activism: Yazoo City and Belzoni officials simply prevented his public appearance.[120] Others endured similar outright denials of free speech. Consider what happened to the *Mississippi Free Press*, a major source of information about the campaign. Organized efforts often prevented distribution of the paper, a kind of censorship reminiscent of the Soviet Union. The reaction in Columbus in late October illustrated what could happen when contents of the paper displeased the authorities. The mayor simply barred anyone from distributing Henry's campaign literature. This included his order not to distribute the *Mississippi Free Press* because its inclusion of material on the "Freedom Vote would only cause a racial disturbance." Later upon seeing a *Mississippi Free Press* headline that read, "Negroes get shackled," the mayor issued an angry denial: "There ain't no damn Negroes getting shackled in Columbus." He then denied the use of a sound truck by the campaign leaders.[121]

A remarkable campaign ensued in many respects, not least for its very execution. Dittmer has said: "Perhaps what was most remarkable was neither Henry nor King was assaulted or arrested throughout the campaign, a unique experience for both men."[122] Nevertheless, a spectrum of segregationists conducted a broad and relentless effort to thwart the campaign. Violence could occur at any time, and student arrests and harassment occurred with regularity during the short campaign. *The Student Voice*, the SNCC newspaper, reported more than one hundred arrests during the mere three weeks of the campaign.[123] The rarely legitimate charges varied—vagrancy, loitering, disturbing the peace, or petty traffic violations such as ignoring stop signs or disobeying an officer. In summarizing the results of the police assaults on campaign workers in the four and a half months of the campaign, the *New York Times* provided this tally. "There were 119 arrests; 63 other harassments, including a church burning, that occurred between October 18 and November 2. This paled against four months past when there were three murders, 35 church burnings, 1000 arrests, 85 beatings, 35 shooting incidents."[124]

Official state and law enforcement actions constituted a large part of the effort to thwart the campaign. Examples went all the way to the U.S. Congress. Henry, Edwin King, and Bob Moses sent a telegram to Senator Eastland charging that he had a "continuing influence in preventing Negroes in Mississippi from registering to vote." They detailed Eastland's actions as chair of the Judiciary Committee in proposing an investigation of the Fifth Circuit Court's "appointments to panels dealing with civil rights." This followed a suit by the U.S. attorney general against Mississippi for denying voting rights to blacks. The telegram charged that Eastland objected to two of the three judges assigned to the hearing panel because they would no doubt favor the government's case. Eventually one of the two judges withdrew from the case and plans for the investigation were dropped.[125]

The COFO put together a partial summary of some of the harassment and other acts perpetrated against the movement leadership and volunteers. The document revealed the scope of the state-orchestrated effort to intimidate, undermine, and exact financial costs against the movement. Virtually all of the incidences reported in the summary involved police and/or other administrative arms of the state—mayors, bureaucrats, and officers of the courts. The summaries are generated from two short intervals late in the 1963 Freedom Vote campaign: the week of October 22–28, and two days between November 1–2. More than thirty-one incidents were recorded in these nine days, and since that number is constructed by bundling events in some individual cities, it seriously underrepresents the true scope of encounters between movement workers and the authorities. Law enforcement officials used considerable ingenuity in creating trumped-up causes for the arrest, detainment, or eviction of activists engaged in campaign work.

In virtually all of these instances of engagement there were considerable consequences for the civil rights workers and the candidates. The continuing summaries from SNCC below provide many examples. Ed King was "fined for four separate traffic 'violations' in one afternoon in Jackson." Auto theft was a particularly specious charge leveled at campaign workers driving cars. The charge was "leveled even at people driving their own cars and carrying the registration papers on their person." Meanwhile, those driving someone else's car could find "themselves detained for long periods." In Indianola twenty-two arrests of workers occurred between October 22 and 24 for "distributing leaflets without a permit." In Clarksdale on the twenty-fourth, a member of Henry's advisory committee and two Yale students received jail time for "violating a curfew" after they parked their car and crossed the street to enter their hotel. Their drive to the hotel followed a meeting at the home of Aaron Henry. Police officers in Jackson used the tactic of "apprehending campaign workers especially enroute to and from campaign offices during the evening hours. [They] trail cars, quiz drivers and passengers and search interiors." Often the workers are taken to the police station and fined. Other times workers were escorted out of town. John Lewis, chairman of SNCC, had this experience in Rosedale. Leaving there with his group for a trip to Cleveland another police escort followed them to the black town of Mound Bayou "and told us not to be in town after sundown." Edwin King and some journalists believed that their phones were tapped, and others charged that "mail of activists was tampered with."[126] Seeing the scale and range of tactics used it seems remarkable that Aaron Henry survived the campaign or that the campaign generated any turnout at all.

It is difficult not to claim success for the Freedom Vote although all the areas of intense activism did not poll as expected. A huge turnout occurred, reaching about two hundred settled towns and communities. Given the harassment and intimidation recounted above, the widespread participation accomplished is noteworthy. Some estimates are that over 90,000 blacks cast ballots, the overwhelming majority of whom, of course, were not officially registered voters. The SNCC newspaper reported that 78,388 votes were cast and that Henry captured all but about 5,000.[127] These citizens easily dispelled charges of disinterest in political participation or the considerable risks borne in order to do so. As expected, highest turnout occurred in Clarksdale, indicating the strength of the mobilization Henry had overseen, but sparse in many other areas where organization or movement presence appeared to be weak. The Jackson area, following the assassination of Medgar Evers, also had an excellent turnout. In the end, about 46 percent of the ballots came from Delta counties, where the strongest cohort of indigenous leaders resided. The two major urban areas (over 50,000 population) contributed over 18 percent of the ballots.[128] However, some notable areas of major civil rights activity generated small turnouts. It is ironic that the smaller turnouts occurred most often in the SNCC and CORE strongholds. Dittmer notes "Leflore County, SNCC's major project, contributed fewer than 2,000 ballots." Moreover, in all counties where SNCC and CORE had ongoing projects fewer than 16,000 votes were cast, less than one-fifth of the total.[129] (See data below.)

TABLE 1

**Freedom Election (mock) for Governor, 1963,
By County 1000+ Votes**

County	Major Town/City	Votes	Percent
1. Coahoma*+	Clarksdale	16,964	20.3%
2. Hinds	Jackson	13,101	15.6
3. Quitman*+		7,168	8.5
4. Panola*+	Batesville	6,339	7.6
5. Forrest	Hattiesburg	3,561	4.2
6. Madison+	Canton	3,518	4.2
7. Washington*	Greenville	3,072	3.6
8. Harrison	Gulfport/Biloxi	2,241	2.6
9. Jackson	Pascagoula	2,208	2.6
10. Lauderdale	Meridian	1,805	2.1
11. Bolivar*	Cleveland	1,723	2.0
12. Leflore*	Greenwood	1,723	2.0
13. Warren	Vicksburg	1,515	1.8
14. Marshall*	Holly Springs	1,261	1.5
15. Lowndes	Columbus	1,058	1.2
16. Tunica*+		1,033	1.2
Delta Counties		38,283	45.8
Urban (50k+)	1	5,342	18.3
Total (Delta and Urban)		53,625	
Grand Total		83,463	100%
Candidates in Regular Poll			
	Johnson (D)	203,760	100
	Phillips (R)	122,917	100

* Delta Counties
+ Counties where Henry/King votes exceeded regular candidates

Source: Adapted from *Mississippi Free Press*, November 16, 1963. 8.

Despite the poor results in some areas, on balance the outcome discredited the hypothetical claims of black apathy. The results also demonstrated that hard-nosed campaigning mattered. Aaron Henry's bailiwick in Coahoma County and the Delta, where much of the campaign centered, turned in the best performance. Coahoma County reported over 20 percent of the poll. Moreover, the turnout for the mock campaign in the county even exceeded that for the state-sanctioned general election (over 16,000 compared to fewer than 3,000 for the sanctioned candidates: Democratic, 1,680 and Republican, 1,084). Other Delta counties adjacent to Coahoma or in the surrounding region had some of the better results too: rural Quitman County (8.5 percent) and neighboring Panola (7.6 percent). Henry's renown in the nearby communities made it easy enough to broadcast the campaign to these places, an area that combined for over 45 percent of the poll. His broad connections in all of the major towns in this region led to a zone of concentrated activity. Aldon Morris labeled such concentrated areas of civil rights movement activity "movement center."[130]

Urbanized places had especially good outcomes in the vote as well. Hinds County, with a sizable vote (15.6 percent) largely from the populous city of Jackson, demonstrated the importance of this area. This capitol city was a stage for many important movement events, and it hosted the secretariat of COFO.[131] However, the outcome here also demonstrated the outsized role of Medgar Evers prior to his assassination.[132] Gulfport/Biloxi (2.6 percent), another rela- tively urbanized setting, had significant previous movement experience and the near 3 percent of the poll is important because a very small black population resided there. Hattiesburg, the largest town in Forrest County in south-central Mississippi, is another excellent example. It had the fifth most impressive turnout at 4.2 percent (some 3,500 voters). The presence of a local grassroots campaign, a string of local leaders, and a significant support base from SNCC and CORE almost certainly contributed to the high turnout. Henry seemed also to favor appearances in Hattiesburg and Jackson because of the concentration of civil rights workers and the accessibility of the areas for mounting events. Almost 20 percent of the voters came from active and urbanized communities.

The outcome also showed the relative potential of the black vote should the franchise become available. In the first place, the votes cast revealed a potential bloc that could be very effective: the overwhelming majority cast their ballots for the Henry/King ticket. This suggested that a would-be electorate attuned to a candidate slate that spoke to its interests. An even more powerful meaning could be drawn from the effect this voting bloc could have on the general election environment. The size of this unofficial vote, if figured into the regular 1963 election poll, which had an unusual two-way contest between a Democratic and Republican candidate, might well have determined the outcome. What if the blacks had strategically voted for the Republican candidate, for example? In this case it could have produced a different winner.

The Freedom Vote put Henry and the movement on the trajectory to make the statewide challenge. It signaled maturity both of the grassroots challengers and the principal leaders. That the mock election put no black officials in office seemed beside the point. It accomplished much more by creating a disfranchised population largely poised to take independent actions, in concert with allies, to make a wholesale challenge against the segregationist elite. Henry gained considerable stature as the public face of the challengers, using the stage to argue for political mobilization as the natural next step in a broadened campaign.

The results made a compelling case for the shift of the movement's priority to political mobilization. Prior to this time the social movement mobilization made most of the headlines; e.g., contested public accommodations and demonstration of the social costs of segregation. But the mock vote heightened attention to the struggle to organize blacks to secure and utilize the franchise. Ivanhoe Donaldson said: "We laid the foundation to establish a really statewide voter registration campaign, . . . It showed the Negro population that politics is not just 'white folks' business, but that Negroes are also capable of holding political offices."[133] Henry's early emphasis on elections had come front and center.

The transition to political mobilization came swiftly, propelled by several factors. Clearly Henry, his cohorts in the Delta, and COFO now focused more on the ballot box. Though COFO had never been a tightly controlled, centralized organization, it held together despite conflicts, especially the hesitancy of the national NAACP, personality clashes between and within groups, and the increasing white involvement in local activity. Their commonality of goals became sufficient to propel the general assault on the racial system. Hardly a town remained untouched by the spirit of the effort. These would-be foot soldiers now provided a momentum difficult to measure especially if they succeeded in obtaining normal access to the vote.

Henry recognized the potential Freedom Vote had for political mobilization as indicated by his sketch of the next move. He planned nothing less than a frontal assault on the wholly segregated state Democratic Party, saying: "There could never be a better time to launch a full-scale effort, and we began to think about a challenge to the right of the regular all-white Mississippi Democrats to represent the state at the party's national convention. It seemed to us that the Mississippi Democratic Party, . . . was, in simple fact, constitutionally illegal."[134]

So what did the future hold? By this time Henry had become a primary figure with the ability and vision to oversee this new phase. He was the leader with the ability to bridge the emerging gap between the movement forces regarding the move from social mobilization to the political phase. He was also the leader with the most dense and elaborate network of alliances, including an array of allies within the National Democratic Party hierarchy, Congress, and within the Johnson administration. Moreover, he was already openly trying to find local social-change-oriented white allies. It was a role he assumed and played with consummate skill.

CHAPTER FIVE

An Alternative to the Segregated State Democratic Party

The MFDP Goes to Atlantic City, 1964

Following Freedom Vote, the civil rights activists and the proponents of segregation ratcheted up their activities. The civil rights forces escalated via a statewide registration campaign, while the white authorities and their supporters met these efforts with intensified violence, murder, and intimidation, while the state legislature produced statutes, initiatives, and other legal/extralegal barriers to forestall equal rights. The confluence of these opposing forces culminated in the most substantive assault on the Mississippi racial system since Reconstruction. In one year the outline for the destruction of racial segregation and political exclusion came into view. Aaron Henry remained at the center of the ensemble that organized and oversaw the evolution.

The immediate postelection object for Henry and the COFO was the upcoming 1964 presidential election. While the Freedom Vote in 1963 focused on state elections, the presidential election and the broad national movement for civil rights created the possibility of making the issue a campaign agenda item for the ruling Democratic Party coalition. The heightened opportunity resulted because blacks were now overwhelmingly identified with the party.[1] This made for an arresting coincidence since the partisan identification of whites in Mississippi also remained with the Democratic Party, a vestige of their rejection of the Republican Party going back to the Civil War.[2] Henry and the civil rights forces now decided to directly challenge the control that whites alone exercised over the party apparatus. Though the whites rejected the increasingly supportive stance of the national party for racial integration, the segregated state party remained officially recognized by the national secretariat. Indeed the whites sought to maintain that privilege, even as they flaunted their disloyalty. The civil rights activists exploited the contradiction by pressing for the disqualification of the state party.

Henry articulated the logic of such a direction back in 1962 when he oversaw the first campaigns to challenge the congressional seats of the Mississippi delegation.[3] Hamlin has perhaps best demonstrated the leading influence of Clarksdale and its leaders (especially Henry) in the mobilization and national attention that followed: "Clarksdale's activists paved the road for COFO's statewide strength. Many of the campaigns waged at the state level before and during 1964's Freedom Summer originated in Clarksdale or Coahoma County. The county's federation of organizations (CCFCO), dating from the early sixties, and its Freedom Vote in August 1963 furnished prototypes for the larger state movement."[4] A week-long COFO workshop began November 11, 1963, to map that project. Henry and Bob Moses remained the chief leaders as they staked even greater claims on remaining unified. A Bob Moses memo captured its importance, saying: "we have no alternative but to work towards a complete supplementation and integration of programs under a unified leadership[,] and organizational conflicts should be decided from this point of view."[5] Henry remained the convening officer of COFO, and Moses referred to the anticipation of an alternative political party for the first time. He lauded the support of the student volunteers in 1963 and anticipated an even greater involvement of them for a massive assault during the summer of 1964.[6] His only question was "how large a force of volunteer summer workers should we recruit? 100? 1,000? 2,000?" The effort subsequently resulted in the emergence of the Mississippi Freedom Democratic Party.[7]

Practically the entire mapping of the organizational details of the intensified campaign occurred in two meetings between December 1963 and February 1964. Minutes of the meetings reveal the important roles of Henry and Moses. Henry very actively helped define the project and presided over meetings. Bob Moses became the day-to-day organizer/manager of affairs, getting people into slots and arranging for meetings. In December Henry led a meeting that planned the arrangements for a COFO headquarters in Jackson. In one half-day the bylaws and a draft constitution were approved.[8] The organizational structure built on its strongest leadership and the dictates of the broad voter registration effort. Henry became president, Robert Moses program director, and David Dennis (CORE) assistant program director. Five teams then formed by organizing around the regional congressional districts. Indigenous leaders served as district coordinators, many of them experienced leaders with long affiliations with early National Association for the Advancement of Colored People chapters, or with the Student Nonviolent Coordinating Committee. Henry then led the participants through very detailed discussions of the mission and short-term objectives. His maturity in organizing and leading groups remained apparent throughout as he skillfully moved the group through the elaboration of a structure and operational details. In his capacity as president, Henry appointed heads of several agreed-upon standing committees. The balance of the week was dedicated to the prospect of running candidates in the congressional races and on how to intensify voter registration efforts "from December 16 to February 28 [1964]." The intent was to register 300,000 blacks by the August national Democratic convention.[9]

The agenda set in the February meeting challenged the segregated political party system. Over one hundred people took part in the planning for participation in the segregated local conventions, down to the precinct level. The challengers also prepared to organize rival conventions if, as expected, the regular conventions denied them participation. They then made a formal decision to run candidates in all five congressional districts, while detailed discussion continued regarding the massive influx of student volunteers anticipated in the summer. In regard to the latter, they sought volunteers for both voter registration and the anticipated alternative freedom schools.[10] During the meeting, various district leaders provided updates of activities in their areas: Reverend Stone of Hattiesburg reported on a campaign led by clergy from national Protestant and Jewish organizations; Edwin King noted the progress in the boycott of merchants in downtown Jackson; and Matt Suarez noted the extreme white backlash in Canton in response to a boycott of downtown merchants.[11]

There is little doubt about the role Henry played in defining the new terms of the Mississippi campaign because many of its outlines had already been well underway in Clarksdale before 1964. The evolution to political mobilization and civic education within the confines of this Delta town is detailed in the "Coahoma Branch Newsletter" of the NAACP of February 8, 1964. It described an intensified voter registration effort, as well as a continuing merchants boycott and a letter-writing campaign to pressure Congress to pass what later became the Civil Rights Act of 1964. The NAACP Political Action Committee served as the organizing body, described in the newsletter as being "chaired by Mrs. Idessa Johnson [and] staff personnel . . . Mr. J. D. Rayford, Jr. and Mr. Gordon Harris"—all well-known activists in the 1962–1963 Clarksdale movement. The planning appeared elaborate with registration leaders designated by each church, neighborhood, and street and with an ongoing weekly "freedom meeting" at local churches for the provision of political education and civic information. In addition to discussion and singing of civil rights songs, other resources such as films and civil rights literature could also be available.[12]

Similarly, a variety of the alternative freedom school concept, barely emerging within COFO, already existed in Clarksdale. Independent black community institutions housed four such schools: two black churches (Chapel Hill M. B. Church and Rayford's Chapel); and two black businesses (Pigee's Beauty Salon and Johnson's Sandwich Shop). They basically functioned as centers for adult literacy and civic education, unlike the later alternative schools that focused on secondary students. Nevertheless, this Clarksdale model showed the extent to which the town had gone in anticipating the next phase of the movement.

While Clarksdale represented a model, neither its foot soldiers nor its indigenous activists across the state had sufficient capacity to mount and sustain the massive campaign planned for the 1964 summer election season.[13] Once again discussion turned to the use of white students from the North, a necessity foreseen by Bob Moses.[14] Notwithstanding the important role these students played in attracting attention to the plight of blacks in 1963, a continuing role caused concern;[15] while they often had civic engagement experience, most lacked a full appreciation of the Mississippi racial system and the dynamics of interracial conflicts within the movement itself.[16] Moreover, Allard Lowenstein, a white activist whose ideas eventually diverged from SNCC, the dominant player in COFO, added another layer of conflict. He sought a greater role for his leadership in engaging external student activists (as opposed to indigenous and grassroots leaders), and he sought a more liberal ideology for the movement over what he perceived as radicalism in SNCC.[17] The decision to invite northern white college students again did not come easily. Nevertheless, the January 1964 decision to recruit more of them went forward with the enthusiastic support from both Henry and Bob Moses.[18] Each saw whites as fundamental to the success of the movement because they, like blacks, had an obligation to work for social justice that legitimized black people in the political community.[19] Henry supported the decision further by arguing that his personal experience of racism revealed how the perpetrators of exclusion usually degraded themselves in the process. Therefore he rued the day that blacks would visit a parallel version of that degradation upon themselves merely to wound others.[20]

The program for Freedom Summer came together quite quickly, and Henry gave the first formal notice of the work plan in a March 15, 1964, announcement of a COFO convention (they called meetings "conventions"). Invitations to attend the Jackson meeting went to heads of all of the national affiliate organizations, including invitations to speak at the event: James Farmer (CORE), James Forman and John Lewis (SNCC), Martin Luther King Jr. (SCLC), and Roy Wilkins (NAACP). They set forth a bold agenda: selection of candidates to challenge all of the state U.S. House and Senate seats; organization of an alternative political party (the "Freedom Democratic Party"; continued "Freedom Registration" (enrolling blacks as for the mock election); and articulation of a prefatory platform demanding welfare relief, employment, and training programs.[21] An undated "prospectus" divided labor into three categories: Voter Registration (including enrolling 400,000 blacks and organizing of the proto freedom party),

Freedom Schools, and Community Centers.[22] The document (authored with activist lawyer Carsie Hall) bore the stamp of Henry's penchant for details about structure and of his routine concern with economic disparity and equity.[23]

The political mobilization never lost sight of the necessity to obliterate the segregation system. Two of the greatest challenges, for example, remained public school education and the dearth of activities to sustain and enrich local community life. In addition to being barred from membership in the NAACP, teachers also could not outwardly introduce "revisionist" or alternative curricula in their classes.[24] Community life, however, was barely existent since the time of most blacks revolved around their instrumental roles servicing the segregated white neighborhoods and businesses. Therefore, movement organizers proposed freedom schools to provide alternative and supplementary educational and civic schooling, with attached community centers with social programs to engage African American children. Henry saw this kind of community engagement as antidotes to a segregated, authoritarian school system that thwarted free and independent thought and that also retarded civic participation.

The school project had high ambitions—twenty-five schools envisioned in as many towns—teaching academics, providing socialization to political work, and studying African American culture.[25] The development and design of community centers sought to enhance learning, job training, and cultural life. Proposed subjects included basic literacy, prenatal care, and nutrition.[26] The detailed curriculum provided illustrations of how it would diverge from the standard existing curriculum and of how it would aid in achieving the broader aims of the summer political project.

This challenge did not go unnoticed by the segregationists, not least the power structure. The impending arrival of the volunteers created a frenzy among state authorities and segregationists to thwart the further development of the movement—from legislation, to terror, to political violence against them and local activists. The legislature floated various proposals, some of which ultimately passed, to deal with increasing local protests and boycotts and in anticipation of the student volunteers. The measures restricted movement and increased penalties, for example, by imposing jail time and fines for violation of any city ordinances. A January proposal that recommended "increasing maximum fines from $100 to $300 and jail sentences from 30 to 90 days" targeted repeat offenders. In order to deal with the expected massive summer arrests, another proposal sought to increase county patrolmen. Still another bill authorized use of the notorious state penitentiary to house municipal offenders. In early February, to thwart boycotts like that of Clarksdale merchants, the legislature tried to make it "unlawful for any persons to willfully or maliciously distribute literature calling for trade boycotts."[27]

The state opposition aimed much of its attack at the pending civil rights bill of 1964. The legislature, at the behest of departing governor Barnett, issued a strongly worded resolution opposing the bill: "The passage of this bill further invading the rights of the states to govern themselves and solve their own problems would do irreparable damage to the already critical race relations, would widen the breech already brought about by efforts to force a social merger of incompatible elements of society and would give untold impetus to the strife and turmoil that has torn our nation asunder." The resolution passed without a single dissent. And Representative C. C. Bullock (Harrison County) deemed this act especially appropriate because "members of Congress were 'bombarded by the insistent voice of the minority' and the state should make its feelings known."[28]

The legislature continued to smart over the integration of the University of Mississippi and tried to undermine or turn back that decision. In late February Senator Edwin Pittman of Hattiesburg threatened to "resegregate" the University of Mississippi by demanding "investigation of the presence of five Negroes last week at a University of Mississippi program." He said, "I hope to find out why the five people were admitted," and threatened to retaliate when the university budget came up for the next appropriation. Meanwhile, a resolution praised the president of the University of Southern Mississippi for "upholding the established regulations of the University" when he denied admission to a black applicant (John Frazier) for the fifth time. The cause indicated for denial was "that he failed to submit the application in time."[29] The proposed freedom schools also appeared on the legislative agenda. A bill, which ultimately failed, would have given school superintendents the authority to "license" schools. That proposed procedure would have allowed them to ban any schools that were "disobedient" to state law. Teachers in such schools could be jailed for six months and fined $1,500.[30]

Henry had a heavy active and oversight functions in all of these activities. While he called Bob Moses the architect of the program, Henry gave public speeches, conducted workshops, and worked telephones. He appeared at the training workshops for the volunteers prior to their arrival in Mississippi, where he gave a short history of the movement.[31] Lemann characterized his role as follows: "He was officially in charge of managing the hordes of Northern college students and civil rights movement ground troops who descended on Mississippi for Freedom Summer, a duty that kept him in a whirlwind of traveling, marching, bailing people out of jail, shepherding visiting dignitaries like Martin Luther King." However, another of his major roles remained "keeping the tensions between the NAACP and SNCC down to a manageable level."[32]

Freedom Summer began with an event that seemed to confirm all of the worst impressions of Mississippi as a state that would go to any length to preserve the racial status quo. Within a day of the arrival in Mississippi (June 21, 1964) of the first group of students who received their orientation for the summer in Ohio, two of the white volunteers (Andrew Goodman and Michael Schwerner) disappeared with a third local Black student activist (James Chaney).[33] Henry had already left the Ohio orientation to attend the national NAACP convention in Washington, D.C.,[34] but the Goodman name struck him as familiar. He recalled him as the enthusiastic Queens College student he encountered on an April recruitment trip. "At the reception following our talk, a sharp-faced, intense young man approached me with his parents. The boy explained to his parents that I was the one who had convinced him that he should spend the following summer in Mississippi."[35]

The signs turned ominous when the burned-out vehicle of Goodman, Schwerner, and Chaney was found the next day without a trace of the volunteers. Confirmation of their murder came forty-four days later, discovered in an earthen dam in August in Philadelphia, Mississippi.[36] It gave Henry one other opportunity to try and prod the Johnson administration to intervene in the South to protect the equal rights of blacks and to prevent acts of violence against those trying to exercise those rights.[37] This time a fairly rapid response came as the administration directed the FBI to take over the investigation.[38]

Despite such an inauspicious start the program did go forward and was a considerable success in many ways and limited success in others. Estimates are that about 1,000 students participated in roughly forty individual projects across the state.[39] They fanned out to do voter registration, using templates that Henry and his local NAACP chapter had developed for soliciting voters in churches: a three-minute speech on the importance of registration and a two-minute version exhorting people to pay their poll tax.[40] However, while many people attempted to register (estimates of 17,000), far fewer succeeded in actually accomplishing the deed (about 1,600).[41] Freedom schools had more obvious success. The organizers had a target of attracting 1,500 students; McAdam estimates that twice as many showed up, in thirty centers (five more than was planned), almost all of which created an attached community center.[42] Henry had a busier schedule during this period than perhaps in the mock election. His considerable charm had to be turned on to gain more from his external network, since the NAACP secretariat remained skeptical of the "over activist" campaign in Mississippi. These vast alignments allowed him to sustain good relations with the other COFO partners and to enhance their own networks of external allies. Joyce Ladner summarized this ability in Henry.

> I would say that he probably was able to read the signals better than most people. He . . . didn't live in a Balkanized world. . . . And even though he was most identified with the NAACP, he didn't say that

there's only one way to achieve this equality and that is through the legal methods of filing suit and so on, which was principally what the NAACP was doing back then. I think he not only could read the lay of the land, but he could reinvent himself and his views as he went along. . . . Some people get stultified . . . in their own little Balkan states, while other people keep seeing new stimuli come along and affect them and if they're open to it, they keep having new experiences and keep evolving. He was a person who kept evolving and that's why he had . . . power for so long.[43]

The preparations for recruitment of the students used the model developed for the mock election. Allard Lowenstein expanded his circle of contacts beyond the extensive ones at a few elite institutions.[44] An array of personal contacts between Henry and a variety of legal, clerical, and governmental resource groups now significantly augmented this base.[45] Meanwhile, SNCC and CORE used their independent and often overlapping contacts to solicit participants.[46] Henry used his considerable statewide contacts to make arrangements for local accommodations, and Clarksdale became one of the first communities to commit to receive multiple volunteers.[47]

The volunteers received assignments prior to their departure from Ohio, so they hit the ground running. Their responsibilities lay in voter registration and/ or freedom schools. All five congressional districts received volunteers. It is evident that the areas of most intensive action were the Delta bailiwick of Aaron Henry and those where SNCC and CORE were concentrated. Thirty percent of the volunteers were located in the center of the Delta—Greenville, Greenwood, Holmes County, Clarksdale, and Ruleville. Local NAACP chapters also remained important to this concentration of resources. Elsewhere concentrations also built on experienced leadership. District Three had the presence of the COFO secretariat in Jackson; in District Four, CORE had dedicated resources concentrated in Canton and rural Madison County. The largest contingent went to District Five in Hattiesburg, which also had a large SNCC presence.[48]

Moreover, this intensive, if short-lived summer, also occurred at a critical moment in the Mississippi movement: the most intense part of the campaign and its transition to a more overtly political mobilization. It brought into focus the comprehensive design Henry earlier envisioned with the Clarksdale movement, where he raised not only the issue of public accommodation in segregated public spaces, but also simultaneously the issues of voting, contestation of political office, and equal employment opportunities. Moreover, this period represented the height of the unity of all of the civil rights forces on the ground—SNCC, CORE, and the NAACP.

Though it may have been little remarked upon at the time, the death of Medgar Evers made the steady hand, experience, working relationship, and usefulness of Henry more important. In order to maintain this critical leadership role, Henry had to ignore or act in defiance of the parent body of the NAACP, the organization to which he was formally tied.[49] The skepticism of the national body quickly turned to outright opposition to COFO, then perceived as a competitor. Indeed, the NAACP formally withdrew from COFO in November 1964, issuing a communiqué with supporting testimonials from prominent chapter leaders in the state. Henry became a major target of some of their objections, one of them asking: "How can he be the head of the organization [COFO] that fights us on every front?"[50] In addition, the NAACP generally opposed the grassroots community empowerment strategies and the more aggressive protest actions being utilized in Mississippi. Some of this came to a head following Medgar's death. NAACP executive director Roy Wilkins expressed concern about "direct action" at the funeral.[51] Henry maintained a more nuanced view of these strategies as he continued his major leadership and support of the evolving political direction of the movement,[52] even as other organizations within COFO struggled with their own crises of leadership. The consequences of a growing schism within SNCC regarding its future direction amplified the importance of Henry's steadiness in keeping sight on changing the racial system in Mississippi.[53]

In this critical time period the power and influence of the local black Mississippi leadership proved especially vital in the transitional phase when political mobilization moved to the foreground. The presence of the volunteers helped in strengthening this group.[54] These outsiders created an opportunity across the state to match the broader range of concerns that Henry had long since articulated in Clarksdale. Their statewide linkage and constant communication helped to broadcast protest activities and bring national identity to sometimes little-known indigenous leaders in the various towns. Sometimes this could be as simple as the issuing of a document chronicling discriminatory encounters with law enforcement officials, by date and town.[55] The impact of the broadcasting could be merely informational, but it could also help maintain a unity of focus. For example, it highlighted the enduring connections that Henry and Medgar Evers had with military veterans largely associated with the NAACP. Amzie Moore is an example of one of these veterans whose influence received broader recognition. He greatly inspired SNCC workers who worked with him in his Delta town of Cleveland.[56] The stories of others are related in a series of historical studies,[57] sociological studies,[58] biographies and memoirs,[59] and political analyses[60] of the period.

The high-water mark of the summer campaign of 1964 came with the emergence of the Mississippi Freedom Democratic Party, a proposed alternative political structure for competing against the white-controlled state Democratic Party. The heightened strength of the confederation of local organizations matched the increased favorable support for its cause from around the country. The final passage in July 1964 of the strongest civil rights law since Reconstruction gave encouragement to the activists. The 1964 Civil Rights Act legitimized aspects of the social movement, particularly protests to gain access to public accommodations and stronger (though limited) enforcement tools.[61] The fight for passage of the law by civil rights forces became one of the significant continuing efforts during the summer, inspired in part by its wholesale denunciation by the state's white power structure.[62] Indeed the campaign for the bill started when President Kennedy introduced it soon after the murder of Medgar Evers.[63]

The momentum for an alternative strategy for the project of black political participation appeared to be significantly enhanced by the actions of the power elite in state government and in the party hierarchy. Their total rejection of any power sharing with blacks caused any inter- and intra-organizational struggles in the movement to pale in comparison. This news hardly mattered since the state party persisted in maintaining a segregated organization (the white primary) in the single-party-dominant state, notwithstanding the 1944 Supreme Court ruling that outlawed the practice.[64] While the first candidates to contest office since Reconstruction won places on the ballot only in 1962 (Merrill/Trammel and Smith), the almost total disfranchisement of blacks left them without much chance. However, leaving nothing to chance the state legislature began a systematic process of racial gerrymandering of voting districts at all levels, and passage of new election laws to guarantee white dominance of the political process. The Delta congressional district where Henry orchestrated the Lindsey/Trammell campaign, with its huge African American population majority, became a first order of business. The legislature promptly redrew the district to split the population between two new districts. Similarly, other procedures shifted individual municipal district elections to at-large contests.[65]

As the civil rights mobilization increased, the power structure realized that prevention of formal participation in the political party process had to be a priority. The broad, sustained resistance to registration of blacks was but the first level of resistance.[66] That strategy became more urgent since Henry now contested not two, but four of the U.S. congressional House seats and one from the Senate.[67] Quickly, the state tactics escalated as Henry and Bob Moses talked more directly about challenging the legitimacy of the segregated party within the national structure. The arrival of Martin Luther King Jr. in July, now riding a crest of popularity as a primary civil rights leader, signaled how aggressive the state's civil rights forces challenged the state organization. King's four-day visit came on the eve of the state party convention, during which he called for the ouster of the segregated delegation. He also lent his support to the emerging alternative party and agreed to raise money for it.[68] As the process for the alternative party fully set into motion over the early summer, it became clearer how the local party sought to deny party status to the MFDP and to fortify the selection process for national delegates against black voting influence.

As the movement forces settled on the organization of the MFDP and agreed to augment its human resources with northern students, Henry's organizational skills and experience as a widely respected indigenous leader became more essential. First his collaborative, noncompetitive style provided him with the pulse of all of the civil rights groups. Confidence in his own role helped him to allow space and facilitate the roles of his cohorts, an increasing number of them indigenous women like Fannie Lou Hamer, Annie Devine, Victoria Gray, and Unita Blackwell.[69] He had an appreciation for the distinct roles others desired to play and worked to see that everyone contributed to the big picture. This mature view resulted from the ubiquity of his work throughout the state, for which his credibility was undisputed.[70] His business acumen proved equally important because it facilitated his earlier development of deep ties with the black economic elites, usually the most active element within the NAACP.[71] Henry also had a reputation for administrative skill. Researching his papers revealed his excellent sense of order, protocol, and formality and his penchant for preparing agendas, parliamentary procedures, and talking points and lists.[72] At the same time, he knew the racial system better than most, and had manifestly confronted of that system. This knowledge of the terrain gave him a storehouse of information to share with young local leaders and external volunteers. This dexterity also earned him the enduring support of his partners.[73] The segregationists confronted in Henry perhaps their fiercest enemy, this cunning, backslapping entrepreneur, whose simple message belied a steely determination to obliterate the racial order.

The first major formal challenge to the primacy of the state Democratic Party, a prelude of a ramped-up campaign, came with the contestation of the congressional seats in the June 1964 primary election. As Henry and his cohorts pondered an agenda for the arrival of perhaps thousands of college students, thoughts turned to the summer primary elections, the contest that generally resolved elections in this one-party state. Mississippi would fill five House and one Senate seats. Henry had continued to persist in getting candidates to contest these seats, whose occupants he regarded as illegitimate. He fulfilled his enduring wish when black candidates agreed to run against the white incumbents—Fannie Lou Hamer against House incumbent Jamie Whitten (Second District); James Houston against incumbent John Bell Williams (Third); Reverend John Cameron against incumbent William Colmer (Fifth); and Victoria Gray against the incumbent senator John Stennis.[74] They all had excellent credentials as active

indigenous leaders in their local communities and as affiliates of the NAACP and/
or SNCC. Despite the symbolic stakes for whites, the candidates gained approval
to go onto the primary ballot. They endured harassment, personal violence, and
economic reprisals. Hamer's eviction from her longtime plantation home was
swift. She also lost her job, all of which added to the permanent physical scars
she received in an earlier gruesome, racial assault from her jailers in Winona.[75]
Reverend Cameron, a young minister, received a jail term and remained incarcerated for much of the campaign.[76]

Meanwhile, even the favorable liberal press termed their candidacies as merely
symbolic,[77] entirely missing the point of how important symbolic acts are in politics.[78] All of the campaigns appeared fledgling, though Henry and COFO gave
the candidates their wholehearted support. Sometimes this came in the form of
small financial contributions from the COFO secretariat (Hamer alone received
$10,000).[79] Henry's activities in their behalf, however, appeared to be the most
resourceful. He seemed tireless in visiting various districts to give speeches and
in using his commanding presence to help seize this moment.[80] His popular,
well-informed, stirring speeches minced few words in boosting morale at the rallies. He brought an arsenal of contacts and personal integrity that could link the
candidates and their local communities to national partisan and civil rights allies,
and he had the leverage to secure legal, financial, and personnel support and to
allocate them.[81]

Despite the predictable outcome of the challenge in the congressional primary elections, it proved important in building momentum for independent
black political action. By and large because they did not have the franchise,
blacks could not win in terms of "real" votes cast. However, they could once
again demonstrate the inconsistency of the racial system to their increasing body
of allies across the country. Activists and their allies could not ignore the glaring
inconsistency when the votes came in. Even the intense registration mobilization of the previous two years had hardly put a dent in black disfranchisement.
Hamer mustered just 621 votes in the Black-Belt Delta District Two, and only
16 of these came from her home county of Sunflower. Houston in District Three
could muster only 1,257 votes, in a district that included urban Hinds County.
Cameron in District Five received 883 votes, and Senate candidate Gray polled
2,783 across four districts.[82]

The level of movement organization, however, guaranteed that the activists
hardly lost a beat in moving on to the next target. Even as planning commenced
to make a stand at the Democratic convention to disqualify the Mississippi
delegation, a parallel strategy ensued to run candidates as independents in the
general congressional elections. Henry anticipated that they might fail in that
effort, and as a result resurrected the idea of running the candidates in another

mock campaign in the fall general election. He referred to being most struck because "the great body of disenfranchised Negroes—the people whom MFDP was designed to represent—was being aroused."[83]

In the meantime, planning continued for the alternative convention. Henry led monthly COFO meetings beginning in early 1964 that culminated with a convention that formally brought the MFDP to life on April 26, 1964. "Approximately 200 delegates from across the state" took their places in Jackson's Masonic Temple, a common venue for mass rallies.[84] They included some of the most active grassroots people, from some of the most highly organized parts of the state. The first business took place with the appointment of a temporary state Executive Committee: twelve members to reflect Mississippi's then five congressional districts. They elected Henry chairman of the body and representative of the Second District. Leslie McLemore (a Rust College student) served with him as co-representative for the district. Well-known indigenous leaders with experience in their communities represented the other districts. Reverend Merrill Lindsey, former candidate for Congress in 1962, represented the First District. District Three, including the populous city of Jackson, had three representatives: Reverend R. L. T. Smith (also a congressional candidate in 1962), Percy Chapman, and Eddie Thomas. Annie Devine (concurrently a candidate for Congress), Samuel Glover, and Charles Robinson represented the Fourth District. Three from the Fifth District rounded out the group: Reverend J. W. Brown, Pinky Hall, and Evelyn Wright. Henry played a key role in presiding over and generally leading this organizational meeting.

The focus quickly turned to the justification for and goals of this alternative party. Henry stated the obvious: "We are not allowed to function effectively in Mississippi's traditional Democratic Party; therefore, we must find another way to align ourselves with the National Democratic Party."[85] He urged this position believing that a future existed for an organization like theirs, composed of likeminded Mississippians of both races, within the national party. He had already begun trying to cultivate some white prospects as he traversed the state. He also calculated that without converting new registrants into members of a regular partisan structure, their mock votes could not be translated into influence. To this end the regular party justified being displaced. The organizers laid out three reasons:

- The long history of systematic and studied exclusion of Negro citizens from equal participation in the political processes of the state grows more flagrant daily.
- The Mississippi Democratic Party has conclusively demonstrated its lack of loyalty to the National Democratic Party in the past, and cur-

rently indicates no intention of supporting the platform of the 1964 Democratic Convention.

- The intransigent and fanatical determination of the State's political power structure to maintain status-quo clearly demonstrates that the "Mississippi closed society," as Professor James Silver of the University of Mississippi asserts, is without leadership or moral resources to reform itself, and hence can only be brought into the mainstream of the twentieth century by forces outside of itself.[86]

They had good evidence: the party controlled all but one elective office, in all three branches of government; used all governmental processes to strictly maintain a racially exclusive public sector; and effectively barred blacks from participation in the only party that mattered in staffing state government.[87]

To demonstrate its seriousness in preparing to bid for membership in the national party, the MFDP convention structure closely adhered to the general rules for organized state parties, in many ways thus paralleling the Mississippi party structure. Unlike the 1963 mock contest, the MFDP sought to operate within the formal structure of the electoral system, providing an alternative slate of delegates that it hoped the national Democratic Party convention would recognize. It represented a direct challenge to the very right of the white delegates to represent the state. Therefore, the MDFP Executive Committee accepted a clear charge for "setting up precinct and other state meetings. These meetings will parallel those of the Mississippi Democratic Party, and every effort will be made to comply with all state laws that apply to the formation of political parties."[88] Eventually, delegate selection processes were set to commence August 2 and to culminate at the state convention on August 9.[89]

This formal challenge, organized within the confines of the regular electoral structure, dictated that the congressional candidates appear on a regular state ballot. The candidates wore the label of the MFDP, and the massive accompanying ongoing voter registration campaign also portrayed that party identification. Despite the inevitability of their loss, the committee reasoned that "This will help to establish the fact that thousands of Negroes are deprived of citizenship participation because of the racist character of Mississippi's voter registration procedures."[90]

A general reading of the organizational activity associated with the birth and early organizational activity of the MFDP makes Henry's central role clear. He presided over these meetings, made major operational decisions, and helped to arrange for the critical tasks of an organizational structure. A careful review of those who occupied the major leadership positions in the organizational structure shows that it included a generation of older men associated with the NAACP, a young cohort of SNCC and CORE activists, and some indigenous women (for the first time). One of the women activists, Annie Devine, who had been affiliated with CORE in her hometown of Canton, served on a three-person executive review committee, the most powerful decision-making group in the young organization.[91] Charles Evers, his brother Medgar's successor at the NAACP, became an official member of the team. This same indigenous group largely assumed financial responsibility for the developing secretariat by providing loans.

Henry had significant footprints stamped on the outlines of the strategy for the summer campaign. His influence probably proved most critical in devising the plan to establish the MFDP, and not the white segregationist party, as the body that was the true, loyal reflection of the interests of the National Democratic Party. He had excellent contacts within the national party organization, and that facilitated access to the Democratic administration in the White House. Even though he often criticized how slowly the administration was moving on civil rights matters, he found its general approach sufficiently practical and thus workable for his goals.[92] Though not all of his COFO partners shared his view, it nevertheless became the prevailing view for the summer campaign.[93] Therefore, the MFDP adopted a platform that looked like a virtual carbon copy of the interests that first Kennedy and then Johnson adopted: "full employment, collective bargaining, food stamp programs, Medicare, civil rights, reapportionment, job training, and anti-poverty programs, the United Nations, foreign aid, and the Peace Corps." Moreover, the MFDP adopted an oath of loyalty to the national party, which the state party defiantly refused to do.[94]

Things did not go well from the start as the MFDP sought to get formal recognition as a party. The secretary of state quickly denied it a charter as a party,[95] arguing that state law allowed one party to use the label "Democratic," while a chancery judge even barred the group "from using that name [MFDP] and its officers from functioning."[96]

Meanwhile, despite repeated rebuffs the challengers made a final effort to participate in the June 16 state Democratic Party convention. The MFDP organized precinct and district conventions and selected delegates that it hoped might be allowed to take part in these ordinarily whites-only events. For the most part that did not materialize. Virtually everywhere blacks encountered barriers. Sometimes party officials simply told them outright that only whites could participate in these events. Other times blacks also encountered dirty tricks, ruses, and alternative procedures: the sudden relocation of convention sites; the conduct of business ahead of the posted date; and the use threats and intimidation.[97]

In the few instances where blacks gained access to the meetings, constraints prevented substantive contributions. Henry's experience at Clarksdale showed how chicanery ruled the process despite the attention his prominence was guaranteed to draw. He and a group of about twenty African Americans arrived early, greatly outnumbering the whites at the official start time. Instead of proceeding, Henry said, the chair of the meeting consulted with the whites there and then announced a postponement until the arrival of secretary Leon Potter, a man "we had just seen in the building. During the delay, whites from the South Clarksdale precinct began straggling in."[98]

The MFDP challengers prepared for eventualities like these and continued to organize their parallel precinct and county conventions. Descriptions from some of these sites suggest that this activity represented one of the greatest examples of participatory democracy that the state had ever seen. Sally Belfrage recounted the setting in Greenwood, a Delta town like Clarksdale, which had been the scene of considerable movement activity. First, the participants there nominated seventeen candidates, from which they selected four delegates and another four alternates. "Nominations were made and seconded by the chairman, a local minister, [who] recognized motions from the floor; resolutions were introduced; each candidate was allowed a few minutes to speak his case; they voted; and with dizzying speed and confidence they grasped the meaning and technique of democracy."[99] In Madison County, according to Dittmer, a similar process played out on a black-owned farm where "convention chair Annie Devine grouped the 300 delegates by precinct under trees."[100]

The state convention met on August 6, and when delegates assembled in Jackson this became a coming-out event for the MFDP. Some estimates put attendance as high as 2,500 in a large meeting with about 800 certified delegates.[101] The event reverberated with the symbolic and cultural frames of its fervent church-going attendees, and it displayed the prevalent elements of defiance and resistance associated with the civil rights movement: part church meeting, part civil rights rally, and part didactic for how to alter a racial history. It also reflected the benefits of the unity efforts that Henry worked so hard to maintain—SNCC, CORE, the SCLC, and the state NAACP arrived in virtual synchrony. The national NAACP demurred, but Henry simply continued to ignore the contrary executive secretary Roger Wilkins and his aide, Gloster Current.[102] Henry, at the height of his visibility in the MFDP, led the convention through to conclusion. The racially integrated delegation, which Dittmer described as including more of the "militant" activists, subsequently elected him its chairman.[103]

The importance of the leadership role Henry played in organizing a network of powerful allies outside Mississippi became clearer after the convention selected its delegates. Since no deal could be struck to integrate the local Mississippi delegation, any future success of the MFDP hinged on making the case that its integrated delegation should be formally recognized at the upcoming national convention in Atlantic City. Henry thus began an intense lobbying campaign, which he fairly much personally conducted, to line up supporters. He traded on his contacts in the White House, among them the president, Attorney General Robert Kennedy, and John Doar, head of the Civil Rights Division of the Justice Department, and members of Congress.[104] In the private sector his NAACP affiliation generated a variety of sources he could tap for support—individual state chapter presidents and national board members who could tap into their broad business and legal networks.[105] Above all he had significant access to the national party hierarchy and influence upon other state convention delegations as they were forming. Henry spoke to many delegations around the country. Among those that committed early to support the MFDP were Massachusetts, Oregon, Michigan, Minnesota, Wisconsin, New York, California, and Washington, D.C.[106]

After researching the rules on making challenges to delegations based on loyalty, Henry and the MFDP leadership believed they had more than an even chance of getting their appeal heard and possibly approved at the convention. The Mississippi Democratic Party had utterly rejected the national party and its candidate; former governor Ross Barnett called Lyndon Johnson a "counterfeit confederate." Preference for the Republican candidate Goldwater or third-party candidate George Wallace had also been flaunted.[107] Therefore, in mid-July after expressing its loyalty to the National Democratic Party Henry formally petitioned chairman John Bailey for representation on July 17, 1964. He told him that a full MFDP delegation would be sent to the convention, adding: "We hereby challenge the delegation of the regular Democratic Party to be seated . . . as the true representative of Mississippi Democrats . . . We request tickets, floor privileges, badges, housing, and all the rights that accrue to a regular delegation."[108] The MFDP delegation was banking on loyalty rules adopted in 1948, when the southern Democrats bolted the party in response to Hubert Humphrey's "civil rights" plank.[109] At that time the party adopted loyalty rules and a low threshold for those making challenges based on loyalty to get a floor vote.[110] For example, if the Credentials Committee, where a challenge was first heard, issued a rejection, it took only 10 percent of its 108 members to force issuance of a Minority Report. In that event the question had to be taken to the convention floor, where it took only eight state delegations to force a roll call. Henry knew that the MFDP already exceeded that number of commitments from delegations.[111]

After busing into Atlantic City, it became clear that the central goal of the MFDP was now being considered in the context of winning the national election, hard for many COFO activists to contemplate. The question was no longer whether the party would get a hearing, but what kind of compromise could be struck to hold together the Democratic coalition. For President Johnson and his forces, the major consideration turned on how to hold onto southern white voters against encroachments from the Republican Party. While Johnson could make strong claims for supporting and taking the initiative on a bold civil rights legislative agenda, winning the presidency at this interval had primacy. He also hoped that his expressed support for civil rights provided some leverage to maintain the support of social change agents in Mississippi (especially Henry), black voters elsewhere and their allies. By this reasoning securing the greater goal of an administration favorable to civil rights would create a constructive climate for a compromise on MFDP seating.[112]

Since the COFO had framed its campaign around the illegitimacy of a white delegation that it deemed racist, an acceptable compromise seemed hard to imagine.[113] At the same time, the white Democrats seemed in no mood to negotiate themselves into oblivion. Johnson felt compelled to try and placate both as the convention proceeded. In the end, he secured his ultimate goal of winning, but at a steep cost for both of the entities he sought to appease. As the drama played out, it became one of the factors that altered the COFO partnership forever, even as it foretold the death of the segregated state party system.

In hindsight, the COFO strategy for winning at the convention proved flawed and perhaps naïve.[114] The strategy rested on trading on Henry's influence and delegate lobbying to mobilize powerful allies among convention delegations and on the use of COFO activists to maintain critical scrutiny of the egregious behavior of the segregated state delegation within the convention and in the general public. Indeed, Henry did his job lining up pre-convention commitments of support,[115] and Bob Moses and the others easily made the case lobbying against the generally unsympathetic elites controlling the state delegation.[116] However, neither of these proved sufficient to match the president's control over the national party apparatus and the convention, and his unabashed willingness to exercise it against the preferred MFDP goal. The president assigned responsibility for the project and its resolution to Senator Hubert Humphrey of Minnesota, a longtime Henry friend and ally. It was widely believed that finding a compromise that Johnson could accept was the price Humphrey had to pay to be selected as the president's running mate.[117] However, leaving nothing to chance, Johnson also instituted a high-level FBI-led intelligence operation (involving about thirty officers) that provided continuous information on all aspects of the convention, including the MFDP challenge.[118]

Giving a public appearance of neutrality on the question of the seating of the MFDP, Johnson had a direct hand in formulating both the compromise on offer to the group and in directing the campaign to get its acceptance. All of this came to a head in the Credentials Committee. Johnson preferred to offer the MFDP some symbolic presence at the convention, with formal representation remaining with the state organized delegation. Soon enough, Johnson's disguise fell away, and he turned up the heat on party elites and state delegations that had committed to favor the MFDP in its challenge.[119] Moreover, Johnson's links to civil rights elites, including Henry, also gave him the potential for exerting undue influence within the MFDP delegation itself. As leader of the delegation Henry became an obvious object of attention as the White House intensified its efforts to generate support. Johnson and his forces knew him and perhaps saw him as more of a moderate partner in the future than SNCC or CORE. Otherwise, Johnson used his influence with some of Henry's long-term civil rights associates to exact their support for a compromise, notably Martin Luther King Jr. (albeit with some reluctance) and Detroit congressman Charles Diggs.[120]

Washington insider Joseph Rauh, with the help of Eleanor Holmes (Norton), (now congresswoman from D.C.) and H. Miles Jaffe presented a legal brief to the Credentials Committee laying out the MFDP case.[121] It recounted the disloyalty of the regular party with the connivance of state officials and under the cover of state law; pledged the commitment of the MFDP to the national party and to work "dauntlessly" for the presidential ticket; and showed how citizenship rights of blacks were violated because they were barred in effect from the only game in town for political participation and representation: the Democratic Party and its primary elections. Rauh began simply, asking rhetorically "whether the National Democratic Party [would take] its place with the oppressed Negroes of Mississippi or their white oppressors." He made a stirring accounting of what led the MFDP to be at the convention as challengers, especially the racism of the state party. He asserted the deep optimism within the MFDP for the agenda of the convention and presidential candidate Lyndon Johnson. In short, he tried to shore up the group's loyalty to the party as he undertook to undermine the credentials of a longstanding racist element within the national party's constituency. He asked for a resolution of this contradiction in favor of the MFDP delegation.[122]

Henry then took his turn before the committee. He spoke of the aberrant actions of the state's attorney general in trying to jail him and other MFDP leaders to prevent even their presence at the party organization to which they felt bound to identify. He then intoned: "But, sir, if jail is the price we must pay for our efforts to be of benefit to America, to the National Democratic Party, and to Mississippi then nothing could be more redemptive." He again hammered home the loyalty of the MFDP, saying: "We want to minimize our differences and maximize our chances for carrying the State of Mississippi and the Nation for President Johnson in November." He proceeded to quote Governor Paul Johnson to show the utter disdain the segregationists had for the national party: "The people of Mississippi have rejected decisively the influence of the Kennedy-dominated National Democratic Party . . . The Mississippi Democratic Party separated itself a long time ago from the National Democratic Party and has fought consistently against everything it stands for."[123]

Henry went on to associate state officials with the sustained violence and mayhem perpetrated against black citizens of the state, merely because they fought to exercise their rights. He argued that the national organization should stand against such illegal forces and the resulting casualties, some of which he detailed. For example, he reminded them that thirty-one churches had been burned since the start of 1964, fifteen murders committed against black activists, and literally hundreds of cross burnings, floggings, and shooting incidents. He said that the segregated delegation had this blood on its hands. He then retold the bitter experience he endured trying to participate in his own precinct convention in Clarksdale when the white official deliberately changed the time of the meeting to buy time for whites to arrive and negate the votes of a black majority.[124]

Henry ended his presentation with a flourish, invoking the poetic expression of Langston Hughes, one the country's greatest poets, who often used his work to expose the faults and contradictions of racial exclusion and prejudice. The poem Henry recited, a device he often used with deftness and great recall of memory, was "Harlem." Its first line asks, "What happens to a dream deferred?" Hughes uses that work to narrate a range of possibilities, from ruin of frustration wrought of pent-up aspiration, to sheer abandonment of hope. In this case he ended by asking rhetorically if the dream "explodes."[125] Henry appeared to be putting the convention on notice that Mississippi blacks arrived at the convention bound to push all the way for the elimination of the lily-white state Democratic Party delegation.[126]

While Henry's presentation hardly left any doubt about the strength of the resolve of the MFDP, Fannie Lou Hamer's personal story drove the point home. She recounted explicitly how severely Mississippi police authorities had beaten her and how she was later ejected from her plantation home. As she began a plea for simple justice and fairness, the cameras suddenly cut away to a presidential news conference. The commanding power of her ability to connect to the convention and television audience allegedly led President Johnson to orchestrate that event to cut off her testimony, thereby ending the compelling drama then unfolding on national television.[127]

Despite all of the promise for success, the seat challenge before the Credentials Committee failed. Neither the influence of Henry among Washington insiders, nor Hamer's oratory proved enough to prevent the committee from postponing its decision, even perhaps indefinitely. Henry ridiculed such a prospect: "That was the most noncommittal way for the issue to be settled, and we were learning quickly that politicians on that high a level don't like to be committed to anything that hasn't got several convenient exits. . . . It seemed outrageous that

Aaron Henry before Credentials Committee of National Democratic Convention, October 1964, Atlantic City, New Jersey. (Courtesy The Image Works/Take Stock.)

they could lack the integrity to face the matter squarely, come to a decision, and provide reasons for that decision."[128] Thereafter "horse-trading" went into high gear to consummate a symbolic, but not substantive deal with which to placate the MFDP. The first formal iteration of the "compromise" deals authorized by President Johnson offered the MFDP the opportunity to take part in the convention "at large" while official representation remained with the regular delegation. It did not take long for the MFDP to reject this option.[129] According to Leslie McLemore, "Henry said that the group would not accept a 'back-of-the-bus compromise.' He was supported by Martin Luther King, Jr., who said 'a natural reaction of Negro voters would be to go fishing on Election Day' if the Freedom Party is not seated."[130]

At this point, consistent with routine elite-led decision processes in national party affairs, Henry became the target to represent his delegation and to bring it along in accepting a compromise. The final resolution of the matter had now been put in the hands of the leadership of the Credentials Committee (Senator Walter Mondale of Minnesota and Congressman Charles Diggs of Michigan, respectively chair and cochair). Henry, of course, being close to both of these men, must have made it seem natural to expect him to be the conduit for getting the MFDP to agree to some face-saving compromise.[131] The whole thing proved to be a spectacular failure.

In many ways, the compromise proposal from the Credentials Committee leadership showed signs of failure from the outset. These leaders both misread the fundamental grassroots nature of the MFDP campaign, and the way in which power relations functioned in the essentially confederal Mississippi movement. While the MFDP delegates did not present themselves as impractical, they nevertheless did not have a favorable disposition toward top-down leadership. They emerged from a process of community-based actions often around local events, only being cemented into a broader movement via various organizational linkages that became the COFO. They emerged principally an ensemble cast. Henry, perhaps more than most, understood this as he presided over an assemblage that went its own way on a number of issues and ideas. He understood and played his role well in providing the guidance and the prestige that held it all together. To be sure he had broader contacts and relationships that yielded more external allies. A major part of his success rested on facilitating other voices and in sharing out the tasks and responsibilities in his state. Moreover, his dexterity at practical politics never allowed him to waver in his criticism of "his friends" Lyndon Johnson and Hubert Humphrey, who now seemed willing to "compromise" on the illegality of the regular state delegation.

The options soon crystallized into two additional compromise proposals before Johnson's final two-seat option prevailed. The first from Representative Edith Green of Oregon offered equal votes to loyal delegates from both groups, with values shared proportionally. The MFDP seemed favorable to the proposal, but Johnson rejected it. He countered with an offer of two nonvoting seats to the MFDP, while other members of the delegation would remain as "honored guests." Two among them, Aaron Henry and Edwin King, would be designated as official "delegates at large." Then in a bare-boned political pressure from the White House, a style of politics that Lyndon Johnson had honed in the Senate, the two-seat option gained favor and "passed" by a voice vote on the floor.[132]

Rumors were rife that Henry, deemed the principal object for accomplishing an MFDP compromise, agreed to the plan.[133] Indeed, the pressure was intense on him and the MFDP to accept a deal, as opposed to losing everything. The challenge already represented the most successful organizational effort the Mississippi movement had achieved, and though perhaps not known at the time, would be the high-water mark of the unified social movement collective. Henry denied collusion in putting the deal together, but seemed persuaded that it was indeed the best payoff for the huge investment, and he believed that the segregated state party had virtually been brought to the point of destruction.[134] After all, almost all of its members rejected a loyalty oath and went home, vowing to vote for anybody but Johnson. Therefore, Henry argued that the two-seat option should not be rejected out of hand, that perhaps there was room for negotiating other civil rights promises as a part of a package. Moreover, he alluded to the prominence of movement allies who were vouching for this plan (Martin Luther King Jr., Humphrey, Labor leader Walter Reuther, Roy Wilkins, and so on). At the same time, he was torn because he knew that the Johnson forces had outmaneuvered him and the MFDP, and that some of the tactics were beyond the pale. Yet on balance, he was practical and wanted to gain leverage for his broader goal of desegregating Mississippi. Gaining two seats in 1964 might be the best deal for gaining all of them down the line, a reality that came to be in 1968.[135]

The fallout within the MFDP delegation from the conflict over the two seats, however, virtually broke the confederation as it had been known. In the process among the indigenous leaders Henry was perhaps the most compromised, though ironically the one who had the most influence in defining the long-term future of racial political mobilization in Mississippi. Perhaps his compromise was inadvertent. Clearly he was trapped in this situation. In some ways this was because of his very success as a leader. Most people in COFO liked and respected him. Nevertheless, there was an element of continuity in his integrationist goals that came to be a mismatch with those of elements in SNCC and CORE. The approaches and different interests evolved over time, but crystallized to a greater degree over the summer and fall of 1964. SNCC, in particular, began to make a radical critique of American society, including some of its liberal allies. Yet, Henry remained focused on obtaining the promises of the equitable, liberal democratic society (symbolized by black access). So the firestorm that accompanied his entreaties for a possible compromise resulted because most of his delegation was grassroots people critiquing that American promise.[136] Henry seemed utterly surprised and appalled. "The SNCC cadre was vehement in the rhetoric that later became typical of the Mississippi Freedom Democratic Party—that the political and economic systems of this country were no good and that the systems had to be replaced before any progress could be made and before an acceptable society could be attained." He termed these views "as foreign to the American system as white supremacy."[137]

The battle for seating at Atlantic City, though lost, nevertheless proved to be a victory of huge proportions. It changed the entire trajectory for the Mississippi movement and for the role of Henry in the quest for political power. Theodore White referred to what was gained as a "larger victory"—having exacted a commitment from the national party to banish racial considerations from criteria for naming future convention delegates.[138] As the confederation that brought the delegates to Atlantic City faltered, the shift in movement focus to the political arena was virtually complete. No longer would social mobilization be privileged over the efforts to seek the political kingdom. The passage of the Voting Rights Act the next year only increased the momentum as blacks gave more attention to acquisition of the vote in all of the assertiveness that the social mobilization had wrought. Few within the Democratic Party coalition doubted that the segregated white political party could not survive another convention, having been so thoroughly discredited before the entire nation. The only remaining question became what the terms would be for the assumption of a degree of power by the new black constituency—shared or on some terms of independence. As the movement forces splintered, over tactics and to some degree over the nature of the goal, Henry continued to focus singularly on a practical means to demolish the Mississippi racial system. It left him with a degree of flexibility that some of the other COFO players could not muster. In the process, though momentum waned for a time, Henry ultimately found a formula that propelled him to a position of unparalleled political influence nationally and in Mississippi.

Since most third parties in American political history have failed, few could have predicted that organizing such an effort in Mississippi would so radically transform the options for black participation in state politics. The loose confederation of COFO attained an unusual degree of unity of purpose, grassroots organization, and marshaled a diverse array of allies to challenge the lily-white state Democratic Party. In the process the MFDP, self-described as a third-party alternative, demonstrated the glaring and egregious denial of black political representation. The merits of the case were easy enough to document. However, the COFO activists also exposed the most unabashed efforts of the segregationists, often led by the highest officials of the state, to ever consider sharing power with blacks. Though they officially affiliated with a national Democratic Party supportive of the franchise for blacks since at least 1948, the Mississippi Democrats refused to accept these principles. When Henry proposed an agenda to defeat them, it provided a platform around which COFO eventually coalesced for making the 1964 challenge. Perhaps not even he realized how this challenge, which looked like a complete disaster, laid the seeds for the integrated political party of his dreams.

CHAPTER SIX

Henry the Public Entrepreneur and Network Tactician

Exploiting National Allies and Cultivating Local Interracial Partners

In the transition and lull that succeeded the failed MFDP effort at the convention, a critical question remained how and on what terms would the momentum of the Mississippi movement be continued. Initiatives decreased from both SNCC and CORE, the anchors for the summer campaign, hastened by the withdrawal of the NAACP from the confederation. The withdrawal came as a blow because despite its demurral at what it regarded as the militancy of COFO, the NAACP had been a critical cog in the summer operation. The national office provided significant support to sustain the infrastructure that surrounded COFO and legal resources to assist activists with court challenges and to obtain releases from jail. Once the NAACP withdrew following the 1964 convention, it exposed the difficulties in sustaining both an organizational structure and a legal framework to support the challengers. As a result some movement momentum did fall off. Some activists left the state and reduced movement activity, while others moved on to related social and rights issues.

Henry lost some momentum during the lull and had also lost his major indigenous partner, Medgar Evers. The similar mind and commitment of these two have been noted; however, the impact of the interruption of their teamwork is little noted. Medgar's absence left a deep void because the two had together set the NAACP on a new path in the late 1950s.[1] Though Henry managed his relationship and power well within the NAACP across the state, it took a toll in that he had to be everywhere as the face of the revitalized organization and to manage a sometimes contrary national office regarding the independence of the Mississippi chapter.

The scope of the undertaking increased for Henry at the time because Medgar's replacement, his brother Charles, did not enjoy the same depth of relationship with Henry. Though the two did a lot of work together, the relationship did not always result in positive and fully collaborative outcomes. They sometimes appeared to be working at cross-purposes, and other times were in complete disagreement. As the political environment evolved, additional difficulties in the partnership emerged because of Charles Evers's tendency to go his own way.[2]

Meanwhile, among the major state movement leaders, Henry's credibility appeared the most sullied because of fallout from his presumed support for the two-seat compromise at the 1964 convention. Following the convention some accused him of being a sellout, and that criticism increased as he cultivated local white partners to integrate the Democratic Party. Moreover, his certainty that the old Democratic Party would cease to be important in the state proved premature since that project took an additional four years.

This part of the narrative shows Henry using his leadership skills to remain trained on the sights of the goal of the equitable society. He focused on activities that shored up and expanded his network of collaborators and would-be partners, state and federal, and he exploited a range of opportunities along these lines that grew as a product of Lyndon Johnson in the White House. Despite the wide skepticism about Johnson's motives and commitments, his period in the White House turned out to be a boon for civil rights legislation and policy initiatives.

Henry trained his sights on how to turn all of these into benefits in Mississippi. To fully appreciate this development it sometimes requires taking a step back in the narration to fill out backstories and parallel activities that occupied him following the 1964 party challenge. While the momentum built for the party challenge, Henry also exploited other avenues for changing the racial system in Mississippi. He worked to deploy the legalistic approach of the NAACP to bring disputes directly to the increasingly friendly federal court system. The major legal challenges on this parallel track included civil liberties, segregated education, and voting and political representation. Moreover, he assiduously used his preference for collaborative partnerships to expand his already legendary network of allies in the national government and Democratic Party—cultivating presidents and congressmen. Finally, while the grand coalition floundered, he began to build the basis for what Edwin King called the next phase of social change activity in Mississippi: the shift from protest to politics. Edwin King saw this phase as especially important for Henry because it maximized his talents at the networking game.[3]

Hence, Henry began his strongest efforts to network with local white partners who expressed sentiments for taking Mississippi beyond the segregation system. While this further contributed to suspicion about his motives from some,[4]

Edwin King suggests that no one had a steadier commitment to cross-racial engagement.[5] In the end this all served Henry well, though the path through a transition of perhaps two years was not always smooth.

While some thought that the failure of the 1964 challenge would break the movement,[6] in reality that seemed unlikely given the spectrum of changes that had already occurred. Many of the areas of changes also remained ripe for further exploitation. For example, since the segregationist state party left no wiggle room for accommodation with the national party, a vacuum opened that forces like Henry's could occupy. Meanwhile, the mobilization activists that challenged the racial system between 1960 and 1964—freedom rides, boycotts, sit-ins, strikes, and so forth—had taken a real toll. They energized legions of external allies that became the stimuli for a bevy of legislation, Executive Orders, and judicial decisions that provided the foundations for redress. With many of the rights to "accommodations" questions established in court rulings, the shift to the franchise was natural. Henry also calculated that continued affiliation with the National Democratic Party remained the best way to capture this wave of social change. The party had strengthened its civil rights profile over time, giving Henry every reason to believe that he and the MFDP could benefit from that refined approach.

Even as the momentum grew for the 1964 challenge, Henry (and practically the entire COFO delegation, some with skepticism) realized the importance of the federal government as an ally. Above all else it seemed clear that black people alone could not win the civil rights struggle in Mississippi and across the South; partners would be necessary. Looking back as far as the Civil War this reality appeared well established.[7] While support for black rights from the federal government did not always materialize and at other times appeared ambivalent, in the period surrounding the 1964 election the signs looked favorable.[8] Henry, being particularly attuned to these conditions, exploited them in all three branches of the federal government. In this effort he succeeded to turn the central government into a major ally. Sometimes he achieved this by direct personal action or intervention, and other times he was simply a good entrepreneur taking advantage of opportunities available in the environment.

As an officer of the NAACP, an organization devoted to using legal challenges to change the American racial system, it is hardly surprising that Henry saw the court system as an important resource for changing Mississippi. He took advantage of major Supreme Court decisions that expanded general civil and human rights to support his broad initiatives for the imagined integrated society. Oftentimes he appeared as a party to legal suits, but just as often used favorable court rulings as the base for testing Mississippi compliance. By the time that Vera Pigee, Henry, and the NAACP youth challenged the trains, buses, and businesses in Clarksdale, they already had reason to believe that the federal courts, though sometimes slow, were on their side. As Henry moved to solidify his position first as state president of the NAACP, and subsequently as the administrative leader of COFO, he always wanted access to a legal team to back up whatever civil rights activities were occurring in the streets. The Supreme Court decisions gave him a lot to build on in a string of civil rights and civil liberties cases. However, a series of decisions about representation that followed the 1964 convention debacle served as the major base of support for the new enfranchised voters.[9]

The legal framework that guided many of the challenges regarding representation came in 1962 when the Supreme Court ruled in *Baker v. Carr* that state legislatures were in violation of the constitutional requirement for decennial reapportionment. Several other cases followed that more fully elaborated what came to be known as the one-man, one-vote principle.[10] Though reapportionment remained a national problem more often based on a rural bias in state legislatures, but the racial dimension in Mississippi and the South added an equally important variable.[11] In part, therefore, the four unsuccessful challengers to the Mississippi congressional delegation (June 1964 primary) contested their loss on the basis of claims about representativeness based on racial exclusion; the Mississippi delegation as constituted represented only white people, violating the one-man, one-vote principle.[12]

The legal contestation by these challengers generated a bevy of federal lawsuits based on disfranchisement and malapportionment.[13] Immediately after losing the congressional primary contests, they requested the right to be placed on the ballot in the general election as independent candidates. However, denial came quickly because of a state law that prevented those who had contested a primary election for a political party to obtain a ballot place in the succeeding general election. Their formal efforts went all the way to Congress before being rejected, again as a product of political considerations of the Johnson administration.[14] The candidates ultimately prevailed on the question in the case of *Clifton Whitley et al. v. Paul B. Johnson*, which vacated this state law.[15] However, the resolution did not come in time to allow them on the ballot that fall.

The reapportionment decisions with the addition of the Voting Rights Act of 1965 (VRA) provided real confidence to Henry that the federal court system was a reliable (if sometimes slow-moving) ally. Of course, he had worked tirelessly (along with a national NAACP and other civil rights organizations) in promoting the voting proposal after President Johnson introduced it.[16] This legislation added significant heft to the reapportionment decisions insofar as it gave significant enforcement power to the federal government to execute the registration of African Americans.[17] Mississippi became perhaps the greatest beneficiary of the legislation because of the size of its African American population and its woeful level of disfranchisement. The combination of this legislation and the reapportionment decisions spurred a wholesale assault on disfranchisement and the racial gerrymandering that previously diminished and skewed the benefits of the franchise.

Henry joined a large contingent in challenging the legislative redistricting process that diluted the value of the African American vote in Mississippi by stacking and packing districts and by gerrymandering. This anticipated the tremendous impact that the open franchise was bound to have on the racial composition of elected officials in Mississippi.[18] The challengers were thwarted early because the state legislature instituted actions to head off the potential impact of black voters, starting after Henry first teamed with Merrell Lindsey to run for a congressional seat in 1962. In executing its plan to head off the potential impact of a restoration of the black franchise, the legislature broke up a compact, racially gerrymandered majority black Delta district that had existed for almost seventy-five years.[19] It first split the Delta district in 1962, then in 1966, according to Frank Parker: "The state legislature divided the heavily-black Delta area horizontally among three of the five districts, depriving black voters of a voting majority in any of the state's congressional districts."[20] The struggle crystallized around the 1966 Connor case, which continued for another ten years. The battle finally ended in victory for the challengers in 1977 when a court decision produced a reasonable reapportionment of the state legislature.[21] It had immediate effect, dramatically increasing the number of blacks in the legislature.[22] Henry himself attained a seat, the service for which will be described later. In this phase, however, the long fight most reflected the reasonable reliability of the federal court as an ally.

Desegregating education also became an enduring target for federal court action, which Henry pushed in his capacity as president of the state NAACP. Indeed, the NAACP maintained continuous primary leadership for school desegregation. Looking backward from the 1964 convention, Henry and Medgar Evers began to intensify their demand for implementation of the 1954 *Brown* decision. After all, since beginning an initial push in 1955, Henry argued that the actions of their reliable judicial ally had hardly changed school segregation. "By the 1964–65 school year, only 57 of Mississippi's almost 280,000 black school children attended formerly all-white schools. By 1965, the overall desegregation rate for Mississippi schools stood at .02 percent—the lowest in the South."[23] Undaunted, Henry worked through the NAACP to institute new lawsuits in 1963 seeking compliance with *Brown*—two by the Justice Department in Biloxi and Gulfport[24] and three by the NAACP Legal Defense Fund (LDF) in Jackson, Leake County, and also in Biloxi.[25]

Henry and the NAACP were pushing hard in these cases to get compliance on this major movement goal. The first of the cases to get to trial appeared in

Biloxi, where a segregated school on a federal military base compelled the federal government to become a partner in the challenge. The nearby Keesler Air Force base had some two thousand school-age children of military personnel in the area. Biloxi had an active NAACP chapter, which teamed with the federal administration, in a suit against Biloxi and Gulfport schools to prevent the segregation of dependents of military personnel or federal employees. The outcome revealed that southern federal judges did not always prove to be reliable. The January 1963 filing received fairly swift attention from district judge Sidney Mize, who ruled in May that "the federal government had 'no standing as a plaintiff in this court and does not have the requisite interest in the subject matter to maintain the action . . . only natural persons are entitled to the privileges and immunities of the Fourteenth Amendment' . . . and that the federal government was not a person and 'could not sue for the deprivation of civil rights of others.'"[26] This forced the complainants to appeal to the next level.

Meanwhile, Henry and Medgar Evers prepared to submit several new cases via the Legal Defense Fund of the NAACP. Just after the Mize ruling they filed a claim in Jackson for Medgar Evers's children. Similarly, Winson Hudson worked to prepare a challenge against the Leake County schools.[27] Eventually the Fifth Circuit Court consolidated all of these cases, but not before Judge Mize dismissed the Biloxi case again, despite the clear "standing" of the new plaintiffs, which Gilbert Mason says included "thirteen parents [including himself] and twenty-five children in Biloxi."[28]

The early 1964 desegregation ruling of the appellate court in the Biloxi case opened opportunities for broad new NAACP-led challenges. It set into motion a trajectory and a model that prevailed into the 1970s. The court required Biloxi to develop a plan for the 1964 school year: desegregation of one grade in the first year (1964–65); three grades in 1965–66; and all grades by the end of 1966–67 school year. Hence, Gilbert Mason was pleased to record that "On Monday, August 31, 1964, for the first time in Mississippi history, black children and white children started to school together in desegregated first-grade classrooms in Biloxi."[29]

Meanwhile, Henry stepped up the efforts in Clarksdale, a challenge he promised back in 1954: "I made it clear that segregation was the cause of all of our problems and that I could no longer go along with it. I told them that I intended to devote all of my energies to implementing the Supreme Court decision."[30] A 1955 desegregation petition he made to the school board had long since been rejected.[31] He now proceeded to sue in the interest of his own child. Rebecca became the plaintiff in a suit against the school district.[32]

He required no afterthought in injecting his personal family circumstances into the struggle. He saw it as the ultimate affront that his own daughter, a defenseless and innocent child, had to accept segregation in a school so obviously inferior to those for whites. Others shared his sentiments, and as a result a large number of Clarksdale parents joined him to seek compliance with the *Brown* ruling. The *Clarksdale Press Register* reported on September 12, 1963, that twenty-one parents petitioned for the desegregation of the schools in the interest of twenty-nine children. If voluntary compliance did not occur, Henry vowed, these parents would institute a lawsuit with the full backing of the national NAACP. The district did not budge, and the challengers duly filed the lawsuit.[33]

Legal relief seemed forthcoming when a court order in 1964 called for a plan for a "unitary, nonracial system of public education." Thereupon negotiations commenced between the challengers and the Clarksdale school board. A "geographic" plan offered by the board proposed that students attend a school only within their zone. Four options within the plans sought to stagger full integration as far out as 1971. The only problem with the plan is that it did not result in any integration, precipitating a new court filing by Henry and his co-plaintiffs. The blacks charged that the board's plan reflected geographic zoning in which the railroad tracks became a natural racial dividing line, and that where this dividing line did not naturally occur, the city acted to create it by a process of selective de-annexation. If left in place, they argued in their court filing, no school integration would ever take place: "In the fall of that year, not a single child in Clarksdale was enrolled in any school with members of the other race. Again, for the spring semester of the 1964–65 year, not a single child was enrolled in a school attended by children of the other race." The details were arresting: "in April 1965, 2800 Negro pupils attended the five 'Negro' schools in Clarksdale and 2100 white children attended white schools along with two Negro girls who had transferred to the white high school to obtain a course, Latin, not available in the Negro high school."[34]

The negotiations were far from over, and several years passed in a slow-moving court process. Eventually, the district offered a plan based on "ability" groupings, designed to achieve desegregation by assigning students on the basis of normed testing. Curiously the court accepted the plan. It created a firestorm among blacks, who called it a tracking system and another stalling tactic by the school board. They refused to allow their children to take the "ability test," risking their removal from school. Henry went on the offensive in a big way, lobbying to a broad cross section of his vast network to help dramatize the continued violations of the law, addressing his legal position paper to "Foundations, National Parties, National Educators, National Churchmen, Civil Rights Organizations, and friends of justice," among others.[35] This battle too proved long, but eventually successful. Alas, the resolution came too late for Rebecca Henry, who had already finished high school when the ruling came in the 1970s.

The upshot is that Henry maintained a continuing profile of leadership in school desegregation efforts through the transition succeeding the failure at the 1964 Democratic convention. While he continued to be at odds with the national NAACP about the way in which he chose issues and his flexibility in choosing partners, he never wavered about the legal avenue as the means for achieving school desegregation. Since this remained a high agenda item for both him and the national organization, Henry had an advantage because of his access to NAACP legal resources with which to sustain the demand for desegregation. The collaboration built a body of law on which all movement activists continued to rely. As the chief point person for many of these legal challenges Henry's profile of leadership and his network of statewide allies greatly increased across the state.

The role of the Supreme Court as an ally for Henry was greatly augmented by an activist executive and a coalition in Congress. An analysis of his interaction with the Office of the President, especially in the last days of Kennedy and then Lyndon Johnson, shows Henry amassing significant power and influence that he put to good use in the regrouping of the movement after the convention. Unlike the courts, Henry had a more direct means of influencing the legislative and executive branches, playing to his peripatetic style. Similar to the deep engagement he had with every element of social change through the 1950s and 1960s in Mississippi, he also associated himself with every conceivable source of support elsewhere. His engagement with the broad national civil rights hierarchy and his entrée to members of Congress and to Presidents Kennedy and Johnson allowed him unprecedented influence for an African American from segregated Mississippi. He laid the groundwork for this early, and it provided him a reservoir of resources that strengthened him as a player in the heady summer of 1964, but it also sustained him as a leader of continuing prominence through the transition after the convention.

The highly charged and increasingly publicized racial contention that emerged in Mississippi early in the tenure of President Kennedy could not be ignored, not least because of the overwhelming identification of black voters (and prospective ones) with the Democratic Party. It seemed prudent for an ambitious president to make some kind of response, especially to egregious racial acts of violence and terror in Mississippi. Numerous and constant opportunities presented themselves, not least widespread arrests of peaceful demonstrations, picketers, and sit-in activists. Early on Henry acted to get both access to Kennedy and to frame the policy debate regarding racial change in Mississippi and elsewhere. He met the president in 1963 when he "was the only Mississippian to attend the White House conference called to discuss racial issues, Saturday [June 22]."[36] In addition, he made himself useful to individuals in the Kennedy cabinet who were charged with drafting the major civil rights policy options for the president. Fortuitously the unfolding daily drama in Mississippi made it a central agenda item for the administration. As the omnipresent leader linked to all of the challengers, Henry became a primary source of information and advice to the administration, cabinet officials, and Congress.[37]

As circumstances compelled President Kennedy to become more involved in civil rights, his administration sought to balance many competing interests. The president, however, had to find willing partners from the movement who appreciated both his expressed interest in civil rights and the necessity of balancing that interest with competing ones.[38] Henry became an important prospect because he appeared more willing to cooperate with the administration than some of the other leaders within COFO.[39] For example, skepticism continued to grow within the administration about the perceived militancy of SNCC, then the organization with much of the day-to-day operating responsibility for COFO.[40] Though Henry's stock rose, the administration's perception of his moderation may have been somewhat misplaced. Henry was as relentless as any of the activists in his pursuit of his goals for comprehensive social change and the racial order in Mississippi. Indeed, he gave no quarter in pressing the Kennedy administration to intervene and give public signals of support for black civil rights. However, Henry's greater experience in networking with national officials and his practical approach clearly gave him an advantage and he used it with consummate skill, even though he did not always win.

A Kennedy biographer, Robert Dallek, captured the difficulty of the political choices for a president intuitively in favor of civil rights. On the one hand, Kennedy "could not quite understand how educated southern leaders could be so impractical as to believe that they could permanently maintain their outmoded system of apartheid. . . . He puzzled over their intransigence in denying the franchise to blacks." On the other hand, "he believed that national security and domestic reforms advancing prosperity, education, health care for all trumped the needs and wishes of blacks . . . With so much else at stake, especially overseas, he felt compelled to make civil rights a secondary concern." But wariness about losing the southern Democratic partisans weighed heavily: "Fears of civil strife across the South, with negative political repercussions for North and South, were enough to make Kennedy a temporizer on an issue he wished to keep as quiet as possible."[41]

Henry suggested that his relationship with Kennedy began a mere month after the inauguration. The president dispatched Justice Department official John Doar and Robert Owens to collect information about problems with Mississippi voting registration, foretelling this issue as an administration priority. Henry and Medgar Evers shared responsibility for finding willing informants to discuss their unsuccessful efforts to register and vote with Doar and Owens. Despite this different quality of access to the highest levels of power, Henry said he was skeptical of the overtures from Kennedy.[42] Yet he and Evers proceeded to collect data on the use of literacy tests for disfranchisement in the Delta. Henry recorded that they canvassed to find people willing to give testimony to support the case Evers was building. He indicated that while "Medgar and I were not permitted in the courtroom during the hearing, . . . we stood outside with those who had come to testify to reassure them of our support."[43] The Justice Department subsequently intervened and filed suit to eliminate the practice in Panola and Tallahatchie Counties. The federal district court ruled that voters were only required to record their name, age, and address, and to copy a brief section of the state constitution. It instructed registrars to also provide all needed assistance to applicants. Subsequently, the court eliminated the requirement to copy a portion of the constitution.[44] Thereafter Henry's ambivalence about Kennedy disappeared.

The path that Henry tread as he cultivated the administration did not always appear smooth. He often lost or experienced significant delays as he tried to curry favor and pressure the government at the same time. The continuing efforts to get the United States Civil Rights Commission to hold hearings on the racial situation in Mississippi is an early example of how tricky simple matters could be. Henry became aware that a 1960 extension of the 1958 legislation that established the commission[45] allowed the receipt of testimony under oath. In light of this new power Henry worked assiduously to get an investigation of Mississippi. He wanted a published report of what he calculated would be damning and explosive public testimony from grassroots African Americans. He hoped that these revelations would be hard for the federal government to ignore. President Kennedy, however, demurred on such a hearing calculating it would inevitably be critical of the powerful Mississippi senators, whose favor the president wanted to curry.[46]

When the full commission did not rush into Mississippi, Henry felt frustration but worked with the Mississippi advisory committee of the commission to get testimony on the record about conditions in Mississippi. The results proved his point. Even the unsympathetic *Clarksdale Press Register* could not ignore the power of the images portrayed by Henry's testimony. The hearings occurred in May 1962, and the paper carried two entries about their content, buried in the last pages of separate editions. On May 16, it reported that the Mississippi state advisory committee was holding its first-ever hearings in Clarksdale. Aaron Henry and Vera Pigee, it reported, testified regarding their arrests for sit-ins and boycotts and to the effect that the local radio had refused to allow them to purchase advertisements for the 1962 congressional campaign of Reverend Merrill Lindsey, a campaign it noted that Henry managed.[47] A day later, documentation from the advisory committee indicated that it heard from another twenty-five people, who complained about equally disturbing measures by state officials to prevent routine exercise of civil and human rights: Circuit clerks refused to allow them to pay poll taxes, and often even denied attempts to register; police abuses during arrests for civil rights demonstrations; and abuses and intimidations on plantations for area movement activity. Though vilified by local segregationists, the advisory body subsequently moved about the state documenting an increasingly hostile environment for blacks, sustained by evermore elaborately wrought informal and formal barriers.[48]

While this exposed the ambivalence and/or recalcitrance of the Kennedy administration from time to time, Henry built a relationship that proved valuable. There is little doubt of the importance of his continuous prodding in getting a full visit from the commission albeit two years later, far too long for his cohorts in SNCC and CORE.[49] Nonetheless, the graphic sworn testimony of egregious violations of rights before the commission in 1965 proved riveting and significantly ramped up the pressure on the federal government to intervene. The timing of the testimony proved auspicious for influencing the debate on the 1965 VRA. The hearings revealed the vast scope of racism, but were especially revelatory about the profligate barriers against black participation. With tongue in cheek Henry addressed the commission: "I am happy to express a welcome to the Commission for coming to Mississippi. We had anticipated your coming over 2 years ago but we are glad you finally made it."[50] He first described the players in the struggle for civil rights—identifying organizations and taking care to describe how a variety of groups worked in solidarity as COFO. He then provided details about voter registration efforts in only a single year—1964. He listed twenty-seven counties, cities, and towns literally stretched from one end of the state to another, where the NAACP had initiated campaigns. He cited nineteen other areas, most in the Delta, where COFO was leading similar efforts. The point was to demonstrate that nowhere in the state were there offices friendly to would-be African American registrants.

He documented how all manner of legislative action had been instituted in this one-year period to thwart efforts to increase black political participation. The governor acquired emergency powers to act against activists, and the highway patrol force was increased from 275 to 475. Powers of municipalities were extended to increased detention powers and increased penalty power for municipal courts. Street movements, including mass assemblages at voter registration offices, were criminalized: printing and circulation of pamphlets/handbills carried a $500 fine and/or six months in jail; there would be strict regulation of picketing at public buildings; and there would be enforced obeisance to police commands during demonstrations. He cited the "outright refusal by registrars to permit Negroes to attempt to register; church burnings; beatings, involving residents and voter registration workers; economic reprisals[;] shootings, bombings, murders, cross burnings, and other forms of intimidation." Many of these "crimes have been committed with the cooperation of local officials." As an example he quoted the lieutenant governor calling for all state officials to "wage a brave, determined, and continuing battle against invasion from any source, that takes from any group, of our heritage, sovereignty, constitutional rights, and Southern Way of life." He also reminded the commission that "The present Governor has the distinction of being the only Governor in the Nation to counsel disobedience to the Federal public accommodations law." Moreover, Kennedy appointee "Federal Judge Harold Cox, from the bench in March of 1964, referred repeatedly to Negro voter registration applicants as a 'bunch of niggers' acting like a bunch of chimpanzees."[51]

Before President Kennedy could respond to the likes of Governor Barnett and Judge Cox, he was assassinated and Vice President Lyndon Johnson stepped into office. Henry immediately sought to establish linkage to the president, albeit in protest. He wasted little time in demanding that Johnson "make it unequivocally clear that the Negro citizens of Mississippi are going to secure the right to vote, now, regardless of how much it takes in terms of Federal force." He used his entreaty to also increase pressure on the Democratic-controlled Congress to pass three bills: (1) putting federal registrars "into any county where any of the adult population is denied the right to vote"; (2) "outlawing the literacy test as a prerequisite to voting"; and (3) holding officials "liable for damages when violence and/or intimidation is directed . . . against persons trying to register to vote or assisting people trying to register to vote." If this failed, he urged the president to "use his full power under Title 10, Section 333 of the Federal Code" to achieve these ends. Indeed a precedent for such action existed since the president acted against Governor George Wallace to secure admission of blacks to the University of Alabama.[52]

Unlike Kennedy, Johnson won the presidency in 1964 by a large margin (61.1 percent), which theoretically allowed him to claim a much firmer mandate for civil rights policies.[53] African Americans voted overwhelmingly for him, and their identification with the Democratic Party rose from 58 percent in 1960 to 82 percent in 1964.[54] His coalition in the legislative branch remained strong with Democrats solidly controlling the 89th Congress: 295 House seats to 140 for the Republicans, a gain of 38; and 68 of the 100 seats in the Senate (over two-thirds of the seats in each body).[55] Therefore, it seemed likely that it would not be as easy for the president to ignore the demands of African Americans.

Henry had some insight into the president because of contact they had when Johnson was vice president, and during the MFDP struggle at the 1964 convention. This access significantly enhanced Henry's position because of the long-term relationship he had cultivated with Vice President Humphrey. Their alliance began during Humphrey's days as a senator and because of his leadership on civil rights within the party hierarchy.[56] Even so, a smooth relationship with the new president did not always exist, especially since transparent political considerations often caused Johnson to place limits on projects that the civil rights coalition deemed fundamental.[57] Thus even when Henry wrote thanking the president for an April 21, 1965, meeting at the White House, he took the occasion to complain. He objected to the appointment of former Mississippi governor James Coleman to the Fifth Circuit Federal Court that handled cases from Mississippi. He reminded the president that Coleman sponsored the literacy law and the internal spy agency known as the State Sovereignty Commission and conspired to eliminate compulsory school attendance to sustain segregation.[58]

President Johnson delivered more than many in the civil rights community had predicted. His proposals directly advanced many parts of the civil rights project reflecting the demands Henry put before the Commission on Civil Rights. Two of the three major bills that Henry argued for, the Civil Rights Act of 1964 and the VRA of 1965, passed with significant support from Johnson. This prompted Lawson to argue that "in his five years as chief executive, Lyndon Johnson fulfilled many of the legislative goals of Negroes. Among the accomplishments was his translation into statutory language the ideas originally conceived during the Truman, Eisenhower, and Kennedy regimes." Lawson then quoted the NAACP lobbyist Clarence Mitchell as saying that Johnson "made a greater contribution to giving a dignified and hopeful status to Negroes in the United States than any president including Lincoln, Roosevelt, and Kennedy."[59]

Implementation by the executive branch did not always come swiftly and sometimes required the intervention of the courts. Two important lawsuits that contested the legitimacy of the Civil Rights Act of 1964 had to be adjudicated before many of the rights to public accommodations were enforced. In *Heart of Atlanta Motel v. United States* the Supreme Court took on the challenge of forcing the desegregation of hotels by invoking the interstate commerce clause.[60] Meanwhile, in *Katzenbach v. McClung* the court used the same reasoning to disallow the segregation of restaurants and eating places that customarily did not serve African Americans or forced them to use a back entrance.[61] In this instance the court came through as a reliable ally, but even then implementation could be halting in Mississippi.

From Henry's point of view, the federal government had finally directly authorized intervention; under the 1964 act everyday segregation of public spaces and accommodations were eliminated; the Justice Department could bring suit to advance desegregation; and the investigative power of the Commission on Civil Rights was beefed up. The 1965 act authorized the government to directly intervene in the registration process, operating a parallel system to restore the franchise to African Americans. Johnson, meanwhile, actively supported his Justice

Department, which aggressively litigated test cases brought by segregationists and affirmatively pursued others to sustain the principles of the law. The deployment of federal registrars, achieved after fierce congressional debate, rapidly altered the franchise status for African Americans.[62] Prior to the VRA just 6.7 percent of the African American population was registered, but this grew to 59.8 percent just two years later.[63] The difference was striking. In thirty-two of the eighty-two counties with federal registrars, 71 percent of the black population enrolled to vote just two years later.[64] The Justice Department continued to bring suits against registration violations. Data show that following the first court challenges, for which Henry and the NAACP lay the foundation in Tallahatchie and Panola Counties, other counties initiated suits, often multiple submissions, by 1965. Alas, these cases usually had to travel through every level of the federal court system through to the Supreme Court.[65]

President Johnson accompanied his aggressive efforts to implement the legal aspects of the two civil rights acts with the "Great Society" and "War on Poverty" projects.[66] Johnson described his economic opportunity legislation as follows: "The Act does not merely expand old programs or improve what is already being done. It charts a new course. It strikes at the causes, not just the consequences of poverty."[67] Many aspects of these policy initiatives proved even more consistent with the inclusive society that Henry envisioned. This easily tapped into his imagination that foresaw the necessity of a diverse complex of means to enable poor people to sustain independence. From Henry's point of view, Johnson seemed to be making the requisite fundamental break with the past to build such a capacity in blacks.

The components of the Johnson program were imaginative and broad. The Job Corps program sought to enhance employment opportunities for the young poor in cities and in the rural South through institutionalized on-the-job training.[68] The Head Start preschool program targeted three- and four-year-old impoverished children with little or no access to preschool. Later as the War on Poverty program progressed, it expanded elements for a comprehensive attack on racial disparity: elementary and secondary education, comprehensive health, elderly care, and housing. Joseph Califano, a special assistant to President Johnson and architect of many of these programs, summarized Johnson's policy initiatives. Commenting on the scope of these projects, he said: "The president submitted, and Congress enacted, more than 100 major proposals in each of the 89th and 90th Congresses." Of course, large portions of the beneficiaries of the Johnson initiatives were newly enfranchised voters of all ages, schoolchildren and college matriculants, the elderly, and the unemployed, among them.[69]

The Johnson initiatives appeared to be a veritable recipe for Henry's idealized world with African Americans free to acquire resources and to cultivate them

Aaron Henry and President Lyndon Baines Johnson, circa 1965, Washington, DC. (Courtesy Aaron Henry Papers, Tougaloo College.)

like other independent and engaged citizens. In this interval it became apparent how Henry's expanded network of national supporters generated real outcomes. Henry immediately adapted and deployed the poverty initiatives to some of his own existing designs in order to advance his version of the "Great Society" in Clarksdale, the Delta, and the rest of Mississippi.

He became the consummate entrepreneur in pursuit of federal programs, and Mississippi became the laboratory for implementation. Some of his early ideas that eventually led to proposals for federal grants were the Southern Educational and Recreational Association (SERA); Coahoma Opportunities Inc., Community Action Program (COI); and the Citizens Crusade Against Poverty (CCAP, sponsored by Organized Labor and discussed later in this chapter). Henry spearheaded all of these homegrown ideas, except SERA, while working with a small cadre of NAACP members, some already entrepreneurs themselves. The rapidity with which the marketplace developed for pursuit of federal support was staggering; virtually all of the ideas generated within these three organizations resulted in multiple proposals for millions of dollars, for a diversity of programs in Clarksdale and the Delta.

The SERA incorporated in 1963 in Delaware, but had many Clarksdale representatives on its board. The project aimed to respond to the disparities among African American youths, many caused by segregation in education and recreation.

Many of the local participants and board members were close associates of Henry: among these were B. F. McLaurin (president of Coahoma Jr. College), Laura Hearn (a dean of the college), Bennie Gooden (confidant and partner on many Henry-sponsored grants), and Andrew Carr (a local white farmer). Despite its local diversity, the presence of nonlocals ("outside agitators") within the group led segregationists to challenge its legitimacy.[70]

The controversy inspired the outsiders to withdraw in mid-June of 1965. The board of SERA then reconstituted as an entirely local operation.[71] Even at this early date it remained an integrated entity, representing a "who's who" among the African American social change agents and moderate whites in Clarksdale. Henry very much desired these local whites on the board, which he then joined after its reconstitution. Locals Bennie Gooden, B. F. McLaurin, Mary Whiteside, H. Y. Hackett (an early NAACP activist), and Charles Stringer (a businessman and NAACP stalwart) also joined. The whites in the group included Andrew Carr, Harvey Ross (a lawyer and later judge), and George Maynard (a lawyer), all of whom Henry perceived as reliable allies.[72] When SERA received its first grant of $200,000 from the Office of Economic Opportunity (OEO), it then became apparent to the white power elite that federal money would likely flow to Clarksdale with or without their approval. The role of an outsider, Jesse Epps, the actual grantee, raised eyebrows. Wilkie described him as "a diminutive man with a Napoleonic complex [and] a smooth speaking style and a lust for publicity" and of suspect qualifications. In any case, this grant illustrated the potential of the federal government (and outside entrepreneurs) as a real option for responding to the claims of the black community in Clarksdale. It also revealed the potential that such largesse could have in increasing the bargaining power for blacks.[73]

For a short while SERA became the conduit for directing many of Henry's proposals to the OEO. However, several other organizations began to emerge, inspiring some competition in this small town where memberships and functions within organizations overlapped. The tremendous scope of the needs of the mobilized but desperately poor, rural blacks of Clarksdale and the Delta precipitated this energy. The local mobilization and the availability of new federal money provided immense opportunities for exploitation, a confluence of circumstances that advanced Henry's broader goals for desegregating Mississippi. He turned on his natural instinct for entrepreneurship, which was basically another dimension of his networking skills.

Meanwhile, the federal Community Action Program (CAP) emerged as the administrative home for a plethora of the new poverty programs. It is striking how much the organization and conceptualization of the program resulted from experimentation, bold risk-taking, and a kind of antibureaucratic bias. Two bold iterations of program decentralization and "maximum feasible participation" became operational constructs. Gillette suggests that the program foremost reflected an effort to help local people develop their own resources for self-improvement. "Local community action agencies (CAAs)—either private organizations or creatures of government—social service professionals, civic leaders, and residents of target areas would develop antipoverty plans tailored to their particular needs." In support of their efforts, OEO would absorb up to 90 percent of the direct costs.[74] All of these elements proved especially attractive to Henry in his role as an agent of social change.

In this heady environment, Henry and the highly mobilized Clarksdale community set out to exploit the "market." SERA and two other organizations that paralleled its development became the conduits for grantsmanship. The COI eventually became the most successful and enjoyed a longer life span. An analysis of its board shows that it had an early capacity to bid for federal programs as a CAP agency. It organized in 1965 and elected white planter Andrew Carr as chair and black businessman Charles Stringer as vice chair. Sensing that he needed to stay in the background because many whites saw him as controversial, Henry declined to accept nomination as chair of the group.[75] He did exercise great influence in selecting the interracial recruitment committee that recommended applicants for the important staff positions of program and assistant program directors.[76] Meanwhile, the full board included a much wider spectrum of locals, among them some whites not known for racial moderation. Semmes Luckett, a local attorney, is an example. He had been appointed just months earlier to the State Sovereignty Commission and was assisting in drafting legislation for state financing of the emerging segregated white academies, a bulwark against public school integration.[77] This illustrated the speed with which African American mobilization inspired broader local engagement with maximum feasible participation by default. Participants now included an odd assortment of bankers, physicians, teachers, clergy, planters, and farmers—across the racial divide in Clarksdale. (See Table 2 below.)

While this did not mean that all of these white citizens had a sudden change of heart, it did illustrate how the prospect of acquiring federal largess engaged even the detractors of Lyndon Johnson's Great Society programs. Wilkie characterized most of them as "conservative white men who had more interest in blocking funds from the likes of Epps than extending aid to the poor."[78] Moreover, it was the beginning of the realization on the part of whites that continued silence would leave these proceeds entirely in the hands of blacks. In the long run this array of participants did not last. Henry's insistence on trying to engage local whites, however, remained his long-term goal for breaking down the segregated society. Notwithstanding his natural tendency to moderation, he recognized that working with this new integrated group was not a panacea. It seemed inevitable under these conditions that Henry's resolve and continued criticism of his local society would inherently weaken this board.

TABLE 2
Clarksdale Opportunities, Inc.
Original Officers and Members

Andrew Carr*	PresidentPlanter; board First National Bank
Chas Stringer	Vice PresidentBusiness [mortuary]/church officer
Marion Reid	Sec./Treas.Teacher, Coahoma Junior College
Chase Chambers Jr.*	Clergyman
Paulene Clark*	Planter
B. T. Cooper	Clergyman
W. N. Crowson*	Physician/surgeon
Fred Crum	Farmer/church official
R. L. Drew	Clergyman/Voters League
Montyne Fox*	Director of Welfare
James Gilliam	Masons Grand Master/fed'l. gov't. (Ret.)
Julian Bloom*	Real estate
Aaron Henry	Pharmacist/state NAACP president
Lillian Johnson	Daycare director/fmr. school supervisor
Frank Marascalco*	Physician
George Maynard*	Attorney and Library Board
B. F. McLaurin	President Coahoma Junior College
Lula Pendleton	Principal (Ret.)
W. A. Pennington	Clergyman
T. J. Perry*	Contractor
J. C. Pettis	Farmer
Haywood Pickel	Mechanic/church official
Harvey Ross*	Attorney
J. W. Stampley	Asst. superintendent of education
M. Carter Stovall*	Planter
Mary Whiteside	Dean Coahoma Junior College

* White members
Source: Benbow Collection 90.24.85. V1: A: 1410. September 10, 1965. "Minutes of Community Action Committee."

The following discussion of COI reveals how the early pursuit of federal funding shaped up in Clarksdale and the surrounding area. The organization quickly made its first application in 1965 for a federal antipoverty program. Marion Reid, COI secretary, described the proposal as a year-round "Early Childhood Day-Care Center" under the auspices of SERA. This Delta-wide project predated the federal Head Start initiative, but was based on a conceptualization under discussion in Washington. (SERA claimed it had run an independent pilot operation that summer.) It aimed to serve one thousand low-income children and to employ low-income citizens, with a budget request of $977,180. The justification seemed simple: the absence of day care for the large number of mostly black children in this impoverished region. Moreover, research authorized by Henry in 1963 indicated the importance of day care for early child development, a finding consistent with what scholars documented.[79] The well-wrought guiding concepts and the content of the curriculum featured the following: social enrichment; building self-reliance and initiative; intellectual stimulation via problem solving; language and storytelling; motor skills; activities to stimulate; field trips; and health.[80]

The preschool project illustrated the engagement of the professional black community in these "civil rights" ventures. For example, faculty at nearby Coahoma Junior College served as experts for the project. Both the president and the dean sat on the board of COI. Dean Mary Whiteside, in fact, had the important role of teacher training on the grant. She planned to conduct teacher-training institutes for the imagined staff of local, largely unlettered staff members. Her role was entirely logical since the college's general education curriculum provided preparation for one of the few occupations to which African Americans could aspire: school teaching. She had a modest amount of resources at her command to assist, including teachers and facilities. Despite all the risks as a state employee, she had excellent connections to the mobilized grassroots community, traversing boundaries often thought off limits. She had an active membership in the NAACP and founding membership status on the SERA board. Obviously she had the support of her boss, President B. F. McLaurin, himself active in this work.[81]

At this point Henry began to make extensive use of external allies to support his comprehensive program for racial change. He aligned with Walter Reuther, president of the AFL-CIO, who initially made the call for a national poverty program. Henry already knew Reuther well because he was a Democratic Party stalwart significantly involved with civil rights and specifically the movement in Mississippi. What developed out of Reuther's call was an organization known as the Citizens' Crusade Against Poverty, which became first the conduit for the articulation and subsequently the sponsoring agency of community-based programs in Clarksdale (and the rest of Mississippi).[82]

The very ambitious CCAP project came into its own during congressional debate about poverty and the "Great Society." The movement allies in Congress and the administration saw the organization as an alternative to placement of these programs under the auspices of traditional state agencies; for example, segregated school districts in Mississippi. This immediately resonated with Henry, who had plenty of reason to be skeptical of local authorities in Clarksdale. The first-rank civil rights leadership among its members also made the CCAP attractive to Henry. For example, Reuther served as its chair, and Richard Boone, a major figure in the conceptualization of the Community Action Program of the Great Society, served as its executive director.[83] Several others completed this high-powered team with excellent civil rights credentials: Rabbi Richard Hirsch of the Union of Hebrew Congregations occupied the position of secretary; Clyde Ellis, director of the National Rural Electric Cooperative Association that of treasurer; and Martin Luther King Jr. that of a vice president (one of six).[84] Otherwise, the membership reflected virtually every level of the social change, labor, government, and business elite of the country. Religious denominations included the National Council of Churches, Presbyterians, Catholics, and Jews. The president of the National Farmers Union and the National Sharecroppers Fund represented Labor. The National Council of Negro Women (NCNW) represented black women, and the Students for a Democratic Society (SDS) represented the political left. Many of the most significant civil rights leaders occupied positions within the CCAP executive committee: Dorothy Height, A. Philip Randolph, Whitney Young, Roy Wilkins, and Bayard Rustin.[85]

An early CCAP proposal illustrated the ambition of the organization and its Mississippi partners: construction of one hundred community centers ($4.6 million) to enhance the independence of the poor. The overall program budget was estimated at $4.6 million. The board referred to its project as a "Proposal to Establish Nation-wide Training Programs for Community Antipoverty Workers," through which the "poor [would] acquire the capacity to participate more effectively in the democratic process, in community life, and in the present national war on poverty." The proposal included a massive ten-week training period to prepare citizens (840 in 200 to 400 locales) to train grassroots community leaders to assume responsibility for local democratic processes. The CCAP bolstered its legitimacy and commitment by providing the $4,000 planning grant, which landed the state's first Head Start program.[86]

During the same period Henry also illustrated that the scope of his vision for an integrated society was comprehensive, including the improvement of education, acquisition of the franchise, and alleviation of economic disparity. To this end he and the COI developed a proposal for basic education for seasonal Delta sharecroppers and day laborers and those displaced by the mechanization of agriculture. The proposal shows the scope and integrated character of the projects he and his collaborators conceived. It went to the heart of the economic problem confronting African Americans—the lack of the economic resources to acquire goods in the marketplace and the lack of skills to compete for other means of survival. The $1.8 million request sought CAP funds to provide day laborers and sharecroppers the basic education necessary to acquire supplemental employment at the end of the farming season.[87]

The disposal of the proposal also illustrated the challenge of getting funding approved over objections from southern legislators. Though the project eventually received funding, it did not come without an intense battle within Congress and a noisy standoff with Henry. The Mississippi congressional delegation (especially Senator John Stennis) strongly objected to such a project. Whereupon Henry lambasted the senator, offering to answer any of his objections and concerns. Most of all, however, Henry wanted Senator Stennis to go on record to explain his objections. If the reasons were merely the usual racist objections, Henry warned, he would not waste time answering that.[88] There is no known documentation that the senator replied. In June 1967 the project did receive funding for almost $1.7 million, covering Coahoma and thirteen other Delta counties.[89]

Johnson's War on Poverty opened a whole new line of activity for Henry and his cohorts, which further splintered the frayed post-1964 Democratic Convention civil rights coalition in the state. Quickly assessing the program's implications for enhancing their civil rights goals, various elements became skilled at negotiating the maze of bureaucratic requirements to effectively compete for projects. The downside of this, however, is that it drew into bold relief the distinction between Henry's model for going forward and that of the more radical elements in the civil rights coalition. Henry's moderation and willingness to compromise as he sought to engage new partners, preferably local whites with some commitment to integration, further drew him away from the remnants of COFO. Fannie Lou Hamer, for example, accused him of betraying the grassroots people because of his willingness to compromise.[90] In the long run the opportunities afforded by Great Society programs made it inevitable that Henry's tactics significantly diverged from those who perceived reliance upon the grassroots as a singular requirement. At this point, major conflicts became more frequent and open as the coalition competed for grants from OEO.

With the implementation of the War on Poverty, the internal struggles in the Mississippi coalition became more intense. Ironically, the greatest fault line developed over a program concept central to the ideals of virtually all of the movement forces—the Head Start preschool program. Coincident with Clarksdale's development of its local day-care operation, the Child Development Group of Mississippi (CDGM) received a pilot grant and subsequently one of the largest federal grants for a multicounty Head Start program in Mississippi. The CDGM project became a bold experiment at community participation, despite its potential for objections from the ruling white elite. Unlike many proposals from Mississippi and elsewhere, CDGM did not derive from a local government or public school system for very good reasons—the segregationist power structure.[91] Instead, the structure emerged this way because federal bureaucrats sought to locate a credible program outside of state strictures,[92] in order to implement this national program that had the strong personal backing of President Johnson.[93] Moreover, despite the deep commitment of Sargent Shriver, the head of the OEO (where Head Start was housed), he hoped to avoid needlessly butting heads with powerful segregationist elites who objected to any civil rights agenda. As such, a small group of interested individuals, ironically all from outside the state, received the offer to draft the proposal.[94] Later a restoration of some semblance of credibility came when local civil rights forces assumed prominent administrative roles. Subsequently local activists from the otherwise skeptical SNCC organization joined CDGM, and eventually "of the fifteen workers in the top administrative positions, thirteen had civil rights credentials. Eight were women and six were black."[95] This set of partners, which did not include Henry, also did not reflect his evolving interest in developing a partnership composed of a locally based, integrated coalition.

Almost immediately the CDGM became the largest and most visible transfer of federal monies that targeted African Americans, specifically structured to avoid direct control of Mississippi state officials. Gillette described it as follows: "The nation's largest Head Start program was launched in May 1965 in Mississippi, with a grant to establish eighty-five centers in forty-six counties to enroll some 6,000 children. The fact that the grantee was Mary Holmes Junior College, a private, historically black institution, enabled OEO to avoid the governor's veto."[96]

The conflict over the CDGM program involved a complex cast of players set against the traditional state power structure. The state element included the Mississippi senators and congressmen, elected by white voters, who remained unprepared to accept the infusion of federal funds largely designated for blacks. The largely white group of activists in New York and Washington who wrote the proposal became another element in the puzzle problem, since they represented the reviled "outside agitators."[97] Another dynamic resulted when the outside agitators joined movement forces to form a diverse, racially integrated team to administer the federal fund. Significantly, some of the more radical black members of COFO who were especially critical of the Johnson administration became CDGM administrators. These included several SNCC workers who signed on despite skepticism about the project as a threat to grassroots participation.[98] In short the liberal and radical white social science professionals, federal bureaucrats, and leftist COFO activists found CDGM a vehicle for continuing an approach reminiscent of the freedom schools started in 1964.[99]

In short order the project set out on a path that foretold its ultimate destruction and exposed the major fault lines within the civil rights coalition. Senator Stennis used his vast power to undermine the CDGM-administered program, with the outcome that an alternative group emerged to supplant it. The Mississippi congressional legislators joined him as he led the legislative opposition seeking the withdrawal of support for the CDGM program, located at Mount Beulah in the small Hinds County town of Edwards.[100] Two months after the May 1965 funding the senator said he had identified illegalities in the administration of the funds, charging that money had been allocated to support civil rights activity. Subsequently a report presented to the Senate in a memorandum from an investigator, Paul Cotter, laid out many of these charges.[101] Stennis then formally requested that Sargent Shriver "withhold funds from the largest Operation Head Start program in Mississippi." He said that there was "evidence of irregular handling of funds . . . (where) freedom marchers occupied common facilities" (with CDGM); that the staff was paid four times above the normal wage for their positions; and that CDGM staff had participated in civil rights demonstrations while being paid. Congressmen William Colmer and John Bell Williams also railed from Washington against the "illegal" use of funds. Apparently they received "insider" information gathered by State Sovereignty Commission informants. The delegation then used rank power to exact penance. On June 29 "the Senate Appropriations Committee, at the urging of committee member Stennis, sent its staff members to Mississippi to inspect CDGM operations."[102]

The occasion for the senator's ire seems likely to have been a June demonstration in Jackson, apparently organized by the MFDP. According to Dittmer, some CDGM staffers did indeed take part, but all but one had requested a leave from work. The matter was complicated when some of those on leave were arrested and used advances on their CDGM salaries to post bail. It was "in the financial ledger as 'bail fund.'"[103] Stennis exploited this, in effect accusing the staff of being involved in a widespread and intentional scheme for misallocation of public funds.[104] While Henry did not have a formal affiliation with the CDGM organization, he supported it and apparently exerted some effort to save a project fundamental to his broad vision. This led him to make entreaties to OEO to try and save CDGM. He wrote to OEO in late August 1966 saying that the efforts to defund CDGM disturbed him, and he offered to help resolve the problems. He asked for a detailed accounting so that he could use his influence to assist. He had effusive praise for CDGM and its staff, saying they had "done a wonderful job and every effort should be made to permit them to carry on the program that they are so effectively promoting."[105] There is also some indication that Henry worked to get the national NAACP office to support CDGM at the outset of the conflict, notwithstanding the organization's later objections. Gloster Current noted this: "At the recent Mississippi State Conference Board meeting this situation was the subject of a firsthand report by the President [Henry] and others. Included in their reports was information to the effect that NAACP officials, state and national, as soon as information was received that CDGM was in trouble had made representations to OEO urging that it be refunded." The report to which Current referred was actually Henry's keynote address to the state conference of the NAACP, a setting that elevated its importance with statewide delegates present.[106]

Meanwhile, after the summer grant came under such heavy pressure from the powerful Mississippi senator Stennis, the Johnson allies of CDGM in the cabinet and OEO sought to find a formula for compromise. The OEO tried to resolve the Stennis charges by removing CDGM staff from Mount Beulah, by now a well-known training ground for civil rights activists. Since official grantee Mary Holmes College in West Point, Mississippi, 150 miles north of Edwards, had facilities like those at Mount Beulah, the OEO proposed moving the central staff there, an idea that proved unworkable.[107]

Meanwhile, the grantee coalition went on the offensive in the face of the barrage of criticism from the Mississippi delegation. Together with support both within the administration and among other civil rights allies, these forces weighed in to try and save the program. The CDGM sent its own delegation of children to Washington and enlisted the help of allies in Congress and powerful labor supporter Walter Reuther and the CCAP (its original private benefactor).[108] It all had little effect; the program received only a six-month renewal that came early in 1966. The administration now seemed reluctant to institutionalize the CDGM and began to favor some kind of alternative.

Ideas for a parallel structure began to emerge, but not without encouragement from some within the Johnson administration. The group was Mississippi Action for Progress (MAP), an organization that some saw as an ideological alternative to the radical sentiments deemed to be reflected in the CDGM. This group had Henry as a major player, as well as a budding group of local white reformers. Its energies were focused on finding a practical alternative that could be supported, which would allow OEO money to continue to flow to Mississippi for a Head Start program.[109] Henry's involvement and support was of little surprise since Head Start was reflective of an earlier Clarksdale initiative that he clearly wanted to see sustained. Moreover, he remained enthusiastic about Johnson's OEO program, but must surely have known that this new organization stood to isolate and perhaps remove the CDGM. Indeed, for the remnants of the SNCC/MFDP coalition his involvement with MAP further compromised him. It did not help that the national NAACP secretariat subsequently publicly opposed continued CDGM funding in favor of MAP. The secretariat sent a memo to all Mississippi branch presidents indicating that a new biracial group—MAP—had taken over the CDGM Head Start activities because of the organization's failure to "discharge its responsibilities in areas of program, management and fiscal procedures."[110]

Henry likely did not agree with all of the assessment of the national NAACP, but being ever practical he perhaps recognized that he was beaten on the CDGM. He kept his eye trained on the acquisition of federal funds to support the broader goals of civil rights and equity for African Americans. So he insisted that if the CDGM could not be refunded, some way should be found to continue to help the children of Mississippi. He wrote to OEO offering a substantial list of alternative sponsors. The list of twenty-five included many of Henry's longtime associates in the civil rights struggle (and whites in the Delta with whom he had established some rapport). Their affiliations overlapped with the RCNL, the NAACP, COFO, and the MFDP—all organizations in which Henry had leadership roles.[111] Lemann said of this compromise list that "Henry had decided once again to side with the liberal elements in the federal government instead of the forces of independent black radicalism, and in so doing he had saved Sargent Shriver's neck."[112]

This revealed more than just Henry's practicality; it also revealed the importance of his influence in the evolving political situation. By taking a middle ground that isolated the radical forces, and by providing options for consideration, Henry positioned Shriver to advance the president's goals. President Johnson wanted to limit conflict with the powerful Mississippi senators, whose help he needed in maintaining the democratic majority in Congress. He also had a keen awareness of the increased power of blacks in the party coalition, as demonstrated by the MFDP challenge. That led him to direct Shriver to keep Head Start going, but with someone else directing it.[113] Jules Sugarman, associate director of Head Start, said, "Part of the issue here was that, when we reached the decision that we could not continue with CDGM, we were reluctant to see a program disappear from Mississippi altogether, so we actively supported the formation of another group called Mississippi Action for Progress, which would develop programs to replace CDGM." He further commented that much of this rested on the backs of Aaron Henry and Hodding Carter III, "progressives . . . who had a certain reputation."[114]

President Johnson had direct involvement in orchestrating the plan for an alternative group. He and Shriver had entrée to both Henry and Carter. Johnson then brought the two to Washington and invited them to assume responsibility for Head Start, given the inevitable elimination of the CDGM.[115] The president

Aaron Henry and Sargent Shriver, director of Office of Economic Opportunity, circa 1965, Clarksdale, Mississippi. (Courtesy Aaron Henry Papers, Tougaloo College.)

also directed his personal emissaries in Mississippi and at the highest levels of the national NAACP secretariat to secure the cooperation of the two.[116] Both confirmed that the initiative from the White House drew them into what became MAP.[117] Finally, after sparring for a time over turf, CDGM accepted being folded into MAP in late 1967.[118] Some parts of its original territory then began to operate under the new organizational name of Friends of Children of Mississippi.[119]

In many ways, the emergence of MAP concretized a local biracial coalition. The MAP subsequently became a conduit for Head Start funds in the state. It was an elite operation, whose rapid organization and chartering foretold the powers behind its creation. Its leadership hierarchy, all local whites, did reflect sufficient moderation to contravene the old racial order. Hodding Carter, a prominent Greenville journalist, ran a newspaper described as "the main integrationist newspaper in Mississippi"; Leroy Percy, his cross-town neighbor, represented the "benevolent" wealthy planter class; and Owen Cooper, who eventually chaired MAP, represented the wealthy entrepreneurial class as head of a fertilizer corporation in Yazoo City.[120] Interestingly, they all resided in the Delta, an illustration that a cohort of "liberal" whites emerged there.

Following approval of the MAP charter by the governor, the hierarchy appointed an interracial governing board. Henry, of course, gained an appointment, not a surprise since he had links to many of the whites on the board. He also largely picked the other four blacks appointees. They all had very close, longtime links to him and the NAACP. Two of them worked with him in the Regional Council of Negro Leadership: brother-in-law Reverend Merrill Lindsey and James Gilliam (Grand Master of the Masons). Reverend R. L. T. Smith of Jackson and Meridian businessman Charles Young both had longtime active NAACP affiliation. (See Table 3) However, Henry remained critical to the entire operation, as Lemann has shown: "Aaron Henry's participation, though, was the real key to MAP's credibility as a replacement for CDGM: he was the one black leader in Mississippi whose civil rights credentials were so unassailable that no organization he lent his name to could be convincingly portrayed as a mere tool of the white power structure."[121] Henry continued on the MAP board and was an active participant for many years, giving his legacy to a program that stills exists. Like the CDGM, MAP had its own administrative problems. Its first grant proposal too was virtually written in OEO offices in Washington.[122] It received funding for one year at just over $3 million in October 1966. It had a goal of serving 1,500 children in one hundred centers. An audit in August 1967 showed that the program, like the CDGM before, was well above capacity. Only eighty-eight of the proposed one hundred centers existed, but they were serving 4,497 children.[123] MAP continued to receive steady funding until it became the virtual face of Head Start in the state. However, the program remained grossly under-funded, a product of the political limits of OEO and the continued influence of the segregated, white power elite in the state.

TABLE 3
Map Board of Directors

Member	Residence	Office
Owen Cooper	Yazoo City	Chair
Merrill Lindsey*	West Point	Vice Chair
Hodding Carter III	Greenville	
LeRoy P. Percy	Greenville	
Aaron Henry*	Clarksdale	
R. L. T. Smith Sr.*	Jackson	
Charles Young*	Meridian	
James Gilliam*	Clarksdale	
W. P. Davis	Jackson	
Oscar Carr	Clarksdale	
Oliver Emmerich	McComb	
Wilson Evans	Gulfport	

Source: MAP Memo. Benbow. 90:24:92: VI:B:1491. July 20, 1967.

The establishment of MAP had broader implications, though it remained fundamentally a Head Start organization. It cemented a working political "coalition of Delta whites and old-line NAACP leaders," with Henry at the center.[124] They originally met earlier in 1965 and formed a new political group: "The Mississippi Democratic Conference (MDC), [with] the announced purpose of challenging the dominance of the state's Dixiecrats and electing candidates loyal to the national party."[125] Henry, Charles Evers, and twenty-five other African Americans attended this meeting of 125 (dubbed "loyalists") who elected a Jackson County Democratic operative as chair, Robert Oswald. The previously mentioned longtime NAACP leader and Henry confidante from Meridian, Charles Young, served as its elected vice chair. Another NAACP stalwart, R. L. T. Smith of Jackson, held the position of treasurer. Claude Ramsay, the white labor leader, attended and represented a new element that subsequently became a part of the biracial coalition.[126] No designated representatives from the MFDP, SNCC, or CORE appeared at this conference. It seemed clear that Henry sought

to develop new partnerships predicated to a degree on the isolation of these former members of the civil rights coalition. While the MDC itself did not flourish,
the MAP became virtually its incarnation by another name. Its Head Start work
became merely the subtext that presaged its emergence as the political force that
eventually superseded the 1964 MFDP coalition.

Henry gained significantly in his ability to influence the direction of Mississippi political affairs from the emerging coalition. He proved to be among the
least disaffected by the loss at the 1964 party convention. Indeed he seemed invigorated by the promise that loyalty to the national party and compliance with its
agenda would again not be forthcoming from the state's segregationist delegates
at the 1968 convention. While he did not take along the entire COFO coalition
with this view, he did have success in engaging the old NAACP alliance. Losing
some of his traditional black allies never diminished Henry's vision of fundamentally changing the racial order in Mississippi. Consequently, he continued
to make overtures locally across racial lines. Those who joined him on the MAP
board all had to accept his terms for fighting the forces that wished to maintain
segregation. This new coalition merely provided him another vehicle for reaching
for that goal. It ultimately provided the outline of the cast that would propel him
to the leadership of the party organization as events continued toward the next
convention challenge in 1968.

The Henry that emerged at this stage looked like a mature specimen poised
to master the forces around him—challenging, cajoling, and ultimately negotiating an array of resources in a game that no black man had played with such
élan in almost one hundred years in Mississippi. His self-effacing manner belied
a political leader fully confident of his mission and committed to accomplishing
it with integrity. Over time in his social movement and political activism his
tentacles spanned the full range of players with a commitment to changing the
racial system in Mississippi. He pursued those segregationists who opposed him
with a relentless campaign to persuade, expose, or subject them to the full force
of the law. On these commitments he never wavered, enlisting help from a web of
personal connections, political networks, and organizational affiliations. In this part
of his story Henry has been observed marshaling support from the White House,
Congress, the hierarchy of the Democratic Party, and a host of supporters among
civil rights, labor groups to structure a formidable network of allies with which to
confront the segregationists. It meant sometimes taking unpopular practical steps,
but he maintained focus on the broader goal of displacing the segregationists.

Meanwhile, as things evolved within Mississippi society his liberal approach
to developing partnerships afforded him entrée across racial lines when potential
collaborators began to emerge in the mid-1960s. This matched his goal, but he

also possessed a style that allowed him to maximize the benefits of a collaboration of which some others remained suspicious. Despite the risks he took and the skepticism his moves generated, this local coalition and the external resources ultimately moved the agenda for racial change in Mississippi further than it had ever gone before he and Medgar transformed the fledgling NAACP of the 1950s.

CHAPTER SEVEN

Private and Public Entrepreneurship for Redistributive Justice

Addressing African American Socioeconomic Disparities

The transition of the Mississippi movement following the failure of the Mississippi Freedom Democratic Party at the Democratic Party convention of 1964 left many within the coalition dispirited. It affected Henry too, but he remained involved in many projects that reflected his enduring comprehensive vision for African American equality in the state. Although he lost favor with some of his chief partners in the Council of Federated Organizations, both the Mississippi Democratic Conference and Mississippi Action for Progress show how he began to cultivate new partners, to obtain federal resources, and to extend his allies within the Johnson administration and the national party. An extensive and significant variety of other social change projects engaged him as well. These may be broadly categorized as social welfare interests (including psychological and physical health and basic welfare of shelter and employment). Among other things, he challenged the license of the WLBT television station in Jackson; established MINACT, Inc., a corporation that developed Job Corps centers to train youths; helped to build a safety net and infrastructure to meet some of the social welfare needs of blacks and poor people in general: housing, health and elder care, and penal reform. The following discussion illustrates how the elaboration of these projects filled out a very comprehensive civil rights vision, though they did not have the visibility or perceived immediacy as his earlier social protest and voter registration work.

Perhaps no sector promoted the racial order as easily and thoroughly as the media, and WLBT television in the state's major market of Jackson illustrated this in a manner that was unmatched. The station served as a highly visible mouthpiece that promoted the racial system and reinforced its symbols and substance. It also had other powerful roles: authority to determine inappropriate behaviors and to interpret them within the racial system, and authority to obstruct alternative narratives. WLBT specifically used its power to denigrate the civil rights movement by filtering it or appropriating it for segregationist counter mobilization. Blacks, however, had no ability to influence the portrait the local media presented. Consequently Henry joined a team to challenge the license of this NBC affiliate, and eventually succeeded in not just taking its license, but ended up with its ownership as well. The process stretched over many years, but it reveals how Henry spent some of his time as the movement was transitioning.

There are various stories about how Henry became a part of the challenge of the station's license. He made his own best case in June 1964 when he testified before the Federal Communications Commission. He first established himself as a consumer of the station's products and then established that he was a community leadership. He told them that as president of the state NACCP, he spoke on "behalf of many other Negroes who live in the area served by WLBT and WJTV." However, he also revealed how he personally had been victimized by the discriminatory practices of the station. He said that when he was a candidate for governor in 1963 his request to purchase airtime was denied. The station manager allegedly told him that "niggers couldn't buy time."[1] The denial of airtime to himself and others left Henry particularly irate. "The net effect of these practices was that my opportunity to appear and to make my views known was negligible." He also fumed at not being acknowledged or treated as the other candidates for governor. The white candidates, he said, "appeared daily" and were given free airtime. And, "contrary to the allegations in WLBT's statement . . . , no free time was either offered or given to either myself or any persons campaigning in my behalf. In my opinion a station is not operating in the public interest when it denies people validly seeking the community's support an opportunity to appear before the public and request this support."[2]

When Henry learned that Tougaloo College planned to seek removal of the license of the station, it took little effort to get him to sign on. The challenge began when the WLBT license (held by the Lamar Broadcasting Company) came up for regular renewal in March 1964. Dr. Everett Parker of the United Church of Christ (UCC, independently and in the interest of a Mississippi affiliate, Tougaloo College), Aaron Henry, and Reverend R. L. T. Smith made the official challenge to the FCC. Their case seemed very compelling. They alleged that "WLBT discriminated against Negroes in its presentation of news and announcements and in selection of program material; in its presentation of controversial issues, especially in the field of race; in its failure to publicize Negro community affairs; in its failure to use Negro entertainers and other participants in locally originated programs; in its failure to use courtesy titles for Negroes; and in its failure to represent Negroes in the presentation of religious programming."[3]

Indeed the status of WLBT as the leading television source in the state made it the primary authority in visually reinforcing perceptions of black racial inferiority and depravity. No other public or private media entities enjoyed its prominence for the daily display of racial bias. Its general manager Fred Beard, "a particularly outspoken [Citizens'] [C]ouncil member, was often perceived as exceptionally militant in his beliefs and expressions." He permitted the white supremacist Citizens' Council to air its segregationist tract on the station every week.[4] Meanwhile, according to Classen, the station (and others in the state capital) regularly restricted programming whose racial content was deemed inappropriate: "[J]uggling of network resources and programming as well as the consistent omission of integrationist or black perspectives were common, routinized professional practices. And these strategies of preemption, omission, and aggressive neutrality were increasingly practiced."[5]

The case for denial of the license appeared to be straightforward. The licensee presented no evidence that contradicted the claims of Henry and Reverend R. L. T. Smith regarding refusal of airtime. Moreover, considerable documentary evidence existed of discriminatory programming. A television-monitoring group organized under the auspices of the UCC provided a considerable part of the documentation. According to Classen, Dr. Everett Parker, then director of the Office of Communication for the UCC, "hired more than 20 volunteers from around Jackson to secretly monitor local television. For one week these volunteers quietly traded off shifts at a location disclosed only to them, transferring television sets, reel-to-reel audio tape machines, and specially designed log books into a local home."[6] Meanwhile, Henry and Reverend Smith testified of their own experiences in seeking airtime and of the general denial of participation to African Americans. Nine other witnesses joined them during more than two weeks of testimony.[7] Their evidence clearly showed that the station refused to air programs when the racial content was deemed offensive to whites or when programs appeared favorable to racial integration. Dittmer relates one blatant example. During an appearance by civil rights lawyer Thurgood Marshall on NBC "Today," WLBT swiftly commenced a total program blackout, which lasted only through this segment. Service was thereafter magically restored.[8] Evidence showed that such occurrences happened all too frequently.

Moreover, well before this challenge, the licensee already had a long history of problems and complaints. The state NAACP, for example, made complaints in the 1950s that the FCC gave short shrift.[9] However, the UCC attained possession of those records that showed that the FCC had an ongoing struggle with WLBT over compliance regulations, and especially those regarding civil rights. Indeed, the station admitted back in the 1950s that it avoided discussion of civil rights because it wished to prevent advocacy of racial integration, even though it persistently advocated segregation. WLBT justified its use of anti-integration

editorials as somehow reflecting a states rights doctrine, asserting that such doctrine trumped other arguments. Some of its claims stretched credibility or ration-
ality. For example, the station argued that it did make significant use of network
programs, and that in doing so it actually balanced out its advocacy of segregation. It neglected to mention that network programs featuring any racial theme
were systematically blocked. An equally ludicrous argument suggested that the
fairness doctrine did not actually apply to statements or personal attacks made by
politicians upon others.[10]

Despite overwhelming evidence, the FCC, already widely seen as a protector
of the media industry, ruled in favor of the station. The ruling proved a strained
attempt to limit the burden of proof for the station, virtually ignoring the evidence brought by Henry and his partners. While the FCC acknowledged problems in the administration of the license, for example, it did not deem them
sufficient to deny the station a license. Instead it extended WLBT an opportunity
for correction. Therefore in May 1964 Lamar Broadcasting was awarded a temporary one-year extension of its license. The FCC issued this ruling without even
a hearing on the substance of the case, citing what it termed "the urgency of race
relations." Specifically, "given the 'sensitivity' of these relations, it reasoned, the
federal intervention and disruption attendant with hearings would be contrary
to the public interest. As for the complainants, the FCC essentially argued that
they had no standing to make claims."[11] The commission went out of its way to
support the industry it had authority to regulate, even when there was prima facie
evidence of violations of its charter and the law. In this instance, the federal allies
that Henry so assiduously courted failed him.

The complainants made an appeal to the U.S. Court of Appeals, D.C.
Circuit, on August 25. They asked that the FCC decision be voided, and also
sought a hearing on the substance of the complaint. The challengers argued that
the justifications WLBT advanced reflected the ultimate in duplicity—a cleverly
designed project to deny racial integration for blacks, but to maintain racial segregation for whites only. The station aired editorials, for example, with abjectly
racist content, clearly espousing an ideology of segregation. The Citizens' Council
not only aired a weekly program that espoused its segregationist ideology on the
affiliated radio station of WJTV, but Lamar Broadcasting operated a bookstore
on its premises that promoted these views. The challengers lambasted the FCC
claim that members of their group had no standing to bring a complaint, since
all of them were direct or indirect consumers in the market and Henry and Smith
were recognized leaders in Mississippi. In sum they contested the accountability
and integrity of the FCC, accusing it of dereliction of duty.[12]

The appeals court issued a resounding defeat for the FCC in March 1966, and
ordered a full hearing on the merits of the case. The judges presented a withering

indictment of the FCC, calling the station's justifications a strained and strange substitute for a public interest finding. In the first place they demolished the argument that Henry and the other complainants could only seek relief from the FCC in this dispute if they had claims based on economic injury or electrical interference from the station. The court found the private interest reasoning archaic, and demonstrated that everything about the FCC complaint process is predicated on the acknowledgment of average consumer voices as arbiters of the public interest as reflected in television media. The ruling said that "[a] broadcaster seeks and is granted the free and exclusive use of a limited and valuable part of the public domain," which then results in a public obligation that is enforceable under the law.[13] At the same time the court gave no support to the FCC arguments that a hearing on nonrenewal of the WLBT license would have been disruptive of the local media, nor that there was any reason to expect the racist practices to change in one year's time.[14] The ruling left little doubt the court found the claims of the complainants compelling.

Despite the clarity with which the judges spoke, when the demonstrably biased FCC issued the rules for the conduct of the hearing it put the burden of proof almost solely on the complainants.[15] The station, on the contrary, had only to answer whether it had used "good faith" in dealing with racial discrimination.[16] Everett Parker said that the order also was "not in line with usual procedures of the Commission. It has, we think, been drawn to disadvantage us in the hearings." Parker proved prophetic. The FCC ruled that the allegations in the complaint "were neither corroborated nor substantiated at the hearing." The examiner said that "the record demonstrated that WLBT had consistently afforded the right of expression over its facilities to persons of contrasting views." It was then concluded that "the record was devoid of any evidence that WLBT misrepresented," its programming policy with respect to racial issues or that it did not act in good faith in the presentation of programming.[17]

It is worth noting that minority voices within the FCC did get on the record, and that the complainants also filed another appeal. Two commissioners rejected the majority decision, calling it "a classic caricature of the FCC at its worst."[18] Henry and his UCC partners, having found the federal court friendly to their arguments, immediately appealed the latest FCC decision. The appeals court, as expected, reversed the FCC in June 1969. It required that the license of WLBT be vacated "forthwith." Judge Warren Burger again castigated the FCC, saying its decision bore "plain errors in rulings and findings," and was thus "beyond repair."[19]

Even before the final outcome, it seemed quite probable that the license of WLBT would be revoked. In anticipation of that eventuality, Aaron Henry joined a racially integrated coalition of business people who contemplated bidding for the license. Two African American NAACP activists, Charles Evers and Charles Young, joined Henry. Charles Evers's business interests preceded his return to Mississippi following his brother's assassination.[20] Charles Young represented a business family that by self-description was "the oldest black hair care manufacturer [established in 1931 in Meridian] in the world."[21] The white Delta newspaperman Hodding Carter III also joined them. All of them, not coincidentally, had primary leadership roles in the integrated "loyal" coalition of Democrats that Henry pursued to take control of the segregated state Democratic Party.

By 1968, and prior to final resolution of the case, the group formed an unincorporated organization, Civic Communications, Inc. (CCI), and began to develop an application for WLBT. By January 1969 they secured the services of Weyman Walker, a recently fired general manager of WHTV in Meridian, who was linked to stockholder Charles Young. Weyman proved an assiduous advocate for the group, using his contacts and influence to secure potential financial backers for the acquisition of the station. He quickly identified Walter Hall, president of Citizens' Bank of Dickinson, Texas, who expressed an interest in extending a $700,000 line of credit for the corporation and individual letters of credit at $5,000 for each of the stockholders.[22] In March 1969 the group prepared an application for the license, though the ruling vacating the license had not yet been issued. Mind you, CCI stockholder Henry also remained a party to the suit before the federal court. None of this deterred Walker and his stockholders, who appeared confident of being far ahead of other competitors in planning for the inevitable availability of the license.[23]

Notwithstanding the confidence of being ahead of the game, Henry and his partners found themselves spurned because the FCC issued only an interim license to give more time for resolution of questions about ownership. Eventually Communications Improvement, Inc. (CII), a racially integrated group that also had civil rights and communications credentials, received approval to run the operation. Ken Dean, a local white Baptist minister well known as director of the Mississippi Council on Human Relations, led the group.[24] The CII team included prominent representations of both races. Several local African Americans joined the team: Aaron Shirley, a physician; George Owens, president of Tougaloo College; and businesswoman Thelma Sanders. Others included Earle Jones and Jack Shuford, white business owners in the hotel and insurance industry, respectively. The UCC, one of the initiators of the challenge, had good representation as well. Church attorney Earle Moore, and chairman of its Office of Communication, Shelby Rooks, joined Everett Parker. Edward Barrett (former dean of the Journalism School at Columbia University), and James Day (a former president of the New York City station WNET) completed the team.[25] Henry subsequently became a part of this group, and the aims of the CII reflected changes he sought in the local media. For example, sometime after 1972 this nonprofit entity reported that it had significantly altered the nature of the staff. It described a staff configuration more than 40 percent black and over 30 percent female. This included William Dilday, whom the group identified as "the first black general manager of an American television station."[26]

This interim arrangement continued for ten years, longer than Henry imagined, while five groups sparred (and sometimes collaborated) to persuade the FCC administrative law judge to resolve the sale. Over time Henry involved himself with more than one of these groups. The *Washington Post* remarked: "The bewildering scramble for control of the TV license has mixed the social idealism of the civil rights movement with another less noble quality—old fashioned, biracial avarice."[27] In this scramble Henry did not always appear to reflect consistent motives. For example, he and the Civic Communications group expressed willingness to collaborate even with Lamar Broadcasting, the entity from which the original license had been withdrawn. Indeed, several odd partnerships emerged as progressives and segregationists alike tried to team with various blacks using a working assumption that any successful partnership would have to include some blacks. Much of the behavior of many of the potential black partners, on the contrary, seemed driven by their need to find associates who could provide capital. They were drawn, therefore, into conversations with an odd assortment of would-be partners who had the financial wherewithal to attract investors.

William Greider describes what happened after two years of hearings: "The judge chose Dixie National Broadcasting Corporation," another insurance company. That decision caused consternation among the original challengers because this group reflected the composition and ideology of the former-broadcasting owners. "Its dominant stockholders [were] white businessmen with no previous record of championing equal employment practices in their businesses." Three blacks, controlling less than 4 percent of the investment, held stockholder positions on the team.[28] During the ten years of the interminable process of competition, the vision and goals that drew Aaron Henry into the conflict in the first place seemed to be lost. He originally joined with the UCC to integrate the media in Mississippi, and now the WLBT media behemoth attracted a large number of suitors whose commitment to these ideals seemed suspicious at best.

Yet as this competition played out, it strengthened the resolve of Henry and the UCC to exact an agreement that guaranteed black majority ownership in the station. When they adopted that approach, it significantly changed the debate and set off a round of bidding and negotiations that focused on the proportion of minority representation among all bidders for a partnership. Even Dixie Broadcasting tried to woo Henry's group with 25 percent equity as late as May 1978, a marked improvement over its 4 percent in 1973.[29] However, Henry held out. He remained confident not just that he could stop Dixie National, but he also seemed equally certain that holding out for 51 percent ownership was reasonable. He noted, from where "I sit and the echoes that I am hearing it appears that our chances of securing the station improves daily. The main reason for this optimism is that more and more pressure is being put on me and Charles Young daily for a settlement that includes us and leaves everybody else of Civic out."[30]

Henry again proved prescient. In just over a year a merger agreement circulated featuring virtually all of the competitors, with Henry as a principal stockholder and board chairman. The partnership included Dixie National Broadcasting (25 percent), Jackson Television (25 percent), Channel 3 (20 percent), and Civic Communications (30 percent), and, it maintained the corporate name "TV-3." Henry's Civic affiliate acquired the largest share. The agreement specified that blacks would hold a majority ownership of 51 percent (combined stock distributions within the individual groups). African American stockholders secured a guarantee for control of four of the eight board seats. With this Henry met the original goal of securing major policy influence for blacks. In fact, the corporation elected five African American board members, including Charles Young as vice president.[31] A month later the administrative law judge agreed, adding that "[t]he public interest cries out for such an action." Everett Parker called it a "resounding victory over deep-seated racial discrimination and a boon to minorities who have long been second class citizens in television and radio."[32] Henry had come full circle from lockout to absolute control of WLBT.

In his first communication to the employees January 31, 1980, Henry struck his usual conciliatory, humane tone. He praised them, saying, "your efforts have been tremendously helpful." With self-effacement he spoke of joining them, exhorting the workers to "soar to even greater heights." Yet, he reminded them that something fundamental had occurred: "As you know the struggle has been long. Let me remind you that every time a person stands up for an ideal, or acts to improve the lot of others, or strikes out against injustice, he sends forth a tiny ripple of hope."[33] In short, he sought to assure them that in the new environment everyone could thrive so long as all accepted that racial injustice in the practices of this media giant was a thing of the past.

Henry's leadership in WLBT again reflected how his coworkers regarded him. In this battle, as in others, he exhibited a special skill for bringing people together, while maintaining integrity to his vision. His focus and integrity allowed him to navigate amid an array of power brokers, to become a valuable ally and conduit to practically every bidding entity. This allowed him to change the focus of the debate from whether African Americans could acquire sufficient resources to bid, to the terms on which they would have a controlling interest. It came, of course, not without costs. His willingness to collaborate and negotiate with some of these strange bedfellows further eroded his standing with COFO affiliates and others. Both longtime civil rights activists Henry Kirksey and Charles Evers expressed criticism of the operation under Henry's leadership.[34]

Henry went on to have a sustained partnership in WLBT, an entity that significantly changed the landscape of media in Mississippi, even as it remained a very profitable operation. He remained president of the board and a major stockholder in the various iterations of the enterprise for the remainder of his life. His steady hand brought together a variety of interests that kept the station at the forefront of social change and enhanced African American participation in the media in an interracial environment. Henry gave to WLBT what he gave to the often-fractious civil rights activists during his lifetime. As a fount of practicality focused on a vision of social change, he oversaw a television station that brought a revolution with the recruitment and training of the widest range of African Americans in influential positions in media anywhere in the United States.

Yet for a variety of reasons, some related to financial interests, and others to racial sentiments, the struggle continued for black majority control of WLBT. Soon enough fissures in the boardroom played out in reference to a sale option. Henry charged that some of the local white board members sought to undermine him with furtive efforts to sell to interests with no commitment to African American ownership. His attorney, Frank Stimley, confirmed Henry's fears, saying that after "reviewing the bylaws and various other documents associated with TV-3, Inc. . . . I determined that although TV-3, Inc. was majority owned by black stockholders, and although the Board of Directors was fifty percent (50%) comprised of black directors, that the bylaws and other documents which I reviewed, completely negated all black control."[35]

Henry's group subsequently bought out its existing partners and established a new partnership in January 1984. Now he and a new set of black partners acquired 95 percent of the station. The principals in this agreement remained Henry and Charles Young, but now included Frank Melton (then also general manager and one of the Texans who acquired stock during the original sale). They bought out all other interests, except "Yazoo City businessman Owen Cooper . . . [with] 5 percent, representing the only remaining white interest in WLBT."[36]

Yet some aspects of the sale arrangement further tarnished Henry's reputation. While no one argued that he had lost his commitment to his civil rights goals, some of his new partners caused controversy. For example, since the African American partners in his group remained undercapitalized, they had to borrow money to acquire stock. In a series of very complex financial maneuvers it appeared that at least Frank Melton, the new majority black owner, served as a front for white bankers in Texas.[37] Suspicions about his interests grew when he chose to fire the popular manager Dilday and assumed the position himself.[38]

Following the firing another labor dispute led to a boycott of the station, which caused Henry to be severely criticized by some of his previous strongest allies: Drs. Aaron Shirley and Dr. James Anderson (physicians and NAACP activists), Claude Ramsay of the AFL-CIO, and black congressman Bennie Thompson.[39] Lamenting this disagreement, Henry waxed philosophical: "It hurts deeply to be on the opposite side of this group. . . . If standing alone is the punishment for being right, then I say as for me slam the door, don't throw the key away as eventually right will prevail over wrong."[40]

The lack of job opportunities for blacks in Mississippi continued to be another concern for Henry. He began to pay attention to it as soon as he began his pharmacy business and sought to use entrepreneurship to generate job opportunities. Henry became a central figure in the development of the Coahoma Opportunities, Inc., the first local, stable organizational structure through which he sought to influence the depressed welfare situation of blacks. The role that the COI played as the conduit for the Head Start operations in Coahoma has already been described. However, the organization had an even deeper involvement in workforce development and training. Hamlin found its scope and accomplishments unprecedented: "It affected thousands of lives in the early years, through employment and services and because of its holistic approach to combating poverty."[41] Henry invested a considerable amount of time in helping to sustain COI and its broad welfare project in the interval between the 1964 and 1968 Democratic conventions.

The workforce development role of the COI emerged even in its operation of the Head Start program. From conception this preschool program in Coahoma County offered a holistic approach for improving the general welfare of the local black community. The COI contracted with local owners of cars and buses for service as drivers for its programs and hired community people as teacher aides and/or other classroom duties. Many of the latter received training on the job. Similarly, black churches (usually the only option) rented their facilities for operation of Head Start centers, and often received funds to upgrade their properties appropriately. This in turn provided local construction jobs for some of the black unemployed, and renovation of church facilities also improved the community infrastructure.

The COI enjoyed great success in large part because of the availability of federal money from President Johnson's Great Society programs. Henry's influence within the administration and his wide network in Washington proved to be an important resource in generating these funding opportunities. The first major COI workforce program for seasonal Delta workers resulted because of Henry's mastery of the federal program (3B) in the Department of Agriculture. Typical of his mode of operation in pulling strings Washington he called upon the important operational bureaucrats in the Department of Agriculture, lobbied Roy Wilkins of the NAACP, and made a direct entreaty to the president.[42] He addressed a letter to President Johnson (and released its contents to the press) asking him to release unused state and federal property for use as shelter; to make surplus food available to these workers; and to establish the 3B program in every county in the Delta area. Henry criticized the president for yielding to presumed pressure from Senator John Stennis in delaying action on the COI proposal already at OEO.[43] The proposal eventually received approval, providing $3.4 million to twelve counties in the Delta.[44] It became only the first of many grants to COI that targeted the welfare part of Henry's vision. A summary report of its proceeds from 1965 to 1969 documented close to $12 million for programs including development of neighborhood centers and credit unions, adult education, legal aid, early childhood development, and emergency food and medical services. A corps of unemployed African Americans, many of them women, acquired some degree of financial independence from working in these programs.[45]

The ideas that Henry and his COI partners worked out in this organization lay the seeds for continuously successful efforts in receipt of federal funds to underwrite workforce development programs. An example of one large outfit on which Henry collaborated (he served as member of the board) is the Systematic Training and Redevelopment, Inc. (STAR). The Catholic Diocese of Natchez-Jackson, another part of Henry's local network of sympathetic collaborators, sponsored this manpower training program. Father Joseph Brunini, who eventually became bishop of the diocese, led the STAR.[46] Not everything was rosy in this collaboration, however. Eventually Henry, as a board member, led an NAACP investigation charging discriminatory operation of the program. Nevertheless, the STAR received significant OEO funding that Henry's influence and good name help to secure. At the time of the NAACP investigation in 1970 the STAR operated sixteen centers across the state that provided literacy and job training.[47]

The Neighborhood Youth Corps is another early example of a COI program through which Clarksdale leaders tried to respond to workforce needs of young people in their own environs. This in-school work program for fourteen- to twenty-one-year-olds provided a minimum wage for these young workers. A second phase of it occurred in summer when participants could receive an eight-week summer job. A complementary component dedicated to school dropouts helped them to earn some income as they made an effort to complete the GED.[48]

However, no workforce development project on which Henry worked exceeded the Job Corps in importance. This OEO program, inaugurated in 1964, responded to the chronic conditions of blacks in the labor market: those less likely to be employed, more likely to be underemployed, and more likely to be concentrated in unskilled jobs.[49] The government defined Job Corps as a "comprehensive residential, education and job training program for such at-risk youth." It offered a holistic approach to the elimination of a broad range of barriers to labor market access—job training, educational qualifications, and access to support for job counseling and placement. In operation the program aimed to create a residential environment akin to boot camp. Recruits lived in dormitory-like settings to facilitate ready access to program activity. The setting also allowed intensive focus on skills preparation, GED classes, and access to counseling and placement staffs. Enrollees had the added incentive of being paid a stipend.[50]

Henry felt vindication for his earlier ideas along these lines, which he began thinking about when SERA and COI received the grant to train displaced farmworkers in the Mississippi Delta in 1966. Now Job Corps provided a broader opportunity by offering contracts to local entities willing to mount programs. What Henry had learned in workforce programs in the mid- to late 1960s gave him sufficient knowledge and a network to make a bid for Job Corps programs in Mississippi. By the late 1970s he had formed a working team to compete for Job Corps contracts, most of which at the time went to a small number of well-financed partnerships.[51] Henry had to find partners who had capital or who were willing to finance a Job Corps bid that empowered minority owners.[52] Jackson physician Robert Smith (dubbed the doctor to the civil rights movement), an early partner on the WLBT team, joined him. The other three partners, two of them African Americans, came from Henry's vast personal network. The three already had experience in the Job Corps program—Booker T. Jones, Jimmie Lee McNeal, and Glen Jent. The African Americans, Jones and McNeal, had Mississippi roots, and Jent knew Jones from their previous employment at a Kentucky Job Corps site.[53]

In February 1978 Henry and these partners organized a corporate structure under the name of MINACT, Inc. to seek funding to train young people for the workforce. The corporation received immediate certification as a business corporation in Mississippi. Among other things, the corporation would "perform all manner of contracts, agreements and obligations for the provision of programs and projects of education, training, counseling, research and other activities and services." To achieve these ends it would "apply for, purchase, receive, acquire, assign, and enjoy any license, power, authority, franchise, concession, right or privilege that any government or authority, Federal, State, or local, or any corporation, person or other legal entity may be empowered to enact." In reality the express aim was to seek Job Corps contracts.[54]

Henry remained primarily interested in making Job Corps accessible to blacks in Mississippi, but it took some time to realize that goal. The first Job Corps contract that MINACT acquired was in Kentucky where several of the partners had contacts at the predominantly black Knoxville College. The corporation also

negotiated a contract for several of its stockholders to run the food service operation of the college. The proceeds from that arrangement would then be used to
repay a $10,000 loan advanced to the company.[55] In some measure this filled a
gap in capital when MINACT could not succeed in acquiring financial backing
from two Jackson, Mississippi, banks (Fidelity and Mississippi Banks).[56]

The MINACT had ambitions for a large-scale, profit-making operation far
beyond the scope of Job Corps. In minutes of its first year, references appeared
about many Job Corps and other contracts for which the partners wanted to
compete. The group aggressively pursued these options. Henry and Jent visited
Minnesota as early as March 18, 1978, where a "Mr. Brent Lewis of the local
Manpower Administration in St. Paul showed them around the city and arranged
a complete tour of the facility." Later they competed for federal training grants
in Appalachia; for contracts with local lawyers for consulting services; for management of apartment complexes in Maryland; and for numerous Job Corps
Centers around the country (Dennison, Iowa; Batesville, Mississippi; Woodstock,
Maryland; St. Paul, Minnesota; and St. Louis, Missouri).[57]

However, in the absence of sufficient capital, MINACT soon turned its focus
to the Small Business Administration (SBA) and its 8(a) program that offered set-
asides for projects that enhanced the education and training of minority populations. As a minority operation, MINACT seemed especially encouraged because
the Labor Department held its regional offices accountable for involvement of
minority firms by requiring documentation prior to approval of funds. As incentive the department provided "up to ten additional evaluation points for subcon-
tracting portions of Job Corps Center operations to SBA 8(a) firms."[58]

Meanwhile, even attaining 8(a) status proved challenging for minority firms.
The initial MINACT application received quick rejection because its 51 percent
minority ownership was composed of multiple stockholders. In the interpretation
of the rule by the Atlanta Regional Office of the SBA the 51 percent had to be
held by a single board member. Henry tried to meet the SBA objection by having
himself and Dr. Robert Smith personally withdraw their stock, after which they
resubmitted the application with Booker T. Jones, MINACT president, assuming
the 51 percent ownership. That did not work, either, and the negotiations for 8(a)
status continued well into 1979.[59]

The MINACT application succeeded only after Henry turned the matter
into a civil rights issue. He looked for help among his substantial network in the
administration. Henry sent letters to various officials pleading his case, a plea he
elevated by strategically distributing copy of his claims to Washington bureau
heads and the White House. In June 1979 he sent a strongly worded letter seeking reconsideration to William Clement at the SBA. He copied the correspondence to Secretary of Labor Ray Marshall and his African American assistant

secretary Ernie Green and others.[60] He continued the barrage of letters through November, when he contacted Hamilton Jordan, assistant to President Carter, and James Dyke, special assistant to the vice president for domestic policy.[61] The pressure worked. In January and February, Louis Martin, an African American special assistant to the president, and Stuart Eisenstadt, assistant to the president for domestic affairs, wrote Henry indicating their delight that the matter had been resolved. The latter said the approval was "well deserved."[62]

In time MINACT took off, acquiring Job Corps contracts all over the country with significant profits for the partners. It became and remains a major player in the Job Corps business and has from time to time expanded into other areas. Its success is indicated by how quickly it exceeded its early goal. In late 1968 it had a goal to acquire only one additional center in each of the next four years. Soon after the initial contract in Knoxville, the first Job Corps Center (JCC) got underway (1980) in the Mississippi Delta—at Batesville, a town about forty miles east of Clarksdale. Before the end of the second year a center in St. Louis, Missouri, became the third acquisition.[63]

Finally, the program made investments from its proceeds to repay some of its loans and to secure letters of credit from major financial institutions. By 1981, MINACT began planning for the construction of its own headquarters building in Jackson, and by the end of the year had assets of almost $650,000 and liabilities of $200,000.[64] Moreover, it continued aggressive pursuit of all manner of opportunities, among them ventures with the federal government, states, and at least one foreign government (Nigeria). Here are just some examples: In 1980 it proposed a three-story housing complex for forty-five units for the elderly in Baltimore, Maryland.[65] Bids followed on a then ineffective JCC in Columbus, Indiana, and on a joint venture in Kentucky to acquire and manage a new center. Meanwhile, active discussions ensued about prospective projects in Alabama, Kentucky, Iowa, and Florida, and multiple sites in Michigan and Mississippi. In addition to JCCs, project options included manpower management consultancies, cable television management, Department of Energy grants, and fertilizer exports to Nigeria. While not all of these worked out, their mere pursuit gave an indication of the aspiration.[66]

The expansion of the MINACT Corporation continued all over the country to the end of Henry's life. While little information about its placement record is available, some measure of success is the continued ability to attract contracts. In 2009 eight centers existed that served 2,900 participants. However, by its self-description the organization is much more. "It has grown from a small company operating one Job Corps Center to the largest minority owned company in the Job Corps business with over 1,100 employees. With key partners the company is involved in providing support services in the auto manufacturing industry."[67]

These centers have evolved into fairly institutionalized operations in most of their majority minority communities. Almost every center provides the following capacity-building training: business clerical, culinary arts, carpentry, and building maintenance. About half of them offer house painting, welding, and brick masonry. A few offer retail sales, auto repair technicians, and advanced career training for those with appropriate skills. Fewer still offer electronics.[68]

Henry's ideas initially articulated in Clarksdale have remained defining elements of MINACT. Its leadership has also remained centered in Mississippi, and headquartered in Jackson. In all of the organization's literature homage is paid to Henry as the principal founding member. He served as chairman of the board virtually from the founding until his death. Moreover, many of the other principals, also recruited in Mississippi, maintain important roles, especially Dr. Robert Smith.[69] The MINACT remains an excellent illustration of the range of Henry activities as he worked through the loss of momentum following the 1964 convention. It also demonstrated how tenacious he remained despite the incremental nature of the changes he pursued.

Perhaps as a product of being involved in the health care industry, Henry also had deep concern for social welfare disparities. He worked tirelessly to attain resource access and reallocation of welfare benefits for the most vulnerable African Americans and others similarly situated. He most consistently exerted energy on gaining equal access to housing and health care, attaining prison reform, and making provisions for the elderly population. Again, this concern arose at the start of his activism in Clarksdale in the late 1950s, and remained an enduring feature of his broad vision.

Concern for the elderly seemed a logical project for Henry. In following the vision for his grand civil rights project, he placed a significant emphasis on the utilization of public support to provide a safety net for those less fortunate because of discrimination and racial exclusion. He saw the elderly African American population as one of the most vulnerable. Henry honed these ideas in the mid-1960s within the COI. As a health professional he also had a keen awareness of the longstanding conversation, going back to the New Deal days, about a national health insurance program. He saw this as possibly the best way to sufficiently respond to the needs of the elderly population he saw around him daily in the Delta. As such Henry inserted himself early in this debate by lobbying for the development of the Medicare program, which passed in 1966.

He and Bennie Gooden, his chief COI partner, lay the groundwork early on for intervening in the local problems of the black elderly. They developed a major proposal to build low-rent housing for this population perhaps as early as 1967.[70] Henry could help advance proposals because he had good connections in the relatively new Department of Housing and Urban Development (HUD), and in

Agriculture where many of these programs resided originally. For example, agriculture secretary Orville Freeman appointed Henry to serve on the department's advisory board as early as 1965.[71] Yet, after several years of promising negotiations Bennie Gooden received the unexpected news that the 1967 project did not get approved due to a lack of funding. The surprise decision left him in disbelief; negotiations had been going so well that local land had already been purchased for the project. Gooden and Henry did not dawdle. They had done their homework and knew that a supplementary appropriation had been authorized. Not missing a beat, the pair immediately requested funds from that pot of money. Gooden asked the black assistant secretary Samuel Jackson, a man well known to them, to assist in making this possible. Eventually, they prevailed and the first housing was built in 1970.[72] Meanwhile, programs serving some of the food and nutrition needs of the elderly had been underway since 1968 in three centers supported by grants received by STAR.[73]

Henry subsequently acquired unparalleled voice and advocacy in influencing federal policy for the black elderly. He observed that this population suffered virtually all of the same problems of social discrimination and economic dislocation as others, except that their situation often seemed worse and their story virtually hidden. Many had been employed in the informal service sector (as cooks, maids, janitors, etc.), or as seasonal rural agricultural laborers and tenant farmers. These jobs more often than not offered no access to the Social Security retirement system. He told this story repeatedly at the White House, to conferences on the elderly, and to multiple committees of Congress from the late 1960s until his death. Here is how he rendered it before Congress in 1976: "In 1973, 37 percent of all blacks over 65 years of age and older were in poverty, which was two and one-half times greater than the proportion of elderly whites in poverty." He said their housing situation was no better: "For example, 60.5 percent of all homes owned by husband and wife aged black families were valued at less than $10,000 according to the 1970 census, while only 28.8 per cent of the houses owned by aged whites husband-wife families were valued at less than $10,000."[74]

Henry not only spoke out forcefully on these issues, he gave considerable leadership to a variety of agencies created to assist the black elderly and to formulate public policy. Most agencies existed, some created by statute, at the national level. The following is a list of key early organizations to which he gave leadership. In the late 1960s he became associated with several rural coalitions that advocated for elderly blacks, especially in the Mississippi Delta. He served on the Boards of the Rural Housing Alliance and the Coalition of Rural America[75] and became a founder of the National Caucus on Black Aged (NCBA), organized in 1970. Throughout the 1970s he played a major role in the National Advocacy Network of the Black Elderly and Elderly Housing, Inc. (a Mississippi organization). In the late 1980s several important federal appointments came: he was nominated to the Federal Council on Aging and also served on the Ad Hoc Leadership Council of Aging Organizations as detailed below.

Perhaps the most visible of the organizations with which Henry affiliated is the NCBA, dedicated exclusively to fending for the black elderly. Its formation in 1970 was *ad hoc*, initiated in anticipation of a 1971 White House–sponsored conference on the aged. The NCBA set out to assure that President Nixon's conference would address the particular needs of black seniors.[76] Henry served as chair of the important Committee on Physical and Mental Health of the Black Aged at the NCBA founding meeting. It established a charge to develop an agenda for a "National Policy on Black Aged," then estimated to be 1.4 million.

The committee issued its report in November 1971, just prior to the White House meeting. The substantive document both staked out a philosophical position and formulated a policy agenda. According to the report black elders lacked housing, education, medical benefits, and social services due to discrimination based on "white supremacy and social Darwinism."[77] It cited data that Henry used over and over in various congressional hearings: life expectancy, for example, was headed in the wrong direction—declining "a full year from 61.1 to 60.1" in the eight-year period 1960–1968, while there was a "greater incidence of stroke, heart disease, mental disability and hypertension than found in the white population; and, there were fewer visits to physicians than the general population."[78]

Under Henry's leadership and guidance the committee suggested a model akin to the notion of a comprehensive social and health care system identified with the Medical Committee for Human Rights (MCHR) in Mississippi and in urban communities in the 1960s.[79] The theory rested on a concept that sought the systematic and simultaneous treatment of the causes and symptoms of the human disparity in the black elderly population. Henry and his RCNL colleagues had given thought to the same notion back in the 1950s. Now he led the NCBA committee in the elaboration of a set of fundamental principles designed for such a broad health system. He first suggested that health services should not just be within the preserve of physicians and nurses (the "traditional health team"). He described this old approach as isolated, instead seeking "a continuous program designed to maintain health with emphasis on prevention, education, treatment and rehabilitation." He saw it as the province of "all who work together for the health of the people." The vision anticipated bringing together the expertise of health personnel and related family experts to uncover the interrelatedness of the problems confronting the elderly.[80] Despite this conceptualization of a comprehensive health care system, the committee recommendations nevertheless focused fairly exclusively on Medicare, no doubt becuase the expansion of Medicare constituted an ongoing topical debate at the time. The committee also argued for inclusion of home and long-term care, certain services for dental and eye care, and the elimination of deductibles and cost-sharing arrangements.[81]

Henry served as a delegate at the White House conference that followed in 1971. The four thousand delegates at the conference included 20 percent minority representation.[82] While not the first such conference, it was the first since passage of legislation such as Medicare and Medicaid and the first being hosted by President Nixon. The new president supported the conference, made a substantive speech laying out some reform proposals, and appointed Dr. Arthur Flemming (Eisenhower's secretary of health, education and welfare) as a senior adviser for the elderly.[83] While Nixon supported a number of items for which the NCBA lobbied, it seemed clear that the president's priority was the elderly in general.[84] Therefore the presence of the caucus proved important for getting its imprint on the nearly two hundred recommendations that delegates eventually produced. For Henry, it also gave him one more avenue of access to the White House.

Henry's influence is perhaps best reflected in his ability to lobby policymakers, gleaned from some of the national testimonies he gave on the special problems of the black elderly. His testimony to the Presidential Public Forum on Domestic Policy in 1975, during the Gerald Ford administration, is typical. After he recited the appalling statistics about the conditions of the African American elderly, he launched into a critique of the Ford administration's "program consolidation and budget reduction" proposal. He told the audience (including Vice President Nelson Rockefeller) that a retrenchment was already underway because while the "total federal budgets have gone up sharply, many programs for the aging have either been cut back or eliminated." Cases in point were the 1975 consolidation of the Comprehensive Employment and Training and the Older Americans Acts, which "had the net effect of eliminating federally administered employment programs for the 45 to 54 year old unemployed low-income workers."

He also rejected revenue sharing, a policy that redirected funding for many of these programs to city and local governments that had no interest in the aged poor.[85] He exhorted this forum to "list as a national priority the rights for Americans to age naturally . . . with the knowledge that their investment in this country will not run out when they need it the most."[86] In a similar forum in 1979 organized by President Carter, Henry made an equally scathing critique of policy for the elderly. He said that declining access to programs designed for elders (e.g., food stamps) resulted because administrators seemed more concerned with the mechanics of program rule application than delivering services.[87] He also did not absolve Congress, finishing his testimony to a House Committee that summer with the following: "I would like to end this statement by reminding us that more than 40 years ago president Roosevelt said that, 'one third of the nation was ill-clothed, ill-housed and ill-fed.' He could make the same statement today about the black aged."[88] He then called "on the Congress to order the Commission on Civil Rights to undertake a comprehensive study of racial discrimination in services, in employment, and in contracts in all programs and activities receiving federal financial assistance which [a]ffect older persons."[89]

The NCBA became an important vehicle for Henry, and he proved a diligent chairman and very effective advocate. In the early days he helped to anchor and institutionalize the NCBA, showing its board members and supporters how to negotiate the thicket of Washington politics and use networks for effective lobbying. For example, he described how he did this via his ongoing and deep relationship with cabinet secretary Joseph Califano and two of his assistants. One of these was Arthur Flemming, whom he had known in both his capacity as an assistant to President Nixon and as chairman of the United States Commission on Civil Rights.[90] He showed similar connections in the Mississippi Council on Aging that allowed him to establish contacts with a variety of other national aging organizations, including the Catholic bishops of the United States. He then discussed the importance of cross-referencing contacts from related experiences. Finally he shared the benefits gained from earlier Clarksdale projects by searching bureaucratic offices and their implementation regulations (with Bennie Gooden of COI).[91]

In 1975 the focus on housing finally resulted in a funded project. Henry's long advocacy attained success when the USDA area director in Jackson requested a preliminary proposal for Delta housing. In July that year Henry sent a detailed description for a substantial construction in five Mississippi Delta counties—Coahoma, Desoto, Tunica, Quitman, and Tallahatchie. Coahoma County would get 66 units of one- and two-bedroom apartments, while 50 would go to Clarksdale. The entire project called for 232 units. Henry told the USDA that he had a plan ready for mixed financing from private and FHA sources, and added some details of the progress of discussions about terms with the latter. He identified the architectural firm in California that had been secured, named an experienced African American contractor for the work, and identified the experienced management group that would operate the facilities. Moreover, he indicated that a social service package (transportation, health, recreation, leisure time, and counseling for elderly and handicapped) was also being designed, but not included within the preliminary proposal at hand.[92]

Henry had other concerns beyond housing for the elderly. He had equal passion about the general housing needs of poor and impoverished African Americans across the Delta. Therefore, when he appeared before the U.S. Senate

Select Committee on Nutrition and Human Needs in 1970 he referred to the lack of government action as "abdication" of responsibility for more than one-half of the nation's poor who lived in rural areas. He referred to two-thirds of their housing as substandard, or what he called "concentration camps for the poor."[93] In Mississippi an additional problem needed to be attended: a ban on many federal programs targeting the poor and blacks. Henry railed that this "is not federalism . . . but feudalism when the state government of Mississippi tells local government[s] that they can't participate in a national program like Urban Renewal unless they enact a specific ordinance to offset a general state-wide ban."[94]

Therefore, he helped form a number of economic development organizations that focused on the development of low-income housing. Not all of the organizations had success in getting projects off the ground. However, it is revealing to see the number of housing organizations he helped to create and/or in which he participated from 1965 to 1970. Among them are the Delta Opportunities Corporation; the Progressive Association for Economic Development and Community Improvement; the Friendship Community Federal Credit Union; the Multi-Racial Corporation; and the Rural Housing Alliance.[95] The Progressive Association for Economic Development and Community Improvement operated from a Philadelphia, Pennsylvania, organization but had a Clarksdale affiliate (1970). It had an aim to both build houses and to improve the physical environment in the Delta.[96] The Friendship Community Federal Credit Union (COI) organized in 1965 and operated "as part of the demonstration grant designed to provide low-cost lending to members . . . while promoting self-help and offering family and personal financial counseling as part of financial education."[97] Henry organized the Multi-Racial Corporation with Robert Clark (Mississippi's first state legislator since Reconstruction) to redevelop the parts of Mississippi, Louisiana, and Alabama that had been devastated by Hurricane Camille in 1969.[98] The Rural Housing Alliance developed from an organizational tie that Henry cultivated through his work with Walter Reuther and labor organizers. He became an active board member of the Alliance and often spoke to its conferences.[99]

He brought his voice of activism to virtually all of the housing organizations to which he maintained attachments. In the end through his ingenuity and energy Clarksdale and the surrounding Delta became virtual conduits for housing and other social and economic programs. In short, he had substantial influence on the availability of housing for the African American poor and displaced families in the Delta. Driving around several of the counties in and about Clarksdale to this day one sees the visible evidence of public housing in many towns.

As a health care professional he naturally gravitated toward advocacy for issues related to health. He began to lay the groundwork for the expansion of health care to the Mississippi Delta when he opened his Fourth Street Drugstore. It will be recalled that he partially established his pharmacy by collaborating with the sparse number of black medical professionals in and around Clarksdale. Dr. T. R. M. Howard, who, like Henry, also combined his medical profession with political activism, had organized a regional health organization in nearby Mound Bayou. Henry learned a great deal from collaboration with Howard, especially seeing the ambition of the latter to establish a medical facility that responded to a comprehensive range of health and related social conditions of his Delta patrons.[100] Although pressure from segregationists forced Dr. Howard to flee Mississippi before complete implementation of the project, Henry remained to see through the realization of a similar dream. This occurred in a piecemeal and halting process, following the election of President Johnson and passage of his Great Society initiative. However, in Clarksdale elements of a vision for comprehensive health, partly influenced by Henry's thinking, accompanied the projects of the SERA and the COI. Quite early on he perceived that the depressed nature of the community resulted from the intersection of poor health care and social deficits. Subsequently the first SERA award for a Clarksdale Head Start program also provided modest medical, dental, and nutrition services. Henry's "national influence and authority" within the OEO and the Democratic Party made him perhaps the single most important resource in getting the funding approved.[101]

Meanwhile, Henry's statewide leadership and visibility situated him to be on the ground floor as the concept of comprehensive health took hold among state activists and allies. For example, he became attached to the labor movement network, which had similar aspirations for workers. Henry helped them to exploit links to one of his closest external labor allies, national labor leader Walter Reuther.[102] Subsequently his conversance with these ideas and experience as a health care professional led him to support efforts to develop a medical arm of the civil rights movement in 1964. These efforts eventually resulted in a facsimile construct of a comprehensive health system resting on the needs of poor Mississippians. Its organizational form became the Medical Committee for Human Rights, a group of largely white physicians from the North. It defined its original purpose in Mississippi as looking after the health of movement activists. However, their experiences on the ground led to more—offering treatment to the poor and opening discussions that gave voice to a comprehensive health model.[103]

The Mississippi's racial system, of course, dictated the development of an organization like the MCHR; few local physicians agreed to treat civil rights activists, and the minuscule number of available black physicians could hardly handle the problem. One of them, Dr. Robert Smith of Jackson, did see movement patients though he increasingly found himself stretched. He subsequently helped get MCHR off the ground. With the impending arrival of the white volunteers for the summer of 1964, Smith tapped into his own network of medical professionals in New York City and, with the approval of Aaron Henry and Bob Moses, arranged to get some to volunteer to come to the state in the summer.[104] From this small start, the MCHU emerged and became an important contributor in the Mississippi civil rights movement. Four sites received teams that summer, and Henry saw to it that Clarksdale acquired one of them. From this modest beginning, and on the strength of the experiential learning and thinking of local, activist health professionals like Robert Smith and Aaron Shirley, the concept of health care encompassing the broadest range of socioeconomic and psychological factors began to emerge. The MCHR implemented some of the earliest models along these lines in Mississippi. Dittmer called this "the most significant and enduring achievement in the field of health care to come out of the civil-rights years."[105] The concept had great appeal to Henry insofar as it resonated with his own thinking about holistic patient care.

As a health care provider responsiveness to health care problems remained a high priority for Henry. This first became evident in the way he developed his pharmacy practice. He designed it to make medicines available to his isolated, segregated Delta community. Even as he focused intensively on problems of the elderly or housing, he always worked health into the package. In the process he became both an expert and a leader in the field, and these provided him an unusual platform. Early in his pharmacy career, he served as president of the National Pharmaceutical Association from 1962 to 1964.[106] Later he augmented his access to national levers of powers with influence within the general health establishment in Mississippi as things opened up in the 1970s and 1980s. He served both on the Statewide Health Coordinating Council and the State Health Planning and Development Agency.[107]

However, perhaps the best example of his thinking about health and racial disparity is reflected in the Aaron Henry Community Health Center, which he helped develop in Clarksdale. The center incorporated in 1979 and received funding for one year by HEW for $346,239. It began operation in 1980 as a nonprofit entity, the culmination of a body of ideas percolating since the 1960s. Henry and partners in the COI made a number of proposals with health components through the years, some of which acquired funding, and within their limits proved quite effective. However, with great stimulus from the work of the MCHR, the concept of comprehensive health gradually gained traction within OEO by 1970. For example, as early as 1967 a preventive health care program received funding in Mound Bayou. Tufts University served as the grantee; Jack Geiger, a medical rights activist, led the project. The closeness of the Tufts–Delta Health Center to Clarksdale put it within Henry's Delta bailiwick, coincidentally a place with some resonance to the earlier ambitions of Dr. T. R. M. Howard.

Following the Mound Bayou project, Dr. Aaron Shirley founded the Jackson-Hinds Comprehensive Health Center in 1970. As Dr. Shirley had been employed at the Mound Bayou center, he obviously drew upon the model for his operation in Jackson.[108]

The Aaron Henry Community Health Center developed in the same mold as Jackson-Hinds. Henry and his prime movers in the black elite attached to the COI led this effort. Indeed, the center leased property from the GHS partnership (composed of Bennie Gooden, Aaron Henry, and Reuben Smith, all of Clarksdale).[109] The failed original application for over a million dollars sought support for five adjacent counties: Coahoma, Quitman, Tallahatchie, Tate, and Panola.[110] A later proposal including only Coahoma County received funding for comprehensive and preventive care services. The proposal made a strong case for the Delta location and copiously documented that it remained a "medically underserved area with morbidity and mortality rates significantly above the national average." Moreover, the proposal took existing services into account and specified how these would be coordinated with the new medical facility; for example, contract services for certain laboratory needs.[111] The funded proposal supported ten staff: administrator, billing clerk/cashier, secretary/receptionist, janitor, two physicians, midlevel practitioner, nurse's aide, medical record clerk, and a social/outreach worker.[112] Things progressed quickly: complete architectural designs arrived in November, with occupancy scheduled to begin in April 1981.[113]

The health center fundamentally and instantaneously altered health care accessibility for African Americans in the north Delta. It brought basic health care within the reach of many in Coahoma and some surrounding counties for the first time. It eliminated the long waits and differential service typical in segregated waiting rooms, where services could also simply be denied. At the same time the center's sliding fee scale significantly reduced the cost of services. The most innovative part about the comprehensive services is how it aimed at the client across the life span. It offered "General medical services, including pediatrics, internal medicine, prenatal care, family planning, physical examinations, minor office surgery, immunizations, pap smears, sickle cell screening, diagnostic x-ray and laboratory, EKGs, health education and counseling, nutrition counseling, preventive and restorative dentistry, and prescriptions."[114]

The Aaron Henry Center continues today with a much-expanded staff and range of activities. Moreover, it is a part of a complex of linked state and national institutions, supported by an array of public and private funds. In March 1998 executive director Aurelia Jones-Taylor described how the project evolved over the years. The original facility soon outgrew demand, and moved to a new location in 1990. Its budget grew from under $500,000 to a multimillion-dollar operation, employing a staff exceeding the original by more than tenfold. Its new pediatric program was added in 1991, an affiliation with the Mississippi Children's Health Project, a project illustrating how collaborative arrangements expanded the range of the operation at the local level. That collaborative relationship also brought the Henry Center into an affiliation with the New York State Children's Health Project. As a result the center acquired a mobile unit that began to attract private foundation support. Otherwise, the expanded center included two school-based clinics and had satellite facilities located at Friars Point and Tunica, nearby Delta towns. The professional staff also expanded considerably by 1998. There are now four primary care physicians, three nurse practitioners, and three social workers. This staff configuration allows the center to also operate a large-scale health education outreach program. According to Jones-Taylor, the clinics are fielding 34,000 encounters with over 10,000 users annually. It has become a health care destination for a significant part of the northwest Delta.[115]

Yet, the health component remained merely part of other associated functions of the Aaron Henry Community Health Center. Its fuller actualization came as close as anything else to Henry's broad vision to create a comprehensive base for the development of the impoverished and previously excluded community. As the health center evolved, it linked a number of key components in the life cycle of blacks in the Delta. As a comprehensive health center, the operation encountered families over the span of their development: birth of children in the pediatric program and primary care for husbands, wives, and extended family members. Access to families through the full life cycle provided opportunities for health care professionals to somewhat alter the cycle of poverty.

This web of community links provided vital information and ultimately support for employment, training, and a host of other family needs. The following example about the linkage between health care and transportation is illustrative. Medical personnel soon noticed irregularity on the part of many clients in keeping medical appointments. An investigation of this recurring problem revealed that most clients did not own vehicles and had to hire someone to bring them to the site. Oftentimes the availability of transportation did not match the patients needs. This led the center to seek alternative means for getting clients to the services as needed. The solution found, also consistent with the holistic model of community development, anyhow, required the center to develop its own transportation service.

Therefore, in 1990 the center developed the Delta Area Rural Transit System (DARTS), to provide transportation to meet a broad range of medical and other needs in the area. It began with "two minivans purchased with funds from the federal Department of Health and Human Services."[116] However, the idea of providing transportation to medical services rapidly expanded, and soon it became available for other family needs. Now 80 percent of the DARTS traffic is not to medical facilities, but to jobs. An array of buses and minivans form a fleet covering a seven-city area, within an eighty-five-mile radius of Clarksdale. The fleet makes 120,000 trips per year. Together with its medical routes, DARTS has become a fee-based system with fixed routes for transportation to places of employment.

The scope and impact of this operation is of profound importance for health care in the Delta, for the employment of an unemployed and underemployed population, and for the economic development of the entire region. Among other things, rural displaced farmworkers have been able to have reliable transportation to the towns where employment opportunities exist. The system offers sufficient flexibility so that it is accessible to the rural working population within an eighty-five-mile radius. This has been especially consequential since the gaming industry became a major source of employment in nearby Tunica.[117] The buses and vans ply the sixty-mile route due north from Clarksdale on an excellent double-lane highway. Otherwise, according to Mrs. Jones-Taylor, Henry remained close to the center as an adviser and in making his vast network of contacts available.[118] Until his death in 1997 "he was resourceful in using his telephone network" and "would intervene as necessary" to assist with fundraising. She indicated that his greatest influence was in the cadre of people cultivated in the Clarksdale movement. Many of them still occupied strategic positions in the area and remained faithful to his ideas and personally loyal to him.[119]

This comprehensive and complex range of activities help to put into perspective the scope of the Henry network and its importance to changing the racial climate in Mississippi. In the earlier analysis of the Clarksdale movement, one could clearly see Henry's command of the social movement dimension of the movement. He marshaled significant resources and challenged the day-to-day aspects of segregation—integrating trains and buses, restaurants, the public library, among others. But what the foregoing analysis revealed in the range of activities that challenged the infrastructure undergirding the intractable differential status of blacks is another dimension all together. In this body of activities Henry is seen to be putting teeth into his promise to fundamentally challenge how the racial system allocated resources. He always said that it was one thing to be able to sit anywhere one wanted on a bus, but that it was quite another to be able to afford the ticket. The efforts to alter the control of media and social communication devices proved to be a major assault on differential resource allocation as he and his partners won control of the major television station in the state's major media market. Similarly, the development of Job Corps sites aimed to prepare a generation of young people to assume new roles in a society, sustained by the bevy of equality legislation now on the books. The same point can be made about the efforts to develop a safety net system for health, housing, and care for the elderly. Although all of these projects involved areas where access was glaringly denied to blacks, but they rarely engaged the hordes of external allies that helped integrate public spaces. Nevertheless, the challenges to the institutional structures that maintained the denial of resources may have been more important. If successful they could situate blacks to become sufficiently independent to force the system to respond to their economic, health, and welfare needs. Henry was far ahead of most other activists at the time in articulating this kind of comprehensive assault on the racial system. Few analysts have taken note of the importance of this superbly balanced vision in making Henry a vital force in leadership of the Mississippi movement following the 1964 convention.

The diverse and complex range of activities that Henry balanced as the broader Mississippi movement fissured provided him significant capital to assume a more central role in the subsequent phase of the movement. He elevated his networking skills to new heights and had more than an equal hand in delivering social, economic, and political resources to blacks. His mastery of the bureaucratic process in Washington allowed him to deliver a sizable amount of largess to the black community, and he effectively situated himself to occupy the mantle of party leadership that he assumed would soon become available in the state Democratic Party. Few stopped to think, least of all Henry, of the tremendous power and influence this implied for this single figure as the gradual transformation of the political process unfolded between 1964 and the next party convention in 1968.

CHAPTER EIGHT

Taking the Reins of the State Democratic Party

Aaron Henry Wrests Power from the Segregationists

Aaron Henry built up tremendous capital in the interval between the 1964 and 1968 national Democratic conventions, but not enough to fundamentally alter the power disparity between the races in Mississippi. While many of the projects that he started after the 1964 convention resulted in considerable resources for the socioeconomic betterment of African Americans, the dream of altering the control of the political process remained unfulfilled. The old maxim established by V. O. Key in 1949 continued to hold: that the maintenance of white political control remained largely animated by the need to prevent the enfranchisement of a large and potentially threatening black electorate.[1] Yet a great deal of change did occur, and to get a perspective on how events evolved toward a reallocation of power requires briefly looking backward in the narrative.

The failure of the MFDP challenge in 1964 created a leadership vacuum that Henry ultimately filled as things evolved. The altered landscape emerged as a product of the disagreement among movement activists about the direction of the social change campaign. As has been shown, some activists saw the MFDP as an alternative and independent party in a state where the only other functioning party denied blacks membership. It exacerbated their chagrin that the parent National Democratic Party did not disavow this disloyalty from the state party.[2] Other disaffected activists went even further rejecting collaboration in a capitalist social order that they deemed inherently biased against power reallocation.[3] Henry had a different perspective, perceiving an opportunity to open up the political process by negotiating with potential local partners and throwing out the segregationists. He elaborated upon this, saying, "My idea of the MFDP in the beginning was that it would be a real political party—a party of inclusion for labor organizations and liberal whites, as well as for much of the black population. I had hoped we could supplant the old-guard Democratic Party in Mississippi."[4]

Henry did not see the convention outcome as a catastrophic failure, but a "painful time," which dictated even stronger leadership "through the times of adjustment."[5] He began to focus on the part of the convention compromise that had implications for the future organization of the state party. The NDC required the state party to open membership to African Americans in the future, and pledged to establish procedures for all states to guarantee and generate open participation for delegate selection.[6] Henry made the calculation that the state party would remain segregated and thus make its ouster a foregone conclusion in 1968. In that case an alternative organization needed to be positioned to take advantage of that circumstance.

Henry worked diligently to take advantage of what he perceived to be the improbability that the national party could again sanction seating the regulars without at least some degree of integration of the state party structure. He evinced an unabashed belief that the best opportunities for blacks lay in the Democratic Party. This was not just blind faith. The party gave his view some credence when it started the process for implementing its loyalty rules less than six months after the convention. The party chairman convened the eighteen-member committee appointed in March 1965, which quickly adopted a rule to require state delegates to vote only for electors pledged to support the election of the party's official nominees. At the same time the committee began a study of state election laws so that policies could be developed to guarantee that racial discrimination was eliminated. The party also anticipated passage of the Voting Rights Act under consideration in Congress, and charged a study group to incorporate that legislation into its discussions.[7] Henry had reasons to be hopeful that he and his cohorts had laid the groundwork for eventual certification as the official state party.

As the presidential campaign went into high gear, Henry signaled his support, writing directly to President Johnson, calling his nomination "the greatest experience in most of our lives. We rejoiced with you and Senator Humphrey in your greatest hour." Henry then asserted his high expectation of the president regarding the future of African American participation in the party in Mississippi: "The problems we have here in Mississippi will come nearer to being solved by the National Democratic Party than any other unit in America."[8] Meanwhile, campaign literature promoting the candidacy of Henry for Congress (as well as the other congressional candidates) started appearing across the state. Some of these flyers included a photo of Henry exhorting citizens to vote for him and for the national Democratic Party ticket of Johnson and Humphrey. Oftentimes the materials accompanied campaign stops that Henry made promoting only the national ticket.[9]

In the short term, despite the soul searching, some indigenous activists in the MFDP also survived the convention. They worked with Henry on several projects that continued a certain degree of mobilization. Indeed, the group made three resolutions to this end prior to departure from Atlantic City: to work for the Johnson-Humphrey ticket; to challenge the seating of the Mississippi congressional delegation; and to challenge the segregationist state party at the 1968 convention.[10]

The first major postconvention act seemed motivated by the activist-protest mode—another mock election. Since most blacks remained disfranchised, they could actually neither vote in the presidential election for which Henry and others were vigorously campaigning, nor in the state congressional elections. In the latter case the slate of black candidates that ran (and lost) in the primary (Aaron Henry, Fannie Lou Hamer, Annie Devine, and Victoria Gray) sought another chance by running in the general election. After being denied places on the ballot, the new mock ballot offered options for participation in both the presidential and congressional races. As such, not only would a spotlight be placed on black disfranchisement, but one would also be placed on the loyalty of black citizens to the Democratic Party. The MFDP developed its own ballot to capture the 450,000 black "voters," including only 28,000 already registered.[11] The ballot carried the names of the Democratic presidential and vice presidential candidates, as well as a slate of African American candidates as alternatives to the regular congressional slate. The foregone electoral failure of the latter would then provide the basis for the challenge against the seating of the all-white delegation.

Despite the unyielding efforts of President Johnson to keep the white Mississippians in the national party, these resulted in a spectacular failure. The local party faithful remained steadfast in maintaining control of the party apparatus and all political offices. They conceded no role for blacks, and maintained unabashed support for the maintenance of white supremacy. The crowning achievement for the party hierarchy occurred when the white electorate rejected Johnson in favor of Goldwater. While Johnson won by a national landslide (61 percent), Goldwater trounced him in Mississippi, capturing over 87 percent of the votes.[12]

After Atlantic City the state party commenced an active campaign to neutralize the threat of an enfranchised black population. Since white segregationists continued to control the power apparatus, they studiously avoided making any concessions to the MFDP, and sought to thwart all its efforts to attain formal recognition.[13] The primary goals continued to be maintenance of control of the state party apparatus and the unity of whites in this one-party dominant region.[14] The state's political leadership led the campaign, adopting Goldwater after fellow segregationist George Wallace withdrew. Fulfilling Henry's prophecy that they

196 TAKING THE REINS

would go their own way, Governor Paul Johnson declared, "Mississippi's debt to the national Democratic Party is now paid in full." He deemed any expression of loyalty to the Democratic Party as offensive—a "blind oath" precipitated by the challenge from "an outside pressure group, which represents no one but itself."[15]

Henry, better than almost anyone else, took advantage of the vacuum created by state party's virtual abdication of membership within the National Democratic Party. The modest work Henry did across racial lines in the state and his stature within the inner circles of the national Democratic coalition made him the prime prospect for leadership of this forming interracial coalition. Bob Moses referred to him as eminently suitable, though Moses himself had lost his enthusiasm for the broader Mississippi project. He credited Henry with a charming affability that easily transcended political differences and with possessing acuity in assessing situations and making decisions with integrity to movement goals. Despite the inherent practicality in such an approach, Moses believed that Henry could always be trusted.[16]

The organization of the Mississippi Democratic Conference (MDC) became a signal event that forecast the possible new interracial political party. While short-lived, it reflected the new dynamics as the contest for power shifted from the hard-line segregationists. The organization generated significant interest because this new coalition seemed at least promising as the grand black civil rights coalition ebbed. Claude Ramsay, the state labor leader, who had cultivated relationships with certain elements of the social change movement, issued the MDC call.[17] Though a curious initiator, Ramsay's moderation gave him entrée to potential white recruits, themselves equally distant from the nitty-gritty of the movement. For example, he had white collaborators among the Delta men linked to Henry, the White House, and/or the national party hierarchy: Doug Wynn (a Regular delegate in 1964 who actually signed the loyalty oath); Oscar Carr (a Clarksdale planter); and Hodding Carter III (whose editorially moderate Greenville newspaper gave him visibility).[18]

Ramsay did not invite those he perceived as representing the radical, left wing (e.g., SNCC and some in the MFDP, whose disenchantment with partisan politics was on the record). Dittmer reminds us that other obvious indigenous stakeholders also lacked representation: "no black sharecroppers, maids, or day laborers were invited."[19] Henry and a string of leaders, who like him were indigenous professionals and longtime NAACP affiliates, did receive invitations: Charles Young, the businessman from Meridian; R. L. T. Smith, the Jackson clergyman and businessman; and Charles Evers, who assumed his martyred brother's position in the NAACP. The clearly elite dominant group reflected the discomfort the emerging interracial partnership felt about including the voices of grassroots leaders. The meeting attracted about 125 participants.

Blacks composed about 20 percent of those present, and two acquired prominent elected positions: Charles Young, vice president, and R. L. T. Smith, treasurer.[20] A white Pascagoula lawyer, Robert Oswald, won election as chair. The other white officers included a second lawyer and a university professor, each deemed moderates at the time.[21]

The stated purpose of the meeting, in collaboration with a willing group of blacks, was to resurrect the state Democratic Party that the unyielding segregationists had brought to the brink.[22] Several factors propelled the development of this direction of political activity. There is ample evidence of high interest in establishing a workable interracial coalition, even within the Johnson White House. The politics of Head Start that resulted in the emergence of the MAP revealed this. While the old-line southern congressional coalition exerted pressure to destroy CDGM, it could not thwart the moderate interracial MAP group orchestrated from the White House.[23] Many elements of this group were involved in the MDC. However, fallout from the convention challenge also provided stimulus for the development of something like MDC. Whether by design or not, the elements of the MFDP dubbed radical after the convention posed a problem because the new alignment aimed to stabilize the volatile climate in Mississippi, which required holding the right and left at bay. A wedge naturally developed that privileged Henry's steady hand. Even though the MDC as such did not survive, the organization laid the groundwork for the formation of the Loyalist group that eventually succeeded the "Regular Democrats."

Following Atlantic City events moved rapidly from social mobilization to electoral politics. With widespread black enfranchisement on the horizon with passage of the 1965 VRA, Henry and the MFDP had reasons for finding common ground for moving through the transition. Numerous voter registration campaigns already existed, aided by the presence of federal registrars. Registration increased significantly in 1966. Morrison and Middleton show that "In the first year after passage of the VRA, the proportion of registered black voters in Mississippi . . . increased from nearly 7% to almost 60%."[24] Suddenly running blacks for office with the prospect of winning appeared highly probable. Perhaps they could even influence the outcome of statewide races. Henry used these prospects to somewhat minimize the tensions dividing indigenous elements within the MFDP and his NAACP cohorts; both had an interest in using the new black votes to gain electoral power. Therefore even as Henry cultivated interracial partners to compose a new state Democratic Party, he maintained an enduring focus on engaging indigenous MFDP activists around the potential gains that blacks could make by mobilizing to vote in local elections.

In the early skirmishing for the election of African American candidates, it appeared that the NAACP and the MFDP were running parallel but distinct campaigns. The NAACP strategy seemed to be under the aegis of Henry and Charles Evers, while Lawrence Guyot remained the titular leader of the MFDP faction. Despite their conflicts (some generational and some personal), each group became intensively involved in the new game of pursuing electoral politics. Indeed, in the interval between 1966 and 1967 the MFDP became the leading proponent of election politics. Lawrence Guyot fought off some internal conflicts to ramp up the organization's involvement in running candidates. The MFDP ran a slate of candidates in all of the congressional elections in 1966, continuing a challenge that Henry introduced in 1960.

Despite the increase in the number of registered black voters, the outcome in these races, as well as that for the seat of Senator James Eastland, did not change; they all lost by wide margins. The disjuncture between the NAACP and the MFDP could be discerned in the outcomes. Charles Evers, whose icono-clastic behavior caused considerable concern to both the MFDP and Henry for that matter, produced the better showing in southwest Mississippi where he had become most active in Claiborne County.[25] At this point Evers often isolated Henry, too, virtually running a one-man show. Sometimes this included collab-oration with segregationist elements, and at others his efforts appeared designed to out flank Henry, at least in the eyes of the national secretariat of the NAACP.[26] Henry's deftness hardly left him sidelined; his hard work sustained reasonable working relationships between the two organizations.

Considerable electoral activity continued the next year (1967), accomplish-ing a mixed outcome, an improvement over the previous absolute failure. In Sunflower County an MFDP campaign generated candidates to contest all but one post. It appeared to be a good test case. The county had a black major-ity on the voting rolls, and Fannie Lou Hamer, the dynamic Delta leader, lived there. Everything seemed favorable for a victory. In an astounding outcome all of these candidates lost due to the intensity of a campaign of harassment, terror, and intimidation from the segregationist planter elite and its allies.[27] Meanwhile, the NAACP's Charles Evers, though increasingly more controversial, had a bet-ter outcome. He focused on organizing a virtual political machine in Black-Belt Jefferson and Claiborne Counties in the Southwest. Despite his iconoclasm, Evers became adept at controlling the new voters he mobilized in this county, seemingly outpacing the remnants of the MFDP in the Delta.[28] The MFDP did nevertheless accomplish an important victory. Robert Clark, a schoolteacher in overwhelmingly black Holmes County, won the first statewide post as a member of the legislature. The MFDP dominated in this well-organized county and maintained strong col-laboration with its NAACP affiliates.[29] A year later Evers ran first for Congress (and lost), but then succeeded in becoming the state's first black mayor of an interracial town (small Fayette in southwest Mississippi) since Reconstruction in 1969.[30]

Meanwhile, the segregated party behaved as Henry predicted, fueling the challenge he intended to make at the 1968 Chicago convention. Despite massive efforts to get the state party's hierarchy to deal with the African American constituency, these fell on deaf ears. Instead, the leadership hardened in its determination to hold the line. The arbiter of this strategy remained Congressman John Bell Williams, by then stripped of his Democratic Party seniority for endorsing Republican Barry Goldwater. Williams returned to a state now in turbulence over the question of segregation. He ran an essentially racist campaign, in which he pulled out all the stops to outmaneuver his major white opponents for the maintenance of the racial system. Though not one of these candidates opposed segregation, Williams outpaced them all at the polls and secured control of the state party machinery. He then maneuvered his loyalists into place in the party structure and disrupted any efforts to compromise on the meaningful inclusion of blacks in the party.[31]

As the party prepared through the winter for the 1968 convention, President Johnson's operatives tried to court them for a compromise. Meanwhile, party leader John Bell Williams, now governor-designate, refused to support the party nominee and fretted with the possibility of not even taking a delegation to the convention. Others, however, tried to make some token nod to inclusion by "hand-picking" an acceptable African American or two for the state convention and perhaps the national confab in Chicago. One Executive Committee member deemed it a "serious mistake to overlook this many [black] voters." He proposed extending them an "olive branch" because "[s]omebody is going to furnish the right kind of leadership to the Negroes and I think we are in the best position to do it." Williams retorted: "I fail to see any purpose behind this other than to create confusion." Moreover, "I think it would do serious damage to the Mississippi Democratic Party and its stature." He then made a veiled reference to supporting the independent candidacy of segregationist George Wallace. In order to fully control the state convention Williams engineered the removal of the long-serving chairman, who was deemed to have a soft position on African American inclusion. This guaranteed an overwhelming delegate majority in support of Williams.[32]

The 1968 state party convention reflected the obstinacy of the segregationists in trying to preserve control over the singular route to political power and the tensions wrought by the challenge of blacks. Some of the precinct and district elections in at least twelve counties could not avoid a few blacks becoming either state delegates or Executive Committee members. Charles Evers became an elected delegate in Jefferson County and chairman of the Executive Committee. He and two others (both physicians) acquired delegates slots—Drs. Gilbert Mason and Matthew Page of Biloxi and Greenville, respectively. Despite these inroads, whites worked to deny African Americans any influence within the state party.

The Coahoma County convention, for example, locked out Henry; most MFDP affiliates elsewhere and white moderates and liberals suffered the same fate.[33]

The invective of party leader John Bell Williams set the Regulars on an almost certain path for national rejection. He gave the convention keynote and railed against the national party for drafting a platform that deviated from its roots. He reminded the delegates that Mississippi aligned with the Democratic Party over "a century ago, in the dark and shameful days of reconstruction." Now, he said, the state "suffered under the political lash of vilification, abuse and constant maligning." In a gibe at the locals wont to compromise, he warned: "Let us avoid the selection of delegates, however, who might be willing to surrender their principles and prostitute their convictions merely to gain favor and national recognition." He evinced no faith in the national party. "My friends, we meet here with the full knowledge that our beliefs and our principles—having met with repudiation, scorn and contempt in previous such conventions—-are hardly likely to be met in this year's convention with any demonstrable degree of enthusiasm. Yet we will not modify those beliefs nor dilute those principles."[34]

Henry complained bitterly to the National Democratic Party (NDP) Committee on Equal Rights, blasting the Regulars for denying blacks meaningful participation in processes at every level—precinct, county, and state. He used his own county as an example, and others corroborated his claims. His request for racial equality at the Coahoma convention "fell on deaf ears" because the county committee claimed not to know of any such requirements or of the national party's Equal Rights Committee. This, Henry said, was likely true since the state party circulated no information about these requirements whatsoever. He cited a range of other problems that strained credibility: inconsistent numbers of precinct delegates and alternates from one county to another; a state convention rule that allowed support of the national nominee to be optional; and a governor-inspired motion that quashed opening the convention to blacks.[35] Bolivar County residents found similar circumstances. In the absence of public notices of the venues for the conventions, the sites could not be located. Those who telephoned the chairman received directions to call later, and were subsequently denied information altogether. Indeed, complainants charged: "It is a fact that at many precincts no convention or meetings were held. The delegates . . . were selected some place else than at the precinct convention."[36]

The acts became so egregious that the token blacks among the delegates trying to influence some changes from the inside felt compelled to withdraw. Charles Evers became very outspoken about his objection and made specific demands in order to continue his participation as a delegate. He demanded that at least ten blacks (about 20 percent) be selected as delegates; that the delegates not be required to vote as a unit; that the entire delegation commit to support the nominee and platform of the convention; and that the problems of racial exclusion in the precinct and district elections be resolved prior to the next state convention. Since his proposition received little consideration, Evers withdrew and later joined Henry and the Loyalists in contesting the seating of the Regulars. Only Gilbert Mason agreed to accompany the delegation to the convention.[37]

In the meantime, a potential problem loomed as the MFDP announced an "independent" challenge of the Regulars.[38] Henry, being acutely aware of the potential disaster that could result from an internal rivalry at this stage, joined Hodding Carter (his co-chair of the "Loyal Democrats of Mississippi") to write a beseeching letter (in Henry's tone) to the MFDP to allay fears that his integrated group sought predominance in mounting the challenge at the national convention. The letter reminded them that a working group of major civil rights organizations met June 7 and proposed a committee "to raise funds to finance the project and making appearances before our friends on the National level of the Democratic Party [asking them] to support us with their votes at the National Convention." The letter listed this proposed committee, which included all of the important figures within the main factions—the MFDP, Loyalists, and the NAACP. The MFDP contingent included Fannie Lou Hamer, Lawrence Guyot, Unita Blackwell, Edwin King, Robert Clark, Victoria Gray, and Clifton Whitley. The NAACP members suggested in addition to Henry were all prominent and longtime affiliates—R. L. T. Smith, Allen Johnson, and Gilbert Mason. The Loyalist list included mostly the liberal-moderate whites who had been publicly identified with the concept of a biracial party—Hodding Carter III, Oscar Carr, Wesley Watkins, and Doug Wynn. The letter then added: "As you will note, the Freedom Democratic Party has the largest number on the Committee." The style is vintage Henry, showing an ability to reach out to those whose aims he believed to dovetail with his own.[39]

The civil rights forces did unite, affirmed in a letter Henry and Hodding Carter sent to the steering committee July 8, 1968.[40] The membership of the committee bode well for the loyal challengers—virtually all of those invited to the original meeting signed on, and apparently with some enthusiasm. Henry announced the purpose of the coalition: "to appear before the Credentials Committee . . . in Chicago on August 26th to prove discrimination by the regular Mississippi Democratic Party from the precinct level up." He said he had "affidavits from Negro citizens from more then 30 counties throughout the state, . . . representing 20,000 Negro voters, who contend they were not allowed free participation in Mississippi State Democratic Party affairs."[41]

In some ways the Regulars made the convention fight easy since the governor persuaded most of them that sufficient efforts had been made to meet the national requirements. He also continued to espouse the view that the candidate selection process for delegates remained fluid, though he personally rejected top contenders Humphrey and Kennedy. His preference could hardly be missed, however, when he said: "sooner or later we are going to have to make a determination if George Wallace's name would be put in nomination."[42]

The challengers thus advanced quite quickly. Their position appeared to be enhanced when the major presidential contenders signaled willingness to give them some form of advance endorsement. Hubert Humphrey, closely allied with Henry, personally committed his support, and so did the remnants of the Kennedy campaign following his assassination. Meanwhile, Eugene McCarthy reminded the challengers: "I have affirmed my support on many occasions in the past, and as we approach the opening of the convention I wish to state it once more in the strongest terms."[43] The chances that the Loyalists could not prevail seemed remote.

They prevailed easily when the Credentials Committee voted ·85–9 to seat them, rejecting the entire claim of the Regulars. Even a last-minute maneuver by the Regulars failed when Henry rejected their offer to double the three seats won by blacks at the Regulars' state convention. He also derided the tokenism represented by the presence of his old friend and NAACP cohort Gilbert Mason, the sole African American delegate who actually accompanied the Regulars to the convention. Clearly the governor, absent from the convention, overplayed his hand. After the victory, an ebullient Henry pronounced himself "highly jubilant" because the party had kept to the promise it made in 1964.[44] Shortly afterward he found himself the head of this party organization.

The convention gave its nod to Hubert Humphrey, who selected Edmund Muskie as his running mate. The Mississippi Loyalist delegation followed suit, although there was some support for the other candidates—McCarthy and McGovern. The major question remained of just how this ticket would fare in Mississippi. Since the Regulars had been so completely rejected at the convention, the white "Democratic" vote would be more than suspect. Already for several election cycles in presidential elections that vote had gone to the Republicans, even as local partisan identification remained solidly Democratic.[45] For the African American voters, however, there remained little doubt about voting for the Democratic presidential candidate, or for local Democratic candidates whose prospects of winning continued to improve. It represented the first presidential poll since Reconstruction with a fairly representative number of black voters in Mississippi. Moreover, when the convention concluded, even the recalcitrant leader of the MFDP, Lawrence Guyot, felt compelled by Humphrey's message and put his weight behind his candidacy.[46]

The new black vote did have an impact even though the Democratic candidate Humphrey received a mere 23 percent of overall Mississippi vote. The Republican candidate Nixon received 14 percent, while the American Independent Party candidate George Wallace received 64 percent. Although the percentage of the vote for Humphrey appears small, it reflected almost a 100 percent increase over the 13 percent of the vote that Lyndon Johnson polled in 1964.[47]

In the meantime an increasing amount of evidence revealed how consequential black voting could be. The 1967 mobilization sent Robert Clark to the State House, and twenty-two other black officials in majority black constituencies. The 1968 Charles Evers campaign for Congress also further demonstrated the tremendous potential of enfranchised blacks. Evers polled the most votes in this special election to replace congressman John Bell Williams, who resigned to run for governor among a crowded field of segregationists. Evers's presence on the ballot forced Williams into a runoff with the top vote getter, Charlie Griffin.[48] Evers captured about 30 percent of the primary vote, carrying five of the twelve counties in the state. In the runoff, though soundly defeated, he improved his total by 10,000.[49] In both instances these votes came largely from blacks. In short, the 1968 election proved to be just as much about local politics as the presidential election. Henry could now foresee the partial fulfillment of a project he launched with Merrill Lindsey in Clarksdale in 1960.

Few had any illusion that the Loyalist victory at the Democratic Party convention in 1968 provided actual control of the state party. In part Governor John Bell Williams assured this. This ardent segregationist now orchestrated a campaign to deny the Loyalists legitimacy and to disparage the NDP.[50] He offered no support whatsoever for the Humphrey-Muskie ticket. The distaste he had for Humphrey went back to 1948 when then-senator Humphrey supported African American participation in the party with which southern segregationists identified. Williams said of him, "every time some civil rights group has cried frog, he's jumped." He then promised to go fishing on Election Day, but instead threw his support to George Wallace.[51]

Henry, named the head of the "new" state organization in December 1968, appeared undeterred by the posture of the Regulars.[52] He had long since announced his desire to bring the two elements together. He had his work cut out, but few were better suited to the task. Henry began by exhorting the Regulars to meet him halfway. He first made an overture to the group by offering to acquire guest passes to the convention floor for these decertified Regulars.[53] Later he invited them to sit down with the interracial group, and he fought tirelessly to participate in their routine affairs—from the precinct level to the state convention. Repeatedly they rejected these efforts or gave them token recognition only to betray them later. Notwithstanding criticism from within his coalition (the MFDP), Henry's keen political sense and practicality led him to believe that resolving the competing claims to legitimacy was the route to progress at the local level. He acknowledged that this would require power sharing, an arrangement he expressed willingness to accept so long as the principle of full participation by African Americans remained protected.

Henry and his Loyalists returned to the state and organized a strong campaign in support of the Humphrey-Muskie ticket. Charles Evers sent an early report to the NDC (January 15, 1969) outlining the Loyalist intentions and efforts in the presidential campaign. In addition to praising the NDC for its support, especially its Equal Rights Committee, he lauded Henry for his yeoman work in leading the local team. Evers added that they turned "about 150,000 votes" for the ticket, noting that in the past this would have been sufficient to carry the state. He repeated what had become a refrain for Henry: "We are determined that the Democratic Party of Mississippi will not be an all Black party, not an all White party (as it has been in the past); but a party for all citizens of Mississippi. The door stands open forever." He gave notice that the official state office for the party was being located at Clarksdale.[54]

The new organization moved with dispatch, despite the lingering divide with the Regulars. It remained rigorously biracial. The Executive Committee had sixteen members equally divided between the races, and inclusiveness characterized its standing committees. The functions of the committees reflected many of the projects and principles for which Henry had worked in the NAACP and his hometown: voter registration, voter education, legal redress, emergency welfare, women's activity, employment, federal programs, and school personnel and education. Clearly the aims of this party of Loyalists had a very different approach to politics than the unrepresentative, single-issue Regulars.[55]

To their surprise Henry and the Loyalists learned that the state party had very little formal organization. Not much of a secretariat existed, nor much discernable active citizen participation, an indication of how tightly the old party had been controlled by elites. There seemed to be little on the agenda beyond the maintenance of racial exclusion, which seemed to relegate other issues, even disagreements, to the background. This means of operation greatly circumscribed the arena for developing new voices within the leadership elite. For example, it privileged populist leaders and charismatic demagogues who relied on small cliques to generate mass support. This simplified world did not require nor deem it desirable to have an elaborate array of structures to carry out the mission. A good charismatic leader like Bilbo or Barnett could always mobilize the troops, even as they masked conflict such as the traditional one between small yeomen farmers in the hills and the Delta planters.[56]

In light of what Henry and his cohorts found, their task as the newly recognized party required the creation of an inclusive formal organization. The interracial leadership elite for the Loyalists met but one part of this requirement. Just after the presidential election Henry and Claude Ramsay wrote to the campaign workers sketching the next stage: "Now that the election is over we must begin the hard work of organizing a bonafide Democratic Party in each county as well as in the state." To this end a planning committee was announced. Its members included Henry, Hodding Carter, Mrs. Paul Derian, Thomas Knight, Charles Evers, Lawrence Guyot, and Oscar Carr. It should be noted that despite conflicts with the MFDP, its leader, Lawrence Guyot, joined this group of NAACP stalwarts and moderate whites. They named a team of local and other volunteer lawyers to assist the committee: Jack Young, Armand Derfner, L. A. Aschenbrenner, Wes Watkins, and Reuben Anderson.[57]

Establishing a secretariat became the first order of business. In the absence of resources or any exchange of documents and other party paraphernalia from the Regular "organization," it made sense to establish the secretariat at Clarksdale where Henry and his cadre of local volunteers could provide some staff support.[58] At the same time the Clarksdale site represented a clear acknowledgment of Henry's position at the head of the organization. Early correspondence shows him focused on establishing party rules and trying to bring some order. He met fairly frequently with the Executive Committee and called on a wide range of contacts. He utilized consultants from myriad sources—Democratic Party operatives, representatives of the NDC, civic organizations focused on social change—and he marshaled information from a variety of sources, collecting documents, NDC edicts, and such.[59]

Another early theme, fundraising, became enduring. The new party came into being literally broke (and remained so for much of Henry's tenure). He sought to establish a financial system that would generate support for operational needs. In almost every memo, including the invitation to the official opening of the secretariat, Henry solicited funds—individual contributions, dues, loans, and so forth.[60] The problem of financing extended to the county organization level as well. Henry's exchange with Amzie Moore, chairman of the Bolivar County Executive Committee, is an illustrative example. He advised Moore that his county was assigned a quota of $2,600 for its annual contribution. He specified that $651 of that should be raised every quarter, with one-half deposited to the county treasurer, one-fourth each to the county treasurer and the state headquarters. Membership cards were also on offer for a dollar apiece, with half the proceeds going to the state treasury.[61]

Meanwhile, Henry always sought to comply with directives from the NDC and to illustrate loyalty to the party platform and aspirations. No doubt a good deal of this was designed to maintain the favor of the national leadership, but also to demonstrate the difference between itself and the "rogue" Regular group. The focus on unity appeared to be one of the best ways to demonstrate the responsible nature of the loyal challengers vis-à-vis their nemesis. The Loyalists sought to reach the broadest constituency of voters in the state; mind you, support for the mission of an interracial society remained a requirement. Henry duly created a Reform Committee, per directive from the NDC, for the purpose of making the party more responsive to the people.[62] The various county chairmen and women constantly received appeals to appoint voter registration committees with strong leadership for the purpose of a continuous campaign to register those denied the franchise.[63]

This proved to be far more than mere lip service. Henry, the MFDP, and the Loyalists exerted great influence on establishing this approach at the national level. In part their two challenges forced the NDC to appoint a commission to open up party processes. Henry became a member of this Commission on Party Structure and Delegate Selection (subsequently known as the McGovern-Fraser Commission). Its 1969 report laid out the specifications for eliminating discrimination in delegate selection in the states: (1) fully open public meetings, absent any conditions that limited membership or participation; (2) publish timely notice of party meetings; (3) seek the broadest possible voter registration; (4) publicize information specifying rules and procedures for selection of party officers and representatives; and (5) publicize information on the qualifications for offices guaranteeing all the opportunity to compete in elections.[64]

Henry's activity on the commission highlighted the prominence of his role as a national party leader and his influence on its social change perspective. Upon completion of the commission report Henry assumed an active role in lobbying for adoption of its most comprehensive form. He prepared a report to the Rules Committee of the NDC exhorting it to give the fullest attention to the recruitment of African Americans. He framed all of this by praising the party for its strong support of civil rights since 1948, citing antilynching, the 1948 civil rights plank, passage of the civil rights laws between 1957 and 1965, and Medicare and Medicaid. He said this was not enough; rather, the party had to make certain that Democrats across the country remained in synchrony with the program.[65]

In lobbying for the McGovern-Fraser plan Henry maintained an eye for his own problem in trying to integrate the various elements of the Mississippi party. He argued that the NDC had to set the "minimum participation that a state party and its officials must adhere to in order to be identified as Democrats." He wanted this written into the state charters, providing a clear basis for revocation in the case of disloyalty. Another Henry demand was that anybody running under the party label should be "required to register with the chartered unit" and that those who wore the party label in Congress be required to have "actively supported" both the presidential ticket and the platform. Similarly, he attacked the seniority system, saying it "must yield to the quality and competence of the individual involved as determined by the Democratic Caucus."[66]

On the state organizational front, in the meantime, active preparation continued on a party constitution. The effort began almost immediately after the 1968 election, with the effect that Henry could announce in April 1969 that he expected the constitution to be ready for adoption the following January.[67] A draft circulated during a late June Executive Committee meeting.[68] Then in February 1970 Henry announced a constitutional convention for March 8, 1970, for adoption, two months shy of his deadline.[69]

The remarkable Constitution document opened up participation in accord with requirements of the NDC and completely diverged from the management pattern of the Regulars. Its greatest claims rested in the preamble: It sought to bring together citizens who "seek the right to support only candidates for local, state and national office in general elections who desire to affiliate, associate, align themselves with and fully support the National Democratic Party." It had rigorous rules for membership participation, and adhered to the principles of affirmative action enunciated by the parent body. The composition of the central committee of the Mississippi Party included three members from each county—one each from the two main racial groups, and one from the state's Young Democratic Clubs. This committee had the function of advising the state Executive Committee—composed of three members elected from each of the congressional districts, plus the committeeman and woman. The president of the Young Democrats received ex-officio member status. Equal representation details adhered verbatim to the rules and principles established by the NDC at its 1964 convention. This included, among other things, specification that the states institute demonstrable procedures for recruitment of a diverse membership and leadership and that barriers such as "unit" voting rules for presidential electors, and the requirement of unusually large numbers of signature to attain candidacy be eliminated.[70]

The consolidation of a new Mississippi Democratic Party after the Loyalists prevailed at the 1968 convention began a long and complex process of fits and starts. At the beginning the imagined unified organization of the new group and remnants of the old party seemed impossible. The Loyalist courtship of the Regulars started soon after the election, however. Just weeks after adoption of the constitution, Henry wrote to the congressional delegation using both carrot and stick: "Our greatest desire is to build a Democratic Party in the State of Mississippi of which we can all be proud and be able to participate. We all realize that there must be a turning of the corner in order that we might accomplish the very necessary achievement." He then encouraged the delegation members to help unify the party as a start by signaling their intentions to run for continuation in office "with the Democratic Party of Mississippi." He asserted a prerogative that nevertheless remained contested—that the Loyalists now alone could officially use the title of "Democratic Party of Mississippi." In order to authenticate his claim Henry never failed to reference the certification that the Loyalists received at the 1968 convention. After offering this olive branch he promised to render the segregationists powerless if they refused: "We intend to have one strong Democratic Party in Mississippi. You can help this effort by filing with us. In the event that you do not, you leave us no alternative but to challenge your right to sit on the Democratic side of the aisle and operate as Democrats when you ignore the party at home." He closed by urging "immediate communication."[71]

The Regulars offered a hardly encouraging response. Not a single member of the delegation filed for reelection with the Loyalist-controlled state party. Henry lamented to national chairman Lawrence O'Brien that despite a "major effort" he did not get any cooperation. "Instead, they filed with the group that was unseated at the 1968 Democratic Convention and is controlled by Governor John Bell Williams. To our knowledge this group has the same racist posture as caused their being rejected in 1968. Since 1968 they have not held a meeting to which any black Democrat was invited nor [of which any were] informed." As a result, Henry told the chairman, the state had no recognized representatives in Congress. He then asked the Democratic caucus in Congress to withdraw recognition from these men and deny them participation when the 1971 Congress convened.[72]

Several weeks later the Loyalists escalated efforts to penalize the congressional delegation by challenging their seating in the 1971 Congress. Chairman Henry, national committeewoman and man Patricia Derian and Charles Evers, and secretary/counsel Wesley Watkins issued the challenge. They referred to themselves as the Henry-Evers-Derian Democratic Party, and dubbed their opponents derisively as "Dixiecrats, Wallaceites, [and] Republicans." They continued the caustic tone that Henry had presented earlier to O'Brien. The document the Loyalists prepared referenced the anomaly of a "bogus" Democrat, James Colmer, being advanced to the chairmanship of the House Rules Committee due to the seniority system. In that position he would "determine what bills come before the full House . . . [where he would have] the authority to block the very bills that the Democratic Party wants enacted. Thus, for example, the Equal Employment Act of 1970 would now be law were it not for Mr. Colmer's refusal to allow the House Rules Committee to vote out a rule on it." Then, evincing some exasperation with the lack of action from the NDP, the Loyalists wondered: "*Is there a national Democratic Party?*" (Emphasis in text.) Or, is it simply open to anybody—even those who represent "a virtually lily-white, Negro-hating, segregationist party?"[73]

These leaders then made a case in a legal memorandum against the continued recognition of the illegitimate Regular organization. It noted that twice the Loyalists had been rebuffed in trying to register its Executive Committee with the secretary of state. Their papers were "returned with the notation that recognition had been extended to the 'regular' organization which had been unseated in Chicago." They quoted state law that required candidates to submit their names to the official party's Executive Committee and said that the attorney general had an obligation to deny candidacy to any person who did not meet the requirements and pay the specified fee. The Loyalists found this ironic since the Regular Party, a "typical executive committee," did not itself comply with any of these regulations.[74]

At the same time, Henry and Counsel Watkins prepared a lobbying campaign among congressional allies that revealed both opportunities and risks. In a mid-November strategy session with Joseph Rauh, Watkins acknowledged that perhaps at most they could force the delegation to recognize the Loyalist Party prior to running for office in the succeeding election. There was optimism about such a compromise because so many prominent Democrats on Capitol Hill promised support since the NDC had already recognized the Loyalists as the state party.[75] However, the senior Mississippi congressional legislators remained powerful on the Hill, and some allies and party operatives warned that continued Loyalist pressure would backfire, being seen as meddling in the internal business of Congress. Meanwhile, the united front of the Loyalists began to fray. Henry remained adamant about stripping seniority from the delegation.[76] Some of the white Loyalists, however, perceived Henry to be pushing too hard, confirming a perception among some whites that he too often alienated latecomers to the civil rights game. Watkins averred: "The more I think about it the more I am convinced that this is a time to put a halter on Aaron and make him more responsive to the wishes of the other leadership of the party." Doubts notwithstanding, Henry's position prevailed and the seating challenge proceeded.[77]

Michigan congressman John Conyers managed the unseating effort, with the help of other congressmen in the liberal Democratic Study Group (DSG).[78] Henry and Watkins called on many allies for support and formal endorsements: Joseph Rauh, then at the NDC, became a leading advocate; Minnesota congressman Don Fraser requested the Library of Congress to research the problem; and the Leadership Conference on Civil Rights agreed to make a public statement.[79] Stories about Henry's many news conferences appeared in regional newspapers available in Jackson, while several congressional offices also sponsored news conferences. In the Senate, lobbyists focused on "various people who [had] ever been mentioned for the presidential nomination." In December 1970 George Agree, a DSG fundraiser, advised Henry that he had "commitments for at least six-thousand dollars to finance the challenge."[80]

In the end though, the NDC warned the Loyalists of its inability to sanction its party adherents, bonafide or not, within Congress. Chairman Larry O'Brien issued the caution: "The question of Members elected this year to the House of

Representatives from the State of Mississippi participating in the Democratic caucus of the House is a question solely for the membership of that caucus to decide. However, it is clearly appropriate for the National Democratic Committee to make a full inquiry." He then raised the specter of another delay to buy time for a stronger prospective mandate: "This is certainly an issue that should be vigorously pursued prior to the next election in the State, and the time when delegates are selected to the 1972 Democratic National Convention."[81]

The challenge to the Mississippi delegation came up for formal discussion only in the House, where the Loyalists had greater support. John Conyers offered the resolution, which labeled the Mississippi delegation "third party representatives." He stopped just short of denying them access to the Democratic caucus, saying: "That the Committee on Committees is hereby directed by this Democratic Caucus to assign the last positions on their respective committees to each of the members of the Mississippi delegation; and in the event any of said members are assigned to any other committee of the House that they be assigned the last positions on said committees." Researchers at the Library of Congress found that in the history of Congress no third-party "members received the normal benefits of seniority. In every instance, freshmen members were placed ahead of veteran third party members."[82] Henry attached his biting affidavit recounting much of the discriminatory history of the Regulars, and lamented that they were doing all of this under the cover of "the law," thwarting the wishes of the NDC.[83]

Henry vigorously pursued the claims of the Loyalists, but failed to unseat the congressional delegation. The House voted by an overwhelming majority to seat the Regular delegation—111–55. The Loyalists came no closer than a resolution offered by Senator Fred Harris, a trusted ally from Oklahoma: that a special Democratic Caucus Committee be established and charged to investigate cases where a successful candidate ran on the party label but refused to support the organization. At a minimum, he suggested, such a member of Congress should be banished from the Democratic caucus.[84] This overall outcome gave the Loyalists little comfort that the national party was fully committed to the ongoing Mississippi crisis.

In the aftermath of the defeat, the Loyalists realized they had to confront the Regulars at the polls. While a good deal had been done to mobilize voters, the Regulars seemed to pay almost no attention. Little headway could be discerned in the efforts to have a conversation with them. Nothing transpired, for example, when gubernatorial term-limits forced segregationist John Bell Williams from the leadership. None of the white Democratic candidates took the initiative to move toward the party. The Loyalists therefore unified around their own candidate, Charles Evers. Though Evers's opportunistic streak gave some of them pause, they lined up behind him with the appearance of vigor. Charles Young

(NAACP) nominated him, and Fannie Lou Hamer (MFDP) joined Oscar Carr (white Clarksdale planter) in seconding.[85] Evers had already demonstrated appeal in two campaigns: winning the Fayette mayoralty in 1967 and polling the largest number of primary votes in a 1968 congressional race. It remained to be tested whether his candidacy could capture the purported bloc of 260,000 black voters, and thereby possibly shift gubernatorial politics from its normal racist strategy[86] and whether it would help other black candidates around whom Henry wanted to form the "Mississippi Coalition for Election '71."[87]

The impact of the Evers's candidacy had a quick effect on the campaign. While the Regular leadership did little, Frank Parker says: "For the first time in modern history in the state the two leading Democratic candidates—William Waller and Charles Sullivan—did not campaign as segregationists."[88] These two candidates drew the overwhelming portion of the vote (Waller 227,424; Sullivan 288,219). This signified a major shift, although the segregationist elite remained influential. Waller and Sullivan, for example, were forced into a run-off because segregationist radio personality Jimmy Swan also captured 128,946 votes.[89] Waller prevailed in the runoff and overwhelmed Evers in the general election. However, the poll showed the potential impact of a fully mobilized African American electorate. Evers received 172,762 (22 percent) of the 780,537 votes cast. He claimed that he inspired the largest turnout in a governor's race in Mississippi history.[90]

Gracious in defeat, Evers accepted Waller as the next governor, adding that he was "the first one ever to like and respect us."[91] The Evers candidacy overall had a larger effect, dramatically increasing other African Americans' candidacies.[92] Blacks ran for multiple offices in over half of the counties, in all sections of the state with the Evers's candidacy producing a coattails effect.[93] Black county supervisors doubled from four to eight between 1968 and 1972; city council members increased from five to thirty-one; and the total black county officials quadrupled from twenty-two to eighty-eight.[94]

At this juncture, nevertheless, organizational matters gave way to planning for the 1972 presidential campaign. Who would make preparations for primaries and such, with both the Loyalists and Regulars claiming legitimacy? Through the balance of 1971 the Loyalists continued to try to engage the Regulars, who continued to presume institutional legitimacy. In early December Henry approached officials who controlled the elections machinery to arrange the customary precinct meeting places for January. He received numerous responses, all denying use of the facilities, often delivered by legal counsel. Many officials responded in language that challenged the legitimacy of Henry and his "alleged group." The reasons for denying space varied. Some proprietors told Henry that only public buildings could be used to meet his request. Often, however, those who controlled facilities located in public buildings simply declared the spaces occupied or unavailable on the requested date.[95]

The Regulars sought an opinion on the matter from the attorney general. According to Henry, a December 22, 1971, opinion barred county officials from providing precinct voting places to the Loyalists, though no direct notice was sent to the these officials. When Henry finally became aware of this he blasted the attorney general's ruling, calling it derogatory and personally impugning. He warned that the two of them would continue to face off in court because the precinct decision only prolonged conflict between the races about a doomed system. Waxing poetic Henry adapted a quote from Robert Frost, calling himself: "A fellow Mississippian determined to make Mississippi what it yet not is but what it can and must become."[96]

On the same date Henry also approached governor-elect Waller with an invitation to a December 12 meeting in the hope of advancing prospects for unity under this new executive leadership.[97] Henry said: "We urge your attendance because initial instructions regarding the national convention have been received. We want to plan the dates of the Precinct, County, District and state meetings in concert with you." To accommodate Waller the Loyalists offered space at both a private home and a hotel in Greenwood, where he could "feel most comfortable." However, neither Waller nor members of the Executive Committee replied.

The meeting proceeded and Henry issued a press release recounting efforts to secure Regular participation in the meeting. He noted the absence of the governor-elect and all fifteen members of the Regular Executive Committee. He reiterated "all [of] our meetings are wide open, and we invite anyone interested in electing a Democratic president in 1972 to join us." He sent the correspondence with return receipts so he had reasonable confidence of its delivery. Henry also reported that he tried successively over three days to reach Waller by telephone and failed Though a Waller intermediary did call with a promise to relay a message, there still was no reply from the governor-elect. Meanwhile, the NDC chairman indicated that his independent efforts to reach Waller had also gone unanswered. Claude Ramsay, the labor leader, tried to arrange a later rendezvous between the principals. That attempt failed because Waller declined. Subsequently Waller and the chairman of the Regulars issued public statements again contesting the legitimacy of the Loyalists and declining to participate in any unity meetings. In utter disregard for the Loyalists, the Regulars then announced separate precinct meetings. They scheduled them for the same date as the Loyalists, only earlier in the day—10 A.M. [98]

Rumors swirled about the avowed intent of the Regulars to create mischief. Henry issued a warning in January that the Regulars were attempting to disrupt the processes on the eve of registration for the 1972 national convention. With their meetings scheduled for the same date, Henry urged leaders to exercise vigilance because Regulars might show up and gain control over these operations. He reminded them to get out their members because these meetings remained open to anyone—loyal or disloyal.[99]

Despite Waller's public remonstrance, many in the Loyalist camp believed circumstances dictated some movement toward unity from the Regulars. By January 17, 1972, the Loyalists sketched a proposed twelve-point agreement. They made it known that an Executive Committee split equally between both races would be acceptable (Waller represented by six whites/one black, and Henry by six blacks/one white). The proposal anticipated cochairs (with Henry as the Loyalist choice for coleader). County delegations would be apportioned on the basis of racial composition, with the national delegation split between Loyalists (60 percent) and Regulars (40 percent), and chosen in compliance with the affirmative-action requirements of the NDC. The governor would automatically be a member of that delegation. Increased African American representation in government agencies also figured prominently in what the Loyalists proposed. They identified state and federal agencies that are sources for employment as targets for hiring unemployed and underemployed blacks. They floated a proposal that such agencies would hire blacks at a rate of two to one until equity was attained (highway patrol, the boards, agencies and commissions, federal judges, and postmasters) and sought a "good faith effort and endorsement" from the governor for a single-member district reapportionment plan.[100] Conciliatory in tone, the proposal assigned the governor a special status in the transition as chief executive and even proposed one-time acceptance of a separate precinct convention, with the proviso that a merger occur prior to county conventions.[101]

The proposal elicited no direct negotiations, and each group proceeded to execute separate delegate selection processes. However, there was a nod toward unity when the Regulars accepted the notion of negotiating with the Loyalists. Henry acknowledged receiving a call from the governor in late February promising to negotiate for unity. Subsequently the two sat down for a two-hour closed meeting, the first time that the Regular leadership tacitly acknowledged the legitimacy of the Loyalists and Henry as leader.[102] This discussion, the first since Reconstruction, appeared to be inconceivable merely one year before. Though it represented progress, it still took years to consummate an agreement.

The next development seemed to portend swift movement toward cooperation. Each camp named negotiating teams. The governor identified an integrated team by February, acknowledging the changed circumstances. The members presumably reflected the views of moderation Waller was thought to possess: J. C. "Sonny" McDonald (chair), Cleve McDowell, (an African American vice chair), Rubel Griffin, Charles Spencer, and Tom Riddell.[103] Days later Henry named a very diverse and experienced interracial team of activists, lawyers and other professionals, political operatives, and clergy: Charles Young (chair), Hodding Carter III, Patricia Derian, and Wesley Watkins. The Reverend Harry Bowie, Father William Morrissey, Barbara Phillips, Winson Hudson, Attorney Fred Banks, Mary Hightower, and Emily Walls rounded out the group, all with good civil rights credentials.

The first negotiation session occurred March 18 in Jackson.[104] While no formal minutes of the meeting have been found, on March 20 Fred Banks summarized the oral presentation made by the Loyalists. It restated most of their extant positions and clarified the size of the Executive Committee: fifty members—twenty-five to each group. He described legislation for party registration and empowerment of the Executive Committee, and a requirement that the Regulars adopt "the constitution and by-laws of the 'Loyalist' party." The delicate issue of delegate selection was sidestepped. Instead the notes described a proposal to simply double the size of the delegation to ninety-six, with each group maintaining forty-eight members, so long as they were in compliance with national party rules for affirmative action. Other clarifications related to substantive policy questions and patronage. In addition to a demand for adoption of single-member legislative districts, the group also sought to have "unified mechanical voting machines in every county" and guaranteed fair employment. Given the disparities in the labor force the Loyalists sought to speed equity via an affirmative-action program with two to one hiring for blacks. Finally, since several governors had used their power to veto community-based federal programs serving African American communities, the Loyalists sought the following provision to diminish that power: "All federal programs which now enjoy substantial or complete community-consumer control should be allowed to remain so controlled."[105]

However, things deteriorated during the Regular state convention with the governor rejecting what the Loyalists thought had been promises. He defended the existing precinct and district systems calling them open and fair. Appearing exasperated with the Loyalists, Governor Waller issued an ultimatum: "We must reach a decision here today. . . . Do we give in to a limited number of individuals who have . . . so far . . . succeeded in frustrating our sincere efforts to negotiate, . . . or do we stick by our convictions in seeking to represent the vast majority of Mississippians . . . both black and white at the national level?" He engineered passage of a resolution to send both delegations to the national convention with the Regular and Loyalist leaders as cochairs. He gave Henry ten days to accept or face a lawsuit and a challenge before the national Credentials Committee.[106]

When Henry received Regular chairman McDonald's letter detailing the ultimatum, he became incensed, scribbling on his copy: "It is a subtle call to violence. The results have [already] manifested themselves in Shaw, Drew, Ocean

Springs, Gulfport, Oxford, and Vicksburg." He exaggerated, although given the level of black mobilization the potential for violence always existed in these contested situations with segregationists. Henry exhibited more control seven days later, reminding McDonald that the governor agreed to establish equal negotiating teams. Nevertheless, he signaled disinterest in entering side deals with the governor through emissaries; and, since McDonald had been sent as a second in command, Henry directed him to take up the matter with his counterpart on the Loyalist team, chairman Charles Young. Henry then sent advance instructions to Young asserting that the ten-day limit could have dire consequences: "assault, violence, intimidation and even death." He said that Waller was demanding "that we give him all he asked for, while he and the 'regulars' [give] nothing in return." Henry advised Young that acceding to this would be "unconditional surrender."[107]

What seemed promising quickly degenerated as the Regulars began a process of conflict escalation. When the Loyalists did not comply with the governor's demands, Waller authorized a formal challenge to the NDC, and later entered a court action to deny the Loyalists seats at the impending convention. J. C. McDonald wrote the NDC on May 1, 1972, disparaging the delegates, saying they had been "selected by a group of individuals in Mississippi calling themselves the 'Loyalists' and headed by Mr. Aaron Henry of Clarksdale." He wrote that since a rumor existed that this bogus party had submitted a list of delegates, a clarification needed to be made because only the Regulars constituted a legal Democratic Party in the state.[108]

McDonald was being disingenuous; he knew perfectly well that a Loyalist delegate slate had been transmitted to Washington. Moreover, the NDC had acknowledged its receipt, repeatedly referencing it as the "Democratic Party of the State of Mississippi." Robert Nelson wrote a letter for the chairman to Henry filled with effusive praise: "Yours was one of the best organized and conducted conventions of the Democratic Party anywhere in the nation. . . . Our national chairman, Mr. O'Brien, respects you and trusts you as much as any member of the Democratic Party that I know of." He heaped equal praise for the delegate list. "The composition of the delegates to the [convention] that your party, the Democratic Party of the State of Mississippi has filed with the DNC is in greatest conformity with the commissions and directives." Nelson said he deemed the work of the Loyalists "A model for the nation to aim for."[109]

The Regulars, anticipating problems at the NDC, instituted a legal suit continuing their claims that the Loyalists constituted an illegal party. Initially, a federal district judge ruled that the Regulars did indeed constitute the official party, but refused to require the NDC to seat them. A special three-judge panel also demurred on the question of seating, and the Supreme Court refused to hear the case.[110] Henry issued a bittersweet response to this legal ambivalence, saying he sat in the witness chair for "almost two full days, but enjoyed every minute of it."[111]

Governor Waller then worked hurriedly to secure a last-minute compromise. He dispatched Claude Ramsay as an intermediary to Henry, but sensing that time was short, allegedly chased down Henry and as many members of both groups as he could find. He proposed to give the Loyalists ten out of twenty-five seats and one of the committeeman/woman slots. Henry issued a riposte saying that the Loyalists demanded a fifty-fifty split and adherence to the affirmative action rules of the NDC.[112] As a result, the two could not consummate the deal.

The national Credentials Committee then proceeded with its hearing on the challenge from the Regulars. After reviewing the documentation from the contenders and giving each a hearing, the NDC issued an absolute rebuke of the Regulars. It found that "the Loyalists are in substantial compliance with the Call for the 1972 Democratic National Convention and the McGovern Guidelines." It found no credible evidence of Loyalist discrimination against whites, lack of posted meetings, or excessive membership fees. Instead the delegation received praise for its diversity. Nevertheless, it found particularly damning evidence against the Regulars, the most important being the absence of democratic participation within the organization. When it came to the matter of racial discrimination the hearers wrote: "There is no evidence that there exist any party rules which include the six basic elements adopted by the Special Equal Rights Committee."[113] Following the report, chairwoman Patricia Roberts Harris called for the committee vote, and heard only complete silence. She did so three times and did not gain a single vote for the Waller delegation. The Loyalists had now prevailed twice against the Regulars.

Still it appeared that Henry and the Loyalists remained stuck. Soon after the rebuke of the Regulars, Governor Waller decided not to go to the convention, or to support George McGovern, the presumptive nominee.[114] Signs of goodwill appeared to evaporate. For example, following a tactic adopted by his predecessor, the governor vetoed some federal programs that had a major impact on blacks. Several Delta programs vetoed by the governor earned the particular wrath of Henry: the Mound Bayou Community Hospital and similar comprehensive health programs. Henry excoriated what he termed the governor's "unethical" tactic, and he associated it with the betrayal of the Tilden-Hayes Compromise that ended Reconstruction.[115] Henry found special irony in the veto of the Mound Bayou project because its hospital remained the only option for blacks denied services at segregated institutions.[116]

The results of the 1972 presidential election did not particularly help the situation. The Regulars' predictions of a huge Democratic loss in the state became a reality. McGovern drew only 20 percent of the vote compared to Nixon's 78 percent. Despite the yeoman efforts of Henry and the Loyalist cadre, McGovern carried only three Black-Belt counties—Claiborne, Jefferson, and Holmes. These counties had become the staging areas for two prominent Loyalists: Charles Evers in Jefferson where he served as mayor of Fayette, and in adjacent Claiborne where he also had high influence; and Robert Clark in Holmes, where he became the first black state legislator since Reconstruction.[117]

Henry evinced deep disappointment, albeit defiant, at the policy implications of the Nixon victory for the South. "I am astounded by the promise of Mr. Nixon and Mr. Eastland that one more appointment to the U.S. Supreme Court would give them a 'virtual lock' on the decisions of that Court." He feared a reversal of many Warren Court decisions. His caustic assertions accused Nixon and the citizens who voted for him as using phony issues (e.g., abortion and amnesty) to tar McGovern. Regarding school desegregation, Henry averred: "Every time President Nixon used the term bussing, that was just another word for 'Nigger' in all of its connotations." He promised continued resistance, saying:

> "any attempt to turn the clock back, will find a massive resistance by the Black and minority communities." He lamented "that the methods that many of us have used trying to work within the constitution, and within the system, will have little appeal the next time around. . . . I hope and pray that this does not become the fate of our nation." He ended this unusually boisterous tone quoting a well known Negro spiritual, one often appropriated for use in movement rallies: "before I'll be a slave, I'll be buried in my grave."[118]

The Loyalists did not give up on unseating the congressional delegation. Henry wrote in mid-November 1972 of readiness to resurrect the campaign to prevent the deceptive delegation from participation in the organization of the new Congress. He castigated them for "continu[ing] to ignore the benefits [e.g., seniority and funding] that they receive from the National Democratic Party, [while] failing to recognize it nor support it on the state or national level." He also associated this view with the newly elected member, David Bowen, who shunned the party even after taking its campaign money. Henry already had a lobbying effort in high gear, planning a four-day trip in Washington, D.C., at the end of the month and in early December. Loyalist attorney Wesley Watkins also planned a week in Washington during the same period.[119]

During 1973, little progress occurred as the Regulars pursued court relief challenging the legitimacy of the Loyalists. From the point of view of the Regulars, the decisions of the National Democratic Party that certified the Loyalists at the convention had no relevance whatsoever. The earlier ambivalence of the federal district and appeals courts inspired them.[120] Meanwhile, the snub that the Regulars perceived after loss of their convention seats only set back fledgling efforts for informal talks with the Loyalists.

Henry, of course, continued trying to engage the dominant elites among the Regulars. He sent letters, made phone calls (some of which remained unanswered), and used intermediaries. This did keep alive some hope since not all of the Regulars broke contact. There is an indication that William Winter, the lieutenant governor, sent a representative to Loyalist meetings. Henry chided him for sending an emissary and not coming himself, and encouraged his direct involvement. He sent Winter a party membership card and urged him to enroll.[121] In early 1974 it is also evident that Henry and the governor again had some contact. Henry wrote to Waller in February, indicating that they had something of a rapport. As party chairman, Henry detailed national procedures for meeting affirmative-action requirements in delegate selection and offered "specific advice . . . on how to get this mess straightened out." This same correspondence also indicated that he had contact with Senator Eastland, who Henry said expressed high interest in achieving unity, and a willingness to come home to lobby for this project. He ended the correspondence in a common flourish, wishing the governor a "Happy Valentine's Day."[122]

The contact between them continued in early 1974 as preparations got underway for the national Conference on Democratic Party Organization, slated for December in Kansas City, Missouri. The conference had significance because the national party slated the adoption of a charter to confirm its reorganization. Loyalist leaders Hodding Carter and Patricia Derian had served on the Fraser-O'Hara Commission that prepared the draft charter, a further illustration of Loyalists influence within the national organization. For the conference the national party allocated twenty-three delegates from Mississippi, six as ex-officio (the governor, the two U.S. senators, and three congressmen). While not noteworthy in other states, in Mississippi this configuration seemed at least contradictory—no Loyalists appeared on the ex-officio delegate list. Even so, the Loyalists did not contest this arrangement because it afforded contact between the warring factions. However, their differences remained stark. In the fact sheets the Loyalists issued regarding the selection process for the other seventeen delegates, they emphasized "Democrats and only Democrats." They clearly sought selection of only those who signed a loyalty oath to the national party, and also indicated that affirmative steps would be taken to prevent nonparty members from voting.[123]

Nevertheless, a larger goal remained to generate the broadest participation possible. Henry urged "all persons who are Democrats to participate in . . . the election of delegates for this important conference. Black, white, male, female, young, and old are welcome. Our meetings are open, we want you, one and all in this Party, in this process." He sent the same message to the Regulars. "We urge the involvement of every single Democrat in Mississippi, from the governor's mansion to the humblest shack. Attend this seminar, read the Fact Sheets, go to your Congressional District Caucus on May 19 to elect your delegates." In order to enhance participation among those normally underrepresented—minorities, Native Americans, women, and youth—Henry appointed a special affirmative-action committee to "Develop, review, and approve all publicity, organizational and educational efforts to make the Delegate Selection Process for the 1973 Conference fully understandable and accessible to all Mississippi Democrats."[124]

The mask of comity soon evaporated, however. Committeewoman Pat Derian stepped aside to allow the governor to serve with Henry as representative at the party's mini pre-conference, a fortuitous circumstance that might kick-start renewed merger efforts. It did not accomplish the desired end. The governor arrived and abruptly resigned as a conference delegate, and called on Henry to do the same. Waller reasoned that as principals in a legal dispute about the status of the party, neither he nor Henry should represent the state.[125] The larger motive, however, remained Waller's refusal to accept that authority resided with Henry and the Loyalists. If he had remained in Kansas City he would have had to acknowledge just that.

The governor's departure did not sever all communication with the Regulars. Congressman Jamie Whitten, whose seating had been contested by the Loyalists, did attend the meeting, and Henry sent him a warm letter lauding his support that made the convention a success. Whitten responded in kind, also telling Henry that a $200 donation for support of the convention had been dispatched to the governor, an ambivalent posture at best about the legitimacy of Henry's party leadership. Henry must surely have been disappointed that the donation did not benefit the financially strapped Loyalists.[126] He did not let on, no doubt hoping to turn this gesture to advantage in moving Waller to cooperate.

Very little additional merger initiative came from Governor Waller before finishing his term at the end of 1975. It appeared that Waller had gone as far as he believed his white constituency and the power of his office would allow him, or perhaps he had not fully accommodated himself to the shift in leadership of the party organization.[127] Yet there remained other signs of his awareness of how the Mississippi electorate had changed with new black voters. Recall that he had come to office pegged as a moderate because he had not run the traditionally avowedly racist campaign, earning African American support in the process.[128] He began his administration making widely praised signals of progress—appointing the committee of Regulars to negotiate with the Loyalists and appointing some African Americans to his administration.[129] To a degree the contradictions that delayed a merger under his single-term administration overshadowed his reform efforts.

The question of a merger remained on the table as the gubernatorial race of 1975 kicked into high gear. The impending change in partisan politics produced a revelatory campaign. It featured populist Democrat Cliff Finch, who courted the African American vote; a serious Republican challenger, Gil Carmichael; and the independent black activist Henry Kirksey. Finch had the slogan "the working man's friend," symbolized by his lunch pail on the campaign trail. Carmichael put up another strong challenge as a Republican, earned on a reputation for racial moderation in his 1972 campaign against segregationist senator James Eastland. In that contest he earned 42 percent of the vote. He again used that approach, capturing many black voters, gaining 45 percent of the gubernatorial poll.[130] Finch won the contest with 52 percent of the vote, and Kirksey drew a minuscule 2.5 percent.[131]

Finch received considerable support among the black electorate and moved with dispatch to secure a merged party. Indeed, the Finch group signaled its merger intentions to both the NDC and Henry in early December, prior to assuming office. Meanwhile, prospects improved for common delegate selection, the critical sticking point during the Waller administration. Henry once again tried to allay the fears of the Regular Executive Committee. "In the quest for unity," he offered to take the "gamble" of using Regular party chairmen in the counties to assist new precinct chairs with less or no experience in conducting the polling. Yet he warned against the lingering propensity of Regulars to take decisions and issue public statements without seeking input from its Loyalist "partners." He reminded them that unity rested on acting as one voice, not a "predominately Black" or "predominately White" organization.[132]

The precinct delegate selection process occurred on January 24, 1976, which Henry described as the "first formal day of our merger efforts." He was conciliatory in acknowledging that there had been some difficulties, citing most of the problems as bureaucratic snafus. He notified county and district chairs that the affirmative-action committee would consider the problems at a regular meeting on February 1, after which he announced the county conventions would take place in two weeks. He praised Governor Finch "for assistance in the quest for Democratic Party unity," and even thanked some members of the press, among them his previously often-vilified hometown newspaper, the *Clarksdale Press Register*.[133]

The formal merger occurred when the governor appeared at the February 29 state convention of the new Democratic Party. He gave a brief, but poignant speech saying he remained "proud to be with this gathering of the leadership of the state at this vitally important convention." Of the efforts of the leadership:

"I want to express to each of you—from my heart—my personal—deep—and lasting gratitude for the brave—patient—and persistent effort you have made to bring the Democratic Party together." He then invoked words attributed to former Democratic U.S. House Speaker Sam Rayburn—"we are Democrats without prefix—suffix—or apology." He heaped praise on Tom Riddell and Aaron Henry, the respective chairs of the Regulars and Loyalists, who he said had done more than any others to bring the state to this point of unity. Finch then addressed the conferees with a grand gesture: "I ask you—I urge you—to call on Mr. Riddell and Dr. Henry to lead us into the future as co-chairmen of the Mississippi Democratic Party."[134]

With the merger consummated, Henry began the complicated dance to cement the two elements. It proved complicated indeed, since members from both factions remained far apart following longstanding distrust wrought of a racial order that customarily excluded blacks. Yet Henry's style, influence, and clarity of goals gave him advantages in negotiating this terrain. Soon enough, he issued a number of letters and statements indicating his willingness to work with the local Regulars and set out to engage the members of Congress whose seats he had earlier contested. One of those to whom Henry made early overtures

Aaron Henry with Mississippi governor Cliff Finch, 1976, Jackson, Mississippi. (Courtesy Aaron Henry Papers, Tougaloo College.)

is Senator James Eastland. His efforts resulted in a meeting that both publicly acknowledged.[135]

Not all activists accepted this Henry-Eastland rapprochement. Owen Brooks of the Delta Ministry reflected the sentiments of many when he used a news release to criticize Henry for making this step toward a man seen as an unapologetic racist.[136] In turn, Henry did not remain silent. He chided Brooks for being an outsider (the "brain from Boston") with a suspect track record of his own. Henry issued a searing, perhaps overheated rejoinder: "I consider Mr. Owen Brooks as much or more of a racist than Senator Eastland." He noted changes in the senator's voting behavior: "In the past year Senator Eastland has supported more human-social legislation than ever before in his life. This political change in Senator Eastland has come because some of us from Mississippi, who are black, not including Mr. Brooks, have visited with Senator Eastland in his office and have tried to point out to him the error of his ways."[137] Henry likely had a simpler calculation in mind, however—if Eastland acknowledged the changed political circumstances, past sins should not be material to the new game; he had to count votes like everybody else in the first truly competitive race of his long tenure.

Consolidating various elements of the two factions seemed daunting on other fronts. Perhaps one of the greatest tests for Henry appeared because of the behavior of a presumed ally: Charles Evers. The always-unpredictable Evers, a self-described man of the Chicago underworld, now began issuing statements anathema to party interests, and even fraternizing with Republicans. He expressed disgruntlement with the Democratic Party, and even endorsed George Wallace for vice president in 1972 and again in 1976. He became notoriously dismissive of some of the efforts of the local Democratic Party when he ran in election campaigns against the wishes of the Loyalists (and anybody else for that matter). In 1979 he formed what he called the Independent Coalition for Mississippi, a self-described nonpartisan lobbying group. Henry bitterly rejected the idea and worked hard to keep Evers in the fold, but to little avail.[138] To Henry's chagrin, when Eastland retired in 1978 Evers ran as an independent. Henry saw this as tantamount to guaranteeing a victory to an increasingly competitive Republican Party. Indeed, Thad Cochran became the first Mississippi Republican senator since Reconstruction.[139]

This problem was not over for Henry since Evers stopped participation in the Democratic Party and officially registered as a Republican. Evers then declared: "I've always thought like a Republican, and I always knew that someday I would register as a Republican."[140] Henry sent him a letter dripping with anger at the betrayal: "if you lay down with Independents you will wake up with Republicans." He accused Evers of "trying to tear down two institutions, the State and National Democratic Party, that you know personally that I have tried to build." Then he pleaded: "I would not do this to you, Charlie, and I want you to stop your uncanny abuse of me, and of the confidence of the Black people who love, respect and trust us both."[141]

Under Henry's leadership the party nevertheless enjoyed success through the Finch administration. The merger agreement provided for party cochairs and the full integration of all affairs. Henry spent much of his time on administrative matters for the well-being of the faithful, as he cajoled wavering Regulars to remain. Considerable success also resulted in the opening of the political system to newly franchised blacks. The number of blacks going to the polls and running for office increased by leaps and bounds. The 8 elected in 1968 paled against the wave of 95 elected coincident with Waller in 1972. That figure doubled in four years to 210 with the Finch election. The success appeared in virtually all areas, except the state legislature where the reapportionment court battle continued.[142] The leadership seemed to be settling into a reasonable working relationship, belying the tension wrought by perceptions of Loyalist privilege in the hierarchy and the lack of enthusiasm by white citizens.

Reapportionment of the state legislature, a problem on which Henry and others worked for many years, now reached a partial resolution. Malapportionment was well documented, and had been litigated since the 1966 legislative sessions of "massive resistance" that sought to thwart the influence of the VRA. Frank Parker termed these dilution measures: stacking (diluting a concentrated black group by combining it with a larger white population); packing (clustering black voters in one district to prevent its influence on adjacent ones); and cracking (fragmenting a concentrated black group).[143] Gradually through the 1970s the Supreme Court rejected dilution based on race. The late May 1977 ruling in the Mississippi case, *Connor v. Finch*, rejected dilution of 16 and 19 percent in the House and Senate, respectively, as inconsistent with the Fourteenth Amendment.[144] It also rejected "combining black concentrations with greater white concentrations [to] submerge the black vote in majority white districts." The malapportionment system as a bulwark of racial exclusion had finally been interrupted, opening legislative spots to competition from black candidates.[145]

Henry, at the pinnacle of power in state and national politics, somewhat curiously contemplated elective office. It was difficult to perceive what a legislative seat could add beyond the power he already enjoyed. He led the state Democratic Party, had tremendous influence in the NDC, and widespread entrée to sources of power in Washington. The deputy chairman of the National Democratic Party, Ben Brown, revealed as much in describing Henry's influence in Washington. He told Henry in a letter that "on any given subject you have demonstrated your ability to secure more votes for your philosophical position from the members of Congress than any of the present members of the Senate or the U.S. House of

Representatives from Mississippi." Regarding the executive branch, Brown continued: "The relationship you have with President Jimmy Carter and his White House staff is wonderful to behold. Your constant relationship with the cabinet members is unparalleled by any other personality whom I know."[146] Moreover, Henry's civil rights credentials remained intact and significant. He already operated with a perch of independence superior to any that might be accorded by occupying a legislative seat.

Yet, having struggled so long, Henry said he felt compelled to seek a legislative seat: "After making a fight for nearly fifteen years through the courts of Mississippi and the Federal System for a redistricting plan in Mississippi that would assure more democracy in the state legislature, I find myself both desirous and obligated to make the race to enter the Mississippi Legislature." He sought a district "wholly within Coahoma County," his home base. He notified his co-party chairman that he would take a leave from duties while campaigning.[147]

In the meantime, the approaching end of the Finch administration in 1979 began a gubernatorial contest within the Democratic Party that improbably set off the greatest challenge to Henry's party leadership. The events that set this in motion related to efforts to halt defections by white Democrats to the Republican Party, a panic caused when the retirement in 1978 of longtime Democratic senator Eastland resulted in the election of the first Republican since Reconstruction, Thad Cochran. William Winter, a previous Democratic gubernatorial candidate, tagged as a "liberal" by segregationists in 1965 and 1975, set off the furor.[148] He had finally become governor in 1980 with the help of a sizable voting constituency of blacks in the Democratic Party, to whom he made direct appeals.[149] The outcome represented a proud moment of achievement for Henry at the head of a party whose interracial coalition had done so well in holding back the emerging Republican Party. However, soon after inauguration Governor Winter called for an end to the delicately negotiated dual leadership of the party. Winter said: "It was my desire that we maintain the strongest possible Democratic Party coalition. Up until that time, there had been two chairs of the party, the white chair and a black chair."[150] As a result he recommended selection of a white person as leader, and proposed Danny Cupit, a young lawyer within an emerging moderate to liberal camp that saw itself as heir to the disrupted segregationist ideology. Winter calculated that a white leader would reassure skeptical white moderates of a place in the organization.[151] It is doubtful that he anticipated the vitriolic response this would elicit from Henry and black Democrats. After all, the new governor had gone some distance earlier to facilitate the merger and had his election assured with the support of black voters.

Henry appeared stunned at this turn of events, and the governor's proposition set off a firestorm, upsetting the carefully orchestrated, if tortured, relationship between the two camps. Henry termed it an ungraceful return to the old days of

white control, and proceeded to go on the offensive against the Winter proposal.
[152] He wrote a plaintive letter to Robert Strauss, NDC chairman, arguing that the
party appeared to be taking a step back to where it was in 1976. In a barely dis-
guised reference to Governor Winter, he said these actions represented the "clever
and cunning moves" by some of the framers of the merger who sought to derail
coleadership from the start. He seemed most galled because blacks had given
their confidence to these same people who now sought their "exodus . . . from
equal leadership roles in the Democratic Party." As Henry saw it, the aim of these
detractors had now become totally transparent. He publicly termed their ideas
racist: "On May 10, 1980, at the State Executive Committee . . . the Governor
blatantly made the racist demand that the Executive Committee of the D. P. S. M.
[Democratic Party of the State of Mississippi] elect a white person to the leadership of the party." He promised noncooperation with this undemocratic move.
"The Black members of the D.P. S. M. have as a unit, decided on no further
participation in the Democratic Party of the State of Mississippi until you and
other National Democratic leaders move to correct this problem. 'The Black
Democrats of Mississippi refuse to be integrated into a burning house.'"[153]

Henry escalated to an even more searing tone when he wrote Governor
Winter. He began noting their lengthy time working together for change in
Mississippi, and said it pained him to write words that might destroy a well-
cultivated friendship. He then told Winter that "it is impossible for me and thousands like me both black and white to ignore your blatant call to racism as you
sought to establish in the leadership role of the Democratic Party of the State
of Mississippi, simply, 'a person who should be white.'" Henry asked Winter
to explain: "What happened to the high standards of qualified, capable, knowl-
edgeable, considerate, energetic and empathetic, that you usually apply when we
talk to you about employing or involving a Black in the leadership roles of the
Economic Development Commission?"

He even expressed doubts that the blacks Winter appointed to positions
would be allowed to perform their leadership roles with authority equal to that
of his white appointees. To back up his presumption Henry advised Winter of an
official complaint with the NDC regarding violation of the national affirmative
action policy. He reminded the governor of some history of interactions between
the races in the state. Blacks who gave their "innocent cooperation" during
Reconstruction, he said, ended up being duped after accepting a "deal" with the
then governors and lieutenants. That deception led to one hundred years of disfranchisement, and he assured the governor that blacks would not go for another
deal where the "duplicity" was so palpable.[154]

The profoundly bitter tone made it difficult to imagine reaching a compromise. Yet, with the stakes so high neither side could maintain the intensity of its
claims. Henry indicated as much when a day later he advised "Fellow Democrats"

that while a formal challenge had been put before the NDC, he would not pub-licly announce it. Indeed, negotiations had already commenced.

However, in the interim things got worse. Charles Evers, now seen more as a mischief-maker than a comrade, endorsed the Winter plan, prompting further caustic ripostes from Henry. "Charles was desirous of everybody understanding that any time he became involved in someone else's behalf, that he was properly compensated for his involvement." He then expressed surprise that Winter would fall for such a deal, even as Henry himself worked hard to secure a compromise.[155]

The party Executive Committee appointed a committee on May 10, 1980, that offered a resolution. It called for two separate offices at the top of the orga-nization, independent of each other—a chair of the party and a chair of the Executive Committee, one occupied by an African American and the other by a white. The former "would be the spokesperson for the party and represent the party in its dealings with all democratic campaigns and with local democratic units. The chairperson of the Executive Committee shall have charge of the func-tioning of the policymaking body of the party, and the conduct of its day-to-day operations."[156] Over the next month Henry and the Winter faction worked out the compromise announced June 21 that created both a party chairman and a substantive vice chairman. Winter's choice, Danny Cupit, became chairman, while Ed Cole, a former black aide to James Eastland, became the executive vice chairman. The two positions had some overlapping powers, though Cole's major responsibilities included the day-to-day operation of the secretariat and chairing the Administrative Committee. The group then elected Henry national commit-teeman and Unita Blackwell as vice chair of the party.[157]

The fix accomplished little of the desired increase in white participation that Winter sought, as the Republicans continued to gain ground in Mississippi and across the South generally.[158] Congressman Trent Lott became a second Repub-lican senator in 1988, and later several Democrats lost House seats to Repub-licans. Moreover, the state's preference for Republican presidential candidates (that began in the 1960s) continued, except when the state voted for Jimmy Carter the year of the merger.[159]

Nonetheless, blacks remained major players in party affairs and continued to enjoy success in local elections. Mike Espy, a black lawyer, won a congress-ional seat in 1987, followed upon resignation in 1993 by another black, Bennie Thompson. Blacks in the state legislature also ballooned after reapportionment, including Henry, who added the title of legislator to the variety of other political hats he wore.[160] This divergent partisan identification of the races signaled an emerging realignment that confirmed V. O. Key's maxim about the South: as the influence (salience) of blacks increased, white anxiety and fear increased. As black

Democrats grew, the whites deserted the old Democratic Party of the Solid South for the party of Lincoln.[161]

This phase of Henry's story brought him close to the goal of cementing a locally based, interracial coalition with the common goal of fundamentally changing the racial system in Mississippi. When Henry began talking about an expanded coalition succeeding the failure at the 1964 convention, few gave him any chance of pulling it off. In this remarkable phase the relentless pressure Henry led against the Regular Democratic Party caused its elites to harden resistance to any change. The hard-line resisters clearly miscalculated the power of their opposition. Henry, on the contrary, remained convinced that his assemblage of grassroots activists, external allies in the public and private sector, and the direction of public opinion would win. They won big. Though the grassroots coalition remained loose, its agreement about ousting a group remained strong. As the Regulars became progressively more outrageous in denying the legitimacy of black claims for representation, it only helped consolidate the Loyalist resisters and their allies. After the Regulars got themselves booted from the 1968 convention, Henry knew that it remained a matter of time before the Loyalists would assume party leadership. It took longer perhaps than he imagined, but inevitability did set in. Though the path remained tortured for years, moderate governor Waller became the first leader among the Regulars to concede the inevitable. Four years later the new governor Finch consummated a deal that fully empowered a new party system, led by Aaron Henry.

Overseeing the merger of the two elements of the Democratic Party became perhaps Henry's greatest achievement. It ushered in a period where electoral politics became the primary focus of racial change in Mississippi. This shift proved easier for Henry than for most of the members of the social movement coalition. However, if that task seemed suspect to some of his movement partners, it appeared daunting for segregationists who traditionally opposed the social change he sought. He differed from his partners and nemeses because he maintained a flexible approach, albeit with an enduring focus on an interracial cast to alter the racial system. Others became frustrated with the details or wavered in the goal, while Henry always focused on a broad goal of integration. Henry's position never wavered about his comprehensive goal, even when he sought to expand his partnership base to include local white politicians. Though a practical strategy, Henry also sought to maintain integrity to the vision of equal citizenship and livelihood for African Americans. The steadiness of this coalition remained an open question, but it must have given him some pride that blacks had membership at the table, with the ability to negotiate as insiders.

CHAPTER NINE

The Summit and Culmination

Henry as a State Legislator and His Political Demise

It may have been inevitable that Henry, the social movement leader, would evolve to compete in the arena of electoral politics. After all, the power of political office is a heralded benefit of the North American democratic experiment. It should be little surprise that he and some other activists in the civil rights movement also sought this prize. Power and representation ran as an undercurrent in the Montgomery bus boycott, and Henry framed his interests around it after military service; he registered to vote and brimmed with pride when he cast his first vote. He had now come to the cusp of its full benefit, after a thorny social movement path, to have a chance at a genuine, not mock, political office. He rode a wave of electoral success by African Americans, especially in the South and in Mississippi. He saw black officials in his state quadruple between 1968 and 1972 (from 28 to 128).[1] All of the cards seemed aligned for his success after election to the legislature in 1980, though ironically it proved to be the last hurrah for his long and distinguished political career. After serving four terms, he lost his seat and concomitantly experienced a significant weakening of his overall political influence.

This new era of electoralism signaled by his assumption of a legislative seat (with a large cohort of other blacks) raised a major question. How could African American social movement leaders, now politicians, maintain integrity to social change goals in the horse-trading arena of electoral politics? In Henry's case, how would he bargain and build coalitions in the then overtly racist environment of the Mississippi legislature? In reality he fairly successfully maintained integrity to social movement goals even as he functioned within the peculiar limits of the difficult, though evolving legislative environment. He could justly claim much credit for changing the membership and character of lawmaking within that body. He continued his now legendary positive and practical approach within this new arena. He said: "For years, those of us in the black community felt the legislature was no friend of black people. Now we have the opportunity to work within the legislative system. You take your chances there, understanding that if you don't win, there will be another chance."[2]

The Loyalist coalition of blacks and moderate whites that oversaw the merger evolved to bring Mississippi back into the fold of national Democratic politics. Democrat Jimmy Carter carried the state in 1976, the first time a Democrat won since 1956. An example of the standing Loyalist coalition members had in national affairs is that President Carter tapped two of its most prominent adherents for service in his administration: Hodding Carter III became assistant secretary for Public Affairs, and Patricia Derian became coordinator for Human Rights and Humanitarian Affairs, both at the State Department.[3] Henry soldiered on as party coleader, nurturing the old guard in the coalition, and a coterie of younger black supporters and officeholders (most too young to have experienced the 1960s social movement). By some measure, these circumstances reflected the fulfillment of a part of Henry's grand vision for the regularization of African American participation—seeking and assuming political office as a routine choice. For many of the new black members in the party, the symbolic act of running had been replaced by very high prospects of winning.[4]

Henry requested leave from his leadership of the party in early June of 1979, signaling the beginning of his campaign for the legislature. He wrote constituents and supporters explaining his decision as the culmination of the fifteen-year reapportionment quest. All those years, he said, he told the courts: "if a District were created within my residential area and which was predominately Black, that I would consider running for the seat." District Twenty-Six in Clarksdale met the criteria and he sought the seat.[5] His longtime collaborator in Clarksdale politics, Bennie Gooden, served as his campaign manager.

Henry campaigned hard. He asked supporters not just to register and vote, but also to canvass, and make "ten" telephone calls, contribute money, and clerical assistance. He did not pretend to have an ordinary campaign, offering himself as an "inside agitator" in the style of the original washing machine "that beats the filth, the dirt and the grime from clothing." He reminded them that his agitation had been done amid "bombings, bullets and fire bombings right here in this community."[6]

By the end of May 1979 he issued his straightforward platform: a desire to "help relieve the miseries of the poor and down-trodden," and to continue to seek "integration, and to combat the evils of racial separatism." He reiterated his party identification saying, "I am running as a DEMOCRAT [emphasis in the original]. I feel that the policies of the National Democratic Party, that are shared by the Democratic Party of the State of Mississippi, are more responsive to a constituency that I represent." He enumerated a list of ideas, programs, and policies that he helped to formulate, the maintenance of which he deemed critical to community development: affirmative action in local government, Head Start, Public Housing, community action programs, summer jobs for youth, and Job Corps. He cited his record in obtaining eligibility for income subsidy; jobs for farmers, indigent families, and the elderly; prevented Social Security cuts; and continuously supported school integration. He also reiterated his record of continuous access to presidents and governors.[7]

Finally, Henry returned to the central idea of racial integration. He made it clear that racial exclusion would not be a factor in the campaign: "The methods used by the Black community in freeing Black citizens from the chains of inequality, must be methods that so appeal to the conscience of our White Brothers and Sisters that they free you in the process and thus this victory becomes a double victory in which all Americans can share."[8]

In a majority black district that included all of Coahoma and a part of Bolivar Counties, Henry ran unopposed. Both of these Delta counties had huge African American population majorities—each right at 70 percent.[9] The Office of Secretary of State did not even report votes in the primary contest since Henry ran unopposed. However, in the general election he received a total of 1,843 votes.[10] When he arrived at the legislature in 1980, it commenced a legislative service tenure that lasted four terms (1980–1996).

Legislative seats had been objects for African Americans since 1960, though few had succeeded. However, when the long-running reapportionment suit (discussed in chapter 6), *Connor v. French*, finally came to conclusion in 1977, it broke the barrier to significant African American representation. As such 1979 became a watershed year for the election of black legislators. That year sixteen others accompanied Henry into the lawmaking body. Their numbers then climbed to twenty in the next election cycle. Regional residential and segregation patterns situated black candidates well to win in the Delta (four seats), the river counties of the southwest part of the state (three), and in urban Jackson (six). In all of these districts blacks exceeded 50 percent of the electorate. One Jackson district had the highest concentration of African American residents with 95 percent, while Henry's Coahoma district had 74 percent (see Table 4).[11]

The Mississippi legislature Henry entered hardly reflected a representative body, though the job had attractions. The body possessed substantial power vis-à-vis the governor and many other state officials. At the time a governor had a single term limit and did not choose the cabinet. Even selection of the lieutenant governors occurred in a separate poll; that office controlled the upper house by appointing its leadership and managing the legislative agenda. Meanwhile, the size of the legislature is large (122 in the house and 52 in the senate), ostensibly bringing it closer to constituents, though the body is unwieldy.[12] As a result, despite the primacy of the large "people's" legislature, a usually small leadership group dominated internal business. Like the lieutenant governor's dominance of the senate, the speaker of the house largely controlled the agendas, assigned tasks, and determined the state's legislative program in the lower chamber.[13] The legislature perforce remained the most parochial institution in government. Henry thus entered an institution woefully unreceptive to the interests he represented or the reservoir of power he customarily experienced as a party leader.

TABLE 4
African Americans in Mississippi Legislature (House), 1980*

Legislator	Dist#	County (*town*)	Black Pop. (%)	Service (Yrs)
Fred Banks	69	Hinds (*Jackson*)	88	4
Horace Buckley	70	Hinds (*Jackson*)	94	4
Credell Calhoun	68	Hinds (*Jackson*)	89	1
Robert Clark	49	Holmes (*Ebenezer*)	70	12
Tyrone Ellis	40	Noxubee/Lowndes/ Oktibbeha (*Starkville*)	68	1
Hillman Frazier	67	Hinds (*Jackson*)	86	1
Isiah Fredericks	119	Harrison (*Gulfport*)	59	1
David Green	98	Wilkinson/Amite (*Gloster*)	61	1
Clayton Henderson	70	Tunica/Quitman (*Tunica*)	70	1
Aaron Henry	26	Coahoma (*Clarksdale*)	74	1
Leslie King	51	Washington (*Greenville*)	80	1
Barney Schoby	95	Adams (*Natchez*)	68	1
Charles Sheppard	87	Claiborne/Jefferson (*Lorman*)	79	1
Percy Watson	104	Forrest (*Hattiesburg*)	73	1
Charles Young	84	Lauderdale (*Meridian*)	71	1

*Two members were elected to the Senate: Doug Anderson and Henry Kirksey, both from the Hinds County/Jackson area.

There is a body of empirical literature about the influence of elected African American officials in state legislatures—how they think about their tasks and behave, and the outcomes they achieve. Haynie suggests that they must be attuned to the specialized interests (alleviation of disparity and inequity) of their racialized constituents and to be challengers to the policy deficits and the incremental approach of legislative institutions.[14] The socioeconomic disparity generally compels these legislators to seek solutions via government intervention. Haynie suggests that this shows up in their "support for legislation and policies favoring social welfare, economic redistribution, and civil rights issues. Specifically, laws that prohibit discrimination in voting, housing, education, and unemployment, and laws that support unemployment compensation, jobs programs, food stamps, and educational assistance are considered to be black interests."[15]

In light of what scholars know, what can be said about Henry's activity as a representative? In part, much of his early influence (and that of his cohort of black legislators) remained symbolic. Mary Coleman's 1993 study of the Mississippi legislature found that virtually none of the average of twenty-six bills per session that black legislators introduced succeeded in getting to the House or Senate floors, let alone becoming law.[16] Byron Orey's comparative analysis of African American legislators and a control group of their white colleagues, in two sessions (1987 and 1988) confirms much of what Coleman suggests: African Americans on average introduced a comparable number of bills (222.5 versus 259.5 for the control group), but had far less success in gaining passage of proposals (8.5 percent versus 25 percent for the control group).[17]

Some scholars, however, believe that significant influence can be vested in symbolic political positions. Katherine Tate argues that a significant amount of what legislators in general do can be termed symbolic. The system of majoritarian government in the United States makes it inevitable that legislators look out for the district, and making laws is not the only means of doing that. Indeed, she argues that it may not be as important as acquiring pork barrel projects for the district, or influencing the debate about questions that affect the district.[18] From this point of view, when a minority of blacks arrived in the legislature after reapportionment they immediately accomplished what had not been done in a hundred years—integrated the all-white body by descriptively representing constituents they mobilized who never voted before. Some success accrued thereby merely because the voters made a decision independent of the preferences or machinations of the segregationists. Therefore, Frank Parker had no uncertainty about the political impact of the arrival of the black legislators. Their seats at the decision-making table changed the conversations about important and mundane matters of governance: "statewide policy making, distribution of state tax dollars, and allocation of state-provided services."[19]

Legislators like Henry performed other functions by being in place. He gave his constituents entrée to the system, enhancing the prospect for formal exchanges within it. Some exchanges proved banal—seeking information about how government worked, or executing state-mandated paperwork. This routine, mundane legislative activity constitutes a major part of what any legislator does. African Americans, however, only attained this significant symbolic leadership in the 1980 legislature; previously no one assumed responsibility for representing their voices. Now black voters had another place to go with the expectation of being heard by a sympathetic agent. With Henry and his cohort being unified around their common interests, they began to modestly change the environment for their causes. They could and did intervene in debate, giving voice to issues that their compatriots could vote down, but could not entirely silence.[20] Over time, acting as a unified black legislative caucus, they influenced the broader agenda of the legislature by strategic voting. For example, by making coalitions with colleagues from urban districts they assured passage of Governor Winters's educational reform package in 1982. Also, their unified actions on suspension bills (those that require a two-thirds vote, or those on revenue) could put blacks in a position to make demands in exchange for support of one side or the other.[21]

Henry had immediate expectations and responsibilities because his public experience exceeded the others in his African American cohort. Clearly they saw him as a first among equals. One junior member explained the importance of his presence within the cohort. Representative Tomie Green found him to be a commanding presence, competent on issues and with dexterity on procedures. His obvious wealth of experience always showed, and according to Green, he shared it generously. At the same time he formulated a body of ideas for legislative programs of broad scope, though she knew perfectly well that his legislative proposals or those he signed onto rarely passed. Nevertheless they illustrated the consistency of ideas to which he dedicated his time. In sum, he seemed to Representative Green to be a tremendous asset in helping them to negotiate their way through the system.[22]

Upon arrival Henry immediately informed the legislative leadership that he had come to represent a large body of interests and that he expected to get started on his agenda without delay. He staked a claim early as unwilling to play the role of the incrementalist, merely accepting the traditional rules of the legislative game. At the outset he sought incorporation into the power bases of the institution by seeking appointment to committees he deemed strategic.[23] He requested some of the choicest committees, among the large number available.[24] He asked the Speaker to assign him two of the most powerful and essential committees: Ways and Means and Appropriations—those that raised money and spent it. He also requested appointment to: Apportionments and Elections, Labor, Pensions, Municipalities, County Affairs, Military Affairs, and Social Welfare and Public Health. These were all areas to which he had devoted time prior to his legislative service, and on which he had considerable professional or other expertise.[25]

Despite the clarity with which he had already stated his interests, Henry sent notice to the Speaker elaborating what he termed "areas of legislative interest." He sent a loaded list, including some of the hot topics within the black community:

human relations, affirmative action, integration, education and economics; problems of poverty, such as justice, equality, dignity, and fairness; increased involvement of racial minorities, youth, and women; and finally police community attitudes. He labeled education, integration, and economics as "Black Citizens Problems and Concerns" and justice, equality, dignity, fairness as "Poor Peoples problems and concerns."[26] He signaled that he expected to be a representative for matters related to African Americans, but also for a broad range of issues critical to many others similarly situated, and that he would bring his considerable expertise and political influence to bear on his service. This is entirely consistent with the attributes that Haynie associates with the "Black interest" orientation of these legislators.[27]

Legislative appointments were in the hands of longtime speaker, Delta segregationist Buddie Newman. Frank Parker sketched this power: "Through his power to appoint committee chairs, make committee assignments, and control the House calendar, Newman single-handedly determined the fate of bills by manipulating their assignment to particular committees, determining their position on the House calendar, and timing floor actions."[28] Henry received only one of the committee assignments he requested: municipalities. However, he did acquire appointments to two others that are regarded as among the most powerful: agriculture and judiciary "A." In addition, he also drew assignment to the Conservation and Water Resources Committee.[29] Table 5 shows the committee assignments Henry obtained at the start of each legislative service year, 1980–1992.

Perhaps the easiest way to assess Henry's legislative activity is by analyzing individual legislation.[30] Through this lens it is possible to understand his commitments and their consistency with the demands and expectations of his constituents.[31] This approach then makes it practical to account for his influence in the broader legislature environment. Henry proved very active as a first-term legislator, despite being pulled in many directions as a state and national party leader. He participated in the committees and on the floor, although like his African American counterparts, he had little success passing legislation.[32] He certainly tried to influence and redefine the agenda of a body that rarely focused on African American or urban interests. During his first term as a principal his name was attached to twenty-four bills. The subject matter fell within the broad interests he communicated to the Speaker: corrections (six bills), education (six), political affairs (three), social services (three), and civil rights (one). He also signed on to five general state business bills. Over time he spent significant time on only one other category not apparent in the first term, "local" issues in his district or the Delta region. Taken together they reflect the grand vision he articulated from the start in the 1950s.

TABLE 5

Henry Committee Appointments, 1980–1992

Year	Committee	Leadership
1980	Agriculture*	
	Conservation and Water Resources*	
	Judiciary "A"*	
	Municipalities*	
1984	Enrolled Bills*+	Vice Chair
	Conservation and Water Resources*	
	Judiciary "A"*	
	Municipalities*	
	Public Health and Welfare*	
1988	Elderly**	Chair
	Council on Aging***	
	Municipalities*	
	Public Buildings, Grounds, and Lands*	
	Public Health and Welfare*	
	Ways and Means*	
1992	Council on Aging***	
	Municipalities*	
	Public Buildings, Grounds, and Lands*	
	Public Health and Welfare*	
	Ways and Means*	

*Standing Committees.
**Interim Study Committee.
***State Board.
+Joint Committee.

Source: *Mississippi Official and Statistical Register*, 1980–1992. Office of Secretary of State, Jackson.

Almost all of the bills he proposed reflected a concern for altering the inequities experienced by African Americans. Yet, he always formulated his ideas within the context of the routines of the legislation system, even though he sought an expansion of the usual norms for setting the legislative agenda. At the same time, he sought to frame a program whose outputs would be especially beneficial to African Americans, though the projects did not exclude other racial groups.

Rather, he adopted a strategy for inclusive distribution of public goods, while allowing blacks to catch up. This positioned him to lay claim as a spokesperson for the general population, and not just blacks.

Meanwhile, Henry, like most legislators, worked to get on with his colleagues, seeking common ground beyond his African American cohort. He wanted to be seen as a bridge between the new dispensation and the past, so long as his counterparts accepted him as an equal. Oftentimes this collegiality played out regarding local issues, which gave him a basis for communication with his counterparts who had their own parochial interests to pursue. Sometimes their local interests dovetailed with his. Therefore, in being attentive to issues in Coahoma County, Clarksdale, and the region, he often found a basis to collaborate across racial lines, where friendships and respectful relations developed.

Therefore, Henry dedicated the bulk of his time on legislation to realize his grand vision of inclusiveness for African Americans, even as he maintained engagement with the general welfare of the state. The legislative categories into which he divided his time are political affairs, education, local affairs, social services, corrections, civil rights, and general subjects.[33] All but two of the seven subject areas (local affairs and general bills) implicitly or explicitly contained components that enhanced the prospects for equity for African Americans.[34] While the frequency count for his general proposals (many of them collaborations with other colleagues) spiked higher in several sessions, the combined frequency of the other categories dwarf the general bills.

In the first term he dedicated almost 75 percent of his time to corrections, education, and political affairs, issues that related to black inclusion. This is extraordinarily high, no doubt related to the importance he attached to the relative absence of these subjects from the legislative agenda for a hundred years. Later he reduced the focus on these to about 50 percent as he introduced more local legislation.[35] The lion's share of his attention overall remained dedicated to education, a focus maintained throughout his lawmaking career. Over sixteen years of legislative service he spent an average of 20 percent of his time on education, although in the first term he also spent about as much time on corrections. The latter emphasis waned, however, in the succeeding years and almost disappeared in the last two terms. Similarly, he gave considerable focus to political affairs in the first two terms, but this too waned to complete absence in the last term. Civil rights and social services remained steady during the sixteen years, even though they rarely exceeded the 20 percent mark in any term.[36] Given this division of his time, Henry maintained a scrupulous consistency with the ideas he propounded during the social mobilization phase of the movement in Clarksdale in the early 1960s. (See table 6.)

TABLE 6

Aaron Henry Legislation Summary, 1980–1995, By Subject (%).

Year	Pol Affs	Educ	Local	Soc Ser	Correc	Civ Rgt	Genl	Total
1980	3 (12%)	6 (25%)	0	3 (12%)	6 (25%)	1 (4%)	5 (21%)	24
1981	3 (14%)	2 (9%)	1 (5%)	1 (5%)	7 (32%)	1 (5%)	7 (32%)	22
1982	3 (18%)	5 (29%)	1 (6%)	1 (6%)	3 (18%)	1 (6%)	3 (18%)	17
1983	3 (13%)	2 (9%)	2 (9%)	3 (13%)	3 (13%)	2 (9%)	8 (34%)	23
1984	3 (15%)	4 (20%)	4 (20%)	2 (10%)	3 (15%)	2 (10%)	2 (10%)	20
1985	2 (10%)	2 (10%)	6 (28%)	2 (10%)	2 (10%)	1 (5%)	6 (28%)	21
1986	1 (4%)	2 (9%)	9 (39%)	3 (13%)	1 (4%)	3 (13%)	4 (17%)	23
1987	1 (6%)	3 (19%)	2 (12%)	0	1 (6%)	6 (37%)	3 (19%)	16
1988	2 (6%)	2 (6%)	12 (36%)	2 (6%)	1 (3%)	5 (15%)	9 (27%)	33
1989	1 (6%)	1 (6%)	3 (20%)	2 (13%)	0	2 (13%)	6 (40%)	15
1990	1 (6%)	3 (20%)	6 (40%)	1 (6%)	0	2 (13%)	2 (13%)	15
1991	0	10 (47%)	5 (24%)	2 (10%)	0	1 (5%)	3 (14%)	21
1992	0	9 (34%)	4 (15%)	1 (4%)	0	2 (8%)	10 (38%)	26
1993	0	10 (34%)	3 (10%)	8 (27%)	0	2 (7%)	6 (20%)	29
1994	0	14 (37%)	5 (13%)	7 (18%)	1 (3%)	1 (3%)	10 (26%)	38
1995	0	1 (16%)	2 (33%)	2 (33%)	0	1 (16%)	0	6
Total	23 (7%)	76 (22%)	65 (19%)	40 (11%)	28 (8%)	33 (9%)	85 (24%)	350

Legend: Pol Affs: Political Affairs; Educ: Education; Soc Ser: Social Service; Correc: Corrections; Civ Rgt: Civil Rights; Genl: General

The education measures that he repeatedly filed and/or cosponsored sought first and foremost to attain an equitable system. He personally knew the conditions of inequity all too well, and had high hopes that these legislative proposals would be especially beneficial for African Americans. Yet, the interests he expressed in education remained far broader than just the interests of his black constituents. He also sought the advancement of the lagging system for the benefit of the entire state: increased financing, development of infrastructure, and the diversification and expansion of the curriculum. By any objective assessment, Mississippi did lag, investing less than any other state, and its students performing significantly below counterparts in many other states. Henry's broad educational proposals, therefore, anticipated the establishment of a well-financed and first-rate learning system for the entire state. The long-term education agenda may be divided into several categories: (1) support for historically black colleges and universities (HBCUs); (2) educational reform; (3) increased financial and employee benefits; (4) equity funding; (5) symbolic and descriptive representation; and (6) local projects (pork barrel).

Henry perceived an immediate opportunity to correct the disparity in state allocations to HBCUs vis-à-vis the white universities. A good deal of documentation already showed the gross disparity, and the state had lost a major court decision that required it to make an affirmative effort to change its allocation pattern in order to achieve equity.[37] He, therefore, took on the issue of allocations to the HBCUs, and it remained an enduring interest. He often collaborated with other black lawmakers to press this agenda, and together they sponsored a variety of bills over the years. In his first term, HB 240 sought an additional appropriation for a construction project at Jackson State University, and it became a model for building projects that he advanced for the three state four-year HBCUs through his legislative career—Jackson State, Alcorn State, and Mississippi Valley State. He saw all of these institutions as his "constituents," though only Mississippi Valley was located near his Clarksdale district.[38] He expressed equal concern for the private four-year colleges of Tougaloo and Rust. In 1984, for example, he joined a coalition of black legislators, urban legislators, and others to try and get tuition grants for state residents who attended "independent" colleges. Henry aimed to provide assistance to students at Tougaloo and Rust because the higher tuition at these schools created greater financial needs for their impoverished, largely black Mississippi students.[39] Overall, most of his legislation, at least that requiring a commitment of resources, died in committee. He remained undeterred, persistently making such capital improvement proposals.

He also sought to advance the education of athletes via a state mandate for pursuit of a bachelor's degree while participating in athletic programs.[40] This represented an early effort to force colleges to treat African American athletes as students first and not as commodities. In this he articulated a view that animated much of the academic literature on this subject. Though superior athletes remained prized on the playing fields by colleges and universities, their academic needs received far less attention and many never obtained college degrees.[41] These and similar measures also died in committee.

Henry made regular use of House resolutions, as opposed to formal bills. He sometimes used this as a tactic in the face of the inevitability of defeat for his regular bills. The resolutions expressed a straightforward point of view (often preliminary to later submission of an appropriation item) or offered accolades for performance, often athletic (symbolic representations).[42] An attempt to get consideration of an Alcorn construction project provides an example of the former tactic. When Henry failed to get financing into a regular bill for an Alcorn assembly hall, he then sponsored a Concurrent Resolution (which also failed) to authorize studies of the need for such construction.[43] Presumably if he could demonstrate the need, his colleagues might be persuaded at some time in the future to actually schedule formal consideration of an assembly hall.

Some of his resolutions did succeed. Those that did more often than not seemed to partially confirm the persistence of the racial myths about black athletic prowess or to reflect acts of symbolism.[44] He enjoyed considerable success when he offered commendations for athletic teams or individual athletes. In general the sport did not seem to matter. In his first term, for example, Henry initiated or cosponsored successful commendations for individual football players and the women's basketball team at Jackson State.[45] In subsequent years commendations succeeded for individuals, teams, and even athletic banquets (viz., Walter Payton and the Jackson State Hall of Fame Banquet in 1984).[46] He also reciprocated and supported his white counterparts in their sport commendations: Ole Miss golfer Randy Watkins and Alabama football coach Bear Bryant, among them.[47] Indeed, white legislators seemed far less interested in the Henry proposals designed to enhance the academic quality of the institutions and the performance of their students. These collaborations on matters of athletic entertainment in no way threatened the segregated educational system that Henry ultimately sought to destroy.[48] Nor did this comity in celebrating athletic achievement have implications for the outlay of financial resources. Otherwise, white legislators seemed far less interested in the Henry proposals designed to enhance the academic quality of the institutions and the performance of their students.[49]

Educational reform remained a high priority for Henry, a part of a strategy to improve the quality and quantity of education for black children. However, he also made proposals to improve the competitiveness of all Mississippi students. In his early years he persistently sought to make school attendance compulsory and proposed state-financed kindergarten.[50] He followed suit in making resolutions to reform the curriculum, including an annual proposal for observance of "Black History Week."[51] In other bills he proposed compensatory curricula to boost student performance, especially those in historically weak schools, and to increase support for training new reading teachers.[52] Interestingly a resolution proposing health education to stem teenage pregnancies and abortions offered by Henry and an interracial coalition produced rare success. However, there is little doubt that many of the conservative colleagues who joined focused more on limiting abortions than on the broader education components of the resolution.[53]

Despite the persistent failures in getting legislation passed, some of the ideas did prevail by other means. Many of the ideas Henry offered in the first two years also figured into Governor Winter's 1980 education reform package. That package failed when first proposed, but succeeded two years later and incorporated some of Henry's ideas. The Educational Reform Act of 1982 created a public kindergarten program, gave attention to reading, and reinstated compulsory school attendance.[54] The passage of this broad legislation is but one example of how

Henry and the 1980 cohort of black legislators influenced the broader legislative agenda quite early in their tenure.[55] They seized opportunities when they arose and thereby often left their fingerprints on projects they could not dream of passing as independent legislative provisions.

Henry remained an unrelenting critic of the state's financial investments in infrastructure for education. He saw such efforts as willful attempts to maintain segregation, even though this starved the school system as a whole of resources. Therefore, many of his education bills sought an infusion of financial resources for teacher salaries and benefits (e.g., insurance). In 1982 he joined an interracial coalition to propose an Education and Economic Development Trust as the means of funding, and also tried to legalize a state lottery with the proceeds directed to education.[56] He offered very detailed plans focused on improving reading by recruitment of new teachers and assistants in the subject.[57] In 1991, for example, he sought to broaden staffs by hiring assistant reading instructors in the kindergarten and first three elementary grades.[58] While the preceding focused on creating an institutional base for teaching fundamentals, Henry also knew that African American teachers were often being displaced by white teachers as integration increased. Therefore, in 1990 he offered a comprehensive project to recruit minority teachers through a four-year scholarship-loan program administered by a "Mississippi Minority Teachers Corps."[59] He put the enhancement of student performance in this equation. To that end, Henry introduced a bill proposing draconian measures against underperforming schools—withdrawal of accreditation and loss of funding.[60] He coupled all this with the provision of appropriate support for improving the skills of teachers.[61]

In the area of civil rights, from his first year in the legislature Henry endeavored to pass legislation that he deemed of interest to his statewide African American constituency. To a degree these proposals reflected a "common good" element, though they clearly had a direct appeal to African Americans. He framed the proposals on the presumption of blacks as equals within the fabric of social and cultural life. However, since that status remained merely an aspiration, it provided the basis for developing a legislative program designed to better align reality and aspirations. Henry produced quite diverse legislative proposals. Some of the bills recognized heroic figures; others focused on substantive expansion of the state's political culture or substantive redistribution of resources. Still others advanced the ideological agenda of the national Democratic Party. These civil rights proposals also more often than others tended to reappear from session to session. Nevertheless, they attracted the least white collaborators and often stood no chance of passage.

Perhaps the most obvious race-centric proposals Henry put forward recognized African American heroic civil rights figures. One of his first (1983) proposals was to recognize Medgar Evers by hanging his portrait in the Capitol building, a place of honor reserved for highly regarded leaders and public figures.[62] Later in the same session he proposed legal holidays honoring Martin Luther King Jr. (January 15) and Evers (July 2).[63] The proposal could not have been more provocative. He put these bold propositions to a body that in 1967 tried to bar the first black member elected since Reconstruction and then, upon finally seating him, physically isolated him from the rest of his colleagues. It evoked little surprise that these proposals died in committee.[64]

However, the losses turned a page for Henry and the black legislative caucus; they decided to make a stand to demonstrate the power they could marshal as a black-voting bloc. The caucus now had eighteen members and all of them unified behind a retaliatory filibuster. The caucus tied up the rest of the session when the proposal for a King holiday did not clear committee. The action commenced during "deadline week," the time when the legislation that the leadership is willing to support must get to the floor. Usually this means that the prospects for passage of those bills are very high. However, any member may request a verbal reading of any such bills before they come to a vote. The caucus requested a reading for every piece of legislation that came to the floor, to the chagrin of their white colleagues. Henry, of course, had another view; he saw this as a blessing, demonstrating the power of the relatively small caucus to frustrate the majority.[65] An estimate is that more than one hundred bills did not get to the floor.[66] It took time for the caucus to get the body to honor King, but in 1987 a compromise bill did pass. Henry joined a large contingent of African American legislators and some of their white colleagues to designate the third Monday of January a holiday celebrating King and Confederate general Robert E. Lee.[67] The combination of honorees was an odd twist, to say the least.

Several other examples of failed civil rights proposals deserve attention. One of Henry's major initiatives proposed a state Human Relations Commission, designed to legitimize the work of the interracial human rights group that started in the 1950s. He envisioned an investigative role for the commission akin to that of the federal Commission on Civil Rights.[68] This did not succeed, but it was another initiative that generated a monumental backlash—the proposal to get rid of the state flag that incorporated the old Confederate flag.[69] The NAACP joined this effort, legally challenging use of the flag as the state emblem. Both the bill and the legal challenge failed. Then the state supreme court punted the legal challenge, arguing that the controversy was moot since there never was an approved state flag. That prompted a hard-fought statewide referendum on the question; maintenance of the "stars and bars" flag received overwhelming support.[70] Undaunted, still another powerful civil rights bill sought to integrate black history into the public school curriculum. Henry introduced a resolution proposing an observation of Negro History Week in February so that all students could learn that blacks "significantly contributed to and have irrefutably been a part of the social, economic, cultural and political growth of the state."[71] This proved too much for his legislative counterparts.

Henry's political affairs legislative efforts often overlapped with civil rights concerns, but endeavored to effectuate power redistribution and equal representation and to build the party's infrastructure. He spent significant time seeking to eliminate underrepresentation of voters who experienced racial discrimination or otherwise had their votes suppressed. For example, despite passage of the 1965 voting law Henry remained suspicious of voter suppression by circuit clerks. He proposed legislation to deputize high school principals as registrars. They would be able to enroll anyone, but especially their eighteen-year-old students. Another related proposal sought to authorize registrars and those deputized for this work to offer their services in a variety of places outside of the normal venues—the intimidating courthouses.[72] Henry's expansive thinking about citizen participation is reflected in still broader measures he sought that would optimize voting opportunities—approval of absentee and mail voting, both also proposals on the agenda of the national Democratic Party.[73]

The efforts to strengthen the institutional structure of the state party infrastructure seemed to relate to Henry's needs and interests in his role as chairman. He proposed several pieces of legislation designed to shore up the financial base of political parties in general, although the focus remained on shoring up the financial health of his fledgling Democratic Party. He offered an option to allow citizens to designate a portion of their income tax refund (one to five dollars) as a political party contribution. The parties would be able to use these funds for operation, as they deemed appropriate.[74]

Reforming the 1890 U.S. Constitution became perhaps the largest political affairs effort to which Henry (and his black colleagues) dedicated time. After all, the document still included language that technically disenfranchised African Americans: a residency requirement, restrictions for those with criminal records, poll tax and literacy requirements, and a long post-registration waiting period before voting.[75] The constitutional reform effort, therefore, was built around the grievance of African Americans and other similarly situated state residents. For example, Henry's first legislative proposal sought to get an equal rights for women amendment into the Constitution, and he followed that with an effort to restore the franchise to those disqualified for committing common crimes. The following year a huge biracial coalition proposed a convention to revise the entire Constitution. Two governors lent support to the idea of a convention: Allain (1984–1988) and Mabus (1988–1992).[76] However, the coalition eventually faltered because of a dispute over tactics with the black caucus. When Henry and his cohorts could not get the liberal white coalition partners to structure a convention around the enhancement of individual rights instead of "efficiency," the caucus withdrew its support. The black caucus then coalesced with a curious assortment of conservative legislators (who had no interest in a convention in the first place) to defeat the bill.[77]

Henry placed high priority on areas of social welfare and compensation for past deficits as well. He presented several proposals on health, housing, and aid for dependent families to support this interest. Circumstances in his hometown of Clarksdale revealed the compelling nature of these needs. In 1986 transfer payments composed 27 percent of total personal income, and unemployment among African Americans (27 percent) hovered slightly above five times that for whites (5 percent).[78] Conditions like these statewide, with a huge differential impact on children in impoverished households, inspired Henry to develop a collaborative proposal to increase aid to families with dependent children. The bill proposed $90 per month for the first child, $154 for a second, and a ceiling of $36 for additional children.[79] Later when welfare policy required parents of dependent children to go to work, Henry joined other legislators in 1995 seeking $750,000.00 in state funds to participate in the federal At Risk Child Care Program, which provided childcare.[80] His experience taught him that unemployment drove these dire conditions. He worked on several bills to boost unemployment compensation, while he suggested use of Job Corps programs to train young families. In 1983, HB 76 proposed increasing the unemployment benefit from "60 percent of the average weekly wage to 66.66 percent."[81] Another variation several years earlier in HB 75 proposed the elimination of the seven-day waiting period before worker compensation benefits funds could be accessed.[82]

Perhaps Henry's persistent efforts to get state adoption of an affirmative-action plan had the most far-reaching implications for altering poverty and exclusion. He joined several African American and four white representatives from urban districts in 1988 to try and create the "Mississippi Fair Employment Act." The bill required state government to institute a hiring plan to "adequately reflect the composition of minorities in the state population." A later version of the plan directed the governor to develop a ten-year plan with goals for all state agencies.[83] Henry and a number of his colleagues believed that they needed to improve this poor state's capital base in order to effectively respond to socioeconomic issues and to create a framework to support his vision for redistribution. Joining the 1986 coalition that proposed a resolution for a state lottery was a part of this.

In the meantime, Henry continued efforts to systematically expand the state's wealth. He tried to institutionalize a framework that would promote aggressive economic growth. He joined other lawmakers in 1988 on a resolution to amend Rule 60 to allow the creation of a new legislative standing committee—"Economic Development." They drafted a proposal to force the state to prioritize economic planning, a process that presumably allowed for both resource reallocation and the generation of new resources.[84] Similarly HB 860 (1988) aimed to force state compliance with federal affirmative-action mandates. It read: "Any agency, board, commission, department, institution, including the State Institutions of Higher Learning, or other governmental entity of the state or any political subdivision of the state which receives federal funds which contains minority set-aside provisions shall expend such funds specifically in compliance with the federal requirements."[85] Here, too, Henry and his collaborators did not succeed.[86]

At another level, as a health care professional and a national leader on the black elderly, Henry had a deep desire to advance policies in these areas. Many opportunities for advancement existed in this poor state with its limits on both trained professional personnel and limited investments in health and elderly services. Therefore, over his legislative career Henry sponsored or collaborated with others on over a dozen bills to enhance these services. One of his early bills (HB 737) authorized the Public Service Commission to supply the sustainable energy needs of elderly and those dependent on life support or confined to wheelchairs.[87] He joined a broad coalition seeking to increase the state's Medicaid appropriation[88] and later supported more favorable rules for disposition of health and accident insurance claims.[89] He repeatedly tried to get the state to do strategic planning to solve some of these problems. For example, he offered a plan to expand hospital beds in some areas and in others to convert beds in underutilized facilities to related purposes like nursing homes.[90] In recognition that this was a problem far broader than Mississippi, he offered a resolution calling on Congress to pass a national health care law.[91]

Most of the legislators could relate to the problems of the elderly in their communities, and this provided a rare opportunity for Henry to succeed on some of his proposals. His status as a recognized national leader on the subject helped. Therefore, when he wrote a resolution calling for a study group to develop a plan for elderly care, the House agreed and in 1988 appointed an interim committee "to prepare a plan which addresses the problems of Mississippi's elderly population, proposes solutions to those problems, and establishes goals and a framework for meeting the specific short-term and long-term needs of that population group."[92] It did not specify housing, which remained an acute problem for the elderly and the poor. Henry tried to influence those policies in the state legislature, just as he had done before congressional committees (as seen in chapter 6). In his first year he proposed increases in state capital investment for affordable and equitable housing for rural residents via a residential mortgage loan program. It also required establishment of a Mississippi Housing Authority to implement a state bond-supported loan program.[93] Henry had a model exhibit on display in Clarksdale. He and his Coahoma Opportunities Incorporated team demonstrated great dexterity in tapping into federal resources from the Great Society Programs to build a housing project similar to what he had in mind for the state.[94] Nonetheless these legislative efforts on housing largely failed because the state power structure in the executive and legislative branches continued to express the view that these programs encroached on states' rights.[95]

The Mississippi criminal justice system and the Parchman penitentiary reflected long-term concerns for Henry (and the national NAACP). Aside from well-known extralegal measures such as lynching, terror, and harassment, the differential impact of the incarceration of African Americans remained arresting.[96] Henry had his own untoward encounters with this system in arrests in Clarksdale and across the state—the two most prominent examples being an arrest with placement on a chain gang in Clarksdale, and jailing in the maximum-security unit of Parchman with the Freedom Riders in 1961.[97] It is not difficult to see why. A 1966 study by historian David Oshinsky referred to Parchman as a place "worse than slavery."[98] The documentation of the experience of the Freedom Riders there brought national attention to a situation that had long plagued African American housed in Parchman.[99] Partly as a product of the actions of Henry and a lawsuit filed by the NAACP, a finding was made against Mississippi for harsh treatment of these demonstrators.[100] The notoriety of prison system, however, compelled Henry, the NAACP, and others to continue to press for its comprehensive reform. This effort commenced well before Henry got to the legislature. Considerable success came when the Supreme Court handed down the *Gates v. Collier* decision in 1972. That decision eventually produced fundamental changes at Parchman, many of them reflecting what Henry proposed for the administration of the facility.[101]

When he arrived at the legislature, he vigorously pursued changes in the criminal justice system, especially the administration of Parchman. First, he sought assignment to the penitentiary standing committee, an assignment that came only in his last term—1992–1995. He sponsored almost all of his legislation on the penal system alone or in collaboration with other African American legislators. His solo authored HB 812 in 1980 required substantive interventions for inmate rehabilitation. He proposed prison access for civic organizations, so they could assist inmates to adjust to prison life and to prepare to reenter society.[102] A related bill sought access for nonprofit volunteer groups to work inside the prisons, another step aimed at preparation for a future beyond prison.[103] Henry's high distrust of poorly trained and unrepresentative prison authorities led him to propose that both the boards of corrections and parole reflect the composition of the inmate population.[104]

Another bill spoke to the abuse of inmate rights. For example, former inmates under the supervision of the Department of Corrections had to pay a monthly fee of ten dollars, ostensibly "for the establishment of restitution centers." Failure to pay resulted in a fine. Henry designed HB 796 to end that policy.[105] The differential treatment of women within the prison system also concerned him. Women had far less access to the minimal programs and supports available for men, such as education and access to appropriate personal hygiene and grooming products. The HB 973 sought to equalize such opportunities for women by regularly providing sanitary napkins monthly and undergarments and beauty shops.[106]

Henry and his customary collaborators on corrections continued to submit these proposals year after year. Despite their persistence, these bills all died in committee, but did have an impact on accountability. Following the creation of a Department of Corrections in 1976 (a partial response to the *Gates v. Collier* decision), a virtually complete turnover occurred in the administrative personnel of the prison by 1984. It included new leadership with training in corrections and a gradual infusion of funds that converted Parchman from a penal plantation of camps to a facility with common rules. Indeed, a study by Hooper shows that "when *Gates v. Collier* began, the corrections budget was about 3 million dollars. In 1984, the state appropriated $52.9 million for corrections."[107] There was considerable improvement in the humane treatment of inmates. Indeed, today the penal system at Parchman is held out as a model for such measures as a tough truth in sentencing law; decentralization of the formerly highly centralized system; and a parole system for nonviolent offenders that reduces the inmate population.[108]

Like any good legislator who expects to be returned, Henry also looked after his Delta district. Though most of his effort focused on regional economic development for his rural constituents, he also made use of the pork barrel for projects. He repeatedly tried to pass legislation for an economic zone for his area: Industrial Area Development Authority for Coahoma County. He and other Delta legislators coalesced to empower county supervisors to issue bonds for land acquisition and improvement with which to cultivate self-reliant entrepreneurs. Notably, this bill passed, but died on the Senate calendar.[109] The purely local concerns he repeatedly fought for included a second judgeship for Coahoma and surrounding counties, a highway Hospitality Station outside Clarksdale, and bonds for construction at the majority black Coahoma Junior College.[110] On these pork projects interestingly he managed to form interracial working relationships with colleagues in the Delta. He relished these opportunities insofar as they demonstrated his practical side, but also because they reflected the possibility of normal interactions, not based on race, in the political process for black leaders and their constituents.

Henry introduced and/or supported an interesting array of other general bills. Some of these supported the work of colleagues from whom he expected reciprocity; some appeared to be simply of a personal interest; and some supported state economic development and infrastructure. He spent considerable effort on these general measures (24 percent), making this work worthy of note. Six general areas of legislative proposals appeared in this amorphous category: transportation, honorary individual designations, law enforcement, recreation, taxes, and veterans' affairs.[111] Henry, like most of his colleagues, often signed onto such projects because the costs of cosponsoring were not high. He calculated that this might well earn goodwill for his own bills and resolutions that focused on the development of African Americans. He cosponsored a broad set of projects on general law enforcement projects: salaries and fees for county sheriffs,[112] authorizing courts to set bond limits, amending the statute for possession of deadly weapons, and maintaining eminent domain.[113] He also supported law enforcement measures desired by the Retail Association to shield small businesses against losses for bad checks. Its importance to Henry resulted because of its direct impact on virtually every business in his impoverished constituency.[114] His support for businesses to advertise alcoholic beverages, in what had been a largely dry state until the 1960s, had a similar aim.[115] Henry dedicated greater diligence on efforts to expand access to public lands for the recreational sports of fishing and hunting, where such access was often denied to blacks.[116] He repeatedly solo authored legislation to open up unleased land to the general public and to vacate leases that expired by the start of the fiscal year after passage. Of course, none of these passed.[117]

Henry also weighed in on the proverbial tax question. His ideas on the subject are obviously another part of the earlier discussion of his proposals for economic development. However, highlighting the tax effort demonstrates the broad scope of his vision, with specific reference to the difficult question of raising taxes in the state. Mississippi has traditionally been a regressive, high-tax state, with relatively low economic development. There is little doubt that this regressive tax system caused the poor to bear an unequal burden. While perfectly aware that Mississippi's poverty made it more dependent on taxes, he also believed that achieving social and economic equity required spending. He generally supported making investments in social change and offered liberal ideas for generating the growth that would sustain such a project. He joined forces with a new brand of state governors who staked claims for economic growth, albeit while underplaying increasing taxes.[118] He had no aversion to increasing taxes, however. He lent his support to a wide variety of measures to raise state taxes, and at the same time to reduce the tax burden of the poor. A proposal in 1980 sought to exempt some interest money from the state's income tax[119] and others (e.g., March of Dimes) from sales taxes. His ideas were expansive and progressive, featuring designs for the redistribution of resources that his white colleagues could hardly fathom. For example, he proposed an income tax surtax to generate additional revenue from those able to pay.[120] In 1988 he went a step further, when he joined other black legislators to propose an expansion of the role of cooperatives in agricultural and industrial development.[121]

Henry and his African American counterparts were unable to get substantive proposals enacted, despite proposing an average of twenty-six bills per member. This appearance of failure is not quite what it may seem though, in light of Mississippi's history of black exclusion. Henry's actual legislative activity tells its own story. A variety of issues remained important throughout his legislative career. He brought those bills back time and again and gradually brought some legislators along, passing a few bills. He struck a clear independent path—introducing the strongest body of race-centric work in the institution's history. At the same time he remained cognizant of other underserved groups and sought to make them beneficiaries as well, though he had no illusions about the prospects for the hoped-for interracial coalition of the working classes. All told, notwithstanding his efforts at collaboration and pragmatism, no one during Henry's tenure had a more directed focus for the extension of benefits to African American constituents. There is little doubt that the white power elite continued to dominate policymaking processes in the legislative body, and that elites acted to marginalize Henry and the cohort of blacks who arrived with him. Moreover, Henry primarily promoted a progressive, social change agenda focused on African American equity, and most of his white colleagues had no commitment to or sympathy for such an agenda. Racism and its residual elements of class and tradition combined to handicap prospects for interracial coalitions and bargaining about resource redistribution.

Nonetheless, an important question is whether Henry's legislative tenure and the projects he supported were a complete failure? The answer is a qualified no. A variety of broader internal political changes in the state created conditions conducive for Henry and his cohort to have an influence on legislative affairs and on policy innovations in the state beyond expectations. The new governors who came to office after 1972 represent one of the most important of the forces. Despite the traditional weakness of Mississippi executives, the nationalization of southern politics wrought by the civil rights movement had an empowering effect on southern governors, including Mississippi.[122] As this unredeemed southern state became more attuned to its expanded electorate and to the development of its stagnated economy, governors in particular became more amenable to a more entrepreneurial spirit and political openness. Arguably this began in 1967 when William Winter minimized race in the campaign against race-baiting candidate John Bell Williams. For his effort candidate Winter earned the disparaging moniker of a "Kennedy"-type liberal. By the next gubernatorial campaign, however, neither Waller nor Sullivan ran a segregationist campaign, nor opposed economic development. Earl Black referred to Waller as an economic "progressive" and to

Sullivan as "adaptive" on economic development.[123] Waller won that intraparty contest among the Democratic Party Regulars, and thus became the first governor to at least contemplate reconciliation with the nationally recognized Loyalists. Though he did not consummate the merger, clearly he made the important opening by commencing negotiations. Moreover, he brought some blacks into his administration without fanfare, and appealed to industry by rolling back some of the state's authoritarian tendencies.[124] Perhaps one of the best examples is his refusal to embrace the State Sovereignty Commission with all of its elements of state organized race-based terrorism. He subsequently vetoed its funding in 1973.[125]

It was left to Waller's successor to cement the merger of the Regulars and the Loyalists. Cliff Finch did so after a campaign in which he avidly sought the blessing of Henry and the African American electorate. He dubbed himself the "working man's" candidate, carrying a lunch pail to prove it, and regularly appeared on the stump with Henry.[126] The climate he created within the executive bureau helped legitimize Henry's party leadership. Segregation ceased to be *de rigueur* for gubernatorial campaigns and soon candidates from a unified Democratic Party became competitive elsewhere within the expanded constituency. William Winter was already waiting in the wings, and several others soon appeared.[127] This phenomenon helped valorize Henry's legislative efforts when he and a cohort of black legislators arrived in 1980.

William Winter became the first of this group of new southern governors to serve during Henry's tenure as a legislator. Notwithstanding the tortured beginning when he challenged African American party leadership, Governor Winter enunciated projects that Henry had long supported—education, jobs, and equal opportunity for blacks. The signature of his campaign and greatest achievement that comported with the interests of Henry is the school reform measure that passed the legislature. While Henry did not get the credit for this bill, the reform package contained several items that could have been taken verbatim from his playbook—kindergarten, compulsory school attendance, and increased funding. Winter's grand achievement occurred in a "Christmas" special session of the legislature (December 6, 1982), where he and his staffers (dubbed the "Boys of Spring") secured passage of a bill passed with a remarkable $110 million tax increase.[128] Henry did not gloat over his fortune in this case, but the importance of the policy shift was not lost on him.

The integrated Henry-led Democratic coalition continued through the next two election cycles. The 1983 contest featured Democratic candidate Bill Allain, state attorney general since 1980, against a wealthy Clarksdale planter, Republican Leon Bramlett.[129] Allain established his credentials as a part of the new wave with his strong advocacy of consumer rights as attorney general. Moreover, he successfully challenged the power of the legislature and extended the separation of powers vis-à-vis the governor, even as entrenched traditionalists remained in control of the legislature.[130] Allain pushed through the Administrative Reorganization Act of 1984 that empowered the governor to significantly advance a legislative agenda while in office. During his tenure a constitutional amendment also passed allowing a governor to succeed him/herself. The significant changes represented progress, but fell short of the constitutional convention Allain had hoped for and that Henry and black legislators had sought as well.[131]

In 1988 another Democrat, Ray Mabus, followed Allain. His victory once again demonstrated the importance of the highly mobilized African American constituency, though it masked the decline in white Democratic Party identifiers in state elections.[132] His tenure also elevated the value of the legislative contribution of Henry and other black legislators. A former chief assistant to Governor Winter, Mabus earned high marks for his role in drafting the 1982 education reform package. Subsequently he became state auditor and firmly established himself as a reformer and crusader for honesty in government. He audited all eighty-two counties during his term, winning huge damages against some.[133]

Mabus was a striking reflection of the profound changes in the profile of candidates for governor. The *New York Times* described him as a young (thirty-nine) Harvard trained lawyer, "whose campaign platform was 'basic, drastic change' and whose dramatic campaign vow was, 'Mississippi will never be last again.'"[134] The Mabus "revolution" promised further education reform, government reorganization per documented county corruption, and nurture of state diversity (read the black constituency).[135] His projects had significant congruence with the long-term interests of Henry. The education sector is one representative example, where Mabus virtually eliminated disparities in teacher salaries. Additionally, he made substantive structural reforms to state government that yielded some resource redistribution. In particular, he centralized county government in a way that removed the traditionalist hierarchy that disadvantaged African Americans and other nonelites in the allocation of county resources.[136] The environment he created also allowed the small cohort of black legislators to leverage their votes on important legislation that advanced the agenda of their largely black constituents.

Henry had clear and significant influence on the legislative agenda of the new generation of governors. He remained at the center of all of the independent legislative reforms, of every judicial mandate, and led the black mobilization that stimulated political action. Among independent legislative actions, perhaps the influence of education reform remained the most important during his tenure; his footprints are all over the particulars from the 1982 reform package of Governor Winter, changes that Governors Allain and Mabus maintained. Henry's leadership as a principal to the *Connor v. Finch* reapportionment decision is well documented. This ruling opened up the legislature for African American repre-sentatives, Henry being first among equals among them. Their presence had sym-bolic and policy consequences large and small—the numbers ballooned allowing strategic bloc votes to alter legislation; they served on committees and changed debates therein; and sometimes their ideas found resonance with others. It seems unlikely that merely being African American will be used as a standard by white racists to bar an elected representative from his or her seat, as was the case when Robert Clark arrived in 1967.

Even as the consolidation of Henry's vision became discernable, the limits of his strategy for a continuous, racially integrated Democratic majority began to emerge. Following the state's rejection of Johnson in 1964, it took just one year before the Republicans broke the Democratic stranglehold on the congres-sional delegations. Prentiss Walker from the southeastern Fourth District won the first Republican seat since 1885. Eight years later both the Fourth and Fifth Districts sent Republicans Thad Cochran and Trent Lott to Washington. Still the interracial turbulence among the Democrats had little impact on their continu-ous election in some other state races, including the governor's office. However, overall the drift of white Democrats to the emerging Mississippi Republican Party continued to increase.[137]

Some pundits referred to this as an emerging Republican revolution in the region. Revolution or not, the gradual increase in Republican officials had broad implications for the fragile coalition that Henry led. It took almost thirty years after the loss of the Democratic monopoly in Congress before the "revolution" arrived at the governor's office. In 1992, Kirk Fordice became the first Republican governor since Reconstruction, an election outcome that signaled a broad parti-san realignment. It seemed ironic that the economic development platform of this businessman-governor mirrored that of the Democratic coalition he defeated. However, the implications for the social change vision of Henry in the legislature were grave. The new governor fiercely fought the imposition of taxes, even those that undergird the progress in education. He expressed contemptuous hostility to a suit against the state for compensatory funding to support its black univer-sities. He promised to call out the National Guard to sustain his objection if the courts forced such a policy.[138] Clearly the interracial coalition faced an unfriendly executive office. In this transitional partisan climate, it became convenient for an increasing number of white Democrats to desert a party they saw as too black.[139] It did not bode well for an aging Henry, whose influence and power in his own Clarksdale base was now challenged by a younger opponent.

The end of Henry's political life came rapidly when he did not prevail in a challenge to his legislative seat in 1995. That may have merely been the most dramatic event in a chapter that had been closing for some time. The decline in power almost coincided with his entry to the legislature in 1980; his political career had arguably reached its zenith when he consummated the merger of the Loyalists and the Regulars. Soon after entering the legislature, he countenanced a major challenge to his party leadership, the very crux of his remaining power. Governor Winter's provocative view about racial power balance spoke to a fundamental unease among white Democratic leadership about the party's survival. Although Governor Winter and Henry struck a compromise, the new power sharing weakened Henry's almost complete, though hardly authoritarian, grip on the state party.

Other signs appeared that an aging Henry no longer remained the force he was within the African American leadership class. For example, the episode with Governor Winter also coincided with the emergence of a larger class of younger blacks assuming roles in the hierarchy of the party and seeking a path to leadership. They had interests and experiences somewhat removed from the social movement mobilization from which Henry sprang. With broad access to the franchise, the younger partisans appeared to be much more imbued with winning electoral offices in small towns, on votes provided by majority African American constituents.[140]

Even the expectations of the local NAACP, in which he had been a major force since the late 1950s, shifted for Henry. Skepticism began to emerge about his leadership for the next generation, and younger leaders became active in seeking a transition in what remained the strongest statewide civil rights organization. These challenges may have been the more serious since they came from within the African American community. In the early 1980s some members first called attention to Henry's inattentiveness to business and urged him to change his ways.[141] Little change occurred, but it took ten years for the claims against him to fully play out.

Younger members felt blocked along the path to leadership because of Henry's failure to step aside. Moreover, the activism of the organization declined as events shifted to electoral politics. The challengers believed this signaled a need for new leadership. Henry was, of course, not oblivious to these murmurings. After being challenged for the presidency in 1984, an office he first acquired in 1960, a rumor suggested that he pledged to serve one additional term and then resign.[142] Nevertheless, if such a deal existed, Henry did not honor it. He signaled his intent to run again in 1985. Once again a challenge ensued, this time by a longtime NAACP partner, Dr. Gilbert Mason, a matter that demonstrated the depth of concern. Mason and others felt frustration with the president's seeming inattentiveness to NAACP affairs, largely because he persistently spread himself too thin.[143] After all, he remained not just an important figure in Mississippi; he also continued to spend considerable time advising the national government and various national private groups. Clearly he had many constraints on his time, especially now that he had added formal legislative responsibilities. Nevertheless, in the contest Henry prevailed.

Remarkably, he soldiered on almost another ten years before resigning in 1993, despite continuing internal challenges.[144] Perhaps the most telling sign of the decline came not when Governor Winter previously challenged his leadership, but when the young black Hinds County supervisor, Bennie Thompson, defeated him for the position of national Democratic Party committeeman in 1980.[145] Subsequently Thompson also defeated Henry for a place on the National Democratic Committee and beat him out for the position of chairman of the Second Congressional District caucus in 1984.[146]

Yet, the loss of Henry's legislative seat signaled the culmination of his political life, though his service there seemed hardly the crowning achievement of his vision. The end came in an ignominious manner after four terms when another African American Democrat, Leonard Henderson, defeated him by seventy-one votes, charging Henry with virtual absence from the district. In fact Henderson had challenged him before. This young educator and lifetime Clarksdale resident first did so in the 1987 primary, and secured a respectable 42 percent of the vote. The turnout was 3,918 voters.[147] In the succeeding election, Henderson again challenged but Henry gained against him (60 percent), when slightly more voters turned out: 3,928. In another four years things changed dramatically as the primary election became much more competitive and turnout rose (Henderson received 2,094 or 51 percent of the vote, while Henry received 2,029 or 49 percent). Despite Henry's competitiveness, he had lost on the turf where it all began.[148]

Meanwhile, Henry's personal frailties began to show. Ailing and less energetic, he could not maintain his usual pace. News reports questioned his physical ability to go on. Henry apparently could not attend many 1995 legislative sessions or even campaign effectively during this period.[149] According to his physician and other public sources, Henry's health had been declining for some time, and after leaving the legislature in January 1996, he declined rapidly. Within the year he had a stroke and surgery for gallstones. In May 1997 he died of congestive heart failure.[150]

Perhaps Henry stayed on too long trying to influence events whose importance to his vision he saw evermore clearly. It had been a long ride—he was seventy-three years old when defeated for his legislative seat. Despite efforts to maintain his usual level of activity, he appeared both partially consumed by illness and in some ways by being swept aside by a tide of changes he originally set in motion. His family was rent with its own struggles—his wife of many years died in 1993, leaving the frayed remnants he rendered secondary in the course of his public life. In the end he virtually lost the semblances of personal control—a family life and the profession of pharmacy. Even before vacating NAACP leadership in 1993, some descriptions had him presiding when too ill—inattentive and nodding off. Louise Bradford captured the last days, showing his resolve to challenge acts of racial discrimination—a 1995 demonstration against hiring practices of the Clarksdale school district:

> And he couldn't [really march]—he was sort of ill, but he wasn't confined [though] he had a lot of swelling. He had some heart trouble . . . so he couldn't walk. We [marched] about 17 miles around town. We started . . . down at Forest Street and we came on around to Martin Luther King Park, and [since] he couldn't walk a great deal—you know, a great distance, we would carry him by van [un]til we got to certain points. And he would get out and make speeches. . . . it was not a concern to us that he didn't walk. . . . he made the speech and got his point across. We got the black superintendent.[151]

Conclusion and Postscript

The Aaron Henry legacy is one of the most significant in the general history of political leadership in Mississippi, and equally significant within the cast of indigenous African American and civil rights leaders the state has produced. As a state leader there simply is no other person who exceeds Henry's importance as the leader of the entirety of the state's population. To be sure, the state has produced a variety of very important political leaders, but many of these have had a far narrower gaze than that of Aaron Henry.

The earliest iteration of his vision and thoughts about political power in Mississippi reflected a bold imagination of a unified constituency, without respect to race. Of course, he was not the first to articulate such a vision; many others did. However, few of those who articulated such a vision had the length of time and breath of influence for implementation. In this regard, Henry is almost unique among leaders in the state who attained sufficient authority to obviate a racial system that thwarted almost any vision based on racial equality. That is a distinction that makes his story so compelling. Over his lifetime he became almost singular in surviving to see many of the elements of segregated social and political life disappear. Though it is clear that the project for the elimination of racial discrimination and disparity remains a work in process, his contribution in advancing such a prospect is huge.

Aaron Henry virtually gave up everything to work full-time to transforming Mississippi and to enhancing a national environment for racial integration. This required giving up much of the personal life he had already constructed. He had a wife and eventually a daughter and grandchildren, had a profession as a pharmacist, and served as an inveterate entrepreneur. Practically as soon as he married Noelle she said he revealed his special commitment to creating racial change in his home state. She willingly accepted that condition, but quickly learned that it had special implications for family life. In addition to responsibilities as a husband and father, his calling required a public career. That resulted in long and frequent absences from home. The child rearing became largely her responsibility, even as she became engaged in helping to realize the goals of his social change project. The personal costs were profoundly consequential. Mrs. Henry maintained a stoic veneer as she endured the absences and sometimes perceived lack of affection. She nevertheless remained unwavering in support of the man she called "Precious," even when the segregationists had her fired from her teaching job in an effort to intimidate her and her husband into silence.

Daughter Rebecca, on the contrary, did not bear up as well. She expressed deep grievance against her father's frequent absence and lack of engagement. The lost opportunities left her with a sense of estrangement that lasted until her father's later years, when she said she gained an appreciation for the substantial role he played in changing Mississippi. In the end, Rebecca did not long succeed her father. Despite a long history of medical crises, her death in 1999 at forty-eight was quite unexpected.

At the same time, the very way in which he initiated his pharmacist career suggested that it too would be in the service of transforming his indigenous environment and the racial system that defined it. He opted to establish the Fourth Street Drugstore in his hometown of Clarksdale, despite possible opportunities to hang out a shingle in a variety of other places. Indeed, location in a wide range of other places, given the paucity of African American pharmacists, may well have generated a much more lucrative income. Instead he chose to return to Clarksdale to serve the needs of a community that he saw as especially needy of his skills. The Mississippi Delta remained a poor place, and in the nature of segregation, had few opportunities for excellent health services. This choice, to stay, as opposed to leave, became very important to the special ability he possessed in helping to change Mississippi.

The location of his pharmacy in Clarksdale gave him an unparalleled opportunity to network with other African American health professionals, and to hone networking skills he deployed as a leader. It occurred to him that through collaboration they could broaden the services available, and possibly transform this underserved region. The other black health professionals concentrated in the area fortuitously had similar commitments. As professionals who were willing to dedicate their high-quality skill to advance the quality of services for their people, they also inherently posed a challenge to the racial system. Henry's participation in the collaborative owed significantly to meeting and developing a relationship with Dr. T. R. M. Howard, then the leader this collection of black health professionals in the Delta axis between Clarksdale and Mound Bayou. The truncated relationship played out in an organization known as the Regional Council of Negro Leadership, which ended when Howard fled due to white harassment. I will return to the defining influence of this organization later.

The Delta, however, became the place where perhaps the largest contingent of indigenous leaders emerged, many of them like Henry, veterans of World War II. Medgar Evers and Henry emerged as the most notable collaborators in this group after Howard's departure. They subsequently rebuilt and led a new and more aggressive NAACP that set a trajectory for a frontal attack on the racial system. This powerful collaboration set a good deal in motion, but was also cut short with the murder of Evers. This left Henry with the challenge to find partnerships and means to carry out the dreams he shared with Evers. In the conduct of his life succeeding that event he proved more than up to the challenge, demonstrating remarkable dexterity in generating partners, collecting allies, and marshaling resources that did indeed transform the racial system in Mississippi.

Similarly, as an entrepreneur Henry had every opportunity and clearly possessed sufficient acumen to have dedicated his life to the acquisition of business ventures. After all, he had grown up in a household that was dedicated to entrepreneurship, partly influenced by the vision of Booker T. Washington as implemented in Tuskegee, Alabama. Following such a path may well have led him to eschew social and political engagement. Instead, he dedicated himself to a life of entrepreneurship in the service of a social movement organization and eventually political mobilization. He dedicated his pharmacy business to poor black clients throughout the Delta, thus utilizing that resource to alleviate some of the worst disparities of the racial system. He went on to engage in a variety of other entrepreneurial ventures, all dedicated to a similar outcome. He used perhaps his first such successful venture in Clarksdale, the Coahoma Opportunities Inc., to develop local businesses that catered to the housing, recreational, health, and educational needs of this depressed Delta community. He and his collaborators never saw COI as a profit-making venture for personal enrichment. Instead they dedicated it to the provision of community services for the poor, the elderly, and schoolchildren. Similarly, the MINACT Corporation acquired Job Corps programs to reduce the huge number of young unemployed people in the adult. It became prior to Henry's death (and remains) a massive corporation providing training and placement of young people in the Delta and beyond. The acquisition of WLBT television station, though it became a source of considerable wealth for Henry and his partners, came about to fundamentally desegregate the racist Mississippi media. In short, Henry conceived of all of these entities as integrally connected to the broader vision of transforming a racial caste system so that racial equality became a value and an operational success.

Given that Henry set out to fundamentally undo a power structure and its racist constituency, it is hard to explain how he survived to see some of it realized. The segregationists demonstrated a willingness to use the ultimate means of destruction to sustain white racial supremacy. When Henry began his journey the scale and scope of violence, terror, harassment, and intimidation deployed to stanch racial change remained high. He became a prime target. Very soon after his public articulation of a project for racial change, the local power structure concocted an utterly false morality charge to try and silence Henry. Among conservatives of both races in Bible-Belt Mississippi, the tactic seemed on its face to be masterful, despite its crassness. The charge that he propositioned a young white male hitchhiker, not withstanding Henry's complex sexual identity, was litigated all the way to the Supreme Court and found to be without merit. Its spectacular failure seemed only to embolden Henry and to inspire his local and national supporters. Even so the efforts to silence him continued. He often found himself in jail; had his personal home shot at or bombed; saw his drugstore set ablaze; and remained subjected to a criminal justice system in his Delta County and city at the time that functioned almost entirely in the breach. Clearly, a varied and highly orchestrated effort existed, including efforts to destroy his family and livelihood, to silence him. Yet, he survived and remained undaunted and courageous. In the end, he became practically the longest survivor in the most sustained movement for social change the state of Mississippi has ever seen.

Aaron Henry had excellent preparation for the role he ultimately played in transforming Mississippi, although perhaps not as a product of strategic planning. Rather, it seems that his actions resulted from a moral commitment to the racial, but ultimately human rights, changes he sought. From this moral vantage point he set out on a path of personal activism, sought the company of others of a similar mind, and tried to persuade opponents of the justness of his cause. He began the journey to leadership by being at the table with anyone committed to changing the racial system in Mississippi. The Regional Council of Negro Leadership in the Delta became perhaps the earliest post-Reconstruction example of a clearly defined activist program that captivated Henry. There had been furtive efforts before, but the RCNL openly offered a new model for mass action. Dr. T. R. M. Howard used it to organize huge rallies and some protests, and also issued direct calls for voter registration and political participation. The RCNL got off the ground about the time that Aaron Henry, one of the returned veterans, opened his pharmacy practice in Clarksdale. He immediately associated himself with the organization, and in short order assumed a major leadership role in its social change activities. That set him on a trajectory of activism and network-building for the broad-scale challenge he later oversaw.

It is hardly accidental that Henry and this like-minded cast of challengers came from the fertile Delta land of plantations. This string of counties, populated overwhelmingly by African Americans sharecroppers, whose very livelihood ebbed away as agriculture became mechanized, stood in startling desperation. The unmet needs of this population cried out for leadership to channel the hardship and frustration. Although Dr. Howard served as the most visible leader at the outset, the group that assembled around him included some of those who became the most important leaders in the subsequent civil rights movement of the late 1950s and 1960s. As the RCNL faded, this group of challengers included seminal leaders like Medgar Evers and Amzie Moore. They joined Henry in bringing the NAACP above ground, the organization that became the vehicle for mounting a sustained campaign for change. Henry among them survived to bring the organization through many transitions as the movement intensified with new partners.

The RCNL really became a defining element in setting a trajectory for high-level leadership of the Mississippi movement albeit through its successor, the NAACP. This put Henry within the midst of the emerging indigenous class of black leaders who first publicly articulated a fundamental post-Reconstruction challenge to the racial system in the state. When the NAACP came above ground and frontally made its case for racial change, Aaron Henry and Medgar Evers were at the helm. They boldly articulated a program of activism for a locally based NAACP that went beyond the moderate and legalistic framework adopted by the parent organization in New York. Their strategies deviated so far from the New York office that Medgar Evers seemed ready to sever ties to the national office. Henry also always prized his independence from the parent body, though it remained his primary affiliation, as he pursued alternate, aggressive strategies for racial change. Looking back it is difficult to imagine the bravery of the move by Henry and Evers—to challenge a segregated political order, sustained essentially by a police state operation. Medgar, of course, paid the price with his life. Henry continued to build on this base of challenge and eventually stood at the center place of virtually all challengers who later assumed roles in helping to transform Mississippi.

Henry had a number of qualities that allowed him to become perhaps the most important sustained leader of that Delta cohort. As the movement evolved in Mississippi and included a great variety of other organizations, supporters, and allies, Henry's indigeneity stood out as singularly important. As a Mississippian he knew the lay of the land, and his lived experience gave him a deeper understanding of the racial system. Moreover, despite push-and-pull opportunities to leave, he remained expressly committed to remaining in the state and staying the course as a challenger. Second, he had significant experience in openly challenging the system, exhibiting all of the courage that acts of defiance required. That experience began when he returned from World War II and registered to vote. He also had a special knack for identifying and finding means for collaboration with those who shared his sentiments. From the RCNL days he evinced a gregarious nature that allowed him to build networks and collect partners and allies. His vast network eventually connected to sources throughout Congress, the White House, and more. Initially this emanated from his vantage point as state NAACP president, but expanded to include every agency of social change that operated in the state. All of the movement organizations and their leaders found their way to him and developed working relationships.

Finally, he had a clear and unwavering project—attainment of a racially integrated society, where the two races functioned as equals and where the allocation of resources fundamentally diminished the differential in quality of life chances for blacks. The elements of practicality in his approach often brought him critics as the movement transitioned through various phases. Yet, his steadfastness combined with an abiding faith in collaboration earned him the enduring respect of many of those who criticized his strategies. For example, SNCC, CORE, and SCLC activists alike reflect on his leadership and reliability as singular in advancing the Mississippi movement.

As for Henry's place in Mississippi's social change and political mobilization, this story shows it to be simply monumental. The first important point, of course, is that over his lifetime as a social and political activist, Mississippi did fundamentally change. The bold outward challenges that he and his Delta cohorts began in the 1950s laid the groundwork for restoration of the franchise to African Americans, the desegregation of public spaces, and the alteration of the political structure. Henry stood at the center of all of these campaigns as they generated changes in perhaps the most racialized system in the United States. Indeed, he seemed to have been at every important event and to have thought about and/or tried to implement virtually all of the big ideas that activists pursued in the transformation. The boldness and aggressiveness of his approach never waned, despite a growing list of partners, whose ideas varied significantly. His registration to vote long before the presence of federal registrars provided a model for local blacks in Clarksdale, though many bystanders appeared awestruck at his audaciousness. The provocative rebuke that he and other black leaders made to Governor White, who had called them ostensibly for "dialogue," reflected a revolutionary act of defiance on the route to transformation. Though these two acts seem simple now, at the time both reflected extraordinary bravery and bore risks of the most extreme acts of violence from segregationists. The characteristics he exhibited then only strengthened as the range of challenges against the racial system increased.

He and colleagues in Clarksdale initiated a bold set of challenges that served as a prelude and often a model to what came later statewide. The early 1960s "Clarksdale movement" of street protests, boycotts, and challenges of segregated spaces utilized virtually every tactic that had acquired some efficacy in a broader southern civil rights movement. With his NAACP youth leader Vera Pigee, and a small group of clergy, they made challenges at bus stations, train stations, and eating establishments all over the small town. Henry brought experience and added to that experience as he extended his leadership skills in his hometown. The skills he brought and built upon have rarely been blended as in this assessment, in accounting for the early success he had in Clarksdale. As that local movement picked up Henry lent his experience from deep engagement with the RCNL, from observing and participating with King in the Montgomery movement, and

most of all from building an essentially new Mississippi NAACP with Medgar
Evers. He already had a national network in 1961 that he brought to bear when
the NAACP Youth Council staged a sit-in at the white waiting room at the
Clarksdale railroad station. A year later when the all-black high school band was
denied its usual place in the annual Christmas parade, it provided Henry and
Clarksdale NAACP activists the catalyst that led to the most sustained and elaborate antisegregation campaign the state had seen in a single town.

The campaign that Henry led in this town subsequently provided important
features that SNCC and CORE adapted or simultaneously organized in building
their own grassroots campaigns. Henry embraced and lent his experience and
knowledge of the state's terrain to all of these groups. That proved critical to his
influence and the sustained role he played in building out the statewide movement. As the leader of the state's most widespread and prominent civil rights
organization (the NAACP), his accessibility to and encouragement of other civil
rights organizations created an environment of sufficient trust and comity that
led to the development of the Council of Federated Organizations. In the hands
of a different person things could have gone completely differently. After all the
national NAACP sought primacy over the national civil rights campaign and
regarded these other organizations as threats. Henry, an indigenous leader close to
the ground, never bought into the argument, and he gave full support to the concept of a statewide federation. The COFO subsequently served as the organizing
base and central clearinghouse for movement activity. The group selected Henry
as president, and then chose the head of SNCC, Bob Moses (an "outsider"), to
lead everyday operational activity. The alliance generated and harnessed a movement that enveloped virtually the entire state. During the relatively short life span
of the organization a social movement built that brought the state to a crisis level
over civil rights. During the time, Henry's presence was reflected everywhere as he
helped to cement these forces.

Thereafter Henry figured into the most important events of the now statewide social movement that quickly morphed into broad questions about the
desegregation of the political structure, the restoration of the black franchise, and
subsequent political mobilization. He had already anticipated and sketched much
of this direction in activities that predated COFO. For example, a good deal of
his focus in the RCNL in the 1950s was the reacquisition of the franchise, and in
1960 he trained his sights on voting as he organized Merrill Lindsey's campaign
for a seat in Congress. In some senses this latter effort anticipated the mock election campaign in 1963, which focused directly on demonstrating the potential
of an enfranchised black electorate. Henry's selection to stand for governor in
that mock contest merely affirmed the high regards his colleagues had for his
leadership and standing within the confederation. He certainly acquitted himself

well in the process. He traversed the state speaking, often facing down hostile law enforcement officials, and encountering orchestrated counterdemonstrations from white segregationists. Similarly, the 1964 Freedom Summer combined the broadest elements Henry had already articulated for an expansion of the social movement and political mobilization through the strategic use of external allies. That summer, of course, culminated in the birth of the Mississippi Freedom Democratic Party, a bespoke alternative for what Henry called the illegitimacy of the state political organization. By this time the widespread challenge to the state racial system could only be described as a profound crisis. Henry should justly be assigned a major responsibility in formulating a vision for racial change and as a primary actor in bringing things to a head.

The MFDP challenge failed to accomplish what COFO activists hoped for—seating at the National Democratic Convention in the place of the avowedly segregated delegation the state party sent to Atlantic City. Despite all the serious negative consequences this had for the unified confederation, the challenge proved to be the death knell for the racial system, as it had been known. At the convention the white state delegation continued to balk at expressing loyalty to the national party, and returned home to campaign largely for the Republican (or a third-party) candidate. The organization's future was in tatters. While the convention did not seat the MFDP challengers, it sent its strongest signal yet that loyalty and compliance with a variety of affirmative measures to diversify delegations would be required at its convention four years later. During that four-year interval the unified civil rights movement in Mississippi floundered some with recriminations about the 1964 convention loss. Nevertheless, work continued on this major project of destroying the white party structure, and it culminated in a successful Henry-led challenge in 1968.

Meanwhile, in the interim Henry worked to formulate an integrated coalition to assume the space that the discredited white party left behind and to augment the movement base. The strategy brought him some controversy because some of his movement collaborators felt that the failure of the MFDP meant that the national party system and its hierarchy had proved an unreliable partner; or, that eliminating the racial system remained a larger project requiring fundamental changes unlikely to occur in a capitalist democracy like the United States. Henry did not agree with his critics and pressed on, maintaining consistency in his object of an integrated society with blacks as equals. He never lost faith in the suitability of the American democratic system, if fully implemented, for achieving his goal.

Henry's leadership role became even larger following the national party's disavowal of the segregated state party (Regulars) in favor of the integrated delegation that the remnants of the MFDP sent to the 1968 convention (Loyalists). Once again, his colleagues turned to him as the leader of the fledgling party organization. Though the group had been awarded bonafide standing by the national party, replacing the Regulars remained an uphill battle because they saw Henry and his supporters as illegitimate. Gradually though with a new governor, William Waller, some halting discussions began about a merger of the two groups. These remained fraught, however, and the job did not get done. For four years Henry functioned as head of a local party only recognized in Washington, while the Regulars tried to figure out how to either hold on or make peace with the changed state electorate. It took the election of a new governor, Cliff Finch, before consummation of the deal ceding recognition to the Loyalists and party leadership to Henry.

Henry then coheaded a state party in which he and his integrated coalition had a clear upper hand. The coalition could now enforce rules about diversity in leadership in the party and to take affirmative steps to integrate the virtually new African American electorate into state political party affairs. On the strength of federal voting registrars and the Voting Rights Act of 1965, a huge portion of the black voting-age population (about 35 percent) had registered by 1970. As early as 1967 the impact showed at the polls when the African American officials were elected to a variety of posts—the state legislature, mayors, aldermen, and county supervisors among them. It must have been some vindication for Henry. He had foreseen this potential when he orchestrated the 1960 campaign of Merrill Lindsey challenging the overwhelmingly black Delta congressional district.

By the late 1960s a good many projects for which Henry worked had indeed come together in a way that allowed him to claim significant progress toward the vision of an equal society. His comprehensive approach had borne fruit in eliminating some elements across the spectrum of differential status in the spheres of social, economic, and political life. Where fruit had not been borne he could point to a trajectory that seemed appropriate, with active vigilance. On the social side Clarksdale and Mississippi joined much of the rest of the country in opening public spaces relatively equally; economically, while the challenges remained substantial, federal programs and other interventions provided safety nets to secure some of the benefits of the "Great Society." Good illustrations existed all around Clarksdale where federal largess had altered housing, health, and preschool education. Perhaps the most significant changes occurred on the political side. A new party, whose leadership Henry dominated, had displaced the racist party. Blacks not only registered to vote in large numbers, but they also exercised the franchise in significant numbers. Again, significant federal intervention and a national civil rights campaign helped, Henry's leadership of the confederation and the high level of indigenous mobilization had a defining role in these outcomes.

Therefore the interval between the 1964 convention and Henry's assumption of coleadership of the Democratic Party in the 1970s had a far greater significance than is often realized. While it took four years after the 1964 convention for the MFDP goal of unseating the Regulars, a good deal happened in the intervening years that undermined other parts of the broader segregated system. Henry organized and oversaw a good deal of this activity. In this period the conventional wisdom has suggested a lull occurred in the movement. While it is true that this represented a transition phase, Henry remained exceedingly busy and on many fronts. He continued his multipronged initiatives laying a foundation for not just the political takeover, but for changing the terms for access to health, housing, education, jobs, elder care, and respect for African American cultural identity and production. When President Johnson introduced the Great Society programs in the mid-1960s, it took Henry little time to seek funding because he and his hometown cohorts had already proposed and tried to implement many similar ideas in Clarksdale. He helped design a preschool project similar to what became Head Start; proposed job training and placement for youths and seasonal workers that resembled Job Corps; contributed ideas to the medical unit of the civil rights movement that ultimately became comprehensive health; and proposed strategies for elder care that became major features of gerontology policy in the Johnson administration.

Education and protection of cultural identity are the other components that filled out Henry's comprehensive vision of racial transformation. Few things reached the level of importance of education, and Henry and Medgar Evers began an active strategy immediately after the 1954 *Brown* decision to desegregate public schools. Despite the heavy personal toll this exacted for his family (his wife lost her job and his daughter never attended an integrated school), Henry stayed the course for fifteen years until a plan, albeit flawed, emerged. The assault on the television station sought to assure that not only would there be access to media, but that the distinct cultural identity and production of blacks would be on an equal footing with the predominant Euro-American cultural narrative. Here too Henry had the satisfaction of being an influential figure in dismantling (then owning) the major media source that perpetrated the segregationists' cultural narrative of black inferiority. The takeover of WLBT represented a huge shift in the messages heard, as well as who presented the messages—stories by and about blacks, of which they could approve, now appeared over the airwaves. This change for the average black person born and reared in Mississippi was as profound as entering a formerly segregated waiting room.

Soon after the long period of fits and starts that resulted in Henry's leadership of the new state Democratic Party, he finally came full circle in assuming an elected legislative seat of his own. Though his personal election to a legislative seat seemed anticlimactic, it is important to recall the boldness of the Lindsey campaign for Congress that Henry managed. He argued back then that the black majority should run for that seat because the current elected official did not represent their interests. He anticipated that this black majority, if given the opportunity, would vote for someone who articulated a platform consistent with their interests. Of course, without the franchise in 1960, they could not accomplish the deed. However, with the franchise restored and a fairer reapportionment of the electoral districts, he could complete the deal by assuming a legislative seat. By the time that happened in 1980, a vast array of other black elected officials held offices at almost every level in the state. They constituted some of the new faces within the new Democratic Party of Mississippi, and the term Loyalist gradually lost its meaning.

While Henry could take some consolation in having set transformative directions in a new social and political order, the success of the project fell short. Some patterns of racial division endured and remained prominent amid the tremendous changes that he wrought while at the very pinnacle of power. He remained keenly aware of this, having seen the halting nature of progress all along. The first disquieting signs occurred before Henry's control over the new political party structure could be consolidated. Governor William Winter noted as much when he called for white party leadership to head off white defections from a ruling party they deemed controlled by blacks. Though the integrated party hierarchy reached a good faith agreement to move forward, whites continued to defect to the Republican Party. As the number of elected black officials identified with the Democratic Party grew, so did the number of white Republican Party identifiers. Similarly, aside from local races controlled by largely black constituencies, the number of white elected officials identified as Republicans grew. The preference of Republican presidential candidates in Mississippi soon followed in congressional districts and in the state executive offices. Finally, in 2012 both houses of the state legislature came under the control of the Republican Party. Though the proportion of African American representatives has held, they remain identified with the Democratic Party and even the potential of a biracial partisan coalition seems remote. It is hardly what Henry or William Winter hoped for.

As a result of these conditions an increasingly important question is can African Americans and whites, largely single-party identifying groups in alternative parties in the South, live in the same party? Historical evidence does not particularly bode well for the world Henry imagined. In the Reconstruction era African Americans largely identified with the Republican Party, while whites formed the "solid South" within the Democratic Party. In short order black citizens completely lost the franchise all across the South, while those elsewhere continued to identify with the party of Lincoln. With the coming of Franklin Roosevelt's New Deal, increasingly black voters began a shift to the Democratic Party, and the organization became more amenable to civil rights interests. The discomfort this caused the "solid South" white Democrats began to be apparent, but significantly increased with the 1960 election. In Mississippi, and many of the other southern states, the single-party identification of the races is almost complete. By and large African Americans identify as Democrats and whites identify as Republicans. This severely limits and tests the transformation of the race-based political system that Henry fought so hard to displace.

Ironically, shifts in the political environment (nationally and locally) had a devastating consequence on the comprehensive vision Henry sketched for destroying the racial system in Mississippi. President Lyndon Johnson's departure from office accompanied a significant decline in Henry's access to the levers of powers to advance his local goals. The Democratic coalition in Washington in which Henry had been so influential faltered, and controversies swirled about reverse discrimination in the application of Great Society programs and the like. However, the access that the informed black electorate in Mississippi and its leaders had acquired continued to successfully bid for their share of a resource base that had significantly expanded with Franklin Roosevelt and culminated with Johnson. Henry used his vast experience and contacts to continue to secure some support for housing, Job Corps, the elderly, and comprehensive health projects. He remained successful even in the evermore constricted environment of Republican presidents, especially Ronald Reagan. On balance, however, it proved harder to attract allies within the national administration following Johnson's departure, inherently limiting expansion of Henry's comprehensive vision for consolidating changes in Mississippi.

Perhaps the greatest sign of the slowdown in commitment appeared in the area of education, arguably the linchpin for preparing young Mississippians for competitive roles in the future. The already slow speed of the integration of the schools seemed virtually overtaken by the emergence of alternative schools for whites in Mississippi (and elsewhere in the South). Long before Henry's public life ended, the dream of quality integrated public schools seemed to be even more distant. In Clarksdale, for example, most white parents withdrew their students from public schools, thereby thwarting the integration plan. All over the state the pattern repeated itself making for perhaps an even greater education crisis than before school integration. Another sort of dual K–12 educational system now exists, neither prong of which is adequately resourced or effective. What is said about education is also true for a wide variety of other interests reflected in Henry's original vision. However, in so many ways education is a key to all the other deficits, and thus it stands as a powerful symbol of Henry's unfinished project. Alas, with the races also locked into separate one-party alignments, the challenge is monumental for restoration of a grand strategy for state development as Henry envisioned.

This inevitably raises the questions of what Henry wrought and whether he had the wherewithal to see his comprehensive vision through. The answer, of course, is that he brought an enormous amount of change to Mississippi by the end of his career through political influence in state and national politics. Moreover, he remained vigilant, defiant, and aggressive to the end in pursuit of comprehensive racial change in Mississippi. This son of the Delta, born with little prospect of even getting to manhood, let alone acquiring an education and a profession, beat all expectations. Improbably he became a leader of his racial community, and in the process demolished the system designed to assign him a role merely defined by his race. The social movement campaign he led ultimately provided him the statewide influence and power to become a political leader for all Mississippians. Improbable, indeed—there is hardly another example of a political leader who better served the entirety of Mississippi's public constituency. When that power started to wane, Henry worked to maintain influence in a party that tottered as whites deserted; and, while his entry to the legislature began a decline in his power, the programs he pursued sought to deepen equal representation for blacks. He showed a path to the cohort of a younger generation of black legislators who arrived with him and/or later served with him. He also desperately wanted to find a means of sustaining a unified biracial majority, dedicated to what he termed the development of all of the state's people. He remained convinced that while he had a superior formula for action, evolving dynamics of the same old racial system prevented its fullest implementation.

Despite the bifurcated, single-party identification of the Mississippi electorate in Mississippi, Henry accomplished changes that fundamentally altered the representation of African Americans in local politics. Indeed that remains the sector where participation and representation are most robust and enduring—mayors, aldermen, supervisors, school board members, and state legislators. Scholars and political pundits alike call attention to the alluring, and perhaps unexpected, ironic fact that Mississippi has the largest number of black elected officials. The struggles required to accomplish this are often forgotten. It left many of the early proponents of political representation murdered; others fled the state; and still others succumbed to horrific terror. The marvel is that Aaron Henry remained standing to realize the dream of representation and the removal of day-to-day indignities of segregation. His accomplishments are far broader, however. This is the first exploration that shows the broader scope of his projects and how it constituted a comprehensive vision for ending the racial system. Therefore, it is quite logical that he had strategies for housing, jobs, the elderly, education, and economic development in the broadest sense. Given the particular disadvantages of African Americans, no one exceeded Henry in delivering resources that altered the status of that part of his constituency. His success in acquiring and implementing federal programs to this end remains outsized. He arguably had greater success than any contemporary Mississippi leader in delivering on the promise of resource acquisition to eliminate some of the most intractable social and economic problems of all of the citizens of his state.

As such, when shortly after losing his leadership of the NAACP and his legislative seat, Henry succumbed May 19, 1997, he had already given the greatest gift to Mississippi. He had achieved an unparalleled legacy in fundamentally shifting the racial order. Though the transformation was not complete, he provided a model of consistency, persistence, and integrity to a goal that is a high bar for those who succeed him. The "celebration of life" that marked his death suggested that there was widespread recognition of the special accomplishments he made; more than two thousand filled the Coahoma Junior College auditorium. The *Clarion Ledger*, the state's largest newspaper, reported that the Speaker of the Mississippi House of Representatives, Tim Ford, lauded him as a "dedicated legislator who worked diligently for better schools, greater job opportunities and human rights issues." High-level political leaders and everyday citizens from all over the country gathered for the service or sent special condolences. Former president Jimmy Carter attended as an honorary pallbearer and President Bill Clinton sent special sympathies. Congressman Bennie Thompson led a group of state officials from executive and legislative offices, and many of the organizations with which Henry had long been affiliated sent representatives, including NAACP executive director Benjamin Hooks and former presidential candidate Jesse Jackson. State representative Robert Clark summed up his personal sentiments as follows: "I had more respect for him, and often told him, than any other living human being on the face of the Earth." The moving tributes were especially fitting for a man who did indeed accomplish what many thought improbable in perhaps the most conservative state in the union. It only remains to see who might assume the mantle to bridge the racial gaps to renew the trajectory he set.

Notes

Introduction

1. Aaron Henry with Constance Curry, *Aaron Henry: The Fire Ever Burning* (Jackson: University Press of Mississippi, 2000).

2. Minion K. C. Morrison, *Black Political Mobilization: Leadership, Power and Mass Behavior* (Albany: SUNY Press, 1987), 10–14; Aldon Morris, *The Origins of the Civil Rights Movement: Black Communities Organizing for Change* (New York: Free Press, 1984), xii.

3. William Scarborough, "Heartland of the Cotton Kingdom," in *A History of Mississippi*, Vol. 1, ed. R. A. McLemore (Hattiesburg: University and College Press of Mississippi, 1973), 329–330; Vernon Wharton, *The Negro in Mississippi, 1865–1890* (Chapel Hill: University of North Carolina Press, 1947), 12; Morrison, *Black Political Mobilization*, 33–34; Charles Sydnor, *Slavery in Mississippi* (New York: Appleton-Century, 1933), 86–101.

4. The notion of redemption is a reference to the "Redeemers," whites who were disfranchised during Reconstruction who set out to reclaim their lost power thereafter. Their success in doing so, of course, left the freed African Americans the least redeemed in consummating the rights presumably guaranteed by the Thirteenth Amendment. Charles Fortenberry and F. Glenn Abney, "Mississippi: Unreconstructed and Unredeemed," in *The Changing Politics of the South*, ed. William Havard (Baton Rouge: Louisiana State University Press, 1972), 472–524. Also see general discussions in Charles Lane, *The Day Freedom Died* (New York: Henry Holt, 2009), 18; Eric Foner, *A Short History of Reconstruction, 1863–1877* (New York: Harper and Row, 1990), 238–260.

5. Gene Dattel, *Cotton and Race in the Making of America: The Human Cost of Economic Power* (Lanham, MD: Ivan Dee Publishers, 2009), 221–358; Neil McMillen, *Dark Journey: Mississippians in the Age of Jim Crow* (Urbana: University of Illinois Press, 1990), 111–150; see also Robert Brandfon, *Cotton Kingdom of the South: A History of the Yazoo Mississippi Delta from Reconstruction to the Twentieth Century* (Cambridge, MA: Harvard University Press, 1967).

6. Wharton, *The Negro in Mississippi*, 146; Buford Satcher, *Blacks in Mississippi Politics, 1870–1900* (Washington, DC: University Press of America, 1978), 25; John Lynch, *The Facts of Reconstruction* (Indianapolis: Bobbs-Merrill, 1970), 44; John Garner, *Reconstruction in Mississippi* (Baton Rouge: Louisiana State University Press, 1968), 305–307.

7. Wharton, *The Negro in Mississippi*, 221; Albert Kirwin, *Revolt of the Rednecks: Mississippi Politics, 1876–1925* (Lexington: University of Kentucky Press, 1951), 25; Morrison, *Black Political Mobilization*, 23–52; Scarborough, "Heartland of the Cotton Kingdom," 310–351.

8. William Hatcher, "Mississippi Constitutions," in *Politics in Mississippi*, 2nd ed., ed. Joseph Parker (Salem, WI: Sheffield Publishing Company, 2001), 33–52; Morrison, *Black Political Mobilization*, 43.

9. Nicholas Lemann, *The Promised Land: The Great Migration and How It Changed America* (New York: Vintage, 1992), 46.

10. David Beito and Linda Royster Beito, *Black Maverick: T. R. M. Howard's Fight for Civil Rights and Economic Power* (Urbana: University of Illinois Press, 2009).

Chapter One: Son of Sharecroppers and Entrepreneurs: Rites of Passage in a Segregated Society

1. John C. Willis, *Forgotten Time: The Yazoo-Mississippi Delta after the Civil War* (Charlottesville: University of Virginia Press, 2000), 145–173.

2. Ibid.

3. Henry, *Aaron Henry*, 4–10.

4. Lemann, *The Promised Land*, 18ff.

5. Henry, *Aaron Henry*, 4.

6. Ibid., 10.

7. Ibid., 16.

8. He subsequently assisted the town through endorsements and interventions that generated considerable government and philanthropic support. Janet Sharp Hermann, *The Pursuit of a Dream* (New York: Vintage, 1983), 232.

9. Louis R. Harlan, *Booker T. Washington: The Making of a Black Leader, 1856–1901* (New York: Oxford University Press, 1972), 218.

10. Washington was sufficiently impressed to make several formal visits to Mound Bayou. Hermann, *The Pursuit of a Dream*, 233.

11. Donald H. Jackson Jr., *A Chief Lieutenant of the Tuskegee Machine: Charles Banks of Mississippi* (Gainesville: University Press of Florida, 2002), xii, and 129ff.

12. McMillen, *Dark Journey*, 188.

13. Hermann, *The Pursuit of a Dream*, 224.

14. Henry, *Aaron Henry*, 79.

15. Brandfon, *Cotton Kingdom of the South*, 25.

16. He was the employer of Charles Banks's parents and may have inspired his business interest. Jackson, Jr., *A Chief Lieutenant of the Tuskegee Machine*, 5–7.

17. Lemann, *The Promised Land*, 11.

18. Ibid., 15.

19. Wharton, *The Negro in Mississippi*, 105.

20. Brandfon, *Cotton Kingdom of the South*, 135–136.

21. Henry, *Aaron Henry*, 5.

22. Ibid., 18.

23. Ibid., 17.

24. Aaron Henry, 1972, Oral history interview conducted in Clarksdale by Neil McMillen, Oral History Program of the University of Southern Mississippi: Hattiesburg, Mississippi (hereafter MSOHA), 2.

25. Henry, *Aaron Henry*, 12.

26. Ibid., 16.

27. Harlan, *Booker T. Washington*, 140.

28. Henry, *Aaron Henry*, 22.

29. W. E. B. Du Bois, "The Talented Tenth," in *Negro Protest in the Twentieth Century*, ed. Francis Broderick and August Meier (Indianapolis: Bobbs-Merrill Company, 1966), 40–48; John Bracey Jr. et al., *Black Nationalism in America* (Indianapolis: Bobbs-Merrill, 1970).

30. Rayford Logan, *The Betrayal of the Negro: From Rutherford Hayes to Woodrow Wilson* (New York: Collier Books, 1965), 323.

31. Carol George, *Segregated Sabbaths: Richard Allen and the Rise of Independent Black Churches, 1770–1840* (New York: Oxford University Press, 1973); Juliet E. K. Walker, "Promoting Black Entrepreneurship and Business Enterprise in Antebellum America: The National Negro Convention, 1830–1860," in *A Different Vision: Race and Public Policy*, ed. Thomas D. Boston (New York: Routledge), 206–261.

32. Du Bois, "The Talented Tenth," 40–48; Brian Kelly, "Beyond the 'Talented Tenth': Black Elites, Black Workers, and the Limits of Accommodation in Industrial Birmingham, 1900–1921," in *Time Longer Than Rope: A Century of African American Activism, 1850–1950*, ed. Charles Payne and Adam Green (New York: New York University Press, 2003), 276–301.

33. Walker, "Promoting Black Entrepreneurship"; see also Juliet E. K. Walker, "Constructing a Historiography of African American Business," in *The African American Experience: An Historiographical and Bibliographical Guide*, ed. Arvarh Strickland and Robert Weems Jr. (Westport, CT: Greenwood Press, 2001), 278–314.

34. McMillen, *Dark Journey*, 177–180.

35. Charles Payne, *I've Got the Light of Freedom: The Organizing Tradition and the Mississippi Freedom Struggle* (Berkeley: University of California Press, 1995), 280–283.

36. The biography of Madame C. J. Walker, herself perhaps the quintessential beautician for African American women, is an apt illustration of the importance of the market for beauty culture and hair care products. A'Lelia Bundles, *On Her Own Ground: The Life and Times of Madame C. J. Walker* (New York: Washington Square Press, 2002). Also see Julia Kirk Blackwelder, *Styling Jim Crow: African American Beauty Training during Segregation* (College Station: Texas A & M University Press, 2003), 14–33.

37. Henry, *Aaron Henry*, 16. The HOLC was formed in 1933 to salvage a mortgage system decimated by the depression. It provided loans to mostly nonurban areas (maximum of $14,000 at 80 percent of the assessed value), with payments averaging between $50–$150 per month.

38. Ibid.

39. C. Lowell Harriss, *History and Policies of the Home Owners' Loan Corporation* (New York: National Bureau of Economic Research, 1951), 20–34.

40. "Oxford Companion to the US Supreme Court: Reconstruction, Federalism, and Economic Rights," www.answers.com/topic/home-owners-loan-corporation (accessed September 17, 2008).

41. Henry, *Aaron Henry*, 16.

42. Stuart Grayson Noble, *Forty Years of Public Schools in Mississippi, with Special Reference to the Education of the Negro* (New York: Negro Universities Press, 1918), 39.

43. McMillen, *Dark Journey*, 72.

44. Henry Bullock, *A History of Negro Education in the South from 1916 to the Present* (Cambridge, MA: Harvard University Press, 1967), 123.

45. Meyer Weinberg, *A Chance to Learn: The History of Race and Education in the United States* (Cambridge, MA: Harvard University Press, 1977), 67.

46. Bullock, *A History of Negro Education in the South*, 138–139; and Horace Mann Bond, *Negro Education in Alabama: A Study in Cotton and Steel* (New York: Atheneum, 1969), 264.

47. Charles Bolton, *The Hardest Deal of All: The Battle Over School Integration in Mississippi, 1870–1980* (Jackson: University Press of Mississippi, 2005), 16 and 21.

48. Bullock, *A History of Negro Education in the South*, 124; Bond, *Negro Education in Alabama*, 264.

49. Bullock, *A History of Negro Education in the South*, 143–144.

50. Ibid., 139.

51. Robert Embree and Julia Waxman, *Investment in People* (New York: Harper and Brothers, 1929), 47.

52. McMillen, *Dark Journey*, 73.

53. Ibid., 79.

54. Bullock, *A History of Negro Education in the South*, 123; Bolton, *The Hardest Deal of All*, 50.

55. Bolton, *The Hardest Deal of All*, 44–45.

56. Allen Ballard, *The Education of Black Folk: The Afro-American Struggle for Knowledge in White America* (New York: Harper and Row, 1973), 13.

57. Bullock, *A History of Negro Education in the South*, 102, 142–143.

58. Bond, *Negro Education in Alabama*, 269–272.

59. Ibid., 269–272.

60. Henry, *Aaron Henry*, 14.

61. There was no comparison between these church schools and those for whites. According to Embree and Waxman: "Often these buildings were in bad repair, the roofs leaked, and cold and rain came through gaps in the rough boards of floors and walls. Many rural children walked miles over bad roads to get to these schools, to shiver away in their threadbare clothes as they repeated their lessons. ... [And] there was little in the way of furniture, blackboards, desks, or textbooks." Embree and Waxman, *Investment in People*, 37–38.

62. Henry, *Aaron Henry*, 21–22.

63. Ibid., 30. Most blacks who could afford high school, like his older sister, had to board. She attended Methodist-supported Rust College in nearby Holly Springs.

64. Ibid., 32.

65. Ibid., 32–33.

66. Ibid., 33.

67. Ibid., 33.

68. It was reminiscent of the trickster in African American literature. This involved encoding a commonly understood language or act so that it produced outcomes subversive of what was undesirable; or, investing what seemed familiar with opposed or alternative meanings. Henry Gates, "The Blackness of Blackness: A Critique on the Sign and the Signifying Monkey," in *Literary Theory: An Anthology*, ed. Julie Rivkin and Michael Ryan (Oxford: Blackwell Publishing, 2004), 990.

69. Henry, *Aaron Henry*, 37.

70. Ibid.

71. Ibid., 36–39.

72. Ibid., 40–41.

73. Ibid., 42.

74. John Brown, interview with the author, July 9, 2004, Clarksdale, Mississippi.

75. Henry, *Aaron Henry*, 39.

76. Ibid., 44. He specifically refers to "Langston Hughes, Benjamin Banneker, Crispus Attucks, Harriet Tubman, Frederick Douglass, George Washington Carver, Charles Drew, and Mark Epps."

77. John Brown, interview with the author.

78. Ibid.

79. Henry, *Aaron Henry*, 55.

80. Ibid., 58.

81. *Missouri ex rel Gaines v. Canada*, 305 U.S. 337 (1938).

82. Bolton, *The Hardest Deal of All*, 16 and 21.

83. Ibid., 33–60. See Oral History with Gladys Noel Bates, MSOHA, in http://digilib. usm.edu/cdm/compoundobject/collection/coh/id/8488/rec/5 (accessed August 5, 2013). Bates was a black Jackson, Mississippi, schoolteacher who unsuccessfully sued the state to obtain equal pay.

Chapter Two: Military Service, Family, and Profession: Challenging Contested Citizenship at War and at Home

1. Henry, *Aaron Henry*, 59.

2. Daniel Kryder, *Divided Arsenal: Race and the American State During World War II* (New York: Cambridge University Press, 2000), 25–85.

3. Carol Anderson, *Eyes Off the Prize: The United Nations and the African American Struggle for Human Rights, 1944–1955* (New York: Cambridge University Press, 2003), 8–57.

4. Gerald Horne, "Race from Power: U.S. Foreign Policy and the General Crisis of White Supremacy," in *Window on Freedom: Race, Civil Rights and Foreign Affairs, 1945–1988*, ed. Brenda Plummer (Chapel Hill: University of North Carolina Press, 2003), 45–66.

5. John Burrus, "Urbanization in Mississippi, 1890–1970," in *A History of Mississippi, Vol. II*, ed. McLemore, 351–355.

6. Arvarh Strickland, "Remembering Hattiesburg: Growing Up Black in Wartime Mississippi," in *Remaking Dixie: The Impact of World War II on the American South*, ed. Neil McMillen (Jackson: University Press of Mississippi, 1997), 151–152; Neil McMillen, "Fighting for What We Didn't Have," Ibid., 98.

7. John Dittmer, *Local People: The Struggle for Civil Rights in Mississippi* (Urbana: University of Illinois Press, 1994), 16.

8. Strickland, *Remembering Hattiesburg*, 151–152.

9. Ibid., 153–156.

10. Henry, *Aaron Henry*, 58.

11. Strickland, *Remembering Hattiesburg*, 154.

12. Charles Hill, interview with the author, January 28, 1998, Clarksdale, Mississippi.

13. Gerald Jaynes and Robin Williams Jr., *A Common Destiny: Blacks and American Society* (Washington, DC: National Academy Press, 1989), 66–67.

14. Charles Hill, interview with the author.

15. Ibid.

16. "Transition Force," History of Fort McClellan 1917–1999, http://www.mcclellan. army.mil/ (accessed September 26, 2005).

17. "Three fifths of the entire number [was] almost equally divided between infantry, engineer and quartermaster units. . . . Truck, service, car, railhead, bakery, salvage, repair, salvage collecting, laundry, fumigation, gas supply, and bath, sterilization, and pack units. . . . Before the end of the war there were more than 1600 Negro quartermaster

companies." Ulysses Lee, *United States Army in World War II, Special Studies: The Employment of Negro Troops* (Washington, DC: United States Army, Office of the Chief of Military History, 1966), 129.

18. "Transition Force," History of Fort McClellan 1917–1999, http://www.mcclellan.army.mil/ (accessed September 26, 2005).

19. Lee, *United States Army in World War II*, 129; Aaron Henry Personnel file, National Archives and Records Administration, Military Personnel Records Center, St Louis, Missouri (hereafter National Archives, St. Louis).

20. Ibid.

21. Henry, *Aaron Henry*, 61.

22. Paula Pfeffer, *A Philip Randolph, Pioneer of the Civil Rights Movement* (Baton Rouge: Louisiana State University Press, 1990), 45–58; Mark V. Tushnet, *Making Civil Rights Law: Thurgood Marshall and the Supreme Court, 1936–1961* (New York: Oxford University Press, 1994), 67–80.

23. Charles Hill, interview with the author.

24. Henry, *Aaron Henry*, 62–63.

25. Charles Hill, interview with the author.

26. Ibid.

27. Henry, *Aaron Henry*, 63.

28. Lee, *United States Army in World War II* (see supplementary Pacific Ocean map in appendices).

29. Henry, *Aaron Henry*, 62–63.

30. Aaron Henry, interview conducted by Neil McMillen (MSOHA), 8.

31. Amzie Moore, 1977, Oral history interview conducted in Cleveland, Mississippi, by Michael Garvey (MSOHA), 1–61, http://digilib.usm.edu/cdm/compoundobject/collection/coh/id/5707/rec/4 (accessed September 18, 2013).

32. Francoise Hamlin, *Crossroads at Clarksdale: Freedom Struggle in the Mississippi Delta after World War II* (Chapel Hill: University of North Carolina Press, 2012), 15–17.

33. Dittmer, *Local People*, 26.

34. Donald Matthews and James Prothro, *Negroes and the New Southern Politics* (New York: Harcourt, Brace and World, 1966), 146.

35. Ibid., 153.

36. U.S. Commission on Civil Rights (CRC), *Voting in Mississippi* (Washington, DC: Government Printing Office, 1965).

37. Henry, *Aaron Henry*, 64. Henry identifies this clerk only by his surname, "Mr. Smith."

38. Dittmer, *Local People*, 24.

39. Henry, *Aaron Henry*, 65.

40. Hanes Walton Jr., *Black Republicans: The Politics of the Black and Tans* (Metuchen: Scarecrow Press, 1975), 46.

41. Neil McMillen, "Perry Howard, Boss of Black and Tan Republicanism in Mississippi, 1924–1960," *Journal of Southern History* 48, no. 2 (May 1982): 205–224.

42. *Smith v. Allwright*, 321 U.S. 649 (1944); Darlene Clark Hine, *Black Victory: The Rise and Fall of the White Primary in Texas* (Millwood, NY: KTO Press, 1979).

43. The Political Graveyard: A Database of American History: Index to Politicians: J.W. Hopkins, http://politicalgraveyard.com/bio/hopkins.html (accessed November 19, 2008).

44. Lillian Pereyra, *James Lusk Alcorn: Persistent Whig* (Baton Rouge: Louisiana State

University Press, 1966); William Harris, *The Day of the Carpetbagger in Mississippi: Republican Reconstruction in Mississippi* (Baton Rouge: Louisiana State University Press, 1971), 347–350.

45. Jackson State University History, http://www.jsums.edu/unite/jsu-history/ (accessed October 28, 2014); Josephine Posey, *Alcorn State University and the National Alumni Association* (Mount Pleasant, SC: Arcadia Publishing Company, 2000), 31–32.

46. Dr. Gilbert Mason explained how this worked: "Because there was no opportunity for its black citizens to attend graduate school or medical school inside of the state, Mississippi offered to pay black medical students a five-thousand-dollar stipend in monthly installments over four years on the condition that the recipients return to Mississippi to practice for at least five years after med school." Gilbert Mason, *Beaches, Blood, and Ballots: A Black Doctor's Civil Rights Struggle* (Jackson: University Press of Mississippi, 2000), 30.

47. Xavier University website, "History of Xavier," http://www.xula.edu/about-xavier/history.php (accessed August 9, 2013).

48. Aaron Henry, interview by Neil McMillen (MSOHA), 4–5.

49. McMillen, *Dark Journey*, 171–172.

50. "A Short History," Howard University Pharmacy School website, http://health-sciences.howard.edu/education/schools-and-academics/medicine/about/mission/short-history (accessed October 27, 2014).

51. Aaron Henry, interview by Neil McMillen (MSOHA), 6.

52. *Xavier Herald* 34, no. 2 (January 1948): 1; and 25, no. 8 (May 1950): 4, Xavier University Archives, New Orleans, Louisiana (hereafter XUA).

53. Ibid., 22, no. 4 (July 1946): 1.

54. Ibid., 22, no. 5 (March 1947): 6; 23, no. 7 (April 1948): 2; 24, no. 6 (March 1949): 8.

55. Ibid., 22, no. 2 (December 1946): 1.

56. Thomas Krueger, *And Promises to Keep: The Southern Conference of Human Welfare, 1939–1948* (Nashville: Vanderbilt University Press, 1967).

57. John Hope Franklin and Alfred Moss Jr., *From Slavery to Freedom: A History of African Americans*, 7th ed. (New York: McGraw-Hill, 1994), 391–394; Walter White, *A Man Called White: The Autobiography of Walter White* (New York: Viking Press, 1948).

58. *Xavier Herald* 22, no. 3 (January 1947): 4.

59. National Students Organization "Preamble" (1949), Box 26, F 87, Allard Lowenstein Papers, Southern Historical Collection, Wilson Library, University of North Carolina at Chapel Hill, (hereafter Lowenstein Papers, UNC-SHC).

60. William Chafe, *Never Stop Running: Allard Lowenstein and the Struggle to Save American Liberalism* (New York: Basic Books, 1993), 93.

61. *Xavier Herald* 22, no. 7 (May 1947): 1.

62. Henry, *Aaron Henry*, 65; *Xavier Herald* 24, no. 2 (January 1949, (XUA), 4.

63. *Xavier Herald* 22, no. 7, May 1947, 1 (XUA); vol. 24, no. 2, January 1949, (XUA), 4.

64. Minutes of Student Conference of University of North Carolina, Lowenstein Papers, April 1946, Box 134, F 101 (Lowenstein Papers, UNC-SHC).

65. Chafe, *Never Stop Running*, 92–93.

66. Minutes of Student Conference of University of North Carolina, Lowenstein Papers, April 1946, Box 134, F 101 (Lowenstein Papers, UNC-SHC).

67. Chafe, *Never Stop Running*, 94.

68. *Xavier Herald* 25, no. 9 (July 1950): 1.

69. Henry, *Aaron Henry*, 66.

70. Ibid., 66.

71. Ibid., 67.

72. Ibid., 68·

73. *Jackson Advocate*, December 30, 1999–January 5, 2000, 1.

74. Henry, *Aaron Henry*, 68·

75. Rebecca Henry, interview with the author, November 18, 1997, Clarksdale, Mississippi.

76. Ibid.

77. Aaron Henry Funeral Program, "A Celebration of the Life of Dr. Aaron Edd Jackson Henry, "Doc.," Coahoma Community College, Clarksdale, Mississippi, May 23, 1997, personal collection of the author.

78. "Noelle Henry Obituary," *Clarksdale Press Register*, November 18, 1993, 2.

79. Her daughter, Rebecca Henry, unless otherwise noted, provided this biographical information on Noelle Henry in this section.

80. Louise Bradford, interview with the author, March 12, 1998, Clarksdale, Mississippi; Brenda Luckett, interview with the author, March 11, 1998, Clarksdale, Mississippi.

81. Louise Bradford, interview with the author.

82. Henry, *Aaron Henry*, 208–209.

83. *Clarksdale Press Register*, March 5, 1962. 1, Box: Aaron Henry vertical file, 1923–1997, Special Collections Mitchell Memorial Library, Mississippi State University (hereafter MSUSC); see also John Howard, *Men Like That: A Southern Queer History* (Chicago: University of Chicago Press, 1999), 159.

84. *Collins, Benford v. Aaron Henry*; and *Pearson v. Henry*, 380 U.S. 356, 992 (1965).

85. Howard, *Men Like That*, 162–165.

86. Ibid.

87. Letter from Noelle Henry to Aaron Henry, ND, Box 73, F 1266, Tougaloo College Archives, Benbow Collection, Tougaloo, Mississippi (hereafter Aaron Henry Papers, TC).

88. Ibid.

89. Hamlin, *Crossroads at Clarksdale*, 133–134.

90. Henry, *Aaron Henry*, 79.

91. Lawrence J. Hanks, "Civil Rights Organizations and Movements," in *African Americans and Political Participation: A Reference Handbook*, ed. Minion K. C. Morrison (Santa Barbara: ABC-CLIO, 2003), 146–147.

92. Anderson, *Eyes Off the Prize*.

93. Minion K. C. Morrison and Richard Middleton IV, "African Americans in Office," in *African Americans and Political Participation*, 267.

94. Byron D'Andra Orey and Reginald Vance, "Participation in Electoral Politics," in *African Americans and Political Participation*, 205ff.

95. Walton Jr., *Black Republicans*; McMillen, "Perry W. Howard," 205–224.

96. Michael Durham, *Powerful Days: The Civil Rights Photography of Charles Moore* (New York: Stewart, Tabori and Chang, 1991).

97. Julian Foster and Durward Long, eds., *Protest! Student Activism in America* (New York: William Morrow and Company, 1979); New Republic, *Thoughts of the Young Radicals* (New Jersey: Harrison Blaine and the New Republic, 1966).

98. Bennie Gooden, interview with the author, November 19, 1997, Clarksdale, Mississippi.

99. Lemann, *The Promised Land*, 46.

100. Payne, *I've Got the Light of Freedom*, 66.

101. Hamlin, *Crossroads at Clarksdale*, 25–27; Henry, *Aaron Henry*, 70.

102. Patricia Hills Collins, *Black Feminist Thought: Knowledge, Consciousness and the Politics of Empowerment* (New York: Routledge), 146–148.

103. Stanley O. Gaines Jr., "Sexuality and Race," in *The African American Experience: An Historiographical and Bibliographical Guide*, ed. Arvarh Strickland and Robert Weems Jr. (Westport, CT: Greenwood Press, 2001), 315–335. See also McMillen, *Dark Journey*, 233–237.

104. Payne, *I've Got the Light of Freedom*, 57–59.

105. Henry, *Aaron Henry*, 71–72. There is a repeated discrepancy in how Henry reports this event. He referred to the women as "girls" and recalled that two men were identified. The Hamlin version of the events clarifies that the women were aged thirty-five and twenty-two, and that a sole perpetrator was identified, E. L. Roach, a truck driver from the Delta town of Greenville. Hamlin, *Crossroads at Clarksdale*, 25.

106. Henry, *Aaron Henry*, 72.

107. Dittmer, *Local People*, 25.

108. Ibid., 26.

109. Payne, *I've Got the Light of Freedom*, 57; Henry, *Aaron Henry*, 72.

110. Payne, *I've Got the Light of Freedom*, 58.

111. Henry, *Aaron Henry*, 73.

112. Dittmer, *Local People*, 26.

113. Henry, *Aaron Henry*, 73.

114. Kevin Anderson, *Agitations: Ideologies and Strategies in African American Politics* (Fayetteville: University of Arkansas Press, 2010), 33–72.

115. Henry, *Aaron Henry*, 73.

116. NAACP Branch File, Coahoma 1953–1954, Correspondence of August 23, 24, 1953; October 5, 28, 1953, Group II, Box C 96, NAACP Papers, Library of Congress, Washington, D.C. (hereafter NAACP Papers, LOC).

117. Elmer Schattschneider, *The Semi-Sovereign People: A Realist's View of Democracy in America* (New York: Holt, Rinehart and Winston, 1960), 61.

118. Beito and Beito, *Black Maverick*, 60.

119. W. E. B. Du Bois, "The Talented Tenth," in *Negro Protest in the Twentieth Century*, ed. Francis Broderick and August Meier (Indianapolis: Bobbs-Merrill Company, 1966), 40–48.

120. Beito and Beito, *Black Maverick*, 76–77.

121. Louis R. Harlan, *Booker T. Washington: The Wizard of Tuskegee, 1901–1915* (New York: Oxford University Press, 1983).

122. David T. Beito, *From Mutual Aid to the Welfare State: Fraternal Societies and Social Services, 1890–1967* (Chapel Hill: University of North Carolina Press, 2000), 69–89 and 197–230.

123. Beito and Beito, *Black Maverick*, 45–68 and 90–114.

124. Ibid., 107.

125. Ibid., 45–69 and 170ff.

126. Regional Council of Negro Leadership Meeting Minutes, Box 90, F 1411, January 22, 1956 (Aaron Henry Papers, TC); Tushnet, *Making Civil Rights Law*, 156.

127. Beito and Beito. *Black Maverick*, 56–57.

128. Ibid., 53–57.

129. E. David Cronon, *Black Moses: Marcus Garvey and the United Negro Improvement Association* (Madison: University of Wisconsin Press, 1955).

130. Beito and Beito, *Black Maverick*, 79.

131. Ibid., 79.

132. Henry, *Aaron Henry*, 81.

133. Ibid., 68.

134. Beito and Beito, *Black Maverick*, 75–81.

135. Ibid., 141ff.

Chapter Three: Aaron Henry, the NAACP, and Indigenous Leadership: The Clarksdale Social Movement

1. Sidney Tarrow, *Power in Movement* (New York: Cambridge University Press, 1994), 23.

2. Franklin and Moss Jr., *From Slavery to Freedom*, 461–476; Cobb, *The Most Southern Place on Earth*.

3. Michael Williams, *Medgar Evers: Mississippi Martyr* (Fayetteville: University of Arkansas Press, 2011), 82, 93.

4. Beito and Beito, *Black Maverick*, 73, 80; Henry, *Aaron Henry*, 73–74.

5. Tarrow, *Power in Movement*, 3–4.

6. David Snow et al., "Frame Alignment Processes, Micromobilization, and Movement Participation," *American Sociological Review* 51 (August 1986): 464–481.

7. Morrison, *Black Political Mobilization*, 1–21.

8. Morris, *The Origins of the Civil Rights Movement*.

9. Stokely Carmichael and Charles Hamilton, *Black Power: The Politics of Liberation in America* (New York: Vintage, 1967).

10. "Integrating Ole Miss: A Civil Rights Milestone," http://microsites.jfklibrary.org/olemiss/controversy/ (accessed August 13, 2013).

11. Raymond Arsenault, *Freedom Riders: 1961 and the Struggle for Racial Justice* (New York: Oxford University Press, 2006), 251–258.

12. Brandfon, *Cotton Kingdom of the South*.

13. James Silver, *Mississippi: The Closed Society*, 3rd ed. (New York: Harcourt, Brace and World 1964).

14. Henry, *Aaron Henry*, 70; Hamlin, *Crossroads at Clarksdale*, 77–78.

15. Aaron Henry, interview by Neil McMillen (MSOHA), 9.

16. Cobb, *The Most Southern Place on Earth*, 175–177.

17. Hamlin, *Crossroads at Clarksdale*, 56–57.

18. Aaron Henry, interview with Neil McMillen, 13.

19. Bennie Gooden, interview with the author; Louise Bradford, interview with the author; Andrew Carr, interview with the author, March 9, 1998, Clarksdale, Mississippi.

20. McMillen, *Dark Journey*, 233; Payne, *I've Got the Light of Freedom*, 34–42; Henry, *Aaron Henry*, 95–97.

21. Henry, *Aaron Henry*, 74–75.

22. Morris, *The Origins of the Civil Rights Movement*, 275–290; Morrison, *Black Political Mobilization*, 7–15.

23. *Brown v. Board of Education of Topeka*, 347 U.S. 483 (1954), 349 U.S. 294 (1955).

24. Henry, *Aaron Henry*, 85–88.

25. Ibid., 92.

26. Mrs. Medgar Evers with William Peters, *For Us the Living* (New York: Doubleday, 1967), 164; Bolton, *The Hardest Deal of All*, 73–76.

27. Henry, *Aaron Henry*, 92.

28. Hamlin, *Crossroads at Clarksdale*, 57.

29. Neil McMillen, *The Citizens' Council: Organized Resistance to the Second Reconstruction, 1954–1964* (Urbana: University of Illinois Press, 1994).

30. Dittmer, *Local People*, 46–54.

31. Henry, *Aaron Henry*, 91; McMillen, *The Citizen's Council*, 19.

32. Henry, *Aaron Henry*, 91.

33. McMillen, *The Citizens' Council*, 216–217.

34. Beito and Beito, *Black Maverick*, 141–145.

35. Williams, *Medgar Evers*, 283–285.

36. Payne, *I've Got the Light of Freedom*, 35–36.

37. Beito and Beito, *Black Maverick*; Payne, *I've Got the Light of Freedom*, 29–67.

38. Stephen Whitfield, *A Death in the Delta: The Story of Emmett Till* (Baltimore: Johns Hopkins University Press, 1991).

39. Bolton, *The Hardest Deal of All*, 33–49.

40. "Integrating Ole Miss: A Civil Rights Milestone," http://microsites.jfklibrary.org/olemiss/controversy/ (accessed August 13, 2013).

41. *United States v. Ross Barnett and Paul B. Johnson, Jr.*, 330 F. 2d 369. 5th Cir. (1963); Dittmer, *Local People*, 139–141.

42. Payne, *I've Got the Light of Freedom*, 60.

43. Henry, *Aaron Henry*, 101.

44. Minutes of Regional Council of Negro Leadership, Mound Bayou, Mississippi, January 22, 1956, Box 85, F 1411 (Aaron Henry Papers, TC).

45. Henry, *Aaron Henry*, 101; Evers, *For Us the Living*, 216; Adam Fairclough, *To Redeem the Soul of America: The Southern Christian Leadership Convention and Martin Luther King, Jr.* (Albany: University of Georgia Press, 1987), 30–33.

46. Martin Luther King in Clarksdale, Mississippi (summary), May 1958, Box 74, F 1272 (Aaron Henry Papers, TC); David Garrow, *Bearing the Cross: Martin Luther King, Jr., and the Southern Christian Leadership Conference* (New York: William Morrow and Co., 1986), 105–106.

47. Gilbert Mason, *Beaches, Blood, and Ballots: A Black Doctor's Civil Rights Struggle* (Jackson: University Press of Mississippi, 2000), 68.

48. Clayborne Carson, *In Struggle: SNCC and the Black Awakening of the 1960s* (Cambridge, MA: Harvard University Press, 1981), 31–44.

49. Hamlin, *Crossroads at Clarksdale*, 59–61.

50. Vera Pigee, *The Struggle of Struggles, Part I* (Detroit: Harpo, 1975), 47ff.

51. Morris, *The Origins of the Civil Rights Movement*; Hamlin, *Crossroads at Clarksdale*, 85; Pigee, *The Struggle of Struggles*.

52. Pigee, *The Struggle of Struggles*, 47–48; Hamlin, *Crossroads at Clarksdale*, 84–85.

53. Pigee, *The Struggle of Struggles*, 49.

54. *Clarksdale Press Register*, January 30, 1962, 1.

55. Miles Wolff, *Sitting at the 5 and 10*, Revised and Expanded (Chicago: Elephant Paperbacks, Ivan Dee Publishers, 1990), 11–57.

56. *Boynton v. Commonwealth of Virginia*, 364. U.S. 454 (1960).

57. Pigee, *The Struggle of Struggles*, 53.

58. Henry, *Aaron Henry*, 111–114; Hamlin, *Crossroads at Clarksdale*, 91.

59. Henry, *Aaron Henry*, 111.

60. Ibid., 113.

61. Lemann, *The Promised Land*, 310–311.

62. Henry, *Aaron Henry*, 112.

63. Ibid., 113.

64. Pigee, *The Struggle of Struggles*, 20, 53–54; *Clarksdale Press Register*, April 4, 1962, 12; Hamlin, *Crossroads at Clarksdale*, 92.

65. Henry, *Aaron Henry*, 113.

66. Pigee, *The Struggle of Struggles*, 55–56.

67. Lemann, *The Promised Land*, 310–311.

68. Pat Watters and Reese Cleghorn, *Climbing Jacob's Ladder: The Arrival of Negroes in Southern Politics* (New York: Harcourt, Brace and World, 1967), 181.

69. Hamlin, *Crossroads at Clarksdale*, 87–91.

70. Henry, *Aaron Henry*, 70; Watters and Cleghorn, *Climbing Jacob's Ladder*, 181.

71. *Clarksdale Press Register*, February 27, 1962, 1. Hamlin has shown that acts such as these have helped to obscure the important role Pigee played in the Clarksdale movement that was dominated by men. The same applies to how women's defining roles have been downplayed generally in the civil rights movement. Hamlin, *Crossroads at Clarksdale*, 87–88.

72. Henry, *Aaron Henry*, 114.

73. *Clarksdale Press Register*, January 22, 1962, 1.

74. Robert Dallek, *An Unfinished Life: John Kennedy, 1917–1963* (Boston: Little, Brown and Company, 2003), 631ff; Dittmer, *Local People*, 167–169; Cobb, *The Most Southern Place on Earth*, 210–212.

75. *Clarksdale Press Register*, January 29, 1962, 1.

76. Henry, *Aaron Henry*, 101; Evers, *For Us the Living*, 216; Fairclough, *To Redeem the Soul of America*, 30–33.

77. Dittmer, *Local People*, 122.

78. Hamlin, *Crossroads at Clarksdale*, 101.

79. Ibid., 93–99; Henry, *Aaron Henry*, 122.

80. Henry, *Aaron Henry*, 120.

81. *Mississippi Free Press*, June 2, 1962, 1.

82. Ibid.

83. Hamlin, *Crossroads at Clarksdale*, 98–99; John Howard, *Men Like That: A Southern Queer History* (Chicago: University of Chicago Press, 1999), 158–166.

84. Henry, *Aaron Henry*, 116–128.

85. Hamlin, *Crossroads at Clarksdale*, 100–102.

86. *Henry v. State*, No. 42652, 253 Miss. 263; 154 So. 2 d 289 (1963); *Henry v. Mississippi*, 379 U.S. 443. 85 S. Ct. 564. L. Ed. 2d. 408 (1965); *Henry v. Pearson*, No. 42758. 253 Miss. 62. 158 2d 695 (1963); *Henry v. Pearson*, 380 U.S. 356. 85. S. Ct. 992. 13 L. Ed. 892 (1963).

87. *Mississippi Free Press*, June 2, 1962, 1.

88. "Campaign Headquarters Reverend Theodore Trammell Candidate United States Congress Third Congressional District of Mississippi," Clarksdale, Mississippi, January 27,

1962, Box 1, F 4, Amzie Moore Papers, State Historical Society of Wisconsin (hereafter Amzie Moore Papers, SHSW).

89. *Clarksdale Press Register*, December 23, 1961, 1.

90. Minutes of Board Meeting of Regional Council of Negro Leadership, February 10, 1957, Box 85, F 1411 (Aaron Henry Papers, TC).

91. *Clarksdale Press Register*, April 4, 1962.

92. *Mississippi Free Press*, April 7, 1962, 1.

93. Rebecca Henry, interview with the author.

94. Hermann, *The Pursuit of a Dream*, 61ff; Neil McMillan, "Isaiah to Montgomery, 1847–1924, Part II," http://www.mshistorynow.mdah.state.ms.us/articles/55/index.php?id=57 (accessed March 27, 2013).

95. *Mississippi Free Press*, April 28, 1962, 4.

96. Frank E. Smith, *Congressman from Mississippi* (New York: Pantheon, 1964); Frank Parker, "Mississippi's 'Massive Resistance' to Black Political Empowerment After Passage of the Voting Rights Act, 1965–1970," Paper presented to the National Conference of Black Political Scientists, April 2–5, 1986, 1–14.

97. Parker, "Mississippi's 'Massive Resistance," 14–16, 1–104.

98. Leslie McLemore, "The Mississippi Freedom Democratic Party: A Case Study of Grassroots Politics" (PhD. diss, University of Massachusetts, Amherst, 1971), 63–64.

99. Carson, *In Struggle*, 45–78.

100. Henry, *Aaron Henry*, 130–131.

101. Carson, *In Struggle*, 48–49.

102. Henry, *Aaron Henry*, 131.

103. Ibid.

104. Payne, *I've Got the Light of Freedom*, 146ff.

105. Carson, *In Struggle*, 77–81.

106. Joyce Ladner, interview with the author, July 31, 1998, Washington, DC; Robert Moses, interview with the author, March 5, 1998, Jackson, Mississippi; Leslie McLemore, interview with the author, February 6, 1999, Jackson, Mississippi.

107. USDA Food and Nutrition Services, Food and Distribution Programs, http://www.fns.usda.gov/fdd/aboutfd/fd_history.pdf (accessed April 6, 2013).

108. Carson, *In Struggle*, 79–80.

109. Dittmer, *Local People*, 144.

110. Carson, *In Struggle*, 80–81.

111. Cleveland Sellers, "Holly Springs: Gateway to the Beloved Community," in *Freedom Is a Constant Struggle: An Anthology of the Mississippi Civil Rights Movement*, ed. Susie Erenrich (Montgomery, AL: Black Belt Press, 1999), 495; Carson, *In Struggle*, 80, 116.

112. Henry Hampton and Steve Fayer, *Voices of Freedom: An Oral History of the Civil Rights Movement from the 1950s through the 1980s* (New York: Bantam, 1990), 149.

113. Hamlin, *Crossroads at Clarksdale*; Henry, *Aaron Henry*.

114. Carson, *In Struggle*, 80.

115. Dick Gregory, *Callus On My Soul: A Memoir* (New York: Kensington Press, 2003), 54–67; Harry Belafonte, *My Song: A Memoir* (New York: Knopf, 2011), 3–10.

116. Dittmer, *Local People*, 145.

117. Carson, *In Struggle*, 70.

118. Henry, *Aaron Henry*, 140.

119. Henry, *Aaron Henry*, 138; Dittmer, *Local People*, 147.

120. Payne, *I've Got the Light of Freedom*, 261–262.

121. Beito and Beito, *Black Maverick*, 107; Charles V. Hamilton, *Adam Clayton Powell, Jr.: The Political Biography of an American Dilemma* (New York: Atheneum, 1992), 181–182.

122. Henry, *Aaron Henry*, 141–143.

123. Ibid., 143.

124. Ibid.; *Clarksdale Press Register*, July 22, 1963, 1.

125. Henry, *Aaron Henry*, 144.

126. Hamlin, *Crossroads at Clarksdale*, 57.

127. Silver, *Mississippi*, 101.

128. Ibid., 100.

129. Henry, *Aaron Henry*, 100–109; Hamlin, *Crossroads at Clarksdale*, 117.

130. Williams, *Medgar Evers*, 282–283.

131. Henry, *Aaron Henry*, 147–151; Williams, *Medgar Evers*, 283–289.

132. Watters and Cleghorn, *Climbing Jacob's Ladder*, 181.

133. Aaron Henry, Letter to Clarksdale Mayor and Board of Aldermen, June 4, 1963, Box 6, F1, Amzie Moore Papers, State Historical Society of Wisconsin (Amzie Moore Papers, SHSW).

134. Ibid.

135. Ibid.

136. Carol George, *Segregated Sabbaths: Richard Allen and the Rise of Independent Black Churches, 1770–1840* (New York: Oxford University Press, 1973), 1–20.

137. Hamlin, *Crossroads at Clarksdale*, 113.

138. David Chappell, *A Stone of Hope: Prophetic Religion and the Death of Jim Crow* (Chapel Hill: University of North Carolina Press, 2004); Pigee, *The Struggle of Struggles*, 57.

139. *Clarksdale Press Register*, June 17, 1963, 1.

140. Charles Marsh, *God's Long Summer: Stories of Faith and Civil Rights* (Princeton, NJ: Princeton University Press, 1997), 131–141.

141. *Clarksdale Press Register*, September 1961–October 1963; Hamlin, *Crossroads at Clarksdale*, 85, 138.

142. There is some suggestion that the *Clarksdale Press Register* did have a positive role. In 1963 Henry, for example, referred to a reporter, Curtis Wilkie, as a friend. He knew him well enough to invite him to his home to interview Congressman Charles Diggs when he visited in April. Henry reported that "the next day the paper carried a fairly prominent story about Diggs's being in town." Henry, *Aaron Henry*, 141; Hamlin, *Crossroads at Clarksdale*, 142–143. Wilkie has written his own account of the period in Clarksdale. Curtis Wilkie, *Dixie: A Personal Odyssey Through Events that Shaped the Modern South* (New York: Scribner, 2001), 113–153.

143. Pigee, *The Struggle of Struggles*, 58.

144. Ibid.

145. Ibid.

146. Lemann, *The Promised Land*, 311.

147. Henry, *Aaron Henry*, 152.

148. Ibid., 152–153.

149. Hamlin uses a figure of fifty-six. Hamlin, *Crossroads at Clarksdale*, 120.

150. Henry, *Aaron Henry*, 153.

151. Ibid.

152. Hamlin, *Crossroads at Clarksdale*, 122.

153. Henry, *Aaron Henry*, 152–153.

154. Hamlin, *Crossroads at Clarksdale*, 124.

155. Letter from Aaron Henry to Roy Wilkins, September 6, 1963, Group 3, Box 243 (NAACP Papers, LOC).

156. Ibid.

157. Ibid.

158. Henry, *Aaron Henry*, 92.

159. *Clarksdale Press Register*, September 17, 1963, 1.

160. Hamlin, *Crossroads at Clarksdale*.

161. John Dittmer, *The Good Doctors: The Medical Committee for Human Rights and the Struggle for Social Justice in Health Care* (New York: Bloomsbury Press, 2009), 38–60; Frank Parker, *Black Votes Count: Political Empowerment in Mississippi After 1965* (Chapel Hill: University of North Carolina Press, 1990), 79–80; Anderson, *Agitations*, 97–98; Doug McAdam, *Freedom Summer* (New York: Oxford University Press, 1988), 66–115; Dittmer, *Local People*, 214–241; Hamlin, *Crossroads at Clarksdale*, 127.

162. Kenneth Andrews, *Freedom Is a Constant Struggle: The Mississippi Civil Rights Movement and Its Legacy* (Chicago: University of Chicago, 2004), 64–107; John Salter Jr., *Jackson, Mississippi: An American Chronicle of Struggle and Schism* (New York: Exposition Press, 1979), 168–184; Chana Lee, *For Freedom's Sake: The Life of Fannie Lou Hamer* (Urbana: University of Illinois Press, 1999), 43–60; Constance Curry, *Silver Rights* (New York: Algonquin Books of Chapel Hill, 1995), 107–151; Emilye Crosby, *A Little Taste of Freedom: The Black Freedom Struggle in Claiborne County, Mississippi* (Chapel Hill: University of North Carolina Press, 2005), 79–90.

163. Carson, *In Struggle*; Dittmer, *Local People*, 204.

164. Joyce Ladner, interview with the author; Robert Moses, interview with the author.

165. Hamlin, *Crossroads at Clarksdale*, 164–165.

166. *Clarksdale Press Register*, July 6, 1964, 1.

167. Ibid., July 7, 1964, 1.

168. Ibid., July 8, 1964, 1.

169. Ibid.

170. Ibid.

171. Ibid., July 10, 1964, 1.

172. Ibid., July 14, 1964, 8.

173. Ibid., July 20, 1964, 1.

174. Ibid., July 21, 1964.

175. Dittmer, *Local People*, 229–230.

176. *Clarksdale Press Register*, July 13, 1964, 1; July 28, 1964, 1. See also Dittmer, *The Good Doctors*, 33–35, 48–53.

177. Jerry Silverman, *Songs of Protest and Civil Rights* (New York: Chelsea House Publishers, 1992), 4.

178. Guy Caravan and Candie Caravan, "Carry it On: Roots of the Singing Civil Rights Movement," in *Freedom Is a Constant Struggle*, 144; Bernice Reagon, "Civil Rights Movement," in *African American Music, an Introduction*, ed. Mellonee Burnim and Portia Maultsby (New York: Routledge, 2006), 598–623. See also "The Student Voice," SNCC Papers, December 19, 1962, 2(62), V3, #4.

179. *Clarksdale Press Register*, July 14, 1964, 8.

180. Ibid., July 29, 1664, 1.

181. Ibid., June 22, 1964, 1.

182. Ibid., June 23, 1964, 1.

183. Ibid., July 7, 1964, 1.

184. *Rebecca E. Henry et al. v. The Clarksdale Municipal Separate School District et al.*, 409 F. 2d 682; U.S. App. (1969). See also *Clarksdale Press Register*, July 28, 1964, 1.

185. *Rebecca E. Henry et al. v. The Clarksdale Municipal Separate School District et al.*, 409 F. 2d 682; U.S. App. (1969).

186. *Clarksdale Press Register*, July 31, 1964, 1.

Chapter Four: Demanding Restoration of the Black Franchise: Henry Heads the Freedom Vote Ticket, a 1963 Mock Election

1. Aaron Henry letter to Roy Wilkins, August 19, 1962, Group III, Box A270 (NAACP Papers, LOC).

2. oyce Ladner, interview with the author; Robert Moses, interview with the author; Hamlin, *Crossroads at Clarksdale*, 102–105.

3. Henry, *Aaron Henry*, 107.

4. Henry, *Aaron Henry*, 109; Len Holt, *The Summer That Didn't End: The Story of the Mississippi Civil Rights Project of 1964* (New York: Da Capo Press, 1992), 31–33.

5. Carson, *In Struggle*, 78.

6. Payne, *I've Got the Light of Freedom*, 129–130.

7. Henry, *Aaron Henry*, 115.

8. Townsend Davis, *Weary Feet, Rested Souls: A Guided History of the Civil Rights Movement* (New York: Norton, 1998), 299–308; Melba Newsome, "Another Ghost of Mississippi Laid to Rest," *The New Crisis*, 1998, in http://findarticles.com/p/ articles/ mi_qa3812/is_199811/ai_n8815983/?tag=content;col1 (accessed May 13, 2009).

9. Joyce Ladner, interview with the author.

10. Robert Moses, interview with the author.

11. Payne, *I've Got the Light of Freedom*, 108–110; Dittmer, *Local People*, 120.

12. Carson, *In Struggle*, 70; Dittmer, *Local People*, 119–120; Payne, *I've Got the Light of Freedom*, 141; Steven Lawson, *Black Ballots: Voting Rights in the South 1944–1969* (New York: Columbia University Press, 1967), 261.

13. Payne, *I've Got the Light of Freedom*, 141.

14. *Clarksdale Press Register*, April 16, 1962, 8 and 14. When Henry and Lindsey appeared at the hearings the Senate was debating literacy tests, a technique long used to deny African Americans the franchise. The two men indicted this system, facing down its southern supporters. Then after the no-holds-barred indictment, they personally called on Mississippi senator Eastland to reject his assertion that "they seek action at the state level [because] the federal government had no roles in these matters."

15. Dittmer, *Local People*, 194–195.

16. Ibid., 196ff.

17. *Clarksdale Press Register*, May 16, 1962, 14.

18. Dittmer, *Local People*, 95–97; Raymond Arsenault, *Freedom Riders: 1961 and the Struggle for Racial Justice* (New York: Oxford University Press, 2006).

19. Dittmer, *Local People*, 176.

20. Salter Jr., *Jackson, Mississippi*, 132–203.

21. Carson, *In Struggle*, 45–55.

22. Tarrow, *Power in Movement*; Doug McAdam et al., "Introduction: Opportunities, Mobilizing Structures, and Framing Processes—Toward a Synthetic, Comparative Perspective on Social Movements," in *Comparative Perspectives on Social Movements: Political Opportunities, Mobilizing Structures, and Cultural Framings,* ed. Doug McAdam et al. (New York: Cambridge University Press, 1996), 1–20.

23. Morrison, *Black Political Mobilization*, 1–23.

24. Dittmer, *Local People*, 201.

25. Carson, *In Struggle*, 97. Some attribute this find to Bill Higgs, a white Mississippi activist and lawyer, who was equally despised by segregationists because of his homosexuality. Edwin King, 1988, Oral history interview conducted in Washington, D. C. and Miami Beach, Florida by William Chafe. Lowenstein Oral History, Columbia University Oral History Research Office, New York, New York (hereafter CUOHR), 31; Hamlin, *Crossroads at Clarksdale*, 31.

26. Morrison, *Black Political Mobilization*, 103, 108.

27. Neil McMillen, "Black Enfranchisement in Mississippi: Federal Enforcement and Black Protest in the 1960s," *Journal of Southern History* 43, no. 3 (1977): 353.

28. Watters and Cleghorn, *Climbing Jacob's Ladder*, 67; McLemore, "The Mississippi Freedom Democratic Party," 101; William Chafe, *Never Stop Running: Allard Lowenstein and the Struggle to Save American Liberalism* (New York: Basic Books, 1993), 180; Carson, *In Struggle*, 97; Henry, *Aaron Henry*, 156.

29. Watters and Cleghorn, *Climbing Jacob's Ladder*, 67.

30. Todd Gitlin, *The Sixties: Years of Hope, Days of Rage* (New York: Bantam, 1987), 150; Carson, *In Struggle*, 98.

31. Aaron Henry letter to "Fellow Citizens of Mississippi and America," October 28, 1963, Edwin King Papers, Box 6, F 414, Tougaloo College Archives, Benbow Collection, Tougaloo, Mississippi (hereafter Edwin King Papers, TC).

32. Dittmer, *Local People*, 202; Hamlin, *Crossroads at Clarksdale*, 129.

33. Henry, *Aaron Henry*, 157–158.

34. Charles Marsh, *God's Long Summer: Stories of Faith and Civil Rights* (Princeton, NJ: Princeton University Press, 1997), 116–151.

35. Dittmer, *Local People*, 156; Henry, *Aaron Henry*, 156.

36. Edwin King, "Mississippi Freedom Vote," unpublished manuscript, ND, Box 8 (Edwin King Papers, TC), 28.

37. "Freedom Vote Platform," ND, Box 8, F 414 (Edwin King Papers, TC).

38. Ibid.

39. Ibid.

40. Davis, *Weary Feet, Rested Souls*, 195–196; "SNCC Memo," September 15, 1963, Box 8, F 412 (Edwin King Papers, TC), 1.

41. It asked nine questions, including date, name, age, citizenship status, state and county residence, time in the county, local address, and if a member of the clergy. "Freedom Registration Form," Clay County Civil Rights Material Folder (MSUSC).

42. News Release, "COFO Maps Vote Fight," October 1963, SNCC Papers Microfilm, Reel 10, State Historical Society of Wisconsin, Madison (hereafter SNCC Papers, SHSW).

43. Arthur I. Waskow, *From Race Riot to Sit-In, 1919 and the 1960s* (Garden City, NY: Doubleday and Co., 1966), 264.

44. "Freedom Vote Platform," ND, Box 8, F 414 (Edwin King Papers, TC).

45. Ibid.

46. "What is COFO?," Box 1, F 1, B 1, ND, Samuel Walker Papers (SHSW).

47. "Freedom Vote Platform," ND, Box 8, F 414 (Edwin King Papers, TC).

48. "Freedom Primer #2," Box 6, Delta Ministry Papers, Mississippi State University, ND (MSUSC).

49. "Freedom Vote Platform," ND, Box 8, F 414 (Edwin King Papers, TC).

50. Dittmer, *Local People*, 64–65.

51. Julius E. Thompson, *The Black Press in Mississippi, 1865–1985* (Gainesville: University Press of Florida, 1993).

52. Dittmer, *Local People*, 124.

53. Stephen Walsh, "Black Oriented Radio and the Civil Rights Movement," in *Media, Culture, and the Modern African American Freedom Struggle*, ed. Brian Ward (Gainesville: University of Florida Press, 2001), 67–81.

54. Fredrick Harris, *Something Within: Religion in African American Political Activism* (New York: Oxford University Press, 1999), 133–153.

55. Dittmer, *Local People*, 65–66.

56. Letter from Robert Moses to L. M. Sepaugh (illegible), Executive Vice President, WLBT News Release, October 15, 1963, SNCC Papers Microfilm, Reel 10 (SNCC Papers, SHSW).

57. Kay Mills, *Changing Channels: The Civil Rights Case That Transformed Television* (Jackson: University Press of Mississippi, 2004), 121–139; Dittmer, *Local People*, 66.

58. Payne, *I've Got the Light of Freedom*, 295.

59. "Operations Statement. SNCC," Box 8, F 412, September 15, 1963 (Edwin King Papers, TC), 5.

60. Ibid.

61. Ibid.

62. Ibid.

63. Ibid.; Mason, *Beaches, Blood, and Ballots*, 49–87.

64. Payne, *I've Got the Light of Freedom*, 295.

65. Henry, *Aaron Henry*, 158–159.

66. Hamlin, *Crossroads at Clarksdale*, 128–132.

67. "Freedom Vote Platform," ND, Box 8, F 414 (Edwin King Papers, TC).

68. "Press release Coahoma County NAACP," SCR: 1–16–1–74–1–1–1, October 19, 1963, Sovereignty Commission Papers, Mississippi Department of Archives and History (hereafter Sovereignty Papers, MDAH).

69. Campaign blurb, Box 8, F 414, ND (Edwin King Papers, TC).

70. "Freedom Vote," Box 8, F 414, ND (Edwin King Papers, TC), 90–98.

71. "Summary of Events in Hattiesburg," B 8, F 413, October 28, 1963 (Edwin King Papers, TC).

72. Ibid.

73. Ibid.

74. "Freedom Vote," Box 8, F 414, ND (Edwin King Papers, TC), 43–44.

75. Ibid., 69.

76. Dittmer, *Local People*, 205; "Freedom Vote," Box 8, F 414, ND (Edwin King Papers, TC), 68.

77. Ibid., 205.

78. Ibid., 23–24.

79. Ibid.

80. "Aaron Henry Vertical File, 1923–1997," newspaper clipping in the *Lexington Advertiser*, October 24, 1963, NP (MSUSC).

81. Salter Jr., *Jackson, Mississippi*, 228–239.

82. Hamlin, *Crossroads at Clarksdale*, 130–131.

83. Letter and Affidavits from Aaron Henry sent to Roy Wilkins, NAACP Executive Director, September 6, 1963, Group 3, Box 243 (NAACP Papers, LOC).

84. Ibid.

85. Ibid.

86. "Freedom Vote," Box 8, F 413, ND (Edwin King Papers, TC).

87. Dittmer, *Local People*, 116–169; Payne, *I've Got the Light of Freedom*, 132–234; Carson, *In Struggle*, 77–79, 111–129; Morrison, *Black Political Mobilization*, 95–122; Lee, *For Freedom's Sake*, 23–44; Constance Curry, *Silver Rights* (New York: Algonquin Books of Chapel Hill, 1995), 47–72.

88. Carson, *In Struggle*, 45–55.

89. Ibid., 81.

90. Ibid., 96.

91. Chafe, *Never Stop Running*, 180–186.

92. Dittmer, *Local People*, 102–103.

93. Carson, *In Struggle*, 98; Henry, *Aaron Henry*, 161.

94. Henry, *Aaron Henry*, 157.

95. Chafe, *Never Stop Running*, 183–184.

96. Carson, *In Struggle*, 45–55.

97. Chafe, *Never Stop Running*, 184.

98. Ibid., 185.

99. Adam Fairclough, *To Redeem the Soul of America: The Southern Christian Leadership Convention and Martin Luther King, Jr.* (Albany: University of Georgia Press, 1987), 152–160.

100. Elmer Schattschneider, *The Semi-Sovereign People: A Realist's View of Democracy in America* (New York: Holt, Rinehart and Winston, 1960).

101. Carson, *In Struggle*, 99; Dittmer, *Local People*, 208–209.

102. This is a reference to Gilbert Mason's protest, retold in his memoir. Mason, *Beaches, Blood, and Ballots*.

103. Carl Arnold Report, Hattiesburg, Mississippi, October 7, 1963, SNCC Microfilm, Reel 5 (SNCC Papers, SHSW), 1–2.

104. Ibid.

105. "Freedom Vote," Box 8, F 413, ND (Edwin King Papers, TC).

106. Chafe, *Never Stop Running*, 185; Harry Fleishman, *Norman Thomas: A Biography: 1884–1968* (New York: Norton and Company, 1969).

107. King, "Freedom Vote," Box 8, F 413, ND (Edwin King Papers, TC), 95.

108. William Kunstler, *Deep in My Heart* (New York: William Morrow and Co., 1966).

109. John Doar interview for Eyes on the Prize Series, November 15, 1985. http://digital.wustl.edu/cgi/t/text/text-idx?c=eop;cc=eop; rgn= main;view=text;idno=doa0015.0543.028 (accessed August 16, 2013).

110. Henry Hampton and Steve Fayer, *Voices of Freedom: An Oral History of the Civil Rights Movement from the 1950s through the 1980s* (New York: Bantam, 1990), 148–149.

111. Douglas Lindner, "Bending Toward Justice: John Doar and The Mississippi Burning Trial," *Mississippi Law Journal* 72, no. 2 (2002): 1–20, www.law.umkc.edu/ faculty/ projects/ftrials/trialheroes/doaressay.html (accessed April 28, 2009).

112. Clayborne Carson, ed., *The Student Voice, 1960–1965: Periodical of the Student Nonviolent Coordinating Committee* (Westport, CT: Meckler, 1990), 160.

113. Clarence Dunnaville Jr., "Fortieth Anniversary of the Lawyers' Committee for Civil Rights," *Virginia Lawyer*, June/July 2003.

114. Ibid., 38. Perhaps the most prominent among them was Frank Parker, who began his involvement as a staff attorney for the United States Commission on Civil Rights in 1967. He arrived in Mississippi in 1968 and went on to successfully litigate some of the most important cases that dismantled the legal architecture of disfranchisement—among them voting rights and reapportionment. He recounts some of these in copious detail in Parker, *Black Votes Count*.

115. Dittmer, *Local People*, 230; National Lawyers Guild, http://nlg.org/aboutus/history. php (accessed April 28, 2009).

116. "Oxford Companion to the US Supreme Court: Reconstruction, Federalism, and Economic Rights," http://www.answers.com/topic/reconstruction-federalism-and-economic-rights (accessed April 30, 2009).

117. Dick Gregory, *Callus On My Soul: A Memoir* (New York: Kensington Press, 2000); Dittmer, *Local People*, 174.

118. SCR, Ibid., 1–16–1–74–1–1–1 (Sovereignty Commission Papers, MDAH).

119. Henry, *Aaron Henry*, 136–141.

120. Dittmer, *Local People*, 205; *Mississippi Free Press*, November 2, 1963.

121. News release (unattributed), October 26, 1963, B 8, F 413 (Edwin King Papers, TC).

122. Dittmer, *Local People*, 205.

123. Carson, *The Student Voice*, 76.

124. *New York Times*, November 16, 1964, 1.

125. The judges originally assigned were Harold Cox (a reliable vote for the segregationists), Brown, and Wisdom. "Telegram to Senator James O. Eastland from Aaron Henry, Ed King and Bob Moses," ND, Box 8, F 413 (Edwin King Papers, TC). Meanwhile, John Salter documents the overt racism often demonstrated by Judge Cox. See Salter Jr., *Jackson, Mississippi*, 69–71.

126. Charles Cobb Field Reports, ND, Reel 5, F 81 (SNCC Papers, SHSW).

127. Carson, *The Student Voice*, 76; McLemore, "The Mississippi Freedom Democratic Party," 106. This author reports the discrepancies regarding the number of participants, ranging from 80,000 to upward of 90,000.

128. *Mississippi Free Press*, November 16, 1963, 8.

129. Dittmer, *Local People*, 206.

130. Morris, *The Origins of the Civil Rights Movement*, 40.

131. Arsenault, *Freedom Riders*, 258–303; Dittmer, *Local People*, 118.

132. Williams, *Medgar Evers*, 237ff. Salter Jr., *Jackson, Mississippi*, dedicates his entire edition to Medgar Evers's role in the Jackson mobilization.

133. Donaldson quoted in Dittmer, *Local People*, 205.

134. Henry, *Aaron Henry*, 163.

Chapter Five: An Alternative to the Segregated State Democratic Party: The MFDP Goes to Atlantic City, 1964

1. Orey and Vance, "Participation in Electoral Politics," 189.

2. In Mississippi from 1932 to 1964, Republican presidential candidates won only once in nine contests. Harold Stanley and Richard Niemi, *Vital Statistics on American Politics, 1999–2000* (Washington, DC: CQ Press, 2000), 31.

3. Henry, *Aaron Henry*, 163.

4. Hamlin, *Crossroads at Clarksdale*, 117.

5. Memo to Mississippi [COFO] Staff, November 1963, B 2, F 2 (Amzie Moore Papers, SHSW); Dittmer, *Local People*, 204; Joseph Sinsheimer, "The Freedom Vote of 1963: New Strategies of Racial Protest in Mississippi," *Journal of Southern History* 55 (May 1989): 204.

6. Memo to Mississippi [COFO] Staff (Amzie Moore Papers, SHSW).

7. Ibid.

8. "Mississippi Reports," December 5, 1963, Box 1, F 4, Jo Ann Robinson Papers (SHSW), 1–5.

9. Ibid.

10. "Mississippi Reports," February 9, 1964, Box 1, F 4, Jo Ann Robinson Papers (SHSW), 1–5.

11. Ibid.; www.prop1.org/2000/ctbtwsp.htm (accessed April 29, 2005). Dagmar Wilson, founder of Women Strike for Peace, explained the focus of the organization that Claire Collins referenced: "Since we came into being 35 years ago as a protest against atmospheric nuclear tests and the danger of radioactive pollution to children's health, WSP has remained a strong voice in the struggle for our unfinished goal—The Comprehensive Test Ban Treaty and for total nuclear disarmament."

12. Coahoma County Branch Newsletter (NAACP), February 8, 1964, Box 6, F 2 (Amzie Moore Papers, SHSW).

13. Sinsheimer, "The Freedom Vote of 1963," 231.

14. Dittmer, *Local People*, 206.

15. Doug McAdam, *Freedom Summer* (New York: Oxford University Press, 1988), 73 and 38; Pat Watters, "Encounter with the Future," *New South* 20, no. 5 (May 1965): 1–34.

16. McAdam, *Freedom Summer*, 66–155; Dittmer, *Local People*, 208–209.

17. Dittmer, *Local People*, 234; James Forman, *The Making of Black Revolutionaries* (Washington, DC: Open Hand, 1985); Anne Romaine, "The Mississippi Freedom Democratic Party Through August, 1964" (MA thesis, University of Virginia, 1970).

18. Dittmer, *Local People*, 232.

19. Sinsheimer, "The Freedom Vote of 1963," 255.

20. Both Joyce Ladner and Robert Moses spoke at length about this view of Henry. Each rendered it as a variety of "pragmatism" wrought of his maturity and long service in leadership positions and his profound commitment to racial change. Joyce Ladner, interview with the author; Robert Moses, interview with the author.

21. Aaron Henry invitation letter, COFO Convention, March 15, 1964, B 2, F 2 (Amzie Moore Papers, SHSW).

22. *Baker v. Carr*, 369. U.S. 186 (1962).

23. "A Program for a Statewide Voter Registration Campaign in Mississippi," authored by Aaron Henry and Carsie Hall for COFO, ca. Spring 1964, Group 3, Box 270 (NAACP Papers, LOC).

24. Charles Bolton, *The Hardest Deal of All: The Battle Over School Integration in Mississippi, 1870–1980* (Jackson: University Press of Mississippi, 2005); Dittmer, *Local People*, 58–59; McMillen, *Dark Journey*, 72–108.

25. "Prospectus for the Mississippi Freedom Summer," ND, F 1, Freedom Information Service Papers (SHSW), 1–7.

26. Ibid.

27. Mississippi Legislation, January 15–April 14, 1964, Series VIII, Reel 20, Folder 129, SNCC Papers Microfilm, 1–2.

28. Ibid.

29. Ibid.

30. *Wall Street Journal*, May 25, 1964, 1.

31. McAdam, *Freedom Summer*, 67.

32. Henry, *Aaron Henry*, 164; Lemann, *The Promised Land*, 312.

33. Howard Ball, *Murder in Mississippi: United States v. Price and the Struggle for Civil Rights* (Lawrence: University of Kansas Press, 2004), 151–155; McAdam, *Freedom Summer*.

34. Henry, *Aaron Henry*, 168.

35. Ibid., 165.

36. Ball, *Murder in Mississippi*, 64; Lottie Joiner, "A Matter of Justice," *Crisis Magazine* (July–August 2004): 35–41; McAdam, *Freedom Summer*, 70.

37. Henry, *Aaron Henry*, 168.

38. Ball, *Murder in Mississippi*, 69–78; Dittmer, *Local People*, 250.

39. He estimates that around 3,000 students altogether participated in the summer projects. Volunteers were concentrated in areas where movement activity was greatest. Henry's influence led to a major contingent in his hometown, and his Delta region received 30 percent of the volunteers. McAdam, *Freedom Summer*, 4, 255–256.

40. "Two and Three Minute Voter Registration Speeches template," ca. Spring 1964, Box 8, F 9, 1963 (Amzie Moore Papers, SHSW). The experience of this work by volunteers is recounted in a number of excellent memoirs. Sally Belfrage, *Freedom Summer* (New York: Viking, 1965); Polly Greenberg, *The Devil Has Slippery Shoes: A Biased Biography of the Child Development Group of Mississippi* (London: Macmillan, 1969); Len Holt, *The Summer That Didn't End: The Story of the Mississippi Civil Rights Project of 1964* (New York: Da Capo Press, 1992); Silver, *Mississippi*; Elizabeth Sutherland, ed., *Letters from Mississippi* (New York: McGraw-Hill, 1965).

41. Carson, *In Struggle*, 117–118.

42. Success did not mean that the state authorities did not try to thwart these schools. Winson Hudson recounted how the Leake County sheriff swiftly barred their use of an abandoned school blacks had appropriated for use as a freedom school. Winson Hudson, *Mississippi Harmony: Memoirs of a Freedom Fighter* (New York: Palgrave Macmillan, 2002), 82; McAdam, *Freedom Summer*, 1988.

43. Joyce Ladner, interview with the author.

44. William Chafe, *Never Stop Running: Allard Lowenstein and the Struggle to Save American Liberalism* (New York: Basic Books, 1993), 180–182.

45. Dittmer, *Local People*, 229; Henry, *Aaron Henry*, 64–66.

46. Dittmer, *Local People*, 230–231.

47. McAdam, *Freedom Summer*, 255.

48. Ibid., 76.

49. His defiance started early. When he and Medgar Evers were elected to the SCLC board in 1957, the national office was clearly displeased and ordered paid NAACP employee Evers to withdraw. Henry not only did not withdraw, but he also flaunted his membership of both organizations. Hamlin, *Crossroads at Clarksdale*, 53; Williams, *Medgar Evers*, 34–136.

50. Gloster Current memorandum to Roy Wilkins, "NAACP Withdrawal from COFO," December 29, 1964 (NAACP Papers, LOC), 6.

51. Crosby, *A Little Taste of Freedom*, 85–86; Dittmer, *Local People*, 164–165; 274–276.

52. Henry, *Aaron Henry*, 162–172.

53. SNCC was interrogating a range of issues that exacerbated internal conflicts: internationalism, interracial cooperation, feminism, etc. Carson, *In Struggle*, 133–152.

54. Robert Moses and Charlie Cobb Jr., *Radical Equations: Math Literacy and Civil Rights* (Boston: Beacon Press, 2001), 80–81.

55. "Mississippi Summer Project: Running Summary of Incidents." Appendix A, Mississippi Freedom Democratic Party Papers, SNCC Papers, 1961–1972, Reel 69, F 492 (Freedom Information Service Papers, SHSW).

56. For example, Bob Moses credited Amzie Moore, whose activism went as far back as the RCNL, as his chief mentor in the Mississippi movement. Moses and Cobb Jr., *Radical Equations*, 38–42; Gilbert Mason, *Beaches, Blood, and Ballots: A Black Doctor's Civil Rights Struggle* (Jackson: University Press of Mississippi, 2000), 162–163. Moreover, women such as Fannie Lou Hamer and Unita Blackwell; Lee, *For Freedom's Sake*, 61–73; Morrison, *Black Political Mobilization*, 99–119.

57. Carson, *In Struggle*; Dittmer, *Local People*; August Meier and Elliott Rudwick, *CORE: A Study in the Civil Rights Movement, 1946–1968* (Urbana: University of Illinois Press, 1975).

58. McAdam, *Freedom Summer*; Payne, *I've Got the Light of Freedom*.

59. Forman, *The Making of Black Revolutionaries*; John Lewis, *Walking with the Wind: A Memoir of the Movement* (San Diego: Harcourt Brace and Company, 1998); Cleveland Sellers, *The River of No Return: The Autobiography of a Black Militant* (New York: Harcourt, Brace and World, 1973); Howard Zinn, *SNCC: The New Abolitionists* (New York: Beacon Press, 1964).

60. Lee, *For Freedom's Sake*; Morrison, *Black Political Mobilization*.

61. Albert Blaustein and Robert Zangrando, eds., *Civil Rights and the Black American: A Documentary History* (New York: Clarion, 1968), 525; Carson, *In Struggle*, 141–142; Hanes Walton Jr., "Protest Politics," in *Americans and Political Participation*, 103.

62. Dittmer, *Local People*, 273.

63. Henry, *Aaron Henry*, 167; Williams, *Medgar Evers*, 299–301.

64. Hine, *Black Victory*, 212–232; *Smith v. Allwright*, 321 U.S. 649 (1944); V. O. Key Jr., *Southern Politics* (New York: Knopf, 1949), 239–253.

65. Parker, *Black Votes Count*, 34–77.

66. Unita Blackwell's powerful story is recounted in Morrison, *Black Political Mobilization*; while Fannie Lou Hamer's is recounted in Lee, *For Freedom's Sake*, 23–42.

67. McLemore, "The Mississippi Freedom Democratic Party."

68. *New York Times*, July 22, 1964, 20; Henry, *Aaron Henry*, 174.

69. Henry Hampton and Steve Fayer, *Voices of Freedom: An Oral History of the Civil Rights Movement from the 1950s through the 1980s* (New York: Bantam, 1990), 179–204; Payne, *I've Got the Light of Freedom*, 425.

70. Dittmer, *Local People*, 121.

71. Dittmer, *Local People*, 29–30.

72. Minutes of COFO Meeting, December 15, 1963, Jackson, Mississippi, Box 1, F 4 (Jo Ann Robinson Papers, SHSW).

73. Hamlin, *Crossroads at Clarksdale*, 133; Moses and Cobb Jr., *Radical Equations*, 61–74; Robert Moses, interview with the author.

74. McLemore, "The Mississippi Freedom Democratic Party," 63–67.

75. Lee, *For Freedom's Sake*, 45–60 and 68–71.

76. McLemore, "The Mississippi Freedom Democratic Party," 66.

77. Lee, *For Freedom's Sake*, 71.

78. Murray Edelman, *The Symbolic Uses of Politics* (Urbana: University of Illinois Press, 1964), 1–21; Murray Edelman, *Politics as Symbolic Action: Mass Arousal and Quiescence* (Chicago: Markham, 1971), 116–154; Katherine Tate, *Black Faces in the Mirror: African Americans and Their Representatives in Congress* (Princeton, NJ: Princeton University Press, 2003), 96–110.

79. Lee, *For Freedom's Sake*, 70.

80. Henry, *Aaron Henry*, 168.

81. Hamlin, *Crossroads at Clarksdale*, 158.

82. Votes for Freedom Candidates in Official Elections, 1962–1966, Box 1, F 11, January 1967 (Freedom Information Service Papers, SHSW).

83. Challenge of Mississippi Freedom Democratic Party, ND, Folder 1 (Freedom Information Service Papers, SHSW), 1–3; Henry, *Aaron Henry*, 168.

84. Challenge of Mississippi Freedom Democratic Party, 13.

85. Ibid.

86. Ibid., 1.

87. Ibid.

88. Ibid.

89. Minutes of Temporary Executive Committee of MFDP, June 7, 1964, B 1, F 2 (James Houston Papers, SHSW), 1–2.

90. Challenge of Mississippi Freedom Democratic Party, 1.3.

91. Minutes of Temporary Executive Committee of MFDP, June 7, 1964 (James Houston Papers, SHSW); Memorandum, Jackson COFO Office, to Field Leaders, Field Staff and Volunteers re: "Freedom Registration," ND, Summer 1964, Box 4, F 14 (Freedom Information Service Papers, SHSW).

92. Henry, *Aaron Henry*, 104–110.

93. Dittmer, *Local People*, 154–156; 196–200.

94. Henry, *Aaron Henry*, 173; McLemore, "The Mississippi Freedom Democratic Party," 121.

95. Henry had already rejected an offer to be registered as a "third party" from the secretary. Henry, *Aaron Henry*, 173.

96. *New York Times*, July 24, 1964, 9; *New York Times*, August 13, 1964, 26.

97. Dittmer, *Local People*, 273.

98. Henry, *Aaron Henry*, 171–172.

99. Belfrage, *Freedom Summer*, 189.

100. Dittmer, *Local People*, 280.

101. Holt, "The Summer That Didn't End," *The Student Voice*, August 12, 1964, 1.

102. Indeed, the national office conspired with field secretary Charles Evers to lead an

alternative effort, wholly NAACP organized, to end run Henry. It failed. Dittmer, *Local People*, 275.

103. Dittmer, *Local People*, 283. Among whites in the group were three Tougaloo employees: President Daniel Beittel, and faculty members Lois Chaffey and Edwin King.

104. His access was such that he had been invited to the White House to provide his opinions on civil rights. This access began with both President Kennedy and his brother, the attorney general T. H. Baker. Aaron Henry, interview with Neil McMillen, 169, 175; Aaron Henry, September 12, 1970, Oral history interview conducted in Clarksdale, Mississippi, by T. H. Baker. *Congressional Record*, June 16, 1964, 13996.

105. Denton Watson, *Lion in the Lobby: Clarence Mitchell Jr.'s Struggle for the Passage of Civil Rights Laws* (New York: William Morrow & Company, 1990).

106. *New York Times*, July 16, 1961, 19. Henry, *Aaron Henry*.

107. Brief Submitted by the Mississippi Freedom Democratic Party, to the Credentials Committee, Democratic Party Convention, Atlantic City, August 1964, Box 32, F 371 (Lowenstein Papers, UNC-SHC), 21–35; Carson, *In Struggle*, 123.

108. Brief Submitted by the Mississippi Freedom Democratic Party, Appendix B, Aaron Henry letter to John Bailey, July 17, 1964, Brief Submitted by the Mississippi Freedom Democratic Party (Lowenstein Papers, UNC-SHC), 67.

109. Everett Carll Ladd Jr. with Charles Hadley, *Transformations of the American Party System*, 2nd ed. (New York: Norton, 1978).

110. "1952 Ruling Is Key to Delegate Fight," *New York Times*, July 9, 1964, 2b.

111. Ibid.

112. Henry, *Aaron Henry*, 177; Dittmer, *Local People*, 285–302; Payne, *I've Got the Light of Freedom*, 360.

113. Henry, *Aaron Henry*, 175.

114. Henry certainly was not naïve about the difficulty, nor was Bob Moses. Ibid., 177; Dittmer, *Local People*, 287.

115. Henry, *Aaron Henry*, 174–175.

116. James Forman ruefully noted how some of the "movement types" had doffed their uniforms of overalls to make appearances before the delegations. Dittmer, *Local People*, 285; Forman, *The Making of Black Revolutionaries*.

117. Dittmer, *Local People*, 290–291.

118. Dittmer, *Local People*, 292; Kenneth O'Reilly, *"Racial Matters": The FBI's Secret File on Black America, 1960–1972* (New York: Free Press, 1989), 261–292.

119. Carson, *In Struggle*, 125–128; Dittmer, *Local People*, 290; David Garrow, *Bearing the Cross: Martin Luther King, Jr., and the Southern Christian Leadership Conference* (New York: William Morrow and Co., 1986), 348; Henry, *Aaron Henry*, 180–192. Garrow shows how support fell away by the day as delegates assembled.

120. Garrow, *Bearing the Cross*, 347–350; Dittmer, *Local People*.

121. Rauh, a liberal lawyer with considerable government experience, headed the Washington, D.C., Democratic Party and had donated his services to the MFDP cause. Dittmer, *Local People*, 281; Henry, *Aaron Henry*, 166. At the beginning of an unexpected six-day process, Rauh made his official presentation of the case and was followed by Aaron Henry and Fannie Lou Hamer.

122. "Brief Submitted by the Mississippi Freedom Democratic Party" (Lowenstein Papers, UNC-SHC), 1.

123. Partial Proceedings of the Democratic National Convention, 1964, Credentials Committee, Atlantic City, New Jersey, August 22, 1964; F 10, FIS, UW, 21–32.

124. Ibid.

125. Abraham Chapman, ed., *Black Voices: An Anthology of African American Literature* (New York: New American Library, 1968), 436–437.

126. Partial Proceedings of the Democratic National Convention, 1964; Credentials Committee, Atlantic City, New Jersey, August 22, 1964; Box 4, F 9 (Freedom Information Service Papers, SHSW), 21–32.

127. Lee, *For Freedom's Sake*, 89.

128. Henry, *Aaron Henry*, 188.

129. Carson, *In Struggle*, 125.

130. McLemore, "The Mississippi Freedom Democratic Party," 148–149.

131. Dittmer, *Local People*, 289.

132. Henry doubted "that a majority of the convention really voted for the proposal" but that was how the chair called it. Henry, *Aaron Henry*, 194.

133. Dittmer, *Local People*, 297–301; Payne, *I've Got the Light of Freedom*; Holt, *The Summer That Didn't End*, 174–175.

134. Watters and Cleghorn, *Climbing Jacob's Ladder*, 291.

135. Henry, *Aaron Henry*, 180–198; Hamlin, *Crossroads at Clarksdale*, 146.

136. Carson, *In Struggle*, 125–129; Dittmer, *Local People*, 301–302.

137. Henry, *Aaron Henry*, 197.

138. Theodore White, *The Making of the President, 1964* (New York: Atheneum, 1965), 294.

Chapter Six: Henry the Public Entrepreneur and Network Tactician: Exploiting National Allies and Cultivating Local Interracial Partners

1. Henry, *Aaron Henry*, 100–101; Williams, *Medgar Evers*, 206–209.

2. Crosby, *A Little Taste of Freedom*, 86–90; Dittmer, *Local People*, 355–362.

3. Edwin King, interview with the author, January 30, 1998, Jackson, Mississippi.

4. Among these were Fannie Lou Hamer, who lamented his role in the withdrawal of the NAACP from COFO and his disconnect with the grassroots. Dittmer, *Local People*, 342; Lee, *For Freedom's Sake*, 114–116.

5. Edwin King, interview with the author.

6. Dittmer, *Local People*, 209; Carson, *In Struggle*, 134ff.

7. John Hope Franklin, *Reconstruction after the Civil War* (Chicago: University of Chicago Press, 1961); William Harris, *The Day of the Carpetbagger in Mississippi: Republican Reconstruction in Mississippi* (Baton Rouge: Louisiana State University Press, 1971).

8. Minion K. C. Morrison and Richard Middleton, "African Americans in Office," in *African Americans and Political Participation*, 244–248.

9. The body of civil rights law grew exponentially following the landmark Supreme Court decisions in the 1944 *Smith v. Allwright* and the 1954 *Brown v. Board of Education of Topeka, Kansas,* which rejected the white primary and school segregation respectively. After 1954 the justification for the separate but equal principle established in *Plessy v. Ferguson*, 163 U.S. 537 (1896) almost completely crumbled. In the process the court expanded general civil liberties, many of which were major sources of protection for civil rights activists.

For example, in *Mapp v. Ohio*, 367 U.S. 643 (1961) illegally obtained evidence during an arrest/interrogation was ruled inadmissible at trial. Two years later *Gideon v. Wainwright*, 372 U.S. 335 (1963) required equal access to an attorney by indigents; and in *Miranda v. Arizona*, 483 U.S. 436 (1966) required defendants to be informed of the right to counsel even before interrogation could take place.

10. *Baker v. Carr*, 369 U.S. 186 (1962). This was followed by two related cases that specifically directed reapportionment in congressional and state legislative districting: *Wesberry v. Sanders*, 376 U.S. 1 (1964); and *Reynolds v. Sims*, 377 U.S. 533 (1964). Also see Morrison and Middleton, "African Americans in Office," 269–271.

11. Gary Cox and Jonathan Katz, *Elbridge Gerry's Salamander: The Electoral Consequences of the Reapportionment Revolution* (New York: Cambridge University Press, 2002), 12–30.

12. Steven Lawson, *Black Ballots: Voting Rights in the South, 1944–1969* (New York: Columbia University Press, 1967), 322–328; Dittmer, *Local People*, 338–341. Henry, who had been a candidate in the original primary contest, later withdrew his name from the ongoing effort to unseat the Mississippi delegation.

13. *Clifton Whitley et al v. Paul B. Johnson*, 270 F. Supp. 630, 630–631 (1966). Indeed they had already challenged the state's continuing use of a poll tax for participation in local elections (the tax in federal law had already been barred), which in its implementation required a convoluted process for voting in national contests. The black candidates prevailed in *Victoria Gray et al. v. Paul B. Johnson*, 234 F. Supp. 743, 743–746, SD-Jackson Division (October 20, 1964).

14. Lawson, *Black Ballots*, 322–328; Dittmer, *Local People*, 338–341.

15. *Clifton Whitley et al. v. Paul B. Johnson*. Another lawsuit in the summer of 1964 also challenged a related matter about representation. The Mississippi legislature passed a law that revised how the state electors to the electoral college would cast the state's official ballots for president following the popular vote in the November 1964 election. The new law provided for these electors to be selected as both "pledged" and "unpledged," giving them maximum flexibility to cast their ballots without regard to the popular election or the nominees of the national parties. This was, of course, directed at Lyndon Johnson, the nominee of the reviled Democratic Party. Victoria Gray and the other candidates for the congressional seats filed a lawsuit to require these electors to cast a "loyal" vote in favor of the chosen party's candidate. *Victoria Gray et al. v. Paul B. Johnson*.

16. Hamlin, *Crossroads at Clarksdale*, 162.

17. "Voting Rights Act, 1965," http://www.ourdocuments.gov/doc.php?flash=true&doc=100 (accessed September 16, 2013); Morrison and Middleton, "African Americans in Office," 271–272.

18. *Peggy Connor v. Paul B. Johnson*, 256 F. Supp. 962 (1966), 962–977.

19. "From 1882 to 1966 the Mississippi Legislature enacted eight major realignments of the state's congressional districts. Although the state lost congressional seats in 1932, 1952, and 1962, each new redistricting plan kept the Delta district intact. Consequently, as late as 1956 this Delta district's Black population was over 65%." Parker, *Black Votes Count*, 85–117; Frank Parker, "The Mississippi Congressional Redistricting Case: A Case Study in Minority Vote Dilution," *Howard Law Journal* 28, no. 2 (1985): 398.

20. Parker, "The Mississippi Congressional Redistricting Case," 399.

21. *Connor v. Finch*, 431 U.S. 407 (1977).

22. Parker, *Black Votes Count*, 138.

23. Henry, *Aaron Henry*, 87; Parker, *Black Votes Count*, 23.

24. *U.S. v. Biloxi* (1963).

25. Parker, *Black Votes Count*, 23.

26. Gilbert Mason, *Beaches, Blood, and Ballots: A Black Doctor's Civil Rights Struggle* (Jackson: University Press of Mississippi, 2000), 152· See also *U.S. v. Biloxi* (1963).

27. Winson Hudson, *Mississippi Harmony: Memoirs of a Freedom Fighter* (New York: Palgrave Macmillan, 2002).

28. Mason, *Beaches, Blood, and Ballots*, 152.

29. Ibid., 157.

30. Henry, *Aaron Henry*, 87.

31. *Clarksdale Press Register*, September 17, 1963, 1.

32. *Rebecca E. Henry et al. v. The Clarksdale Municipal Separate School District et al.*, 409 F. 2d 682, U.S. App. (1969). This case was consolidated twice: First in *U.S. v. Biloxi* (1963), 691–697; and further elaborated in *United States v. Jefferson County Board of Education, et al.*, 5 372 F. 2d 836 (1966).

33. *Clarksdale Press Register*, September 17, 1963, 1. Prior to the June 1963 assassination of Medgar Evers, the two had already begun to circulate petitions in a number of other school districts and legal assaults were widespread: e.g., *Evers v. Jackson Municipal Separate School District*, 328 F. 2d 408 (1964).

34. *Rebecca E. Henry et al. v. The Clarksdale Municipal Separate School District et al.*

35. "Legal Position Paper," signed by Aaron Henry and Melvyn Leventhal, Counsel for the NAACP, October 29, 1969, Box 131, F 2299 (Aaron Henry Papers, TC).

36. *Clarksdale Press Register*, June 25, 1963, 1.

37. Henry, *Aaron Henry*, 104, 122, 148, 169.

38. Lawson, *Black Ballots*, 288–289.

39. Carson, *In Struggle*, 83–87; Lawson, *Black Ballots*, 296–298.

40. Carson, *In Struggle*, 38–39; Dittmer, *Local People*, 119–120, 197–198.

41. Robert Dallek, *An Unfinished Life: John Kennedy, 1917–1963* (Boston: Little, Brown and Company), 518.

42. Henry, *Aaron Henry*, 104–105.

43. Henry, *Aaron Henry*, 105.

44. *United States v. Cox*, Civil no. D-C–53–61, N.D. Miss. (1964), 46.

45. Albert Blaustein and Robert Zangrando, eds., *Civil Rights and the Black American: A Documentary History* (New York: Clarion Press, 1968), 472–483.

46. Dittmer, *Local People*, 195–197.

47. *Clarksdale Press Register*, May 16, 1962, 14.

48. Ibid. Also see "Report: Administration of Justice in Mississippi," issued by the Mississippi Advisory Committee to the United States Commission on Civil Rights, January 1963, Jane Schutt Papers, Box 1, F 22, Tougaloo College Civil Rights Collection at Mississippi Department of Archives and History (hereafter Schutt Papers, TC).

49. Dittmer, *Local People*, 194–198.

50. U.S. Commission on Civil Rights, *Hearings Before the United States Commission on Civil Rights*, vol. 2 (Washington, DC: Government Printing Office, 1965), 155ff.

51. Ibid., 155. In fact, Kennedy had appointed Cox to the bench, at the urging of Mississippi senator James Eastland. Dittmer, *Local People*, 180.

52. U.S. Commission on Civil Rights, *Hearings Before the United States Commission on Civil Rights*, 159.

53. Harold Stanley and Richard Niemi, *Vital Statistics on American Politics, 1999–2000* (Washington, DC: CQ Press, 2000), 28.

54. Orey and Vance, "Participation in Electoral Politics," 189.

55. Stanley and Niemi, *Vital Statistics on American Politics*, 37.

56. Lawson, *Black Ballots*, 305.

57. Henry, *Aaron Henry*, 180. Lawson, *Black Ballots*, 306.

58. Aaron Henry, Letter to President-elect Richard Nixon, ND, Box 59, F 1032 (Aaron Henry Papers, TC). See also Yasuhiro Katagiri, *The Mississippi State Sovereignty Commission: Civil Rights and States' Rights* (Jackson: University Press of Mississippi, 2001).

59. Lawson, *Black Ballots*, 299–300.

60. *Heart of Atlanta Motel Inc. v. United States*, 379 U.S. 241 (1964).

61. *Katzenbach v. McClung*, 379 U.S. 294 (1964).

62. Lawson, *Black Ballots*, 318–322.

63. U.S. Commission on Civil Rights, *Political Participation* (Washington, DC: Government Printing Office, 1968), 223.

64. Ibid.

65. Ibid.; Lawson, *Black Ballots*, 329–330.

66. Lawson, *Black Ballots*, 329.

67. Public Papers of U.S. Presidents, Lyndon B. Johnson: 1963–1964, V I. 375–380, http://www.fordham.edu/halsall/mod/1964johnson-warpoverty.html (accessed September 20, 2013).

68. U.S. Department of Labor, Manpower Administration. *Leaving the Future Open— Job Corps, the First Decade* (Washington, DC: Government Printing Office, 1975), 1–12.

69. Joseph Califano Jr., October 1999, "What Was Really Great about the Great Society: The Truth Behind the Conservative Myths," *Washington Monthly*, http://www.washingtonmonthly.com/features/1999/9910.califano.html #byline (accessed September 20, 2013); Also see Jonathan Oberlander, *The Politics of Medicare* (University of Chicago Press, 2003), 29–35; Hugh Davis Graham, *The Uncertain Triumph: Federal Education Policy in the Kennedy and Johnson Years* (Chapel Hill: University of North Carolina Press, 1984).

70. Letter from Andy Carr to Semmes Luckett, September 30, 1965, Box 85, VI: A:1414 (Aaron Henry Papers, TC).

71. Ibid.

72. Ibid.

73. Wilkie also suggests that Henry was worried about Epps's shadowy past. However, it is doubtful that this detracted from his intent of getting a share of the Great Society to further his lofty goal of equality. Curtis Wilkie, *Dixie: A Personal Odyssey through Events That Shaped the Modern South* (New York: Scribner, 2001), 167.

74. Gillette, *Launching the War on Poverty*, 189. See also Wilkie, *Dixie*, 167.

75. *Clarksdale Press Register*, July 8, 1965, 1.

76. "Minutes of Community Action Committee," Coahoma Opportunities, Inc., September 10, 1965, Box 85, V1: A: 1410 (Aaron Henry Papers, TC).

77. *Clarksdale Press Register*, May 8, 1965. Additional discussion of the role of this segregationist can be found in Wilkie, *Dixie*, 132–153.

78. Wilkie, *Dixie*, 166–167.

79. Salter Jr., *Jackson, Mississippi*, 78–79.

80. Letter from Marion Reed, Secretary, Coahoma Opportunities, Inc. to Board, September 15, 1965, Box 90, 25–85 (Aaron Henry Papers, TC).

81. Henry, *Aaron Henry*, 73.

82. Gillette, *Launching the War on Poverty*, 287.

83. Ibid., 17.

84. "Community Centers for the South," Proposal for Citizens Crusade Against Poverty (CCAP), ND, Box 85, V1: A: 1410 (Aaron Henry Papers, TC).

85. Citizens Crusade Against Poverty, Statement of Policy and Program, October 13, 1964, F 3, B 4 (Amzie Moore Papers, SHSW).

86. "Community Centers for the South," Box 85, F 1410 (Aaron Henry Papers, TC); Gillette, *Launching the War on Poverty*, 279–281; Polly Greenberg, *The Devil Has Slippery Shoes: A Biased Biography of the Child Development Group of Mississippi* (London: Macmillan Company, 1969), 34.

87. Application of Coahoma Opportunities Inc. for Community Action Program for Seasonal Farm Workers, ND, Box 85, F 1410 (Aaron Henry Papers, TC).

88. Letter from Aaron Henry to Senator John Stennis, August 12, 1965, Box 85, F 1410 (Aaron Henry Papers, TC).

89. Ibid.

90. Dittmer, *Local People*, 378.

91. Gillette, *Launching the War on Poverty*, 279–281.

92. Greenberg, *The Devil Has Slippery Shoes*, 34.

93. Gillette, *Launching the War on Poverty*, 234. President Johnson had associated the idea with what he had accomplished as a young teacher of American children in his early career.

94. Greenberg, *The Devil Has Slippery Shoes*, 28.

95. Dittmer, *Local People*, 370.

96. Gillette, *Launching the War on Poverty*, 279.

97. Greenberg, *The Devil Has Slippery Shoes*, 3–5.

98. Dittmer, *Local People*, 369–370.

99. Ibid., 370–371.

100. Mount Beulah, in the small town of Edwards, was the site of the former Southern Christian Institute (SCI), a private Disciples of Christ junior college, the denomination with which Tougaloo College was affiliated. Indeed, after closing, a formal merger took place and Tougaloo became Tougaloo Southern Christian College. The SCI was a plot of 1,200 acres, and the generally well-maintained buildings were more than sufficient to provide residential facilities to accommodate the CDGM staff and to board teacher trainees and other organized groups. Clarice Campbell and Oscar Rogers Jr., *Mississippi: The View from Tougaloo* (Jackson: University Press of Mississippi, 1979), 181–182.

101. Memorandum from Paul Cotter to Senators Hayden, Stennis, and Pastore, August 5, 1966, Box 1, Hodding Carter Papers, Special Collections Department, Mitchell Memorial Library, Mississippi State University (hereafter Hodding Carter Papers, MSUSC).

102. Dittmer, *Local People*, 371.

103. Ibid.

104. Greenberg, *The Devil Has Slippery*, 224.

105. Letter from Aaron Henry to Oscar Berry, OEO, August 27, 1966, Box 1, F 2, Aaron Henry Papers, Walter Reuther Library, Wayne State University (hereafter Aaron Henry Papers, WRL).

106. Letter from Gloster Current to Mississippi NAACP Branch Presidents, October 14, 1966, Box 1, F 2 (Aaron Henry Papers, WRL).

107. Lemann, *The Promised Land*, 325.

108. Dittmer, *Local People*, 374; Lemann, *The Promised Land*, 327.

109. Dittmer, *Local People*, 377–381.

110. Letter from Gloster Current to Mississippi NAACP Branch Presidents, October 14, 1966, Correspondence B, Box 1, F 2 (Aaron Henry Papers, WRL).

111. Later from Aaron Henry to Ted Berry, OEO (Aaron Henry Papers, WRL).

112. Lemann, *The Promised Land*, 326.

113. Dittmer, *Local People*, 376.

114. Gillette, *Launching the War on Poverty*, 287–288.

115. Letter from Jule Sugarman, Associate Director Program Head Start to Owen Cooper, Chair of MAP, November 5, 1996, Box 92, F 1489 (Aaron Henry Papers, TC).

116. Greenberg, *The Devil Has Slippery Shoes*, 640.

117. Dittmer, *Local People*, 377; Henry, *Aaron Henry*, 237; Owen Cooper, 1972, Oral history interview conducted in Yazoo City, Mississippi, by Graham Lee Hales Jr. (MSOHA), 1–47.

118. The CDGM did not go quietly. The forces it mobilized were successful in getting partial restoration of its funding until its final dissolution in 1967. It helped that the CDGM dispatched two busloads of children and teachers to Capitol Hill, according to Dittmer, "turning the House Education and Labor committee into a kindergarten." Dittmer, *Local People*, 374–375.

119. Correspondence between Leslie Dunbar of the Field Foundation and Helen Bass Williams, Executive Director of MAP, July 26, 1967, and July 31, 1967, Box 92, F 1491 (Aaron Henry Papers, TC).

120. Lemann, *The Promised Land*, 325. Dittmer, *Local People*, 377; Jo G. Prichard III, *Making Things Grow: The Story of Mississippi Chemical Corporation* (Jackson: University Press of Mississippi, 1998); Lemann, *The Promised Land*, 325.

121. Lemann, *The Promised Land*, 326.

122. Gillette, *Launching the War on Poverty*, 277–288.

123. MAP Grant Approval, ND, Box 92, F 1489; Auditor's Report, Roy Wigfield of Ernst & Ernst, August 25, 1967, Box 92, F 1491 (Aaron Henry Papers, TC); Letter from Owen Cooper to MAP Board, October 14, 1966, Correspondence B, Box 1, F 2 (Aaron Henry Papers, WRL).

124. Dittmer, *Local People*, 378.

125. "This Week in Mississippi," July 25, 1965, Box 1, F 7 (Freedom Information Service Papers, SHSW).

126. *Clarksdale Press Register*, July 19, 1965, 1.

Chapter Seven: Private and Public Entrepreneurship for Redistributive Justice: Addressing African American Socioeconomic Disparities

1. Henry, *Aaron Henry*, 167–168.

2. Appellant Brief in the U.S. Court of Appeals, District of Columbia Circuit, #19,409, ND, Box 122, F 2079 (Aaron Henry Papers, TC), 4.

3. Ibid.

4. Steven Classen, *Watching Jim Crow: The Struggles over Mississippi TV, 1955–1969* (Durham, NC: Duke University Press, 2004), 36.

5. I bid., 50.

6. Ibid., 61.

7. Ibid., 130.

8. Dittmer, *Local People*, 65.

9. Classen, *Watching Jim Crow*, 114.

10. Brief for Appellants, in U.S. Court of Appeals, District of Columbia Circuit, August 24, 1965, Box 122, F 2079 (Aaron Henry Papers, TC), 7–9.

11. Classen, *Watching Jim Crow*, 126.

12. Brief for Appellants, in U.S. Court of Appeals, District of Columbia Circuit, August 24, 1965, Box 122, F 2079 (Aaron Henry Papers, TC), 7–9.

13. *Office of Communication of the United Church of Christ, et al. v. Federal Communications Commission*, 359 F. 2d. 994 (1966). The presiding judge at the time was Warren Burger, who later became chief justice of the Supreme Court.

14. Ibid., 1007–1008.

15. Application for Renewal of License of Lamar Broadcasting Company, before the FCC, May 26, 1966, Box 119, F 2004, FCC Docket # 16663, File # BRCT–326 (Aaron Henry Papers, TC), 4.

16. Memo from Everett Parker (Office of Communication, United Church of Christ-UCC) to Aaron Henry et al., June 21, 1966, Box 119, F 2004 (Aaron Henry Papers, TC), 1.

17. Classen, *Watching Jim Crow*, 129.

18. Press Release from Office of Communication, UCC, ND, Box 120, F 2040 (Aaron Henry Papers, TC).

19. Press Release from Office of Communication, UCC, ND, Box 120, F 2040 (Aaron Henry Papers, TC).

20. Charles Evers, 1973, interview conducted by Dr. Robert Smith (MSOHA), vol. 7, 9–20.

21. Charles Young, interview with the author, January 21, 1996, Jackson, Mississippi.

22. Memo from Weyman Walker to CCI stockholders, April 7, 1969, Box 119, F 2007 (Aaron Henry Papers, TC), 1.

23. Ibid., 4.

24. McMillen, *The Citizen's Council*, 260; Silver, *Mississippi: The Closed*, 358.

25. Letter from Earle Moore and Communications Improvement, Inc. (CII) Application for Interim Operation of WLBT, April 25, 1970, Box 119 F 2040 (Aaron Henry Papers, TC); Lew Powell and Edwin E. Meek, "Mississippi's WLBT: After the License Challenge," *Columbia Journalism Review* (May–June 1973): 51.

26. Press Release from Office of Communication, UCC, ND, Benbow, Box 120, F 2040 (Aaron Henry Papers, TC).

27. William Greider, "TV Reform Slowing," *Washington Post*, July 17, 1973, 1.

28. Ibid.

29. Letter from Counsel for Dixie National Broadcasting, Channel 3, and Jackson Television, to Counsel Martin Firestone for Civic Communication, May 17, 1978, Box 119, F 2016 (Aaron Henry Papers, TC).

30. Letter from Aaron Henry to Walter Hall, July 22, 1977, Box 119, F 2016 (Aaron Henry Papers, TC).

31. Settlement Agreement to Administrative Law Judge of FCC Leonore Ehrig, October 25, 1978, Box 119, F 2016 (Aaron Henry Papers, TC), 1–16.

32. "Black Group Awarded a License for a Television Station in Mississippi," *New York Times*, December 7, 1979, Box 122, F 2090 (Aaron Henry Papers, TC).

33. Aaron Henry to "Fellow Employees of WLBT," January 30, 1980. 90.24.119. X. A. 2019 (Aaron Henry Papers, TC).

34. Classen, *Watching Jim Crow*, 165–168.

35. Memo from Frank Stimley, to Aaron Henry, Charles Young, and Frank Melton, February 15, 1984, Box 120, F 2033 (Aaron Henry Papers, TC), 1–4.

36. "WLBT Buyout Ends 22 year Siege," *Clarion-Ledger/Jackson Daily News*, October 5, 1986, Section G1.

37. *New York Times*, May 29, 1984, newspaper clipping, Box 123, F 2101 (Aaron Henry Papers, TC).

38. "Dilday named manager of Jackson's WJTV," *Clarion Ledger*, May 7, 1985, Box 123, F 2103 (Aaron Henry Papers, TC).

39. "Henry's Loss Partly Due to Channel 3 Controversy," *Jackson Daily News*, May 7, 1984, Box 123, F 2101 (Aaron Henry Papers, TC), 6c.

40. Henry memo to "Friends of WLBT," March 26, 1984, Box 120, F 2033 (Aaron Henry Papers, TC).

41. Hamlin, *Crossroads at Clarksdale*, 224.

42. Aaron Henry letter to Roy Wilkins, February 9, 1966, #5133, Group 4, B 7 (NAACP Papers, LOC). Another cause for the exchange with Wilkins was to allay fears that the state NAACP was involved in a worker takeover of a former military base outside Greenville. Henry assured him that the NAACP was not behind the affair though its cause was surely justifiable.

43. NAACP Proposes Aid Program for Displaced Negro Farmers, Press Release, February 26, 1966, Group 4, A 38 (NAACP Papers, LOC).

44. Hamlin, *Crossroads at Clarksdale*, 227.

45. Minutes of Regular COI meeting, December 15, 1969, Box 5, Coahoma Opportunities Industrialization, Inc. Folder (Aaron Henry Papers, WRL). Hamlin has described some of the various federally funded COI programs. She shows that not all of the programs fulfilled their intended purposes, especially the legal services assistance; large sums went to local white lawyers unsympathetic to Henry's vision. Hamlin, *Crossroads at Clarksdale*, 224–230.

46. Michael Namorato, *The Catholic Church in Mississippi, 1911–1984: A History* (Westport, CT: Greenwood Press, 1998), 131–146.

47. STAR Hearing Transcript, December 7, 1970, Box 8, F 165, Patricia Derian Papers, Special Collections Department Mitchell Memorial Library, Mississippi State University (hereafter Patricia Derian Papers, MSUSC); Memo from Aaron Henry to Gerald Davis, February 17, 1971; News Release from STAR challenging Henry's letter, February 19, 1971, Box 13, NF, Wilson Minor Papers, MSUSC.

48. Hamlin, *Crossroads at Clarksdale*, 229.

49. Jaynes and Williams Jr., *A Common Destiny*, 271–324.

50. Fragment of Comprehensive Employment and Training Act of 1973 (CETA), Description of Job Corps, ND, Box 95, F 1556 (Aaron Henry Papers, TC).

51. Letter from Booker T. Jones, MINACT President, to Charles Creel, Small Business Administration (SBA), Birmingham, Alabama, August 4, 1978, Box 95, F 1557 (Aaron Henry Papers, TC).

52. Dittmer, *The Good Doctors*, 23–25.

53. Application for SBA, 8(a) status, August 4, 1978, Box 95, F 1557 (Aaron Henry Papers, TC).

54. MINACT, "Articles of Incorporation," February 22, 1978, Box 95, F 1556 (Aaron Henry Papers, TC).

55. MINACT Minutes, December 29, 1978, Box 95, F 1557 (Aaron Henry Papers, TC).

56. Letter from MINACT President Booker T. Jones to Charles Creel, SBA, August 4, 1978, Box 95, F 1557 (Aaron Henry Papers, TC).

57. MINACT Minutes, March 24, 1978, Box 95, F 1556 (Aaron Henry Papers, TC).

58. MINACT Minutes, December 29, 1978, Ibid.

59. Henry letter to Wiley Messick, SBA, Atlanta, Georgia, June 15, 1978; MINACT Minutes, May 27; Letter from Booker T. Jones to Charles Creel, Business Development Specialist, SBA, August 4, 1978, Box 95, F 1557 (Aaron Henry Papers, TC).

60. Letter from Aaron Henry, to William Clement, June 25, 1979, Box 95, F 1557 (Aaron Henry Papers, TC).

61. Variously between October–November 1979, Box 96, F 1560 (Aaron Henry Papers, TC).

62. Letters from Louis Martin to Aaron Henry, January 31, 1980; and Stuart Eisenstadt, Assistant to the President for Domestic Affairs, February 8, 1980, Box 96, F 1561 (Aaron Henry Papers, TC).

63. Audit Report, Kolheim, Rogers and Taylor, CPAs, December 11, 1978, Box 95, F 1557 (Aaron Henry Papers, TC).

64. Financial Statements, Benbow, April 25, 1981, Box 95, F 1545; and December 31, 1981, Box 96, F 1562 (Aaron Henry Papers, TC).

65. Architectural drawings for Baltimore housing development, November 13, 1980, Box 95, F 1555 (Aaron Henry Papers, TC).

66. Minutes, June 23, 1979, December 14, 1979; April 18, 1980; November 17, 1981, Box 96, F 1558; and November 17, 1981, Box 96, F 1562 (Aaron Henry Papers, TC).

67. "MINACT Incorporated website—Welcome," http://www.minact.com (accessed October 30, 2009).

68. Ibid.

69. "MINACT Incorporated website—"Welcome," http://www.minact.com/people.htm (accessed October 30, 2009).

70. Letter from Bennie Gooden to Samuel Jackson, Assistant Secretary, of Department of Housing and Urban Development, February 19, 1970, Box 106, F 1756 (Aaron Henry Papers, TC).

71. Letter from Aaron Henry announcing Agricultural Committee appointment by Secretary Freeman, June 1, 1965, Correspondence B, F 2 (Aaron Henry Papers, WRL). HUD was established by President Johnson in 1966 and named Robert Weaver secretary, the first black to hold a cabinet level appointment. http://portal.hud.gov/hudportal/HUD?src=/about/hud_history (accessed September 20, 2013).

72. Hamlin, *Crossroads at Clarksdale*, 230.

73. Memo from C. L. Stahler to the President of the Board of STAR, January 31, 1969, Box 9, File Star Inc. (Aaron Henry Papers, WRL).

74. Aaron Henry Testimony at Hearings before the Subcommittee on Housing and Consumer Interests of the Select Committee on Aging, House of Representatives, Washington, D.C., 94th Congress, 2nd Session, May 14, 1976 (Washington, DC: Government Printing Office, 1979), 12–16.

75. The purpose of the Alliance was to seek "meaningful answers to housing needs of low income families everywhere, particularly in rural America." January 29, 1970, Box 9, File Rural Housing Alliance (Aaron Henry Papers, WRL).

76. www.ncba-aged.org/about/history (accessed April 27, 2007).

77. Report of White House Conference on Aging, December 2, 1971, Box 108, F 1802 (Aaron Henry Papers, TC), 1.

78. Ibid., 1–2.

79. The Mississippi part of this movement was something to which Aaron Henry had been privy insofar as the medical committee organized a major project in Mound Bayou, the nearby Delta town where Henry had been professionally engaged in medical affairs since the 1950s. Dittmer, *The Good Doctors*, 81–83, 229–230.

80. Ibid.

81. Report of Committee on Health of the National Caucus on the Black Aged, December 2, 1971, No venue given, Box 108, F 1802 (Aaron Henry Papers, TC).

82. Hearings before the Subcommittee on Housing Consumer and Consumer Interests, House Select Committee on Aging, 94th Congress, 2nd Session, May 14, 1976, Box 108, F 1811 (Aaron Henry Papers, TC).

83. Dr. Flemming was well known in Republican politics. He served as secretary of Health, Education and Welfare under President Eisenhower, and later became Nixon Commissioner on aging, http://en.wikipedia.org/wiki/Arthur-Sherwood-Flemming (accessed June 26, 2013).

84. Richard Nixon, "Remarks to the White House Conference on Aging," December 2, 1971, www.presidency.ucsb.edu/ws/index.php?pid=3242 (accessed June 26, 2013).

85. President Richard Nixon inaugurated this program in October 1972. See his "Statement About The General Revenue-Sharing Bill," http://www.presidency.ucsb.edu/WMS/? PID = 636 (accessed June 26, 2013).

86. "Testimony to the Presidential Forum on Domestic Policy," Washington, D.C., October 29, 1975, Box 108, F 1803 (Aaron Henry Papers, TC), 1–9.

87. Box 79, F 1343, "Comments by Dr. Aaron Henry," Chairman, The National Black Caucus on the Aged, White House Meeting of the Ad Hoc Leadership Council of Aging Organizations with the President, October 10, 1979, Washington, D.C. (Aaron Henry Papers, TC).

88. "Statement of Aaron Henry," Hearing before the Subcommittee on Housing and Consumer Interests of the Select Committee on Aging, House of Representatives, 94th Congress, 2nd Session, May 14, 1976, Box 108, F 1811 (Aaron Henry Papers, TC), 12–16.

89. Hearings before the Subcommittee on Aging of the Committee on Human Resources, U.S. Senate, 95th Congress, 2nd Session on S. 2850 (Older Americans Act of 1978), New Orleans, Louisiana, February 1–8, and April 21, 1978 (Washington, DC: Government Printing Office, 1979), 420–444.

90. In his advocacy for the aged, Henry appeared before multiple committees—among them, the House Select Committees on Aging multiple times, the House Committee on the Budget, and the Congressional Black Caucus. Similarly, in the Senate he appeared before multiple committees, including Education, Labor, Agriculture, Forestry, and Human Resources. In all of these he brought the same passion to the subject of the elderly, presented strong critiques of public policy, and offered the widest range of recommendations for programs and policy changes. See Box 108, F 1795 (Aaron Henry Papers, TC).

91. Ibid.

92. Letter from Aaron Henry to James Boland, Area Director USDA, Jackson, Mississippi, July 18, 1975, Box 106, F 1761 (Aaron Henry Papers, TC).

93. "Statement of Aaron Henry," Hearing before the Subcommittee on Housing and Consumer Interests of the Select Committee on Aging, House of Representatives, 94th Congress, 2nd Session, May 14, 1976, Box 108, F 1811 (Aaron Henry Papers, TC), 12–16.

94. Ibid.

95. Delta Opportunities Corporation sought to build houses for farm laborers across the Delta (1969). See Executive Committee Meeting, September 24, 1969, Box 5, File Coahoma Opportunities Industrialization. (Aaron Henry Papers, WRL); and "Charter of Incorporation of Delta Opportunity Corporation," ND, Box 4, F 7 (Amzie Moore Papers, SHSW).

96. Minutes of meeting of Progressive Association for Economic Development and Community Improvement, February 24, 1970, Box 85, F 1409 (Aaron Henry Papers, TC).

97. Ibid.; Hamlin, *Crossroads at Clarksdale*, 230.

98. Letter from Thomas Karter to Aaron Henry and Representative Robert Clark re. Multi-Racial Corporation, December 19, 1969, Box 2, File Correspondence K (Aaron Henry Papers, WRL).

99. Aaron Henry handwritten speech to Rural Housing Conference, December 4–7, 1977, Box 77, F 1322 (Aaron Henry Papers, TC), 1–8.

100. Beito and Beito, *Black Maverick*, 43–63.

101. Hamlin, *Crossroads at Clarksdale*, 218.

102. Nelson Lichtenstein, *The Most Dangerous Man in Detroit: Walter Reuther and the Fate of American Labor* (New York: Basic Books, 1995), 370–395; Walter Reuther, "Address Before the Annual Convention of the National Association for the Advancement of Colored People," in *Walter Reuther: Selected Papers*, ed. Harry Christman (New York: Macmillan Company, 1961), 195–208; Walter Reuther, "Medical Care for the Aged," Statement to the House Committee on Ways and Means, Ibid., 283–298; Dittmer, *The Good Doctors*, 239.

103. Dittmer, *The Good Doctors*, 61.

104. Ibid., 31.

105. Ibid., 156, 229.

106. The National Pharmaceutical Association was founded 1947 to meet the professional needs of black pharmacists who were not welcome in the American Pharmaceutical Association (1852). http://nationalpharmaceuticalassociation .org/about/, (accessed June 27, 2013).

107. Minutes of Statewide Health Coordinating Council, July 31, 1970, Box 90, F 1466 (Aaron Henry Papers, TC).

108. Dittmer, *The Good Doctors*, 229–236, 280–281.

109. GHS merely reflected the first letter of the surname of each partner in alphabetical order. The board included Lucy Boyd, Joe E. Jackson, Carl Pitts, Lucille Powell, Ezra Towner, Ben E. Jones, Ethel Jones, Sylvester Reed, and Bennie Gooden (who subsequently resigned). Letter from Addie Peterson, MPH, Executive Director, Aaron Henry Community Health Services Center, Inc., January 13, 1981, Box 90, F 1468 (Aaron Henry Papers, TC).

110. Grant application: Title 3, Section 330: Public Health Service Act, Rural Health Initiative Program, April 13, 1979, Benbow, Box 88, F 1448 (Aaron Henry Papers, TC).

111. Transmittal letter for health center grant from Lawrence Peaco, Consultant, Medicus Systems, Washington, D.C., March 24, 1980, Box 89, F 1461 (Aaron Henry Papers, TC).

112. Letter from G. A. Reich, Regional Health Administrator, HEW, Atlanta, Georgia, to Interim Director M. C. Martin, July 14, 1980, Box 90, F 1464 (Aaron Henry Papers, TC).

113. Minutes of Board of Directors, Aaron Henry Community Health Center, November 18, 1980, Box 94, File 1464 (Aaron Henry Papers, TC).

114. Ibid.

115. Aurelia Jones-Taylor, interview with the author, March 12, 1998, Clarksdale, Mississippi.

116. U.S. Department of Transportation, "Building Livable Communities Through Transportation" (Washington, DC: Government Printing Office, 1996), 8–11.

117. Sharon Wright Austin, *Transformation of Plantation Politics: Black Politics, Concentrated Poverty, and Social Capital in the Mississippi Delta* (New York: SUNY Press, 2006), 61–139.

118. Aurelia Jones-Taylor, interview with the author.

119. Louise Bradford, interview with the author.

Chapter Eight: Taking the Reins of the State Democratic Party: Henry Wrests Power from the Segregationists

1. Key Jr., *Southern Politics*, 239–253.

2. McLemore, "The Mississippi Freedom Democratic Party."; Hanes Walton Jr., *Black Political Parties: An Historical and Political Analysis* (New York: Free Press, 1972).

3. Dittmer, *Local People*, 293–302; Carson, *In Struggle*, 123–129; Lee, *For Freedom's Sake*; Robert Moses, interview with the author.

4. Henry, *Aaron Henry*, 197–198.

5. Ibid.

6. Dittmer, *Local People*, 296.

7. *New York Times*, March 24, 1965, 34.

8. Dittmer, *Local People*, 320.

9. Clay County Civil Rights Material, "Clay County" Folder (MSUSC).

10. Walton, *Black Political Parties*, 103.

11. *New York Times*, November 1, 1964, 52.

12. "Dave Leip's Atlas of U.S. Presidential Elections," http://uselectionatlas.org/ (accessed September 20, 2013).

13. Dittmer, *Local People*, 323.

14. "Resolution Rejecting Platform of National Party in 1964," September 9, 1964, Box 4. Election–1960-President-Democrats Folder; and Election–1963-Governor Folder, Wilson F. Minor Papers (MSUSC).

15. *New York Times*, Aug 26, 1964, 1.

16. Robert Moses, interview with the author.

17. Claude Ramsay, April 28, 1961, Oral history interview conducted in Jackson, Mississippi, by Orley Caudill (MSOHA) 50ff.

18. McLemore, "The Mississippi Freedom Democratic Party," 410–411.

19. Dittmer, *Local People*, 299, 346–347.

20. *Clarksdale Press Register*, July 19, 1965, 1; Charles Young, interview with the author.

21. McLemore, "The Mississippi Freedom Democratic Party," 410–411.

22. Freedom Information Service, F 7, UW, July 25, 1965; Dittmer, *Local People*, 346.

23. McLemore, "The Mississippi Freedom Democratic Party," 409.

24. Morrison and Richard Middleton, "African Americans in Office," 272.

25. Dittmer, *Local People*, 398; Crosby, *A Little Taste of Freedom*, 176.

26. Crosby, *A Little Taste of Freedom*, 188–206.

27. McLemore, "The Mississippi Freedom Democratic Party," 368–377.

28. Charles Evers and Andrew Szanton, *Have No Fear: The Charles Evers Story* (New York: John Wiley and Sons, 1997); Grace Halsell, *Evers* (New York: World Publishing Company, 1971); Dittmer, *Local People*, 410.

29. McLemore, "The Mississippi Freedom Democratic Party," 339–391; Dittmer, *Local People*, 415–416.

30. K. C. Morrison and Joe C. Huang, "The Transfer of Political Power in a Bi-racial Mississippi Town," *Growth and Change* 4, no. 2 (1972): 25–29; McLemore, "The Mississippi Freedom Democratic Party," 339–391.

31. Wilson Minor, "Eyes on Mississippi," *Times-Picayune*, May 19, 1967. See also "Eyes on Mississippi," *Times-Picayune*, May 21, 1967.

32. Wilson Minor, *Times Picayune*, April 17, 1968; and, July 3 1968. See also Minor, "Eyes on Mississippi," *Times-Picayune*, January 28, 1968.

33. James Bonney, "Negro Delegates Elected to Miss. Democratic Convention," "*Times-Picayune*, May 22, 1968; and Wilson Minor, *Times-Picayune*, July 3, 1968.

34. *Clarion-Ledger*, July 3, 1968, 4.

35. Letter from Aaron Henry to Governor Richard Hughes, Committee on Equal Rights, National Democratic Committee, May 28, 1968, Box 7, F 136 (Aaron Henry Papers, TC).

36. Complaint from Bolivar County Loyal Democratic Party, Notarized by Aaron Henry, May 27, 1968 (Amzie Moore Papers, SHSW).

37. "Miss. Democratic Party Plans to Chart Course," *Times-Picayune*, July 2, 1968, 2, sec. 2.

38. Dittmer, *Local People*, 418.

39. Letter from Aaron Henry and Hodding Carter III, Co-chairmen Loyal Democrats of Mississippi, June 21, 1968, Box 9, F 188 (Aaron Henry Papers, TC).

40. Letter from Aaron Henry and Hodding Carter to Steering Committee of the Loyal Democratic Party of Mississippi, July 8, 1968, Box 90, F 159 (Aaron Henry Papers, TC).

41. Letter from Aaron Henry to "Dear Friend," July 19, 1968, Box 9, F 188 (Aaron Henry Papers, TC).

42. Minor, "Bi-Racial Step Taken By Demos," *Times-Picayune*, April 17, 1968.

43. "Support Cited by Aaron Henry," *Times-Picayune*, August 1, 1968.

44. Minor, "Miss. Biracial Delegation, Regulars Argue for Seats," *Times-Picayune*, August 20, 1964; Minor, "Credentials Moved Back," *Times-Picayune*, August 27, 1968.

45. Richard Scher, *Politics in the New South: Republicanism, Race and Leadership in the Twentieth Century*, 2nd ed. (Armonk, NY: M. E. Sharpe, 1997), 100–106.

46. Minor, "Loyalists Hail Speech by HHH," *Times-Picayune*, August 30, 1968.

47. Sher, *Politics in the New South*, 102.

48. Charlie Griffin had worked in Washington for eighteen years for Congressman John Bell Williams. In his memoir, Evers characterized the outcome as follows: "the first primary had about six white racist candidates, and the white vote split pretty good. I got all the Negro vote and won the primary by a plurality of seventy-five votes." Evers and Szanton, *Have No Fear*, 234.

49. McLemore, "The Mississippi Freedom Democratic Party," 395–408.

50. Minor, "Entire Loyalist Challenge Unit from Miss. is Seated," *Times-Picayune*, August 21, 1968, 4.

51. John Pearce, "Will Be Seated, Says Williams," *Times-Picayune*, July 4, 1968; http:// uselectionatlas.org/RESULTS/national.php?off=0&year=1968 (accessed September 4, 2007).

52. Leroy Morganti, "Henry to Head Miss. Loyalists," *Times-Picayune*, December 16, 1968.

53. Minor, "FDP Chief Not Looking for Conference Walkout," *Times-Picayune*, August 26, 1968.

54. "Report of Charles Evers to the NDC," January 15, 1969, Box 3, F 5 (Patricia Derian Papers, MSUSC).

55. Letter from Aaron Henry, Chairman of Democratic Party of the State of Mississippi, to Amzie Moore, March 5, 1969 (Amzie Moore Papers, SHSW).

56. Key Jr., *Southern Politics*.

57. Letter from Aaron Henry and Claude Ramsay, Democrats for Humphrey-Muskie Campaign to Leaders of the Mississippi Democratic Party, November 11, 1968, Box 5, F 5 (Amzie Moore Papers, SHSW).

58. Letter from Aaron Henry to "Democratic Party Leader," July 9, 1970, Box 8, F 161 (Aaron Henry Papers, TC).

59. See, for example: Aaron Henry memo to Executive Committee of the Democratic Party of Mississippi, April 10, 1969, Box 8, F 160 (Aaron Henry Papers, TC).

60. Letter from the Democratic Party of the state of Mississippi . . . , Invitation to opening of first State party office, February 16, 1969, Box 8, 160 (Aaron Henry Papers, TC).

61. Aaron Henry letter to Amzie Moore, March 13, 1969, Box 5, F 5 (Amzie Moore Papers, SHSW).

62. Letter from Henry to Democratic Party Executive Committee, June 28, 1969, Box 8, F 160 (Aaron Henry Papers, TC).

63. Aaron Henry letter to Amzie Moore, March 13, 1969, Box 5, F 5 (Amzie Moore Papers, SHSW).

64. "Official Guideline for Delegate Selection," Commission on Party Structure and Delegate Selection, Democratic National Committee (DNC), November 18–20, 1969, Box 4, DNC Folder (Aaron Henry Papers, WRL).

65. Aaron Henry letter to Amzie Moore, March 13, 1969, Box 5, File 5 (Amzie Moore Papers, SHSW).

66. Report of Aaron Henry to the Rules Committee of the National Democratic Party, Atlanta, Georgia, February 21, 1970, Box 8, F 161 (Aaron Henry Papers, TC).

67. Memo from Aaron Henry and District Chairmen to County and District Leaders, August 27, 1969, Box 8, F 160 (Aaron Henry Papers, TC).

68. Minutes of Mississippi Democratic Party Executive Committee, June 28, 1969, Box 2, File 160 (Aaron Henry Papers, TC).

69. Letter from Aaron Henry to State, County, and Local Leader[s] of the Democratic Party of Mississippi, February 19, 1970 (Amzie Moore Papers, SHSW).

70. "Constitution of the Democratic Party of Mississippi," Adopted March 8, 1970, Jackson, Mississippi, Box 5, Democratic Party of Mississippi Folder (Aaron Henry Papers, WRL).

71. Letter from Aaron Henry to Congressional Delegation (by individual name), March 25, 1970, Box 7, F 178 (Aaron Henry Papers, TC).

72. Letter from Aaron Henry to Lawrence O'Brien, November 24, 1970, Box 4, F 1 (Patricia Derian Papers, MSUSC).

73. "The 1971 Mississippi Challenge," Memorandum from Aaron Henry et al., December 14, 1970, Box 4, F 1, MSU (Patricia Derian Papers, MSUSC).

74. Ibid.

75. Letter from Wesley Watkins to Patricia Derian, December 18, 1970, Box 4, F 1 (Patricia Derian Papers, MSUSC).

76. George Lardner Jr., newspaper clipping in the *Washington Post,* December 4, 1970, Box 4, F 1 (Patricia Derian Papers, MSUSC).

77. Letter from Wesley Watkins to Pat Derian, November 27, 1970; Letter from Aaron Henry to Attorney Wesley Watkins, Secretary and Legal Counsel of Democratic Party of Mississippi, December 20, 1971, Box 4, F 1 (Patricia Derian Papers, MSUSC).

78. This group was originally established by liberal Democrats in 1959 in the House of Representatives as a counterweight to the power of conservative southern Democrats. Arthur G. Stevens Jr., Arthur H. Miller, and Thomas E. Mann, "Mobilization of Liberal Strength in the House, 1955–1970: The Democratic Study Group," *American Political Science Review* (1974): 667–681.

79. The Leadership Conference on Civil Rights was originally organized in 1950 by A. Philip Randolph (Brotherhood of Sleeping Car Porters), Roy Wilkins (NAACP), and Arnold Aronson (National Jewish Community Relations Advisory Council) to lobby for civil and human rights legislation. It now is known as the Leadership Conference on Civil and Human Rights, with some two hundred affiliated organizations. http://www.civilrights. org/about/history.html (accessed July 3, 2013).

80. Letter from Wesley Watkins to Patricia Derian, December 18, 1970, Box 4, F 1 (Patricia Derian Papers, MSUSC).

81. Letter from Lawrence O'Brien to Aaron Henry, December 30, 1970, Box 7, F 138 (Aaron Henry Papers, TC).

82. "The Mississippi Challenge," Democratic Study Group Special Report, January 14, 1971, Box 4, F 1 (Patricia Derian Papers, MSUSC).

83. "Affidavit of Aaron Henry," in DSG Report to Congress, January 12, 1971, Box 4, F 1 (Patricia Derian Papers, MSUSC).

84. Letter from Senator Fred Harris to Senate Colleagues, February 1, 1971, Box 4, F 1 (Patricia Derian Papers, MSUSC).

85. James Saggus, *Jackson Daily News,* April 1, 1971, Box 3, File 19 (Patricia Derian Papers, MSUSC).

86. *New York Times,* June 6, 1971, Box 3, File 19 (Patricia Derian Papers, MSUSC).

87. Letter from Aaron Henry to Charles Evers, May 3, 1971; and Letter from Aaron Henry to Wesley Watkins, May 18, 1971, Box 3, F 6 (Patricia Derian Papers, MSUSC).

88. Parker, *Black Votes Count,* 200.

89. Oral History with Mr. Jimmy Swan, March 23, 1977, University of Southern Mississippi Digital Collection, http://digilib. usm.edu/cdm4/document.php?CISO-ROOT=/coh&CISOPTR=7125&CISOS (accessed December 21, 2009).

90. Evers and Szanton, *Have No Fear,* 271.

91. Ibid.

92. Charles S. Bullock III, "The Election of Blacks in the South: Preconditions and Consequences," *American Journal of Political Science* 19, no. 4 (November 1975): 727–739.

93. James Saggus (Patricia Derian Papers, MSUSC).

94. Parker, *Black Votes Count*, 158–164. Also see F. Glenn Abney, "Factors Related to Negro Voter Turnout in Mississippi," *Journal of Politics* 36, no. 4 (November 1974): 1057–1063.

95. Letter from Aaron Henry to Democratic Party (Regular) County Chairmen, etc., December 7, 1971; Letter from S. H. Roberson, Attorney for the Coahoma County Board of Supervisors, to Aaron Henry, December 28, 1971, Box 7, F 139 (Aaron Henry Papers, TC).

96. Letter from Aaron Henry to A. F. Summer, Attorney General, January 8, 1972, Box 7, F 139 (Aaron Henry Papers, TC).

97. Letter from Aaron Henry to Governor-elect William Waller, December 3, 1971, Box 7 F 139 (Aaron Henry Papers, TC).

98. Press Release from Aaron Henry, December 13, 1971; Letter from Aaron Henry to Wesley Watkins, December 20, 1971, Box 3, File 6 (Patricia Derian Papers, MSUSC).

99. Letter from Henry to "Fellow Democrat," January 17, 1972, Box 8, F 162 (Aaron Henry Papers, TC).

100. Mississippi used an array of procedures and laws to dilute the black vote, including the use of multimember districts requiring at-large elections—hence the focus on single-member districts. Frank Parker has documented these procedures and laws in detail in Parker, *Black Votes Count*, 35–77.

101. "Another Effort to Unite the Democratic Party of the State of Mississippi," January 17, 1972, Box 5, F 1 (Patricia Derian Papers, MSUSC).

102. Letter from Aaron Henry to J. C. McDonald, April 17, 1972, Box 7, F 141; "A White and Black Talk—And that's News" (editorial), *The News* (Durant, Mississippi newspaper), March 9, 1972, Box 11, F 214 (Aaron Henry Papers, TC).

103. *Delta-Democrat Times,* newspaper clipping, February 27, 1972, Box 11, F 213, Box 9, F 189 (Aaron Henry Papers, TC).

104. Memorandum from Aaron Henry appointing Unity Committee, March 8, 1972; "Democratic Party Negotiating Committee Meeting," March 14, 1972; Letter from Aaron Henry to J. C. McDonald, April 17, 1972, Box 5, F 1 (Patricia Derian Papers, MSUSC).

105. "Notes on Democratic Party Negotiating Team, prepared by Fred Banks, March 7, 1972, Box 11, F 214 (Aaron Henry Papers, TC).

106. Governor William Wallace Address to the State Democratic Party Convention. Municipal Auditorium, Jackson, Mississippi, April 8, 1972, Box 11, F 215 (Aaron Henry Papers, TC); Letter from J. C. McDonald to Aaron Henry, April 10, 1972, Box 5, F 1 (Patricia Derian Papers, MSUSC).

107. Letter from Aaron Henry to J. C. McDonald, April 17, 1972, Box 7, F 141; Letter from Aaron Henry to Charles Young, April 23, 1972, Box 11, F 214 (Aaron Henry Papers, TC).

108. Letter from J. C. McDonald to the Credentials Committee of the Democratic National Committee, May 1, 1972, Box 14, F 290 (Aaron Henry Papers, TC).

109. Letter from Robert Nelson to Aaron Henry, April 25, 1972, Box 3, F 6 (Patricia Derian Papers, MSUSC).

110. *Riddell v. National Democratic Party*, 344 F. Supp. 908 (S.D. Miss. 1972, 508 F.2d 770 (5th Cir. 1975); *Clarion Ledger*, July 10, 1972, 1, Derian Box 5, NF (Patricia Derian Papers, MSUSC).

111. Letter from Aaron Henry to the District and County Leaders and the State Executive Committee of the Loyalist Party, June 12, 1972, Benbow. Box 9, F 189 (Aaron Henry Papers, TC).

112. A. B. Albritton, *Commercial Appeal*, newspaper clipping, July 3, 1972, Box 10, F 196 (Aaron Henry Papers, TC).

113. "Tom Riddell, Jr., Chairman, et al. vs. Delegation of the Loyalist Democratic Party of the State of Mississippi," Before the Credentials Committee of the Democratic National Convention, Findings of Fact, ND, Box 4, File 3 (Patricia Derian Papers, MSUSC).

114. A. B. Albritton, July 10, 1972, *Commercial Appeal*, newspaper clipping, Box 5, NF (Patricia Derian Papers, MSUSC).

115. The reference is to the 1876 presidential election in which Rutherford B. Hayes, the Republican candidate, agreed to the removal of troops from the "reconstructing" South in exchange for votes from southerners congressmen that allowed him to win the election. William E. B. Du Bois *Black Reconstruction in America* (New York: Meridian of the World Publishing Company, 1935), 691–693.

116. Fragment of a letter from Aaron Henry to Governor William Waller, August 15, 1972, Box 7, F 141 (Aaron Henry Papers, TC).

117. "Dave Leip's Atlas of U.S. Presidential Elections," http://uselectionatlas.org/RESULTS/state (accessed September 20, 2013); Will Campbell, *Robert Clark's Journey to the House: A Black Politician's Story* (Jackson: University Press of Mississippi, 2003).

118. "Response to the Press by Aaron Henry . . . ," November 8, 1972, Box 5, F 1 (Patricia Derian Papers, MSUSC).

119. Letter from Aaron Henry (no salutation), November 16, 1972, Box 9, F 189 (Aaron Henry Papers, TC).

120. Minor, *Times-Picayune*, newspaper clipping, April 24, 1973, Box 5, F 11 (Patricia Derian Papers, MSUSC).

121. Letter from Aaron Henry to Lieutenant Governor William Winter, August 1, 1973, Box 7, F 142 (Aaron Henry Papers, TC).

122. Letter from Aaron Henry to Governor William Waller, February 14, 1974, Box 7, F 142 (Aaron Henry Papers, TC).

123. Press Kit issued from State Democratic Party of Mississippi, January 27, 1974, Box 3, F 7 (Patricia Derian Papers, MSUSC).

124. Ibid.

125. Elliott, Jack, *Clarion Ledger*, newspaper clipping, ca. December 1, 1974, Box 9, F 190 (Aaron Henry Papers, TC).

126. Aaron Henry letter to Jamie Whitten, December 19, 1974, Box 9, File 190; and Letter from First District Congressman Jamie Whitten to Aaron Henry, December 23, 1974, Box 9, F 190 (Aaron Henry Papers, TC).

127. Sher, *Politics in the New South*, 278ff; Bill Waller, *Straight Ahead: The Memoir of a Governor* (Brandon, MS: Quail Ridge Press, 2007).

128. Alexander P. Lamis, *The Two-Party South* (New York: Oxford University Press, 1984).

129. Rickey L. Cole and Kimberly S. Adams, "Mississippi: An Emerging Democracy Creating a Culture of Civic Participation among Formerly Oppressed Peoples," *Nebula* 4, no. 3 (September 2007): 341; Waller, *Straight Ahead*.

130. Cole and Adams, "Mississippi."

131. Our Campaigns website, Mississippi Governor campaign, 1975, http://www.ourcampaigns.com/RaceDetail.html?RaceID=51902 (accessed August 17, 2011).

132. Letter from Aaron Henry to J. C. McDonald, January 1, 1976, Box 3, F 9 (Patricia Derian Papers, MSUSC).

133. Memorandum from Aaron Henry to County, District, Chairmen, and Affirmative Action Compliance Review Committee, *inter alia*. January 25, 1976, Box 3, F 9 (Patricia Derian Papers, MSUSC).

134. Remarks of Governor Cliff Finch to State Convention of Democratic Party of the State of Mississippi, February 29, 1976, Box 3, F 228 (Aaron Henry Papers, TC).

135. Letter from Aaron Henry to Governor William Waller, February 14, 1974, Box 7, F 142 (Aaron Henry Papers, TC); Christopher Asch, *The Senator and the Sharecropper: James O. Eastland and Fannie Lou Hamer* (London: New Press, 2008), 287–288.

136. "Delta Ministry Fact Sheet," January 1965, Box 2, F 4 (Harry Bowie Papers, SHSW).

137. Letter from Aaron Henry to Attorney Clell G. Ward, Greenville District Attorney, March 13, 1976, Box 77, F 1320. He was responding to a letter from Attorney Clell of March 12, 1976, both in Box 77, F 1320 (Aaron Henry Papers, TC).

138. Evers and Szanton, *Have No Fear*, 273–294.

139. Crosby, *A Little Taste of Freedom*, 222.

140. Evers and Szanton, *Have No Fear*.

141. Letter from Aaron Henry to Charles Evers, November 27, 1978, Box 7, F 147 (Aaron Henry Papers, TC).

142. Kenneth Andrews, *Freedom Is a Constant Struggle: The Mississippi Civil Rights Movement and Its Legacy* (Chicago: University of Chicago Press, 2004), 178.

143. Frank Parker, "Racial Gerrymandering and Legislative Reapportionment," in *Minority Vote Dilution*, ed. Chandler Davidson (Washington, DC: Howard University Press, 1984), 85–113.

144. *Connor v. Finch*, 431 U.S. 407 (1977).

145. Parker, *Black Votes Count*, 125.

146. Letter from Ben Brown, Deputy Chairman, National Democratic Party, to Aaron Henry, September 6, 1978, Box 78, F 1327 (Aaron Henry Papers, TC).

147. Letter from Aaron Henry to Tom Riddell, May 5, 1979, Box 7, F 148 (Aaron Henry Papers, TC).

148. Winters sought to brunt the effect of the liberal tag in 1967 by declaring his own segregationist credentials in a contest where blacks remained disfranchised. Dittmer, *Local People*, 416.

149. Scher, *Politics in the New South*, 153, 331.

150. William Winter, interview with the author, Jackson, Mississippi, May 13, 1998.

151. Scher, *Politics in the New South*, 325–326.

152. Wilson Minor, *Capitol Reporter*, "Eyes on Mississippi," February 23, 1978, Box 12, F 234 (Aaron Henry Papers, TC).

153. Letter from Aaron Henry to Robert Strauss, Chairman of the NDC, May 14, 1980, Box 79, F 1339. Henry also dispatched letters to Louis Martin, a presidential aide at the White House, and to Senator Ted Kennedy. And he prepared a letter to the black members of the state Executive Committee urging them to lobby national leaders. Benbow. Box 12, F 235 (Aaron Henry Papers, TC).

154. Letter from Aaron Henry to Governor William Winter, May 16, 1980, Box 7, F 149 (Aaron Henry Papers, TC).

155. Aaron Henry to "Fellow Democrats," May 19, 1980; Aaron Henry to Coalition of Determined Democrats, June 2, 1980, Box 7, F 149 (Aaron Henry Papers, TC).

156. "Proposed report of the Special Committee on the Structure of the Democratic

Party of the State of Mississippi," May 10, 1980, Box 8, F 173 (Aaron Henry Papers, TC).

157. *Commercial Appeal*, newspaper clipping, June 22, 1980, Box 12, F 236 (Aaron Henry Papers, TC).

158. Ronald Keith Gaddie, "Realignment," in *The Oxford Handbook of Southern Politics*, ed. Charles Bullock III and Mark Rozelle (New York: Oxford University Press, 2012), 289–313, 296–310.

159. Lawrence Moreland and Robert Steed, "The Southern Presidential Elections," *The Oxford Handbook of Southern Politics*, 472.

160. Parker, *Black Votes Count*, 138.

161. Stanley Berard, "Southern Influence in Congress," *The Oxford Handbook of Southern Politics*, 502.

Chapter Nine: The Summit and Culmination: Henry as a State Legislator and His Political Demise

1. Voter Education Project Report, "Black Elected Officials in the South" (Atlanta, GA: Voter Education Project, 1973).

2. Legislative Committee Appointments, February 1, 1980, Box 39, F 731, (Aaron Henry Papers, TC); David Hampton, "Legislature Gives Blacks Voice: Henry," *Jackson Daily News,* June 17, 1980, 1.

3. "Department of State Nomination of Patricia M. Derian to be Coordinator for Human Rights and Humanitarian Affairs," online by Gerhard Peters and John T. Woolley, *The American Presidency Project*—March 5, 1977, http://www.presidency.ucsb.edu/ws/?pid=7121 (accessed September 13, 2013); Claire Crawford-Mason and Joyce Leviton, "As State's Man, Hodding Carter Used to Meet the Press," *Archive,* June 15, 1981, 15:23, http://www.people. com/people/archive/article/0,,20079520,00.html (accessed September 13, 2013).

4. Coleman and McLemore, "Black Independent Politics in Mississippi: Constants and Challenges," in *The New Black Politics*; Gary Brooks, "Black Political Mobilization and White Legislative Behavior," in *Contemporary Southern Political Attitudes and Behavior: Studies and Essays*, ed. Laurence Moreland et al. (New York: Praeger Publishers, 1982), 221–238.

5. Letter from Aaron Henry to "Dear Friend," June 7, 1979, Box 37, F 718 (Aaron Henry Papers, TC).

6. Ibid.

7. Ibid.

8. Ibid.

9. James Marshall, *Student Activism and Civil Rights in Mississippi: Protest Politics and the Struggle for Racial Justice, 1960–1965* (Baton Rouge: Louisiana State University Press, 2013), 36.

10. Mississippi Official and Statistical Register, 1992–1996, Secretary of State, Jackson, 1993, 590.

11. Parker, *Black Votes Count*, 136–140; Minion K. C. Morrison, "Federal Aid and Afro-American Political Power in Three Mississippi Towns," *Publius* 17, no. 4 (Autumn 1987): 51–52.

12. Douglas Feig, "The State Legislature: Representatives of the People or the Powerful?" in *Mississippi Government and Politics: Modernizers versus Traditionalists*, ed. Dale Krane and Stephen Shaffer (Lincoln: University of Nebraska Press, 1992), 112.

13. Tip Allen Jr., "The Enduring Traditions of the State Constitutions," *Mississippi Government and Politics*, 43–59; Thomas Hardy, "The 'Weak 'Governor," *Mississippi Government and Politics*, 132–155.

14. Kerry Haynie, *African American Legislators in the American States* (New York: Columbia University Press, 2001), 4–6. See also Kenny Whitby, *The Color of Representation: Congressional Behavior and Black Constituents* (Ann Arbor: University of Michigan Press, 1997); Tyson King-Meadows and Thomas Schaller, *Devolution and Black State Legislators: Challenges and Choices in the Twenty-First Century* (Albany: State University Press of New York, 2006).

15. Haynie, *African American Legislators*, 24.

16. Mary DeLorse Coleman, *Legislators, Law and Public Policy: Political Change in Mississippi and the South* (Westport, CT: Greenwood Press, 1993); Earl Black and Merle Black, *Politics and Society in the South* (Cambridge, MA: Harvard University Press, 1987); Carol Swain, *Black Faces, Black Interests: The Representation of African Americans in Congress* (Cambridge, MA: Harvard University Press, 1993;) Robert Singh, *The Congressional Black Caucus: Racial Politics in the U.S. Congress* (Thousand Oaks, CA: Sage Publications, 1998).

17. Byron D'Andra Orey, "Black Legislative Politics in Mississippi," Faculty Publications: Political Science, Paper 5, http://digital commons.unl.edu/poliscifacpub/5, 2000, 16–17.

18. Katherine Tate, *Black Faces in the Mirror: African Americans and Their Representatives in the U.S. Congress* (Princeton, NJ: Princeton University Press, 2003), 4–5, 96–110.

19. Parker, *Black Votes Count,* 133.

20. Kenneth Wald and Carole Southerland, "Black Public Officials and the Dynamics of Representation," in *Contemporary Southern Political Attitudes and Behavior: Studies and Essays*, ed. Laurence Moreland et al. (New York: Praeger Publishers, 1982), 239–254.

21. Parker, *Black Votes Count*, 134.

22. Tomie Green, interview with the author, January 20, 1998, Jackson, Mississippi.

23. King-Meadows and Schaller, *Devolution and Black State Legislators,* 109–146; Haynie, *African American Legislators*, 39–62.

24. Feig, "The State Legislature," 117.

25. Henry Requests to the Speaker of the House for Committee Assignments, December 5, 1979, Box 37, F 718 (Aaron Henry Papers, TC).

26. Ibid.

27. Haynie, *African American Legislators*, 24.

28. Parker, *Black Votes Count*, 130.

29. *Mississippi Legislature, 1980 House Journal*, 1533.

30. Haynie, *African American Legislators*, 4–6.

31. Gary Brooks refers to these demands and expectations as "black interests as defined by the black community." Brooks, "Black Political Mobilization," 223.

32. Coleman, *Legislators, Law and Public Policy*, 113.

33. I surveyed Henry's legislative proposals from 1980 to 1995, analyzing 350 bills. I analyzed them according to the six substantive subject areas and one miscellaneous category. I then made a frequency count and summed them by category, generating a percentage score to determine how he distributed his time on the issues of primary engagement. (1) **Political Affairs**: bills relating to elections, and procedures and processes of political parties. His goals were expansion of the electorate and strengthening the institutional base of political parties. (2) **Education**: bills designed to expand public education, increase

teacher salaries and rights, improvements for black colleges. (3) **Local Affairs:** bills specific to Clarksdale, Coahoma County, or the surrounding Delta counties, many associated with economic development. (4) **Social Services**: bills related to housing, health, and welfare. (5) **Corrections**: bills to improve services, rights, and rehabilitation of inmates. (6) **Civil Rights**: bills that sought to obliterate racial exclusion. (7) **General Issues**: bills on broad general subjects—taxes, recreation, judicial processes, institutional legislature rules, and state economic development and infrastructure.

34. Henry's legislative efforts compare favorably to his other colleagues in the legislative black caucus. Orey has shown that education was by far the most important emphasis of proposals by blacks in the state legislature in two sessions in 1987 and 1988. Civil rights issues, socioeconomic concerns, and issues related to law enforcement and court proceedings were all significantly represented. Orey, "Black Legislative Politics in Mississippi," 18.

35. Henry's last year (1996) was an anomaly since he was often absent due to illness. In this entire session he submitted six bills, compared to his yearly average of about twenty-two.

36. Henry's resolutions activity is equally revealing. Many of these are in the general category reflecting commendations members make for constituents or prominent figures. Fifty-five percent of those Henry signed onto are of this nature. The second prominent category, however, is civil rights, most of which are Henry commendations for African American personalities and their racial achievements—academic, cultural, or athletic (24 percent). Education resolutions are among these—resolutions seeking commitment of resources to explore enhanced educational needs, many at the HBCUs. During his legislative career (1987–1996) Henry was active in sponsoring or cosponsoring 224 resolutions. The highest percentage (23 percent) was in the area of civil rights; 10 percent were in education; 7 percent dealt with national politics; and 5 percent focused on political affairs and social services.

37. *Ayers v. Fordice*, 879 F. Supp. 1419 (N.D. Miss. 1995); *Ayers v. Fordice*, 1111. 3d 1183 (1997).

38. *Mississippi House Journal*, HB 240, 1980; and HB 1650 and 1651, 1994.

39. *Mississippi House Journal*, HB 474, 1984.

40. *Mississippi House Journal*, HB 240, 1980; and HB 1650 and 1651, 1994.

41. David Wiggins, *Glory Bound: Black Athletes in White America* (Syracuse, NY: Syracuse University Press, 1997), 197.

42. Tate, *Black Faces in the Mirror*, 5–22; Whitby, *The Color of Representation*, 6.

43. *Mississippi House Journal*, HCR 36 and HCR 37, 1980.

44. Wiggins, *Glory Bound*, 197.

45. *Mississippi House Journal*, HCR 62 and HCR 63, 1980.

46. *Mississippi House Journal*, HCR 107, 1984; HCR 66, 1985.

47. *Mississippi House Journal*, HCR 13 and HCR 66, 1983.

48. Payton did receive his own commendation, agreed to by the entire membership. *Mississippi House Journal*, HCR 66, 1985.

49. Harry Edwards, "The Sources of the Black Male Athlete's Superiority," *Black Scholar* 3, no. 3 (1971): 32–41.

50. *Mississippi House Journal*, HB 1007, 1982; HB 936, 1982; and HB 815, 1991. Bolton has shown how the impending *Brown* decision actually derailed a pre–civil rights movement legislative proposal for compulsory attendance. Bolton, *The Hardest Deal of All*, 217.

51. *Mississippi House Journal*, HCR 5, 1983.

52. *Mississippi House Journal*, HB 724, 1991.

53. *Mississippi House Journal*, HCR 109, 1986. This was a resolution that encouraged "the State Board of Education to consider a comprehensive plan for the implementation of health education, emphasizing the responsibility of human sexuality, as a part of the curriculum for elementary and secondary education in the state."

54. Bolton, *The Hardest Deal of All*, 217.

55. Parker, *Black Votes Count*, 136.

56. Bolton, *The Hardest Deal of All*, 217; *Mississippi House Journal*, HB 739, 1992; and HB 815, 1991. Regarding the lottery, see *Mississippi House Journal*, HCR 70, 1986. This resolution died in committee, but was subsequently approved in 1992, as Mississippi joined the nationwide gaming movement. In 1991 HB 722 called for an educational requirement (high school diploma), and specialized training (a complementary School Executive Management Institute administered by the State Department of Education) for school boards. *Mississippi House Journal*, HB 722, 1991. Meanwhile, once lottery legislation passed it did not yield the benefits for education or impoverished communities that Henry imagined. See Sharon Austin, *The Transformation of Plantation Politics: Black Politics, Concentrated Poverty, and Social Capital in the Mississippi Delta* (New York: SUNY Press, 2006).

57. *Mississippi House Journal*, HB 77, 1988.

58. *Mississippi House Journal*, HB 724, 1991; *Mississippi House Journal*, HB 1239, 1994.

59. *Mississippi House Journal*, HB 1346, 1990. These were four-year scholarship loans to black high school seniors who agreed to become teachers in areas where there were shortages. Reimbursement on the loans was forgiven if recipients agreed "to teach in a critical shortage area and in a school district having a substantial disadvantaged student population as defined by the free and reduced lunch program and as determined by the State Department of Education." They would also be required to teach in such a setting for five years within the first six years of degree completion, and funds could only be used at Mississippi institutions, including junior colleges.

60. *Mississippi House Journal*, HB 726, 1991.

61. His proposal focused on achieving best practice for teacher-student ratios and support for librarian and school counselors. The same was true for school board members. He believed they should be better equipped for their duties. *Mississippi House Journal*, HB 723, 1991.

62. *Mississippi House Journal*, HCR 9, 1983.

63. *Mississippi House Journal*, HB 93, 1983. A precedent existed with legal holidays for the birthdays of Confederate general Robert E. Lee and President Jefferson Davis, and a memorial day for Confederates.

64. Will Campbell, *Robert Clark's Journey to the House: A Black Politician's Story* (Jackson: University Press of Mississippi, 2003), 120–123.

65. *Clarion Ledger*, February 15, 1986, 10-A (MDAH).

66. Parker, *Black Votes Count*, 135; Orey, "Black Legislative Politics," 15–17, puts the figure at about 120 for legislation that died.

67. *Mississippi House Journal*, HB 379, 1987.

68. McMillen, *The Citizen's Council*, 260. *Mississippi House Journal*, HB 1088, 1980.

69. Robert Bein, "Stained Flags: Public Symbols and Equal Protection," *Seton Hall Law Review* 28 (1998): 897–923; Gökhan R. Karahan and William F. Shughart II, "Under Two

Flags: Symbolic Voting in the State of Mississippi," *Public Choice* 118 (January 2004): 105–124. See also *Mississippi Division of the United Sons of Confederate Veterans v. Mississippi State Conference of NAACP Branches, et al.*, 774 So. 2d 388 (MS 2000).

70. Byron Orey et al., "Accounting for 'Racism': Responses to Political Predicament in Two States," *State Politics and Policy Quarterly* 7, no. 3 (Fall 2007): 235–255.

71. *Mississippi House Journal*, HCR 38, 1980; Lorenzo Greene and Arvarh Strickland, *Working with Carter G. Woodson, the Father of Black History: A Diary 1928–1930* (Baton Rouge: Louisiana State University Press, 1989).

72. *Mississippi House Journal*, HB 858, 1981; *Mississippi House Journal*, HB 858, 1988.

73. *Mississippi House Journal*, HB 1081, 1981; *Mississippi House Journal*, HB 793, 1987.

74. *Mississippi House Journal*, HB 1140, 1981.

75. Coleman, *Legislators, Law and Public Policy*, 27.

76. *Mississippi House Journal*, HCR 34, 1987; *Mississippi House Journal*, HB 317, 1988.

77. Parker, *Black Votes Count*, 135.

78. Tekie Fessehatzion and Bichaka Fayissa, "Public Assistance and Job Search Behavior of the Rural Poor—Evidence from the Mississippi Delta," *Review of Black Political Economy* 18, no. 3 (Winter 1990): 79–91.

79. *Mississippi House Journal*, HB 734, 1980.

80. *Mississippi House Journal*, HB 1712, 1995. Also see "The At Risk Child Care Program," reviewed at www.eric.ed.gov:80/ERICDocs/data/ericdocs2sql/ content_storage_01/0000019b/80/13/37/d8.pdf (accessed September 20, 2013).

81. *Mississippi House Journal*, HB 76, 1983.

82. *Mississippi House Journal*, HB 75, 1983.

83. *Mississippi House Journal*, HB 665, 1988.

84. *Mississippi House Journal*, HR 13, 1988.

85. *Mississippi House Journal*, HB 860, 1988.

86. Coincident to these direct efforts to integrate affirmative action into state policy was Henry's efforts to protect legal services for the poor. He cosponsored a resolution to maintain funding for the Legal Services Corporation. It urged the congressional delegation to support continued funding for this independent agency. Henry feared that conservative forces would weaken the program or bury it within an unsympathetic executive bureau. The HCR 105 therefore made the case for continued "vigorous, competent and quality legal services to poor citizens," because of a "duty to guarantee equal access to the courts and judicial system." *Mississippi House Journal*, HCR 105, 1981.

87. *Mississippi House Journal*, HB 737, 1980.

88. *Mississippi House Journal*, HB 386, 1984.

89. *Mississippi House Journal*, HB 838, 1993.

90. *Mississippi House Journal*, HB 463, 1989; *Mississippi House Journal*, HB 1284, 1994; *Mississippi House Journal*, HB 868 and HB 1743, 1995.

91. *Mississippi House Journal*, HCR 88, 1994.

92. *Mississippi House Journal*, HCR 12, 1988.

93. *Mississippi House Journal*, HB 955, 1980.

94. Hamlin, *Crossroads at Clarksdale*, 229–231.

95. Fragment of a letter from Aaron Henry to Governor William Waller, August 15, 1972, Box 7, File 141 (Aaron Henry Papers, TC).

96. Henry spoke bitterly of an early case in which he was involved. Clyde Kennard, a young black veteran, applied to what was then Mississippi Southern University and was

denied admission. He was subsequently jailed at Parchman on the totally false charges of stealing, a plot devised to prevent his continuing efforts to integrate the school. He subsequently developed cancer while incarcerated, for which he was denied treatment. Several months after suspension of his sentence and release he succumbed in 1963. It was a case that clearly met Oshinsky's description. Henry, *Aaron Henry*, 134–135. Dittmer, *Local People*, 82ff. In one of the typical means for removal of threats to the racial system, Clyde Kennard was arrested and jailed on trumped-up charges of stealing chicken feed. In an ironic twist, in 2006 a Mississippi judge finally exonerated Kennard by throwing out the former charges. "Kennard, who died of cancer in 1963 while on an 'indefinite suspended sentence,' was declared innocent in the same Hattiesburg courtroom where he was convicted in 1960 and sentenced to 7 years' hard labor for stealing $25 worth of chicken feed, a charge disproved this year when the lone witness against him recanted." Dan Gibbert in the *Chicago Tribune*, May 18, 2006. http://www6. district125.k12.il.us/~bbradfor/clydek-ennardreso.html (accessed September 20, 2013).

97. Henry, *Aaron Henry*, 108 and 153; Hamlin, *Crossroads at Clarksdale*, 122–124.

98. David M. Oshinsky, *Worse Than Slavery: Parchman Farm and the Ordeal of Jim Crow Justice* (New York: Free Press, 1996).

99. Raymond Arsenault, *Freedom Riders: 1961 and the Struggle for Racial Justice* (New York: Oxford University Press, 2006), 348–361.

100. Columbus Hopper, "The Impact of Litigation on Mississippi's Prison System," *Prison Journal* 65, no. 1 (Spring–Summer 1985): 61.

101. This 1972 ruling from a federal district court called for sweeping changes at Parchman. Among other things it barred censorship of mail, the elimination of corporal punishment, and the abolition of the notorious trustee system. It also called for renovation of the facility, and other changes that the court called "unconstitutional conditions in inmate housing . . . water, sewer . . . firefighting equipment, [and] inadequate hospital." *Gates v. Collier*, 349 Fed. Supp. 881 N.D. Miss. (1972). See also *Gates v. Collier*, 501 F. 2d 1291 (1972).

102. *Mississippi House Journal*, HB 812, 1980.

103. *Mississippi House Journal*, HB 944, 1980.

104. Then the composition of the seven-member board was specified: "one member of the clergy, a woman, an ex-offender whose voting privileges were restored, a leader of a human rights group, and a professor of criminal justice from a Mississippi university." He also asked that the member from the medical profession be drawn from a broader list of candidates. The parole board would have a similar composition. *Mississippi House Journal*, HB 943, 1980; *Mississippi House Journal*, HB 945, 1980.

105. *Mississippi House Journal*, HB 796, 1980.

106. *Mississippi House Journal*, HB 973, 1980.

107. Hopper, "The Impact of Litigation on Mississippi's Prison System," 61.

108. "Mississippi's Corrections Reform," by John Buntin, August 2010, http://www.governing.com/topics/public-justice-safety/courts corrections/mississippi-correction-r eform.html (accessed July 15, 2013).

109. A 1983 version targeted "depressed areas." The Department of Economic Development would compose criteria for the depressed designation based on "per capita income, unemployment, income distribution, manufacturing activity, and migration." *Mississippi House Journal*, HB 715, 1983.

110. *Mississippi House Journal*, HB 467, 1983 (see also HB 733, 1982); HB 857, 1988.

111. Some of the transportation proposals dealt with highway construction (outside Henry's district) such as HB 187 for building four-lane highways. Many others were honorary highway naming projects—e.g., the Gus Williams Memorial and the Owen Cooper Highways in 1988. Among his bills honoring individuals were those for named public facilities, such as renaming the Agriculture Museum for its founder, Jim Buck Ross; and the Veteran's Memorial stadium for A. C. "Butch" Lambert Sr., the legendary football and basketball referee in the segregated Southeastern Athletic Conference. *Mississippi House Journal*, HB 187, 1987; *Mississippi House Journal*, HB 855, and HB 1225, 1988; *Mississippi House Journal*, HB 147, 1991; *Mississippi House Journal*, HB 324, 1985.

112. *Mississippi House Journal*, HB 535 and 536, 1993.

113. *Mississippi House Journal*, HB 787, 1980; HB 219 and HB 649, 1992; and HB 1211, 1989.

114. *Mississippi House Journal*, HB 885, 1986; Feig, *The State Legislature*, 125–127. It is of note that while the House support for this measure began in 1986, it twice went down to defeat in the Senate before final passage in 1988.

115. *Mississippi Business Journal*, April 26, 2004, reviewed at http://goliath.ecnext.com/coms2/gi_0199–89634/Private-biz-not-state-ought.html (accessed September 20, 2013).

116. Leases for "Sixteenth (16th) Section" land, held in trust by the state for support of local public education. www.sos.state.ms.us/PublicLands/16th/16l_faq.asp (accessed September 20, 2013).

117. *Mississippi House Journal*, HB 404, 1981. He also proposed HB 683 in 1984 to open up lands controlled by levee boards, especially important in towns in his district that bordered the Mississippi River. *Mississippi House Journal*, HB 264, 1989.

118. Richard Sher, *Politics in the New South: Republicanism, Race and Leadership in the Twentieth Century*, 2nd ed. (Armonk, NY: M. E. Sharpe, 1997), 325; Earl Black, *Southern Governors and Civil Rights: Racial Segregation as a Campaign Issue in the Second Reconstruction* (Cambridge, MA: Harvard University Press, 1976), 145–183.

119. *Mississippi House Journal*, HB 1080, 1980.

120. *Mississippi House Journal*, HB 1172, 1983.

121. *Mississippi House Journal*, HB 859, 1983.

122. Black, *Southern Governors*, 145–160.

123. Ibid., 165.

124. Jack Bass and Walter De Vries, *The Transformation of Southern Politics: Social Change and Political Consequence Since 1945* (Athens: University of Georgia Press, 1995), 211–213; Waller, *Straight Ahead*, 136–137.

125. Christopher Lehman, "Mississippi's Incredible Month: The Demise of the Sovereignty Commission and of Unprofessional Leadership at the Mississippi State Penitentiary, " *Journal of Mississippi History* (1973): 1–20.

126. Bass and de Vries, *The Transformation of Southern Politics*, 215; Chris Danielson, *After Freedom Summers: How Race Realigned Politics, 1965–1986* (Gainesville: University of Florida Press, 2011), 89–96.

127. Jere Nash and Andy Taggart, *Mississippi Politics: The Struggle for Power, 1976–2006* (Jackson: University Press of Mississippi, 2006), 151–162, 186–199.

128. The full bill "mandated statewide kindergartens, created a new reading aide program by placing teaching assistants in the first three grades of elementary schools, enacted a compulsory attendance law, provided teacher pay raises, created the initial accreditation system for public schools, established powers and responsibilities of the new Board of Education,

created a training program for school administrators . . ." Nash and Taggart, *Mississippi Politics*, 144–145.

129. Candidate Allain was the victim of a scurrilous attack from some GOP party activists on the eve of the election. They leveled a charge, later discredited, that Allain patronized black male prostitutes. Ibid., 152–159.

130. *Alexander v. State of Mississippi by and through Allain*, 441 So. 2nd 1329 (Miss. 1983).

131. "Governor Allain's key proposals," January 26, 1984, Box 41, F 763 (Aaron Henry Papers, TC) ; Nash and Taggart, *Mississippi Politics*, 163–167.

132. Sher, *Politics in the New South*, 118–159.

133. Gokhan Karahan, Laura Razzolini, and William F. Shughart II, May 2003, "No Pretense to Honesty: County Government Corruption in Mississippi," http://www.olemiss.edu/depts/economics/Pretense.pdf (accessed May 30, 2008); Nash and Taggart, *Mississippi Politics*, 196–197.

134. "The Yuppies of Mississippi," February 28, 1988, *New York Times*, http://query.nytimes.com (accessed May 29, 2008).

135. Nash and Taggart, *Mississippi Politics*, 196; Danielson, *After Freedom Summer*, 217–218.

136. Karahan et al., "No Pretense to Honesty."

137. Ronald Keith Gaddie, "Realignment," in *The Oxford Handbook of Southern Politics*, 289–313.

138. Kevin Sack, "An Underdog Democrat is Gaining in Mississippi," *New York Times*, November 4, 1995. The reference about compensatory funding refers to the Ayers case in which the Supreme Court determined that the state had systematically underfunded the historically black colleges and universities. *Ayers v. Fordice* (1997). As a result the court required that the state invest $500 million in these institutions to compensate for the differential impact the discrimination had on their growth and development. A settlement was reached in *Jake Ayers, et al. v. Ronnie Musgrove, Governor, State of Mississippi et al.*, Civil Action number 4:75CV9-B-D. U.S. District Court for the Northern District, Greenville Division. http://www.ihl.state.ms.us/ayers/downloads/settlement_agreement_ayers.pdf (accessed September 24, 2013).

139. Danielson, *After Freedom Summer*, 220.

140. Morrison, *Black Political Mobilization*; Danielson, *After Freedom Summer*, 151–154; Parker, *Black Votes Count*, 151–166.

141. Letter from Morris Kinsey, Chair Education Committee, to Aaron Henry, June 21 1982, Box 65, F 1126 (Aaron Henry Papers, TC).

142. At the time terms were for one year. Later and after Henry's resignation, terms were increased to two-year terms. Interview with Bea Branch, who was elected president of the state chapter of the NAACP in 1993 to succeed Henry. Bea Branch, interview with the author, August 6, 1998, Jackson, Mississippi.

143. *Clarion Ledger*, June 6, 1985, "Aaron Henry vertical file, 1923–1997," Special Collections Department, Mitchell Memorial Library, Mississippi State University (MSUSC).

144. *Clarion Ledger*, November 5, 1993, Ibid.

145. *Clarion-Ledger*, May 20, 1997. Thompson had risen from mayor of the small town of Bolton. Cf. Morrison, *Black Political Mobilization*, 58–95.

146. *Jackson Daily News*, May 7, 1984, 6c. Thompson was later elected to the U.S.

Congress (1993) representing the Delta district that Henry had been helping blacks to contest since 1960. Morrison and Middleton, "African Americans in Office," 278–279.

147. *Mississippi House Journal*, Biographical Data, House of Representatives, 1999, 1562.

148. *Mississippi Official and Statistical Register*, 1992–1996. Secretary of State, Jackson, 1993, 540.

149. *Commercial Appeal*, May 19, 1997, B-1.

150. Ibid.; *Clarksdale Press Register*, May 24, 1997, 1.

151. Louise Bradford, interview with the author.

Bibliography

Primary Sources

MANUSCRIPT COLLECTIONS

Austin, Texas

Lyndon Baines Johnson Library Oral History Collection. Austin, TX.
T. H. Baker. September 12, 1970. Interview with Aaron Henry. Clarksdale, MS.

Chapel Hill, North Carolina, University of North Carolina at Chapel Hill

Allard Lowenstein Papers, Southern Historical Collection, Wilson Library.
Rauh, Joseph. August 1964. Brief Submitted by the Mississippi Freedom Democratic
  Party.

Hattiesburg, Mississippi, University of Southern Mississippi

Mississippi Oral History Archive.

Madison, Wisconsin, State Historical Society of Wisconsin

Amzie Moore Papers.
Harry Bowie Papers.
Freedom Information Service Papers.
Jo Ann Robinson Papers.
Samuel Walker Papers.
SNCC Papers Microfilm.

Jackson, Mississippi, Mississippi Department of Archives and History

Sovereignty Commission Papers.
Tougaloo, Mississippi, Tougaloo College, Benbow Civil Rights Collection.

Starkville, Mississippi, Mississippi State University

Special Collections Department. Mitchell Memorial Library.
Aaron Henry Vertical Files.
Clay County Civil Rights Material.
Delta Ministry Papers.
Hodding Carter Papers.
Patricia Derian Papers.
Wilson F. Minor Papers.

New Orleans, Louisiana , Xavier University

Xavier University Archives.

New York City, New York, Columbia University

Allard Lowenstein Oral History Project, Oral History Research Office.

"The Reminiscences of Edwin King." Taken by William Chafe of Duke University. March 10 and October 30, 1988, Washington, DC, and Miami Beach, Florida.

Tougaloo, Mississippi, Tougaloo College Benbow Civil Rights Collection

Aaron Henry Papers.
Edwin King Papers.
Jane Schutt Papers.

Washington, DC.

NAACP Papers. Library of Congress.

Detroit, Michigan, Wayne State University

Archives of Labor History and Urban Affairs. Walter Reuther Library.

St Louis, Missouri, National Archives

National Archives and Records Administration. Military Personnel Records Center.

Middletown, Connecticut, Wesleyan University

Collection of Legal Change. Civil Rights Litigation Records of the 1960s.

PUBLISHED PRIMARY WORKS

Aptheker, Herbert, ed. *Selections from the Crisis*, vol. 1. Millbank, NY: Kraus-Thomson, 1983.
Bates, Daisy. *The Long Shadow of Little Rock: A Memoir*. New York: David McKay, 1962.
Belafonte, Harry. *My Song: A Memoir*. New York: Knopf, 2011.
Cohn, David. *Where I Was Born and Raised*. Notre Dame, IN: University of Notre Dame Press, 1967.
Commission on Civil Rights, U.S. (CRC a-b). *Hearing Before the United States Commission on Civil Rights*, vols. 1 (Voting) and 2 (Administration of Justice). Jackson, Mississippi. Washington, DC: Government Printing Office, 1965.
Commission on Civil Rights, U.S. (CRC). *Voting in Mississippi*. Washington, DC: Government Printing Office, 1965.
Douglass, Frederick. *The Narrative and Selected Writings*. Edited by Michael Meyer. New York: Modern Library (Random House), 1984.
Evers, Charles, and Andrew Szanton. *Have No Fear: The Charles Evers Story*. New York: John Wiley and Sons, 1997.
Evers, Mrs. Medgar. *For Us the Living*. With William Peters. New York: Doubleday, 1967.
Greene, Lorenzo, and Arvarh Strickland. *Working with Carter G. Woodson, the Father of Black History: A Diary, 1928–1930*. Baton Rouge: Louisiana State University Press, 1989.
Gregory, Dick. *Callus on My Soul: A Memoir*. New York: Kensington Press, 2003.
Handy, W. C. *W. C. Handy, Father of the Blues: An Autobiography*. New York: Da Capo Press, 1989 (1941).
Henry, Aaron. *Aaron Henry: The Fire Ever Burning*. With Constance Curry. Jackson: University Press of Mississippi, 2000.
Hudson, Winson. *Mississippi Harmony: Memoirs of a Freedom Fighter*. New York: Palgrave Macmillan, 2002.
Joint Center for Political Studies. *National Roster of Black Elected Officials*. Washington, DC: JCPS, 1981.

Lynch, John. *The Facts of Reconstruction.* Indianapolis: Bobbs-Merrill, 1970.

Lewis, John. *Walking with the Wind: A Memoir of the Movement.* San Diego: Harcourt Brace and Company, 1998.

Mississippi, State of. *Mississippi Official and Statistical Record, 1992–1996* (MS Statistical Record). Jackson: State of Mississippi, 1993.

Neale, Thomas. "The Eighteen Year Old Vote: The Twenty-sixth Amendment and Subsequent Voting Rates of Newly Enfranchised Age Groups." Library of Congress. Congressional Research Service, 1983.

Percy, William A. *Lanterns on the Levee: Reminiscences of a Planter's Son.* New York: Alfred Knopf, 1941.

Sellers, Cleveland. *The River of No Return: The Autobiography of a Black Militant.* New York: Harcourt, Brace and World, 1973.

Silver, James. *Mississippi: The Closed Society*, 3rd ed. New York: Harcourt, Brace and World, 1966.

Sutherland, Elizabeth, ed. *Letters from Mississippi.* New York: McGraw-Hill, 1965.

Waller, Bill. *Straight Ahead: Memoirs of a Mississippi Governor.* Brandon, MS: Quail Ridge, 2007.

White, Walter. *A Man Called White: The Autobiography of Walter White.* New York: Viking Press, 1948.

PERSONAL INTERVIEWS

Banks, Fred. Interview with the author, January 21, 1998, Jackson, Mississippi.

Bolden, R. L. Interview with the author, January 31, 1998, Jackson, Mississippi.

Bradford, Louise. Interview with the author, March 12, 1998, Clarksdale, Mississippi.

Branch, Bea. Interview with the author, August 6, 1998, Jackson, Mississippi.

Brown, John. Interview with the author, July 9, 2004, Clarksdale, Mississippi.

Carr, Andrew. Interview with the author, March 9, 1998, Clarksdale, Mississippi.

Gooden, Bennie. Interview with the author, November 19, 1997, Clarksdale, Mississippi.

Green, Tomie. Interview with the author, January 20, 1998, Jackson, Mississippi.

Harris, Jonathan. Interview with the author, November 19, 1997, Clarksdale, Mississippi.

Henry, Rebecca. Interview with the author, November 18, 1997, Clarksdale, Mississippi.

Hill, Charles. Interview with the author, January 28, 1998, Clarksdale, Mississippi.

Jones-Taylor, Aurelia. Interview with the author, March 12, 1998, Jackson, Mississippi.

King, Edwin. Interview with the author, January 30, 1998, Jackson, Mississippi.

Ladner, Joyce. Interview with the author, July 31, 1998, Washington, DC.

Luckett, Brenda. Interview with the author, March 11, 1998, Clarksdale, Mississippi.

McLemore, Leslie. Interview with the author, February 6, 1999, Jackson, Mississippi.

Moses, Robert. Interview with the author, March 5, 1998, Jackson, Mississippi.

Winter, William. Interview with the author, May 13, 1998, Jackson, Mississippi.

Young, Charles. Interview with the author, January 21, 1996, Jackson, Mississippi.

NEWSPAPERS AND PERIODICALS

Chicago Tribune
Clarksdale Press Register
Commercial Appeal
Jackson Advocate

Jackson Clarion-Ledger
Jackson Daily News
Lexington Advertiser
Mississippi Free Press
New York Times
Times-Picayune
Washington Post

Court Cases

Alexander v. State of Mississippi by and through Allain. 441 So. 2nd 1329, Miss. (1983).

Baker v. Carr. 369 U.S. 186 (1962).

Jeremiah Blackwell, Jr., et al., v. Issaquena County Board of Education, et al. 363 F2.d 749, 5th Cir. (1966).

Boynton v. Commonwealth of Virginia. 364 U.S. 454 (1960).

Brooks v. Winter. 461 U.S. 921 (1983), 604 F Supp. 807, N.D. Miss. (1984).

Brown v. Board of Education of Topeka. 347 U.S. 483 (1954), 349 U.S. 294 (1955).

John E. Cameron v. Paul B. Johnson. 244 F. Supp. 846. 846–856. SD-Hattiesburg. July 10, 1964, July 11, 1964 (1964).

Chambers v. Florida. 309 U.S. 227, 241 (1940).

City of Clarksdale, Mississippi v. Marie Gertge. 237 F. Supp. 213. U.S. Dist. (1964).

Benford Collins v. Aaron Henry. # 5725, Apr 25, 1962. 121: Docket #21:p 74. Mississippi Circuit Court, District 11 (1962).

Connor v. Finch. 431 U.S. 407 (1977.)

Connor v. Johnson. 256 F. Supp. 962 (1966.)

Evers v. Jackson Municipal Separate School District. 328 F.2d 408 (1964).

Gates v. Collier. 349 Fed. Supp. 881 N. D. Miss. (1972).

Gates v. Collier. 501 F.2d 1291 (1972).

Gideon v. Wainwright. 372 US 335 (1963).

Gomillion v. Lightfoot. 364 U.S. 339 (1960).

Victoria Gray et al. v. Paul B. Johnson. 234 F. Supp. 743. 743–746. SD-Jackson Division (October 20, 1964).

Victoria Gray et al. v. State of Mississippi. 233 F. Supp. 139. 139–142. Civil A # GC 6437. ND. Greenville (August 24, 1964).

Guinn v. United States. 238 U.S. 347 (1915).

H. Y. Hackett and Rev. J. D. Rayford v. Mayor W. S. Kincade. 36 F.R.D. 442; U.S. Dist. LEXIS 9870. 2 (1964).

Heart of Atlanta Motel v. United States. 379 U.S. 241 13 L. Ed. 2nd 258; 85 Sup. Ct. 348. (1964).

A. Henry v. Collins, and Henry, A v. Pearson. 380 U.S. 356, 85 S. Ct. 992 (1965).

R. Henry v. Clarksdale Municipal Separate School District. 5th circuit. 480 F.2d 583 (1973).

Rebecca E. Henry et al. v. The Clarksdale Municipal Separate School District et al. 409 F.2d 682; U.S. App. (1969).

Henry v. Pearson. No 42758. 253 Miss. 62. 158 2d 695 (1963).

Henry v. Pearson. 380 U.S. 356. 85. S. Ct. 992. 13 L. Ed. 892 (1963).

Henry v. State. No 42652. 253 Miss. 263; 154 So. 2d 289 (1963).

Henry v. Mississippi. 379 U.S. 443. 85 S. Ct. 564. L. Ed. 2d. 408 (1965).

Cora Hicks v. Bond Cafe. U.S. District, NOR, Reel 151 (1965).

Interstate Commerce Commission v. City of Jackson, Mississippi, et al. 206 F. Supp. 45. 45–50. SD, Jackson Division (April 26, 1962).

Jordan v. Winter. F. Supp. 1135, N.D. Miss. (1982).

Katzenbach v. Gulf State Theatres, Inc. 256 F. Supp. 549. 549–558. # GC6450, ND, Greenville (1966).

Katzenbach v. McClung. 379 U.S. 294 (1964).

Willie King v. City of Clarksdale. No. 44042. Supreme Court of Mississippi. 186 So. 2d. 228, Miss. (1966).

Loewen v. Turnipseed. 488 F. Supp. 1138, N.D. Miss. (1980).

Mapp v. Ohio. 367 U.S. 643 (1961).

Miranda v. Arizona. 483 U.S. 436 (1966).

Mississippi Division of the United Sons of Confederate Veterans v. Mississippi State Conference of NAACP Branches, et al. 774 So.2d 388, MS (2000).

Mississippi Republican Executive Committee v. Brooks. 469 U.S. 1002 (1984).

Missouri ex rel Gaines v. Canada. 305 U.S. 337 (1938).

Mitchell v. United States. 313 U.S. 80 (1941).

Morgan v. Virginia. 328 U.S. 373 (1946).

National Association for the Advancement of Colored People v. Alabama. 357 U.S. 449 (1958).

T. Pearson v. A. Henry, #5724, April 25, 1962, 120: Docket #21: p 73 (1962).

Plessy v. Ferguson. 163 U.S. 537 (1896).

Reynolds v. Sims. 377 U.S. 533 (1964).

Riddell v. National Democratic Party. 344 F. Supp. 908, S.D. Miss. (1972). Rec'd 508 F.2d 770, 5th Cir. (1975).

Smith v. Allwright. 321 U.S. 649 (1944).

South Carolina v. Katzenbach. 383 U.S. 301 (1966).

Stewart v. Waller. 404. F. Supp. 206, N.D. Miss. (1975).

Sweatt v. Painter. 339 U.S. 629 (1950).

Terry v. Adams. 345 U.S. 461 (1953).

USA, Interstate Commerce Commission v. City of Jackson, MS, et al. 206 F. Supp. 45 (1962) 45–50; S.D., Jackson Division (April 26, 1962).

United States v. Cox. Civil no. D-C–53–61, N.D. Miss. (1964).

United States v. Duke. 332 F. 2nd 759, 760. 5th Cir. (1964).

United States v. Ross Barnett and Paul B. Johnson, Jr. 330 F.2d 369. 5th Cir. (1963).

Wesberry v. Sanders. 376 U.S. 1 (1964).

Clifton Whitley et al. v. Paul B. Johnson. 270 F Supp 630. 630–631 (1966).

Secondary Sources

BOOKS

Anderson, Carol. *Eyes Off the Prize: The United Nations and the African American Struggle for Human Rights, 1944–1955.* New York: Cambridge University Press, 2003.

Anderson, Kevin. *Agitations: Ideologies and Strategies in African American Politics.* Fayetteville: University of Arkansas Press, 2010.

Andrew, Rod. *Long Gray Lines: The Southern Military Tradition.* Chapel Hill: University of North Carolina Press, 2001.

Andrews, Kenneth. *Freedom Is a Constant Struggle: The Mississippi Civil Rights Movement and Its Legacy*. Chicago: University of Chicago Press, 2004.

Arsenault, Raymond. *Freedom Riders: 1961 and the Struggle for Racial Justice*. New York: Oxford University Press, 2006.

Asante, Molefi, and Mark Mattson. *The Historical and Cultural Atlas of African Americans*. New York: Macmillan, 1992.

Asch, Chris. *The Senator and the Sharecropper: The Freedom Struggles of James O, Eastland and Fannie Lou Hamer*. New York: New Press, 2008.

Ashmore, Harry. *The Negro and the Schools*. Chapel Hill: University of North Carolina Press, 1954.

Austin, Sharon. *The Transformation of Plantation Politics: Black Politics, Concentrated Poverty, and Social Capital in the Mississippi Delta*. New York: SUNY Press, 2006.

Bailey, Harry, Jr., ed. *Negro Politics in America*. Columbus, OH: Charles Merrill, 1967.

Ball, Howard. *Murder in Mississippi: United States v. Price and the Struggle for Civil Rights*. Lawrence: University Press of Kansas, 2004.

Ballard, Allen. *The Education of Black Folk: The Afro-American Struggle for Knowledge in White America*. New York: Harper and Row, 1973.

Barry, John M. *Rising Tide: The Great Mississippi Flood of 1927 and How It Changed America*. New York: Simon and Schuster, 1997.

Bass, Jack, and Walter De Vries. *The Transformation of Southern Politics: Social Change and Political Consequence Since 1945*. Athens: University of Georgia Press, 1995.

Beito, David T. *From Mutual Aid to the Welfare State: Fraternal Societies and Social Services, 1890–1967*. Chapel Hill: University of North Carolina Press, 2000.

Beito, David, and Linda Royster Beito. *Black Maverick: T. R. M. Howard's Fight for Civil Rights and Economic Power*. Urbana: University of Illinois Press, 2009.

Belfrage, Sally. *Freedom Summer*. New York: Viking, 1965.

Bettersworth, John K. *Confederate Mississippi*. Baton Rouge: Louisiana State University Press, 1943.

Bettersworth, John K. *Mississippi: A History*. Austin: Steck-Vaughn Co., 1959.

Black, Earl. *Southern Governors and Civil Rights: Racial Segregation as a Campaign Issue in the Second Reconstruction*. Cambridge, MA: Harvard University Press, 1976.

Black, Earl, and Merle Black. *Politics and Society in the South*. Cambridge, MA: Harvard University Press, 1987.

Blackwelder, Julia Kirk. *Styling Jim Crow: African American Beauty Training during Segregation*. College Station: Texas A & M University Press, 2003.

Blaustein, Albert, and Robert Zangrando, eds. *Civil Rights and the Black American: A Documentary History*. New York: Clarion, 1968.

Bolton, Charles. *The Hardest Deal of All: The Battle over School Integration in Mississippi, 1870–1980*. Jackson: University Press of Mississippi, 2005.

Bond, Horace Mann. *The Education of the Negro in the American Social Order*. New York: Prentice-Hall, 1934.

Bond, Horace Mann. *Negro Education in Alabama: A Study in Cotton and Steel*. New York: Atheneum, 1969.

Bracey, John, Jr., et al. *Black Nationalism in America*. Indianapolis: Bobbs-Merrill, 1970.

Brandfon, Robert. *Cotton Kingdom of the South: A History of the Yazoo Mississippi Delta from Reconstruction to the Twentieth Century*. Cambridge, MA: Harvard University Press, 1967.

Brieger, James. *Hometown, Mississippi*. Jackson, MS: Town Square Books, 1997.

Broderick, Francis, and August Meier, eds. *Negro Protest in the Twentieth Century*. Indianapolis: Bobbs-Merrill Company, 1966.

Browning, Rufus, et al. *Racial Politics in American Cities*. 2nd ed. New York: Longman, 1990.

Bullock, Charles, III, and Mark Rozell, eds. *The Oxford Handbook of Southern Politics*, New York: Oxford University Press, 2012.

Bullock, Henry. *A History of Negro Education in the South from 1916 to the Present*. Cambridge, MA: Harvard University Press, 1967.

Bundles, A'Lelia. *On Her Own Ground: The Life and Times of Madame C. J. Walker*. New York: Washington Square Press, 2002.

Burner, Eric. *And Gently He Shall Lead Them: Robert Parris Moses and Civil Rights in Mississippi*. New York: New York University Press, 1994.

Burnim, Mellonee, and Portia Maultsby, eds. *African American Music, an Introduction*. New York: Routledge, 2005.

Cagin, Seth, and Philip Dray. *We Are Not Afraid: The Story of Goodman, Schwerner, and Chaney and the Civil Rights Campaign for Mississippi*. New York: Macmillan, 1998.

Campbell, Will. *Robert Clark's Journey to the House: A Black Politician's Story*. Jackson: University Press of Mississippi, 2003.

Carmichael, Stokely, and Charles Hamilton. *Black Power: The Politics of Liberation in America*. New York: Vintage, 1967.

Carson, Clayborne. *In Struggle: SNCC and the Black Awakening of the 1960s*. Cambridge, MA: Harvard University Press, 1981.

Carson, Clayborne, ed. *The Student Voice, 1960–1965: Periodical of the Student Nonviolent Coordinating Committee*. Westport, CT: Meckler, 1990.

Cell, John. *The Highest Stage of White Supremacy: The Origins of Segregation in South Africa and the American South*. Cambridge: Cambridge University Press, 1982.

Chafe, William. *Never Stop Running: Allard Lowenstein and the Struggle to Save American Liberalism*. New York: Basic Books, 1993.

Chapman, Abraham, ed. *Black Voices: An Anthology of African American Literature*. New York: New American Library, 1968.

Chappell, David. *A Stone of Hope: Prophetic Religion and the Death of Jim Crow*. Chapel Hill: University of North Carolina Press, 2004.

Classen, Steven. *Watching Jim Crow: The Struggles over Mississippi TV, 1955–1969*. Durham, NC: Duke University Press Books, 2004.

Cobb, James C. *The Most Southern Place on Earth*. New York: Oxford University Press, 1992.

Coleman, Mary DeLorse. *Legislators, Law and Public Policy: Political Change in Mississippi and the South*. Westport, CT: Greenwood, 1993.

Collins, Patricia Hill. *Black Feminist Thought: Knowledge, Consciousness, and the Politics of Empowerment*. 2nd ed. New York: Routledge, 2000.

Coody, A. S. *Biographical Sketches of James Kimble Vardaman*. Jackson, MS: A. S. Coody Publishers, 1992.

Cronon, E. David. *Black Moses: Marcus Garvey and the United Negro Improvement Association*. Madison: University of Wisconsin Press, 1955.

Crosby, Emilye. *A Little Taste of Freedom: The Black Freedom Struggle in Claiborne County, Mississippi*. Chapel Hill: University of North Carolina Press, 2005.

Curry, Constance. *Silver Rights*. New York: Algonquin Books of Chapel Hill, 1995.

Dallek, Robert. *An Unfinished Life: John Kennedy, 1917–1963*. Boston: Little, Brown and Company, 2003.

Danielson, Chris. *After Freedom Summers: How Race Realigned Politics, 1965–1986*. Gainesville: University of Florida Press, 2011.

Dattel, Gene. *Cotton and Race in the Making of America: The Human Cost of Economic Power*. Lanham, MD: Ivan Dee Publishers, 2009.

Davis, Allison, et al. *Deep South: An Anthropological Study of Caste and Class*. Chicago: University of Chicago Press, 1941.

Davis, Townsend. *Weary Feet, Rested Souls: A Guided History of the Civil Rights Movement*. New York: Norton, 1998.

Dittmer, John. *Local People: The Struggle for Civil Rights in Mississippi*. Urbana: University of Illinois Press, 1994.

Dittmer, John. *The Good Doctors: The Medical Committee for Human Rights and the Struggle for Social Justice in Health Care*. New York: Bloomsbury Press, 2009.

Dollard, John. *Caste and Class in a Southern Town*. New Haven, CT: Yale University Press, 1937.

Du Bois, William E. B. 1964. *Black Reconstruction in America*. New York: Meridian of the World Publishing Company.

Durham, Michael. *Powerful Days: The Civil Rights Photography of Charles Moore*. New York: Stewart, Tabori and Chang, 1991.

Edelman, Murray. *The Symbolic Uses of Politics*. Urbana: University of Illinois Press, 1964.

Edelman, Murray. *Politics as Symbolic Action: Mass Arousal and Quiescence*. Chicago: Markham, 1971.

Embree, Edwin. *Julius Rosenwald Fund: Review of Two Decades, 1917–1936*. Chicago: University of Chicago Press, 1936.

Embree, Robert, and Julia Waxman. *Investment in People*. New York: Harper and Brothers, 1929.

Erenreich, Susan, ed. *Freedom Is a Constant Struggle: An Anthology of the Mississippi Civil Rights Movement*. Montgomery, AL: Black Belt Press, 1999.

Fairclough, Adam. *To Redeem the Soul of America: The Southern Christian Leadership Convention and Martin Luther King, Jr.* Atlanta: University of Georgia Press, 1987.

Ferris, William. *Blues from the Delta*. New York: Da Capo, 1978.

Fleishman, Harry. *Norman Thomas: A Biography, 1884–1968* New York: Norton and Company, 1969

Foner, Eric. *A Short History of Reconstruction, 1863–1877*. New York: Harper and Row, 1990.

Forman, James. *The Making of Black Revolutionaries*. Washington, DC: Open Hand, 1985.

Foster, Julian, and Durward Long, eds. *Protest! Student Activism in America*. New York: William Morrow & Co., 1979.

Franklin, John Hope. *Reconstruction after the Civil War*. Chicago: University of Chicago Press, 1961.

Franklin, John Hope, and Alfred Moss Jr. *From Slavery to Freedom: A History of African Americans,* 7th ed. New York: McGraw-Hill, 1994.

Garner, John. *Reconstruction in Mississippi*. Baton Rouge: Louisiana State University Press, 1968.

Garrow, David. *Bearing the Cross: Martin Luther King, Jr., and the Southern Christian Leadership Conference*. New York: William Morrow and Co., 1986.

Genovese, Eugene. *The Political Economy of Slavery*. New York: Pantheon, 1967.

George, Carol. *Segregated Sabbaths: Richard Allen and the Rise of Independent Black Churches, 1770–1840*. New York: Oxford University Press, 1973.

Gillette, Michael. *Launching the War on Poverty*. New York: Twayne, 1996.

Gitlin, Todd. *The Sixties: Years of Hope, Days of Rage*. New York: Bantam, 1987.

Gosnell, Harold. *Negro Politicians: The Rise of Negro Politics in Chicago*. Chicago: University of Chicago Press, 1967 (1935).

Graham, Davis. *The Uncertain Triumph. Federal Education Policy in the Kennedy and Johnson Years*. Chapel Hill: University of North Carolina Press, 1984.

Greene, Lorenzo, and Arvarh Strickland. *Working with Carter G. Woodson, the Father of Black History: A Diary, 1928–1930*. Baton Rouge: Louisiana State University Press, 1989.

Halsell, Grace. *Evers*. New York: World Publishing Company, 1971.

Hamilton, Charles. *The Black Preacher in America*. New York: William Morrow, 1972.

Hamilton, Charles. *The Bench and the Ballot: Southern Federal Judges and Black Voters*. New York: Oxford University Press, 1973.

Hamilton, Charles V. *Adam Clayton Powell, Jr.: The Political Biography of an American Dilemma*. New York: Atheneum, 1992.

Hamlin, Francoise. *Crossroads at Clarksdale: Freedom Struggle in the Mississippi Delta after World War II*. Chapel Hill: University of North Carolina Press, 2012.

Hampton, Henry, and Steve Fayer. *Voices of Freedom: An Oral History of the Civil Rights Movement from the 1950s through the 1980s*. New York: Bantam, 1990.

Harlan, Louis R. *Separate and Unequal: Public School Campaigns and Racism in the Southern Seaboard States, 1901–1915*. Chapel Hill: University of North Carolina Press, 1958.

Harlan, Louis R. *Booker T. Washington: The Making of a Black Leader, 1856–1901*. New York: Oxford University Press, 1972.

Harlan, Louis R. *Booker T. Washington: The Wizard of Tuskegee, 1901–1915*. New York: Oxford University Press, 1983.

Harris, Fredrick. *Something Within: Religion in African American Political Activism*. New York: Oxford University Press, 1999.

Harris-Lacewell, Melissa. *Barbershops, Bibles, and BET: Everyday Talk and Black Political Thought*. Princeton, NJ: Princeton University Press, 2004.

Harris, William. *The Day of the Carpetbagger in Mississippi: Republican Reconstruction in Mississippi*. Baton Rouge: Louisiana State University Press, 1971.

Harriss, C. Lowell. *History and Policies of the Home Owners' Loan Corporation*. New York: National Bureau of Economic Research, 1951.

Havard, William. *The Changing Politics of the South*. Baton Rouge: Louisiana State University Press, 1972.

Haynie, Kerry. *African American Legislators in the American States*. New York: Columbia University Press, 2001.

Hermann, Janet Sharp. *The Pursuit of a Dream*. New York: Vintage, 1983.

Hine, Darlene Clark. *The Rise and Fall of the White Primary in Texas*. Millwood, NY: KTO Press, 1979.

Holt, Len. *The Summer That Didn't End: The Story of the Mississippi Civil Rights Project of 1964*. New York: Da Capo Press, 1992.

Howard, John. *Men Like That: A Southern Queer History*. Chicago: University of Chicago Press, 1999.

Hugh Greenberg, Polly. *The Devil Has Slippery Shoes: A Biased Biography of the Child Development Group of Mississippi.* London: Macmillan, 1969.

Huie, Bradford. *Three Lives for Mississippi.* Jackson: University Press of Mississippi, 2000.

Jackson, Donald H., Jr. *A Chief Lieutenant of the Tuskegee Machine: Charles Banks of Mississippi.* Gainesville: University Press of Florida, 2002.

Jaynes, Gerald, and Robin Williams Jr. *A Common Destiny: Blacks and American Society.* Washington, DC: National Academy Press, 1989.

Katagiri, Yasuhiro. *The Mississippi State Sovereignty Commission: Civil Rights and States' Rights.* Jackson: University Press of Mississippi, 2001.

Key, V. O., Jr. *Southern Politics.* New York: Knopf, 1949.

King-Meadows, Tyson, and Thomas Schaller. *Devolution and Black State Legislators: Challenges and Choices in the Twenty-First Century.* Albany: SUNY Press, 2006.

Kirwin, Albert. *Revolt of the Rednecks: Mississippi Politics, 1876–1925.* Lexington: University of Kentucky Press, 1951.

Krider, Daniel. *Divided Arsenal: Race and the American State during World War II.* New York: Cambridge University Press, 2000.

Krueger, Thomas. *And Promises to Keep: The Southern Conference of Human Welfare, 1939–1948.* Nashville, TN: Vanderbilt University Press, 1967.

Kunstler, William. *Deep in My Heart.* New York: William Morrow and Co., 1966.

Ladd, Everett Carll, Jr. *Negro Political Leadership in the South.* Ithaca, NY: Cornell University Press, 1966.

Ladd, Everett Carll, Jr. *Transformations of the American Party System.* 2nd ed. With Charles Hadley. New York: Norton, 1978.

Lamis, Alexander P. *The Two-Party South.* New York: Oxford University Press, 1984.

Lane, Charles. *The Day Freedom Died.* New York: Henry Holt, 2009.

Lawson, Steven. *Black Ballots: Voting Rights in the South 1944–1969.* New York: Columbia University Press, 1967.

Lee, Chana. *For Freedom's Sake: The Life of Fannie Lou Hamer.* Urbana: University of Illinois Press, 1999.

Lee, Ulysses. *United States Army in World War II, Special Studies: The Employment of Negro Troops.* Washington, DC: United States Army, Office of the Chief of Military History, 1966.

Lemann, Nicholas. *The Promised Land: The Great Migration and How it Changed America.* New York: Vintage, 1992.

Lewis, David Levering. *W. E. B. Du Bois: Biography of a Race, 1868–1919.* New York: Henry Holt, 1993.

Lichtenstein, Nelson. *The Most Dangerous Man in Detroit: Walter Reuther and the Fate of American Labor.* New York: Basic Books, 1995.

Loewen, James, and Charles Sallis, eds. *Mississippi Conflict and Change.* New York: Pantheon Books, 1974.

Logan, Rayford. *The Betrayal of the Negro: From Rutherford Hayes to Woodrow Wilson.* New York: Collier Books, 1965.

Lomax, Alan. *The Land Where the Blues Began.* New York: Dell, 1993.

Marsh, Charles. *God's Long Summer: Stories of Faith and Civil Rights.* Princeton, NJ: Princeton University Press, 1997.

Marshall, James. *Student Activism and Civil Rights in Mississippi: Protest Politics and the Struggle for Racial Justice, 1960–1965.* Baton Rouge: Louisiana State University Press, 2013.

Mason, Gilbert. *Beaches, Blood, and Ballots: A Black Doctor's Civil Rights Struggle*. Jackson: University Press of Mississippi, 2000.

Matthews, Donald, and James Prothro. *Negroes and the New Southern Politics*. New York: Harcourt, Brace and World, 1966.

McAdam, Doug. *Freedom Summer*. New York: Oxford University Press, 1988.

McLemore, Richard, ed. *A History of Mississippi*. Vol. II. Hattiesburg: University and College Press of Mississippi, 1973.

McMillen, Neil. *Dark Journey: Mississippians in the Age of Jim Crow*. Urbana: University of Illinois Press, 1990.

McMillen, Neil. *The Citizens' Council: Organized Resistance to the Second Reconstruction, 1954–1964*. Urbana: University of Illinois Press, 1994.

McMillen, Neil, ed. *Remaking Dixie: The Impact of World War II on the American South*. Jackson: University Press of Mississippi, 1997.

Meier, August, and Elliott Rudwick. *CORE: A Study in the Civil Rights Movement, 1946–1968*. Urbana: University of Illinois Press, 1975.

Meredith, James. *Three Years in Mississippi*. Bloomington: Indiana University Press, 1966.

Mills, Kay. *Changing Channels: The Civil Rights Case That Transformed Television*. Jackson: University Press of Mississippi, 2004.

Morris, Aldon. *The Origins of the Civil Rights Movement: Black Communities Organizing for Change*. New York: Free Press, 1984.

Morrison, Minion K. C. *Black Political Mobilization: Leadership, Power and Mass Behavior*. Albany: SUNY Press, 1987.

Morrison, Minion K. C., ed. *African Americans and Political Participation: A Reference Handbook*. Santa Barbara, CA: ABC-CLIO, 2003.

Mosley, Donald, and D. C. Williams Jr. *An Analysis and Evaluation of a Community Action Anti-Poverty Program in the Mississippi Delta*. State College: College of Business and Industry, Mississippi State University, 1967.

Namorato, Michael. *The Catholic Church in Mississippi, 1911–1984: A History*. Westport, CT: Greenwood Press, 1998.

Nash, Jere, and Andy Taggart. *Mississippi Politics: The Struggle for Power, 1976–2006*. Jackson: University Press of Mississippi, 2006.

Nelson, William, Jr., and Philip Meranto. *Electing Black Mayors: Political Action in the Black Community*. Columbus: Ohio State University Press, 1977.

New Republic. *Thoughts of the Young Radicals*. New Jersey: Harrison Blaine and the New Republic, 1966.

Noble, Stuart Grayson. *Forty Years of Public Schools in Mississippi, with Special Reference to the Education of the Negro*. New York: Negro Universities Press, 1918.

Oberlander, Jonathan. *The Politics of Medicare*. Chicago: University of Chicago Press, 2003.

Oshinsky, David M. *Worse Than Slavery: Parchman Farm and the Ordeal of Jim Crow Justice*. New York: Free Press, 1996.

Osur, Alan. *Blacks in the Army Air Forces*. Washington, DC: Office of Air Force History, 1977.

Parker, Frank. *Black Votes Count: Political Empowerment in Mississippi After 1965*. Chapel Hill: University of North Carolina Press, 1990.

Payne, Charles. *I've Got the Light of Freedom: The Organizing Tradition and the Mississippi Freedom Struggle*. Berkeley: University of California Press, 1995.

Payne, Charles, and Adam Green, eds. *Time Longer Than Rope: A Century of African American Activism, 1850–1950*. New York: New York University Press, 2003.

Penick, Mary, ed. *The Invisible Soldier: The Experience of Black Soldiers in World War II*. Detroit: Wayne State University Press, 1975.

Pereyra, Lillian. *James Lusk Alcorn: Persistent Whig*. Baton Rouge: Louisiana State University Press, 1966.

Perry, Huey L. *Race, Politics, and Governance in the United States*. Gainesville: University Press of Florida, 1996.

Pfeffer, Paula. *A. Philip Randolph, Pioneer of the Civil Rights Movement*. Baton Rouge: Louisiana State University Press, 1990.

Pigee, Vera. *The Struggle of Struggles, Part I*. Detroit: Harpo, 1975.

Plummer, Brenda, ed. *Window on Freedom: Race, Civil Rights and Foreign Affairs, 1945–1988*. Chapel Hill: University of North Carolina Press, 2003.

Posey, Josephine. *Alcorn State University and the National Alumni Association*. Mount Pleasant, SC: Arcadia Publishing Company, 2000.

Powdermaker, Hortense. *After Freedom: A Cultural Study of the Deep South*. New York: Russell and Russell, 1968.

Prichard, Jo G., III. *Making Things Grow: The Story of Mississippi Chemical Corporation*. Jackson: University Press of Mississippi, 1998.

Preston, Michael, et al. *The New Black Politics: The Search for Political Power*. 2nd ed. New York: Longman Group, 1987.

Rivkin, Julie, and Michael Ryan, eds. *Literary Theory: An Anthology*. Oxford: Blackwell Publishing, 2004.

Salter, John, Jr. *Jackson, Mississippi: An American Chronicle of Struggle and Schism*. New York: Exposition Press, 1979.

Satcher, Buford. *Blacks in Mississippi Politics, 1870–1900*. Washington, DC: University Press of America, 1978.

Schattschneider, Elmer. *The Semi-Sovereign People: A Realist's View of Democracy in America*. New York: Holt, Rinehart and Winston, 1960.

Scott, James. *Weapons of the Weak: Everyday Forms of Peasant Resistance*. New Haven, CT: Yale University Press, 1985.

Sher, Richard. *Politics in the New South: Republicanism, Race and Leadership in the Twentieth Century*. 2nd ed. Armonk, NY: M. E. Sharpe, 1997.

Silver, James, Jr. *Mississippi in the Confederacy: As Seen in Retrospect*. Baton Rouge: Louisiana State University Press, 1961.

Silverman, Jerry. *Songs of Protest and Civil Rights*. New York: Chelsea House Publishers, 1992.

Singh, Robert. *The Congressional Black Caucus: Racial Politics in the U.S. Congress*. Thousand Oaks, CA: Sage Publications, 1998.

Skates, John Ray. *Mississippi: A Bicentennial History*. New York: Norton, 1979.

Smith, Frank E. *Congressman from Mississippi*. New York: Pantheon, 1964.

Smith, Kenneth, and Ira Zepp Jr. *Search for the Beloved Community: The Thinking of Martin Luther King, Jr*. Valley Forge, PA: Judson Press, 1974.

Stanley, Harold, and Richard Niemi. *Vital Statistics on American Politics, 1999–2000*. Washington, DC: CQ Press, 2000.

Suggs, Henry L., ed. *The Black Press in the Middle West, 1865–1985*. Westport, CT: Greenwood Press, 1996.

Swain, Carol. *Black Faces, Black Interests: The Representation of African Americans in Congress*. Cambridge, MA: Harvard University Press, 1993.

Sydnor, Charles. *Slavery in Mississippi*. New York: Appleton-Century, 1933.

Tarrow, Sidney. *Power in Movement*. New York: Cambridge University Press, 1994.

Tate, Katherine. *Black Faces in the Mirror: African Americans and Their Representatives in Congress*. Princeton, NJ: Princeton University Press, 2003.

Thompson, Julius E. *The Black Press in Mississippi, 1865–1985*. Gainesville: University Press of Florida, 1993.

Thompson, Julius E. *The Black Press in Mississippi, 1865–1985: A Directory*. West Cornwall, CT: Locust Hill Press, 1988.

Tooze, Sandra. *Muddy Waters: The Mojo Man*. Toronto: ECW Press, 1997.

Tushnet, Mark V. *Making Civil Rights Law: Thurgood Marshall and the Supreme Court, 1936–1961*. New York: Oxford University Press, 1994.

Twentieth Century. 2nd ed. Armonk, NY: M. E. Sharpe. 118–159.

Viorst, Milton. *Fire in the Streets*. New York: Simon and Schuster, 1979.

Walton, Hanes, Jr. *Black Political Parties: An Historical and Political Analysis*. New York: Free Press, 1972.

Walton, Hanes, Jr. *Black Republicans: The Politics of the Black and Tans*. Metuchen, NJ: Scarecrow Press, 1975.

Walton, Hanes, Jr., and Robert C. Smith. *American Politics and the African American Quest for Universal Freedom*. 3rd ed. New York: Longman Publishing Group, 2006.

Ward, Brian, ed. *Media, Culture and the Modern African American Freedom Struggle*. Gainesville: University Press of Florida, 2001.

Waskow, Arthur I. *From Race Riot to Sit-In, 1919 and the 1960s*. Garden City, NY: Doubleday and Co., 1966.

Watson, Denton. *Lion in the Lobby: Clarence Mitchell Jr.'s Struggle for the Passage of Civil Rights Laws*. New York: William Morrow and Co., 1990.

Watters, Pat, and Reese Cleghorn. *Climbing Jacob's Ladder: The Arrival of Negroes in Southern Politics*. New York: Harcourt, Brace and World, 1967.

Weinberg, Meyer. *A Chance to Learn: The History of Race and Education in the United States*. Cambridge, MA: Harvard University Press, 1977.

Weyl, Nathaniel, and William Marina. *American Statesmen on Slavery and the Negro*. New York: Arlington House, 1971.

Wharton, Vernon. *The Negro in Mississippi, 1865–1890*. New York: Harper Torchbook, 1965.

Whitby, Kenny. *The Color of Representation: Congressional Behavior and Black Interests*. Ann Arbor: University of Michigan Press, 1997.

White, Theodore. *The Making of the President, 1964*. New York: Atheneum, 1965.

Whitfield, Stephen. *A Death in the Delta: The Story of Emmett Till*. Baltimore: Johns Hopkins University Press, 1991.

Wiggins, David. *Glory Bound: Black Athletes in White America*. Syracuse, NY: Syracuse University Press, 1997.

Wilkie, Curtis. *Dixie: A Personal Odyssey through Events That Shaped the Modern South*. New York: Scribner, 2001.

Williams, Michael. *Medgar Evers: Mississippi Martyr*. Fayetteville: University of Arkansas Press, 2011.

Williamson, Joel. *A Rage for Order: Black-White Relations in the American South since Emancipation*. New York: Oxford University Press, 1986.

Willis, John C. *Forgotten Time: The Yazoo-Mississippi Delta after the Civil War*. Charlottesville: University of Virginia Press, 2000.

Wolff, Miles. *Sitting at the 5 and 10*, Revised and Expanded. Chicago: Elephant
   Paperbacks, Ivan Dee Publishers, 1990.
Woodard, C. Vann. *Tom Watson: Agrarian Rebel*. New York: Rinehart, 1955.
Zinn, Howard. *SNCC: The New Abolitionists*. New York: Beacon, 1964.

ARTICLES

Abney, F. Glenn. "Factors Related to Negro Voter Turnout in Mississippi." *Journal of
   Politics* 36, no. 4 (November 1974): 1057–1063.
Aiken, Charles. "Race as a Factor in Municipal Underbounding." *Annals of the Association
   of American Geographers* 77, no. 4 (December 1987): 564–579.
Bein, Robert. "Stained Flags: Public Symbols and Equal Protection." *Seton Hall Law
   Review* 28 (1998): 897–923.
Branton, Wiley. "To Register to Vote in Mississippi." *New South* 20, no. 2 (February 1965):
   10–15.
Bullock, Charles S, III. "The Election of Blacks in the South: Preconditions and
   Consequences." *American Journal of Political Science* 19, no. 4 (November 1975):
   727–739.
Cole, Rickey L., and Kimberly S. Adams. "Mississippi: An Emerging Democracy Creating
   a Culture of Civic Participation among Formerly Oppressed Peoples." *Nebula* 4, no. 3
   (September 2007): 341.
Cunnigen, Donald. "Black Radicals vs. White Southern Liberals: The Charter Battle for
   the Young Democratic Clubs of Mississippi." *Southern Studies* 10, no. 3–4 (September
   2003): 95–112.
Dunnaville, Clarence, Jr. "Fortieth Anniversary of the Lawyers' Committee for Civil
   Rights." *Virginia Lawyer* (June/July 2003).
Engstrom, Richard. "The Supreme Court and Equi-Populous Gerrymandering: A
   Remaining Obstacle in the Quest for Fair and Effective Representation." *Arizona
   State Law Journal* 2 (1976): 277–319.
Fessehatzion, Tekie, and Bichaka Fayissa. "Public Assistance and Job Search Behavior of the
   Rural Poor—Evidence from the Mississippi Delta." *Review of Black Political Economy*
   18, no. 3 (Winter 1990): 79–91.
Henderson, Gordon. "The New Republicans of Mississippi." *New South* 20, no. 6 (June
   1965): 3–7.
Hopper, Columbus. "The Impact of Litigation on Mississippi's Prison System." *Prison
   Journal* 65, no. 1 (Spring–Summer 1985): 61.
Joiner, Lottie. "A Matter of Justice." *Crisis Magazine* (July–August 2004): 35–41.
Karahan, Gökhan R., and William F. Shughart II. "Under Two Flags: Symbolic Voting in
   the State of Mississippi." *Public Choice* 118 (January 2004): 105–124.
Lehman, Christopher P. "Mississippi's Incredible Month: The Demise of the Sovereignty
   Commission and of Unprofessional Leadership at the Mississippi State Penitentiary."
   Journal of Mississippi History (November 1973): 1–20.
McMillen, Neil. "Perry W. Howard, Boss of the Black and Tan Republicanism in
   Mississippi, 1924–1960." *Journal of Southern History* 48, no. 2 (May 1982): 205–224.
McMillen, Neil. "Black Enfranchisement in Mississippi: Federal Enforcement and Black
   Protest in the 1960s." *Journal of Southern History* 43, no. 3 (1977): 351–372.
Morrison, Minion K. C., and Joe C. Huang. "The Transfer of Political Power in a Bi-racial
   Mississippi Town." *Growth and Change* 4, no. 2 (1972): 25–29.

Morrison, Minion K. C. "Federal Aid and Afro-American Political Power in Three Mississippi Towns." *Publius* 17, no. 4 (Autumn 1987): 97–111.

Orey, Byron, et al. "Accounting for 'Racism': Responses to Political Predicament in Two States." *State Politics and Policy Quarterly* 7, no. 3 (Fall 2007): 235–255.

Parker, Frank. "The Mississippi Congressional Redistricting Case: A Case Study in Minority Vote Dilution." *Howard Law Journal* 28, no. 2 (1985): 397–415.

Powell, Lew, and Edwin E. Meek. "Mississippi's WLBT: After the License Challenge." *Columbia Journalism Review* (May–June 1973): 50 55.

Salamon, Lester. "The Time Dimension in Policy Evaluation: The Case of the New Deal Land Experiments." *Public Policy* 27 (Spring 1979): 129–183.

Salamon, Lester, and Stephen Van Evera. "Fear, Apathy, and Discrimination: A Test of Three Explanations of Political Participation." *American Political Science Review* 67 (December 1973): 1288–1306.

Schmidt, William. "The Impact of Camp Shelby on Black Soldiers in World War II on Hattiesburg, Mississippi." *Journal of Mississippi History* 39 (February 1977): 41–50.

Snow, David et al. "Frame Alignment Processes, Micromobilization, and Movement Participation." *American Sociological Review* 51 (August 1986): 464–81.

Stevens, Arthur G., Jr., Arthur H. Miller, and Thomas E. Mann. "Mobilization of Liberal Strength in the House, 1955–1970: The Democratic Study Group." *American Political Science Review* (1974): 667–681.

Watters, Pat. "Encounter with the Future." *New South* 20, no. 5 (May 1965): 1–34.

Winter, R. Milton. "Division and Reunion in the Presbyterian Church, U.S., A Mississippi Retrospective." *Journal of Presbyterian History* 78, no. 1 (Spring 2000): 67–86.

BOOK CHAPTERS

Allen, Tip, Jr. "The Enduring Traditions of the State Constitutions." In *Mississippi Government and Politics: Modernizers versus Traditionalists*. Edited by Dale Krane and Stephen Shaffer. Lincoln: University of Nebraska Press, 1992.

Berard, Stanley. "Southern Influence in Congress." In *The Oxford Handbook of Southern Politics*. Edited by Charles Bullock III and Mark Rozell. New York: Oxford University Press, 2012.

Bond, Julian. "The Media and the Movement: Looking Back from the Southern Front." In *Media, Culture and the Modern African American Freedom Struggle*. Edited by Brian Ward. Gainesville: University Press of Florida, 2001.

Brooks, Gary. "Black Political Mobilization and White Legislative Behavior." In *Contemporary Southern Political Attitudes and Behavior: Studies and Essays*. Edited by Laurence Moreland et al. New York: Praeger Publishers, 1982.

Burrus, John. "Urbanization in Mississippi, 1890–1970." In *A History of Mississippi*, vol. 2. Edited by Richard McLemore. Hattiesburg: University and College Press of Mississippi, 1973.

Caravan, Guy, and Candie Caravan. "Carry it On: Roots of the Singing Civil Rights Movement." In *Freedom Is a Constant Struggle: An Anthology of the Mississippi Civil Rights Movement*. Edited by Susan Erenreich. Montgomery, AL: Black Belt Press, 1999.

Coleman, Mary, and Leslie McLemore. "Black Independent Politics in Mississippi: Constants and Challenges." In *The New Black Politics: The Search for Political Power*. Edited by Michael Preston et al. New York: Longman, 1982.

Dittmer, John. "The Politics of the Mississippi Movement." In *The Civil Rights Movement in America*. Edited by Charles Eagles. Jackson: University Press of Mississippi, 1986.

Du Bois, W. E. B. "The Talented Tenth." In *Negro Protest in the Twentieth Century*. Edited by Francis Broderick and August Meier. Indianapolis: Bobbs-Merrill Company, 1966.

Edwards, Harry. "The Sources of the Black Male Athlete's Superiority." *Black Scholar* 3, no. 3 (1971): 32–41.

Feig, Douglas. "The State Legislature: Representatives of the People or the Powerful?" In *Mississippi Government and Politics: Modernizers versus Traditionalists*. Edited by Dale Krane and Stephen Shaffer. Lincoln: University of Nebraska Press, 1992.

Fortenberrry, Charles, and F. Glenn Abney. "Mississippi: Unreconstructed and Unredeemed." In *The Changing Politics of the South*. Edited by William Havard. Baton Rouge: Louisiana State University Press, 1972.

Gaddie, Ronald Keith. "Realignment." In *The Oxford Handbook of Southern Politics*. Edited by Charles Bullock III and Mark Rozell. New York: Oxford University Press, 2012.

Gaines, Stanley O., Jr. "Sexuality and Race." In *The African American Experience: An Historiographical and Bibliographical Guide*. Edited by Arvarh Strickland and Robert Weems Jr. Westport, CT: Greenwood Press, 2001.

Gates, Henry. "The Blackness of Blackness: A Critique on the Sign and the Signifying Monkey." In *Literary Theory: An Anthology*. Edited by Julie Rivkin and Michael Ryan. Oxford: Blackwell Publishing, 2004.

Hanks, Lawrence J. "Civil Rights Organizations and Movements." In *African Americans and Political Participation: A Reference Handbook*. Edited by Minion K. C. Morrison. Santa Barbara, CA: ABC-CLIO, 2003.

Hardy, Thomas. "The 'Weak' Governor." In *Mississippi Government and Politics: Modernizers versus Traditionalists*. Edited by Dale Krane and Stephen Shaffer. Lincoln: University of Nebraska Press, 1992.

Hatcher, William. "Mississippi Constitutions." In *Politics in Mississippi*. Edited by Joseph Parker. 2nd ed. Salem, WI: Sheffield Publishing Company, 2001.

Henry, Aaron. "Economic and Political Power." In *Mississippi, 1990*. Edited by Walter Matthews. Jackson: University Press of Mississippi, 1981.

Hopper, Columbus. "The Impact of Litigation on Mississippi's Prison System." *Prison Journal* 65, no. 1 (1985): 61.

Horne, Gerald. "Race from Power: U.S. Foreign Policy and the General Crisis of White Supremacy." In *Window on Freedom: Race, Civil Rights and Foreign Affairs, 1945–1988*. Edited by Brenda Plummer. Chapel Hill: University of North Carolina Press, 2003.

Kelly, Brian. "Beyond the 'Talented Tenth': Black Elites, Black Workers, and the Limits of Accommodation in Industrial Birmingham, 1900–1921." In *Time Longer Than Rope: A Century of African American Activism, 1850–1950*. Edited by Charles Payne and Adam Green. New York: New York University Press, 2003.

McAdam, Doug, et al. "Introduction: Opportunities, Mobilizing Structures, and Framing Processes—Toward a Synthetic, Comparative Perspective on Social Movements." In *Comparative Perspectives on Social Movements: Political Opportunities, Mobilizing Structures, and Cultural Framings*. Edited by Doug McAdam et al. New York: Cambridge University Press, 1996.

McMillen, Neil. "Fighting for What We Didn't Have." In *Remaking Dixie: The Impact of World War II on the American South*. Jackson: University Press of Mississippi, 1997.

Moreland, Lawrence, and Robert Steed. "The Southern Presidential Elections." In *The Oxford Handbook of Southern Politics*. Edited by Charles Bullock III and Mark Rozell. New York: Oxford University Press, 2012.

Morrison, Minion K. C., and Richard Middleton IV. "African Americans in Office." In *African Americans and Political Participation: A Reference Handbook*. Edited by Minion K. C. Morrison. Santa Barbara, CA: ABC-CLIO, 2003.

Orey, Byron D'Andra, and Reginald Vance. "Participation in Electoral Politics." In *African Americans and Political Participation: A Reference Handbook*. Edited by Minion K. C. Morrison. Santa Barbara, CA: ABC-CLIO, 2003.

Parker, Frank. "Racial Gerrymandering and Legislative Reapportionment." In *Minority Vote Dilution*. Edited by Chandler Davidson. Washington, DC: Howard University Press, 1984.

Parker, Frank, David Colby, and Minion K. C. Morrison. "Mississippi." In *Quiet Revolution in the South*. Edited by Chandler Davidson and Bernard Grofman. Princeton, NJ: Princeton University Press, 1994.

Reagon, Bernice. "Civil Rights Movement." In *African American Music, an Introduction*. Edited by Mellonee Burnim and Portia Maultsby. New York: Routledge, 2006.

Reuther, Walter. "Address Before the Annual Convention of the National Association for the Advancement of Colored People." In *Walter Reuther: Selected Papers*. Edited by Harry Christman. New York: Macmillan Company, 1961.

Reuther, Walter. "Medical Care for the Aged: Statement to the House Committee on Ways and Means." In *Walter Reuther: Selected Papers*. Edited by Harry Christman. New York: Macmillan Company, 1961.

Sellers, Cleveland. "Holly Springs: Gateway to the Beloved Community." In *Freedom Is a Constant Struggle: An Anthology of the Mississippi Civil Rights Movement*. Edited by Susan Erenreich. Montgomery, AL: Black Belt Press, 1999.

Strickland, Arvarh. "Remembering Hattiesburg: Growing up Black in Wartime Mississippi." In *Remaking Dixie: The Impact of World War II on the American South*. Edited by Neil McMillen. Jackson: University Press of Mississippi, 1997.

Thompson, Julius E. "The African American Press." In *The African American Experience: An Historiographical and Bibliographical Guide*. Edited by Arvarh Strickland and Robert Weems Jr. Westport, CT: Greenwood Press, 2001.

Walker, Juliet E. K. "Promoting Black Entrepreneurship and Business Enterprise in Antebellum America: The National Negro Convention, 1830–1860." In *A Different Vision: Race and Public Policy*. Edited by Thomas D. Boston. New York: Routledge, 1997. 206–261.

Walker, Juliet E. K. "Constructing a Historiography of African American Business." In *The African American Experience: An Historiographical and Bibliographical Guide*. Edited by Arvarh Strickland and Robert Weems Jr. Westport, CT: Greenwood Press, 2001. 278–314.

Walsh, Stephen. "Black Oriented Radio and the Civil Rights Movement." In *Media, Culture, and the Modern African American Freedom Struggle*. Edited by Brian Ward. Gainesville: University of Florida Press, 2001.

Washington, Booker T. "The Atlanta Exposition Address." In *The Negro American: A Documentary History*. Edited by Leslie Fishel Jr. and Benjamin Quarles. Illinois: Scott, Foresman, and Company, 1967.

UNPUBLISHED THESES AND DISSERTATIONS

Cobbins, Sam. "Industrial Education for Black Americans in Mississippi, 1862–1965." Ph.D. diss., Mississippi State University, 1977.

Humphrey, George Duke. "A History of the Public School Funds in Mississippi." MA thesis, University of Chicago, 1931.

McLemore, Leslie. "The Mississippi Freedom Democratic Party: A Case Study of Grassroots Politics." Ph.D. diss., University of Massachusetts, Amherst, 1971.

Reynolds, Charles Felder, Jr. "The Economic and Social Structure of the Yazoo- Mississippi Delta." Ph.D. diss., University of Virginia, 1946.

Romaine, Anne. "The Mississippi Freedom Democratic Party Through August, 1964." MA thesis, University of Virginia, 1970.

Smith, Richard Kent. "The Economics of Education and Discrimination in the U.S. South: 1870–1910." Ph.D. diss., University of Wisconsin, 1973.

Legislative Bill and Resolutions

HOUSE BILLS

Mississippi Legislature. House Journal. HB 240. 1980.

Mississippi Legislature. House Journal. HB 734. 1980.

Mississippi Legislature. House Journal. HB 737. 1980.

Mississippi Legislature. House Journal. HB 787. 1980.

Mississippi Legislature. House Journal. HB 796. 1980.

Mississippi Legislature. House Journal. HB 812. 1980.

Mississippi Legislature. House Journal. HB 943. 1980.

Mississippi Legislature. House Journal. HB 944. 1980.

Mississippi Legislature. House Journal. HB 945. 1980.

Mississippi Legislature. House Journal. HB 955. 1980.

Mississippi Legislature. House Journal. HB 973. 1980.

Mississippi Legislature. House Journal. HB 1080. 1980.

Mississippi Legislature. House Journal. HB 1088. 1980.

Mississippi Legislature. House Journal. HB 1533. 1980.

Mississippi Legislature. House Journal. HB 404. 1981.

Mississippi Legislature. House Journal. HB 858. 1981.

Mississippi Legislature. House Journal. HB 1081. 1981.

Mississippi Legislature. House Journal. HB 1140. 1981.

Mississippi Legislature. House Journal. HB 733. 1982.

Mississippi Legislature. House Journal. HB 936. 1982.

Mississippi Legislature. House Journal. HB 1007. 1982.

Mississippi Legislature. House Journal. HB 75. 1983.

Mississippi Legislature. House Journal. HB 76. 1983.

Mississippi Legislature. House Journal. HB 93. 1983.

Mississippi Legislature. House Journal. HB 467. 1983.

Mississippi Legislature. House Journal. HB 715. 1983.

Mississippi Legislature. House Journal. HB 859. 1983.

Mississippi Legislature. House Journal. HB 1172. 1983.

Mississippi Legislature. House Journal. HB 386. 1984.

Mississippi Legislature. House Journal. HB 474. 1984.
Mississippi Legislature. House Journal. HB 683. 1984.
Mississippi Legislature. House Journal. HB 324. 1985.
Mississippi Legislature. House Journal. HB 885. 1986.
Mississippi Legislature. House Journal. HB 187. 1987.
Mississippi Legislature. House Journal. HB 379. 1987.
Mississippi Legislature. House Journal. HB 793. 1987.
Mississippi Legislature. House Journal. HB 77. 1988.
Mississippi Legislature. House Journal. HB 317. 1988.
Mississippi Legislature. House Journal. HB 665. 1988.
Mississippi Legislature. House Journal. HB 855. 1988.
Mississippi Legislature. House Journal. HB 857. 1988.
Mississippi Legislature. House Journal. HB 858. 1988.
Mississippi Legislature. House Journal. HB 860. 1988.
Mississippi Legislature. House Journal. HB 1225. 1988.
Mississippi Legislature. House Journal. HB 264. 1989.
Mississippi Legislature. House Journal. HB 463. 1989.
Mississippi Legislature. House Journal. HB 1211. 1989.
Mississippi Legislature. House Journal. HB 1346. 1990.
Mississippi Legislature. House Journal. HB 147. 1991.
Mississippi Legislature. House Journal. HB 722. 1991.
Mississippi Legislature. House Journal. HB 723. 1991.
Mississippi Legislature. House Journal. HB 724. 1991.
Mississippi Legislature. House Journal. HB 726. 1991.
Mississippi Legislature. House Journal. HB 815. 1991.
Mississippi Legislature. House Journal. HB 219. 1992.
Mississippi Legislature. House Journal. HB 649. 1992.
Mississippi Legislature. House Journal. HB 739. 1992.
Mississippi Legislature. House Journal. HB 535. 1993.
Mississippi Legislature. House Journal. HB 536. 1993.
Mississippi Legislature. House Journal. HB 838. 1993.
Mississippi Legislature. House Journal. HB 1239. 1994.
Mississippi Legislature. House Journal. HB 1284. 1994.
Mississippi Legislature. House Journal. HB 1650. 1994.
Mississippi Legislature. House Journal. HB 1651. 1994.
Mississippi Legislature. House Journal. HB 868. 1995.
Mississippi Legislature. House Journal. HB 1712. 1995.
Mississippi Legislature. House Journal. HB 1743. 1995.
Mississippi Legislature. House Journal. HB 1562. 1999.

HOUSE CONCURRENT RESOLUTIONS

Mississippi Legislature. House Journal. HCR 36. 1980.
Mississippi Legislature. House Journal. HCR 37. 1980.
Mississippi Legislature. House Journal. HCR 38. 1980.
Mississippi Legislature. House Journal. HCR 62. 1980.

Mississippi Legislature. House Journal. HCR 63. 1980.
Mississippi Legislature. House Journal. HCR 105. 1981.
Mississippi Legislature. House Journal. HCR 5. 1983.
Mississippi Legislature. House Journal. HCR 9. 1983.
Mississippi Legislature. House Journal. HCR 13. 1983.
Mississippi Legislature. House Journal. HCR 66. 1983.
Mississippi Legislature. House Journal. HCR 107. 1984.
Mississippi Legislature. House Journal. HCR 66. 1985.
Mississippi Legislature. House Journal. HCR 70. 1986.
Mississippi Legislature. House Journal. HCR 109. 1986.
Mississippi Legislature. House Journal. HCR 34. 1987.
Mississippi Legislature. House Journal. HCR 12. 1988.
Mississippi Legislature. House Journal. HCR 88. 1994.

HOUSE RESOLUTIONS
Mississippi Legislature. House Journal. HR 13. 1988.

Presentations/Events
Dunnaville, Clarence, Jr. "Fortieth Anniversary of the Lawyers' Committee for Civil Rights." *Virginia Lawyer*. June/July 2003.
Parker, Frank. "Mississippi's 'Massive Resistance' to Black Political Empowerment After Passage of the Voting Rights Act, 1965–1970." Paper presented to the National Conference of Black Political Scientists. April 2–5, 1986.
Slocum, Fred. "Connecting the Past and the Present: Historical Realities and Current Political Trends in the South." Paper presented at the Southern Political Science Association annual meeting. January 2006, Atlanta, GA.

Government Documents
"Comments by Dr. Aaron Henry," Chairman, The National Black Caucus on the Aged. White House Meeting of the Ad Hoc Leadership Council of Aging Organizations with the President. October 10, 1979, Washington, D. C.
Congressional Record, June 16, 1964.
Hearing before the Subcommittee on Housing and Consumer Interests of the Select Committee on Aging. House of Representatives. 94th Cong. 2nd Sess. May 14, 1976.
Richard Nixon, "Remarks to the White House Conference on Aging." December 2, 1971. Hearings before the Subcommittee on Housing Consumer and Consumer Interests of the House Select Committee on Aging. 94th Cong., 2nd Sess. May 14, 1976.
Public Papers of U.S. Presidents, Lyndon B. Johnson, 1963–1964. V I. Washington, DC: Government Printing Office, 1965.
"Testimony to the Presidential Forum on Domestic Policy." Washington, D.C. October 29, 1975.
U.S. Commission on Civil Rights. *Voting in Mississippi: A Report*. Washington, DC: Government Printing Office, 1965.

U.S. Commission on Civil Rights. *Hearings before the United States Civil Rights Commission.* Volume I, "Voting." Jackson, Mississippi. February 16–20. Washington, DC: Government Printing Office, 1965.

U.S. Commission on Civil Rights. *Political Participation.* Washington, DC: Government Printing Office, 1968.

U.S. Department of Labor. Manpower Administration. Leaving the future open—Job Corps, the first decade. Washington, DC: Government Printing Office, [1975.]

Index

L

71–76; Clarksdale movement involvement, 81, 262–63; and Council of Federated Organizations (COFO), 120–21, 137; electoral politics, 60, 197–98, 253, 294*n102*; indigenous leadership, 103, 164; intimidation campaign, 53–54; Jackson convention, 128; leadership arrests, 58–59; legal activism, 139–40; Legal Defense Fund, 104, 142; and Medgar Evers, 50, 52–53, 258–59, 261, 293*n49*; media discrimination complaints, 169–70; Mississippi, xv–xvii; and Mississippi Action for Progress (MAP), 160–61; mock election project and campaign, 90, 94–95, 106–7; New Orleans chapter, 28; Political Action Committee, 115; prison reform, 246; revitalization efforts, 24, 50, 52–53, 55, 82, 258–59, 261; school desegregation, 141–44; separate-but-equal doctrine, 17; sit-in demonstrations, 56–57, 74; social change movement, xv–xvii; state voter registration campaign, 66, 115, 120, 147; student membership, 15, 56–57; voter registration, 60, 73; Youth Council, 60, 72, 263
National Caucus on Black Aged (NCBA), 182, 183–85
National Council of Churches, 103, 156
National Council of Negro Women (NCNW), 156
National Democratic Party: constitutional convention, 207; exclusion and equality, 200; and Henry, 127, 205–6; illegitimate party representation challenge, 208–10, 214–18; and the Mississippi Democratic Party, 125–26; and the Mississippi Freedom Democratic Party (MFDP), 129–36, 193–97; new Democratic Party reorganization and reform, 205–8. See *also* Democratic Party
National Farmers Union, 156
National Lawyers' Guild, 80
National Pharmaceutical Association, 188, 306*n106*
National Rural Electric Cooperative Association, 156
National Sharecroppers Fund, 156
National Students Association (NSA), 29–30
National Youth Administration, 29
Native Son (Wright), 15
NBC network, 94
Negro Convention Movement, 6
Negro History Week, 242–43
Neighborhood Youth Corps, 177
Nelson, Robert, 215
Neshoba County, 96
networking skills: Atlantic City convention, 129–36, 194–95, 264; board examinations, 32; civil rights coalitions, 46–47, 85–89, 119–20, 128–29, 263; congressional and

executive influence, 112, 128–29, 138, 144–49, 165, 176–87, 223–24, 261, 268; Council of Federated Organizations (COFO), xvii, 66, 78, 86–90, 92–93, 101, 263; federal government support, 139–52; Greenwood campaign, 68–69; health professionals network, 80, 187–89; importance, 138, 191–92; interracial partnerships, 30, 39–40, 90, 138–39; Job Corps programs, 178; Justice Department, 60–61; Kennedy administration, 60, 65, 69, 88, 144–47; legal networks, 80; local civil rights street campaign, 60, 66–67, 71–74, 78–80, 83; Martin Luther King, Jr., 55, 61; Medgar Evers, 60–61; Mound Bayou, 39–40, 43, 46–47; NAACP membership, 107, 119–20, 129, 144, 263; as NAACP president, 60, 85, 144; personal style, 165–66, 261–62; pharmacy career, 39–40, 258; poverty initiatives, 151; Regional Council of Negro Leadership (RCNL), xvi–xvii, 46, 55, 260–61; school desegregation, 143; Southern Educational and Recreational Association (SERA), 151–52; as state legislator, 237, 265–67; transportation services, 191; workforce development and training, 176–81. See *also* indigenous leadership
Newman, Buddie, 235
New Orleans, Louisiana, 26–32
New Orleans NAACP Youth Council, 28
news conferences, 100
Newson, Charles, 68
newspapers, 94
Newton, 96
New York, 129
New York State Children's Health Project, 190
New York Times, 108, 251
Nigeria, 180
Nixon, Richard, 183, 184, 185, 203, 216–17
nonsouthern military bases, 21–22
North Carolina Central University, 29
North Carolina Council of Christians and Jew, 30
North Carolina State University, 29
Noxubee County, 232

O

Oakhurst Baptist Church, 79
Oakhurst Church of Christ, 79
O'Brien, Lawrence, 208, 209–10, 215
odd job experiences, 12–13
Office of Economic Opportunity (OEO), 152, 153, 157, 158, 159–61, 163–64, 188
Ohio orientations, 119, 120
Oktibbeha County, 232
Older Americans Act (1965), 184